Business Government and Society

Dr. N. Mohan MBA, MA(Eco.), Ph.D
Associate Prof., Department of Management Studies,
SJC Institute of Technology,
Chickballapur.

Dr. Priyadarshini Pillai
MBA, LLB, M.Sc(Biotech), M.Phil, Ph.D
Former Dean
RK Institute of Management and Science
Bengaluru.

Archana B. S. M.Com, PGDBA, (Ph.D)
Asst. Prof., Department of Commerce & Management,
MLA Academy of Higher Learning,
Bengaluru.

Himalaya Publishing House
ISO 9001 : 2015 CERTIFIED

First Edition : 2015
Reprint : 2022
Reprint : 2024

Published by : Mrs. Meena Pandey
for **HIMALAYA PUBLISHING HOUSE PVT. LTD.,**
"Ramdoot", Dr. Bhalerao Marg, Girgaon, Mumbai - 400 004.
Phone: 022-23860170, 23863863; **Fax:** 022-23877178
E-mail: himpub@bharatmail.co.in; **Website:** www.himpub.com

Branch Offices :

New Delhi : "Pooja Apartments", 4-B, Murari Lal Street, Ansari Road, Darya Ganj, New Delhi - 110 002.
Phone: 011-23270392, 23278631; Fax: 011-23256286

Nagpur : Kundanlal Chandak Industrial Estate, Ghat Road, Nagpur - 440 018.
Phone: 0712-2721215, 2721216

Bengaluru : Plot No. 91-33, 2nd Main Road, Seshadripuram, Behind Nataraja Theatre,
Bengaluru - 560 020. Phone: 080-41138821; Mobile: 09379847017, 09379847005

Hyderabad : No. 3-4-184, Lingampally, Besides Raghavendra Swamy Matham, Kachiguda,
Hyderabad - 500 027. Phone: 040-27560041, 27550139

Chennai : No. 34/44, Motilal Street, T. Nagar, Chennai - 600 017. Mobile: 09380460419

Pune : "Laksha" Apartment, First Floor, No. 527, Mehunpura,
Shaniwarpeth (Near Prabhat Theatre), Pune - 411 030.
Phone: 020-24496323, 24496333; Mobile: 09370579333

Cuttack : Plot No 5F-755/4, Sector-9, CDA Markat Nagar, Cuttack - 753 014,
Odisha. Mobile: 09338746007

Kolkata : 3, S.M. Bose Road, Near Gate No. 5, Agarpara Railway Station,
North 24 Parganas, West Bengal - 700109. Mobile: 09674536325

DTP by : *SPS,* Bengaluru.

Printed at : M/s. Sri Sai Art Printer, Hyderabad. On behalf of HPH.

PREFACE

We have great pleasure in presenting First edition *"Business, Government and Society"* written for MBA students. The related matters are written in a simple and easily understandable language with sufficient support from real business world information.

This volume is an attempt to provide the students with thorough understanding of corporate governance, public policies, environmental concerns, business ethics, corporate social responsibility and various business laws.

We have presented the subject matter in a systematic manner with liberal use of charts, diagrams and case studies where ever necessary so as to make it more interesting to the students.

We are sure this book will prove extremely useful to students and teachers alike. This book would not have seen the light, but for the grace of God and the blessings and support of our family members and friends.

Our work would not attain its fulfilment if we fail to thank the management of SJC Institute of Technology, RK Institute of Management and Science and MLA Academy of Higher Learning for providing us valuable support and encouragement to take up such a task.

We present our heartfelt gratitude to Mr. Niraj Pandey and Mr. Vijay Pandey of Himalaya Publishing House Pvt. Ltd. who intimated the idea for this book and for the best efforts put forth by the matter of publication of this book.

We respectfully acknowledge that the critical comments and constructive suggestions for the improvement of this book are most welcome and will be greatly appreciated. We believe that, there is always some scope for further improvement and to that end, sincerely invite valuable suggestions which would be thankfully incorporated in the edition to come.

Bengaluru
Feb, 2015

Authors

CONTENTS

Module-1

The study of Business, Government & Society

Syllabus

Importance of BGS to Managers – Models of BGS relationships – Market Capitalism Model, Dominance Model, Countervailing Forces Model and Stakeholder Model – Global perspective – Historical perspective.

Introduction

In the universe of human endeavor, we can distinguish subdivisions of economic, political, and social activity i.e., business, government, and society-in every civilization throughout time. Interplay among these activities creates an environment in which business operate, the business-government-society (BGS) field is the study of this environment and it is important for managers.

The study of Business in the context of government policy and studying business in any nation in connection with social system (of a nation) and economic philosophy accepted in a nation is an integrative study. The concept of business has emerged, ever since the exchange activity took place or from the stage of barter economy in the economic process. The business is an activity which is primarily pursued with the object of earning profit. A business activity involves production, exchange of goods and services to earn profits or earn a living. The word 'Business' literally means a state of being busy. Every person is engaged in some kind of occupation, a farmer works in the field, a worker works in the factory, a clerk does his job in the office, a teacher teaches in the class, and a salesman is busy in selling the goods. The main goal of all these personalities is to earn their livelihood while doing some work.

Business "comprises all profit-seeking activities and enterprises that provide goods and services necessary to an economic system. It is the economic pulse of a nation, striving to increase society's standard of living. Profits are a primary mechanism for motivating these activities.

Therefore, business is the profit motivated activity involving buying, producing and selling of goods and or services. Organizations that create benefits for their owners are also to be considered as business enterprises. ***For example***, student's cooperative society in a college, employees housing society in a factory and a consumer co-operative society in your locality are business enterprises. To sum up business may be understood as the organized efforts of enterprises to supply consumers with goods and services and to make profit in the process.

Business

It is a profit-making activity that provides products and services to satisfy human needs. Business is a broad term encompassing a range of actions and institutions. It covers management, manufacturing, finance, trade, service, investment, and other activities. The fundamental purpose of every business is to make a profit by providing products and services that satisfy human needs.

A business also known as enterprise or firm is an organization engaged in the trade of goods, services, or both to consumers. Businesses are predominant in capitalist economies, where most of them are privately owned and administered to earn profit to increase the wealth of their owners. A business owned by multiple individuals may be referred to as a company.

The etymology of "business" relates to the state of being busy either as an individual or society as a whole, performing commercially viable and profitable work. The term "business" has at least three usages. Depending on the scope-the singular usage to mean a particular organization; the generalized usage to refer to a particular market sector, and the broadest which encompasses all activities by the community of suppliers of goods and services. However, the exact definition of business is a matter of debate and complexity of meanings.

Definitions of Business

"Business is profit , can be more the main objective of a business than betting is the main of making profit and acquiring wealth through the satisfaction of human wants". – ***R. Urwivk***

"Business comprises all profit seeking activities and enterprises that provide goods and services necessary to an economic system. It is the economic system. It is the economic pulse of a nation, striving to increase society's standard of living. Profits are a primary mechanize for motivating these actives". – ***Boone Louis E. and David L. Kurtz***

Government

A group of people that governs a community or unit. It sets and administers public policy and exercises executive, political and sovereign power through customs, institutions, and laws within a state. A government can be classified into many types--democracy, republic, monarchy, aristocracy, and dictatorship are just a few. Structures and processes in society that authoritatively make and apply policies and rules. Like business, it encompasses a wide range of activities and institutions at many levels, from international to local.

Society

The term society is the most fundamental one in sociology. In common parlance, the term society refers to the members of specific groups. For example, we speak of Harijan Society, Teacher's Society, and Students society and the like. Similarly, the word is used to refer to some specific institution like, Brahma Samaj, Arya Samaj, etc. The term "Society" refers not to group of people but to the complex pattern of the norms of interaction that arise among them. People are only the agents of social relationship, they are regarded as things. A society is intangible as it is a process rather than a thing and motion rather than structure. Society is a web of social relationships, the pattern of norms of interaction by which the members of the society maintain themselves.

Some scholars are of the opinion that society exists only when the members know each other and possess common interests or objects. For instance, two persons travelling in the same train, in the same compartment, in the same seat, do not form society, because they are not socially related and do not have mutual recognition. But as soon as they come to know each other, the element of society is created.

Definitions of Society

"Society is a system of usages and procedures, authority and mutual aid, of many groupings and divisions, of human behavior and of liberties". - ***Maclver and Page***

"Society refers to complex of forms or processes in wich each of which is living and growing by interaction with the other, the whole being so unified that, what takes place in one part affects all the rest". - ***Cooley***

"Society is the union itself, the organization, the sum of formal relations in which associating individuals are bound together". - ***Giddings***

"A Society is a collection of individuals united by certain relations or modes of behavior which mark them off from others who do not enter into these relations or who differ from them in behavior". - ***Ginsberg***

"The term Society refers not to group of people, but to the complex pattern of the norms of interaction, which arise among and between them". - ***Lapiere***

According to ***G.D.H. Cole*** "Society is the complex of organised associations and institutions within the community".

If we analyse these definitions it will understand that all these fall under two types:

(i) The functional definition which views a society as a process and

(ii) The structural definition which views Society as a structure.

From the functional point of view, Society is defined as a complex of groups in reciprocal relationship, interacting upon one another, enabling human organism to carry on their life -activities. From the structural point of view, society is the total social heritage of folkways and institutions, of habits, sentiments and ideals. Maclver, Cooley and Lapiere have given functional definition of society while Ginsberg Giddings and Cole take a structural view of society.

The BGS field is the study of interactions among the three broad areas defined above. The primary focus is on the interaction of business with the other two elements. The basic subject matter, therefore, is how business shapes and changes government and society, and how it is, in turn, molded by political and social pressures.

Importance of BGS to Managers

1. To understand the role of business in society.
2. To understand the business power in society.
3. It becomes criteria for managerial decisions.
4. To understand the extent of corporate social responsibility.
5. To know the ethical duties of managers and the need for regulations.
6. To succeed in meeting the objectives of business.
7. To excel in managerial performance.
8. To monitor the non-economic environment by taking stock of the situation before anything happens.
9. By recognizing that a company operates not only within markets but within a society is critical.
10. To think beyond profit in order to understand the forces governing social responsibility.

Nature of Business

The concept of "Business" has emerged ever since the exchange activity took place or from the stage of "Barter Economy" in the economic evolution process. When we observe the three different stages of economic evolution, we understand as to how the concept of "Business" was conceived and developed.

(i) Ethics: Business ethics demands that business should be conducted according to certain self-recognized moral standards. Every business unit tries to conduct businesses following certain element of moral standard. This is true nature of business. Business houses, which have followed ethical aspects, have lived for long. Tata group of companies, General Electric, (popularly know as GE), The Hindu (over 120 year) etc, have lived on certain ethical values. As Peter F. Drucker (Modern Management Guru) has said "There neither is a separate ethics of business nor is one needed".

(ii) Culture: Culture greatly influences every business activity. When we speak of nature of business, we try to analyse the culture of a business activity. Culture is a critical component of business. "Culture of civilization is that complex whole which includes knowledge, belief, art, morals, law, custom, and other capabilities and habits acquired by a man as a member of society". The ethics and culture of those countries have to be followed in the respective countries for their success. Therefore, culture is imbibed in the nature of business.

(iii) Professionalism: Professionalism is another character or nature of business. Increased management education is the main cause for growing Professionalism in business. Professionalism involves (i) specialized knowledge and skill for management, (ii) Authority and freedom to take the right decision, (iii) Ideological bias in the discharge of functions and (iv) Following ethical aspects in decision-making and business actions. It may be observed that family owned companies are gradually handing over their business to professionals. Belief in professionalism is the true nature of business.

(iv) Customer delight: Today, the business is a "customer-centered" operation. Delighting the customer is the real nature of business. Customer being quality conscious, it is the primary responsibility of the business to provide quality product or service to the customers. Otherwise, business will not survive. This is a natural factor. Buyers market is emerging at a faster rate. Every business house is trying to satisfy its customers fully. If the customer is delighted, not only he becomes the loyal customer, but he also brings in many more to that business house. Therefore, the nature of business is to attract customers through quality service and providing quality goods.

Scope of Business

Business is a vast and fascinating subject. The subject business encompasses the use of latest scientific know-how and technology, challenges and difficulties encountered in converting raw materials into saleable products, problems confronted with financial management (raising and spending of money for the goods of business), human resource management (recruitment, selection, training and development of employees), sleepless nights spent in the development of strategies for better marketing the products, the stupendous task of complying with business law, and discharging obligations to the community.

The word objective denote desired out-comes for entire business entity or for a specific business unit. Business objectives are written in terms of out-comes (rather than action), clear as to a time frame, challenging but attainable and communicated to entire organization or at firm level to all members. All the objectives of business which are measurable or quantifiable often called as goals. The very first step in business plan is defining broader business objectives (mission), organizational and functional level objectives and quantifying the overall, functional, objectives in terms of goals.

In the business management literature the word objective means quantification (if possible) or more precise statement of goals or the plans for achieving the desired business results. Business being an economic activity has certain objective to be achieved.

Objectives of Business

The objectives of business are as follows:

- Increasing market-share with respect the product/service in which the business is conducted.
- Profit maximization.
- Sales maximization.
- Improving a good business reputation.
- Increasing financing stability and ensuring financial liquidity.
- Achieving growth of business in terms of products markets integration (backward or forward)
- Achieving increased productivity.
- Achieving diversification.
- Achieving employee's development and good industrial relations.
- Attainting social responsibility through community service, family welfare and auxiliary industry development rural development.

1. Profit

Profit is the backbone of any business enterprise. It is the excess of income over expense. Profit is the main motivator, strong sustainer, and judicious allocator of resources, objective indicator of efficient productivity and a solid basis for growth, expansion and survival. It enables a businessman to realize his other objectives. *For examples*, hospitals, schools, charitable institutions and government agencies are not basically concerned with the acquisition of profits. The non-profit enterprise customarily relies on gifts, endowments, receipts from money-rising projects, subsides or taxes for sustenance. The basic objective of these establishments is the provision of a service which is socially desirable and useful.

2. Growth

It is another primary objective of business. It should grow in all directions over a period of time. An enterprise which remains stagnant fro long is presumed to suffer from an organic defect. The strategies adopted to achieve growth are:

- Add more products or markets
- Integration forward or backward
- Increase market share
- Diversify into new areas
- Expand markets
- Cut sown and increase productivity

3. Power

Business has vast resources such as money, materials, men and know-how. These resources confer enormous economic and political power on owners and managers of business ventures.

4. Employee satisfaction and development

The Chinese proverb says, "If you want to plan for a year, plant corn. If you want to plan for thirty years plant a tree. But if you wan to plan for 100 years plant a men". Carrying for employee satisfaction and their development has been one of the objectives of enlightened business enterprises.

5. Quality products and services

This is one of the major objectives of business. Those who insisted on and persisted in quality survived competition and stayed ahead of others on the market. Persistent quality earns brand loyalty, a vital ingredient of success.

6. Market leadership

To earn market leadership is yet another objective of business. To earn a niche for oneself in the market, innovation is the key factor. Innovation may be in product, advertising, distribution, finance or in any other field.

7. Challenging

Business offers vast scope and poses formidable challenges. Success in a business venture speaks of the abilities of individuals who own and manage and failure, their inability and incompetence. The real worth of an individual is tested more in business than in any other profession.

8. Service to society

Business is a part of society and has several obligations towards it. Some of them are:

- Providing safe and quality goods at reasonable prices
- Providing employment
- Patronizing cultural and religious activities
- Maintaining and protecting ecology

9. Good corporate citizenship

Citizenship implies that the business unit complies with the rules of the land, pay taxes to the government regularly discharges its obligation to society and cares for its employees and customers. Bending rules of the land, evading tax payments by under invoicing exports and dubious tax-planning, cornering licenses at the cost of others, adulating quality of products and indulging in other unethical practices may earn money. But such practices hardly speak highly of corporate citizenship

Forms of Business

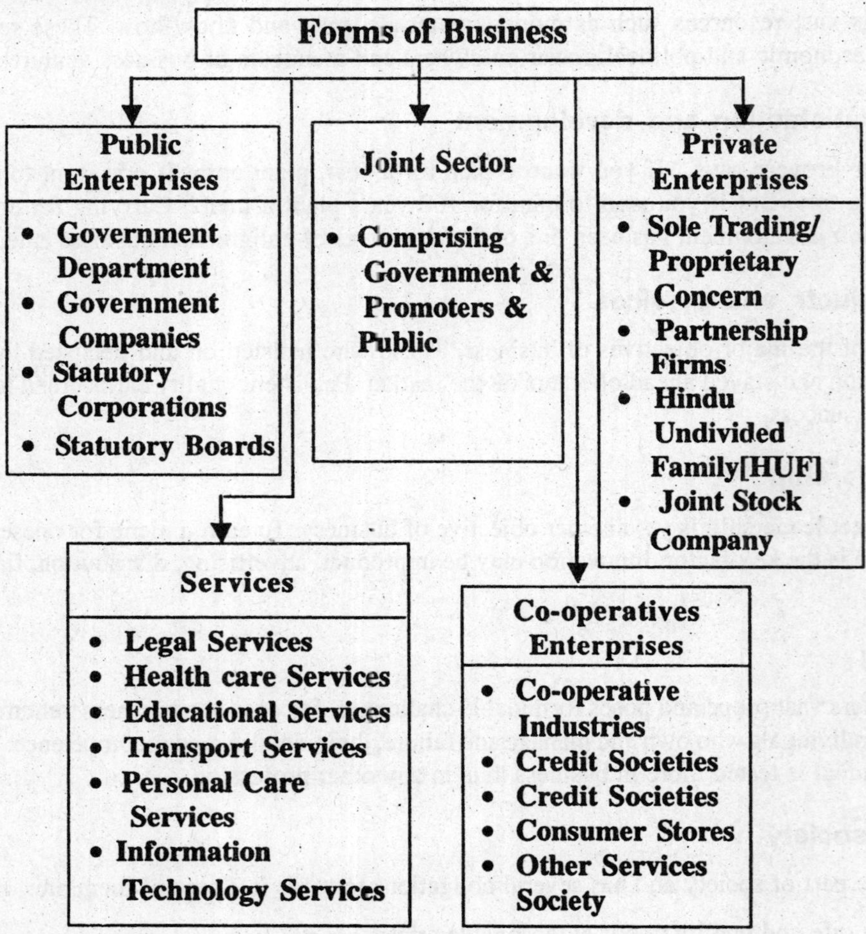

Sole Trading / Proprietary Concerns

Where the size of the business operation is small, this form of enterprise works well, this is managed by an individual. The capital employed is less. The capital can be either his own or borrowed. The individual bears the risks and enjoys all the profits, or suffers all the losses. Thus, proprietary concern otherwise called sole trading concern is run by only one person who organizes, manages finances, bears the risk, and controls the entire activity. He is the decision maker. He operates the business skillfully and makes a profit.

The form of business is the oldest and simplest of all the forms. Even today it enjoys the confidence of business people and has its utility. Any one who is having skill, initiative and drive can start this type of business with little capital. But it has the limitation regarding availing huge funds, obtaining economies of large scale operation etc.

Nature/ Features of Proprietary Concern

1. *Single Partnership:* This is run by an individual. He will be the monarch of the situation. He enjoys all profits and suffers all losses.

2. ***Capital Contribution:*** The capital is contributed by the individual. It may be own or borrowed.

3. ***Management and Control:*** The whole show is run by the individual. He or she takes the decision and faces the consequences. The complete control of the unit will be in one hand. It can be managed in any way.

4. ***Profit or Loss:*** The profit or loss of the concern is borne by the individual alone and will not be shared by any one.

5. ***Economic Risk:*** Even the business risk is to be borne by the individual alone and cannot be shared by any other person.

6. ***No special Law:*** This is not governed by any law. One can start the business at one's will and dissolve it at any time when one wants. This is not covered by any other legislation. General business laws are also applicable to them. Any person competent to enter into a contract can start the sole trading concerns. An insolvent cannot run the business in his name.

Merits of Sole Trading Concerns

The sole trading concern enjoys several advantages. They are –

(*i*) ***Easy to Form*** : No legal formality are needed to be observed to form the sole trading concerns. It is the easiest type of concern to form. Any person competent to enter into contract can organize this business. A formal license from the local authority is required and there will be no legal interference from any quarter in the day-to-day operations.

(*ii*) ***Quick Action*** : A sole trader takes his own business decision quickly. He need not consult any body or take the opinion of any person before he decides the business affairs of his units. He can take quick decisions and prompt actions in all matter like pricing, credit expansion, discount policy, stock position etc. this will help the proprietor to take advantage of business opportunities for gain.

(*iii*) ***Personal Supervision*** : Personalized service can be rendered to the consumers in this form. Good rapport between the customer and the business will increase the turn over and profit. At every level the owner will have personal supervision of the business and personal relationship with employees and customers will facilitate the owner to know their needs. Sole trader can take immediate steps to satisfy such needs of the customer.

(*iv*) ***Incentive*** : In a sole trading concern, the effort and benefit has a direct relationship. The sole trader puts on his heart and soul to the business as he knows that he is the sole beneficiary of the business. Whatever the profit earned in the business will be fully enjoyed by him. Hence this will act has incentive to the owner to work and zeal and it will be the driving force to secure economy and efficiency.

(*v*) ***Secrecy*** : A sole trader need not render annual accounts to anybody except to the tax authorities. There is no necessity to make public the accounts maintained by him. In this form of business, one can have privacy and business secrecy of the firm. Hereditary business is run on these lines.

(*vi*) ***Flexibility*** : As the whole show is run by an individual, the business is highly flexible in character. Whenever the sole trader feels that the business pattern has to change or price has to be refined or any business policy has to be changed he will be free to do it. He can quickly effect the changes to make business highly profitable and efficient. Thus sole trading concern is highly flexible in character and has quick access to changes.

(*vii*) ***Low Cost Profile*** **:** As every business activity is controlled and managed by the individual, the cost of operation will be less. Most of the business activity is conducted by the owner and his family people. He need not have to pay extra for the work rendered. In some of the big sole trading concerns there will be paid employees and the cost of these employees will be comparatively less. Hence, a sole trading concern has the advantage of running the business at a low cost.

(*viii*) ***Business Freedom*** **:** As the ownership of the business is single, there are no other authorities to come in his way of taking decisions and implement them. He will be free to take any action in the interest of the firm.

(*ix*) ***Social Relevance*** **:** From the stand point of society sole trading concern provides an opportunity for self-employment. It is a means of earning livelihood independently. Sole trader will be the master by himself. Another important social aspect is that the business is scattered in this case and hence there will be no concentration of economic power in few hands. Sole trading concern develops the qualities of self-reliance, self-confidence, responsibility, tact, and initiative in the individuals. Thus it generates social values.

Limitations of Sole Trading Concerns

Besides having several advantages, the sole trading concern has certain disadvantages

(i) **Capital Limitation:** As discussed already, sole trading concern is convenient to form when the capital employment is less. If we want to invest large capital, it is not possible in this case. The personal savings of the individual will be merger and borrowing on a large scale is not possible as he cannot provide required security for it. Expansion of business becomes difficult as it requires heavy capital investment.

(ii) **Limited Business Skill:** Besides providing capital, the business also requires organizing ability and managerial skill. The further growth of business needs extra managerial ability and skill which may not be found in one individual. The founder may have the ability and skill. But the successor is not likely to have the same. Even the employees may not work to the expected level. Efficient management of business needs the coordination of capital, technical skill and organizing ability. But every sole trader cannot have all these things in him. The owner of the capital will have no managerial ability and those who are having skill will not have capital and hence the business fails.

(iii) **Unlimited Liability:** Unlimited liability is in of the main deficiencies of the sole trading concerns. Whatever may be the size of the liability, it has to be borne by the sole trader. If the business assets are not sufficient to meet the business liability, the personal property of the sole trader is liable for clearing the business debts. Thus the sole trader will have to be very cautious in dealing with the debts, as his personal property is constantly in danger.

(iv) **No Legal Protection:** The future of sole trading concern is uncertain as it is not having legal status. If the proprietor becomes sick, insolvent the business hampers. There will be no continuity of the business. Disability of prolonged sickness of the proprietor results in the business coming to a close unless the successors have the business ability and acumen.

(v) **Not Suitable for Big Business:** Sole trading concern is well suited for small business. It is not adaptable to big business and hence economic of large scale manufacturing, buying and selling cannot be obtained on account of small size of the business. The degree of specialization is also small. Hence specialized services cannot be obtained.

(vi) **Span of Management:** As the operational area is limited in sole trading concerns, there will be limited span of management. If the span of management increases, inefficiency creeps in and business becomes unmanageable and the efficiency is lost.

(vii) **No Judicious Management :** As the owner has to look after every aspect of business, he cannot pay equal attention to each and every aspects of business activity. Some aspects or the other loses attention and it hampers the business activity. There cannot be judicious management of the business activity.

(viii) **Wrong Decision:** The owner is the sole decision maker in sole trading concerns. Whatever decision he takes, he abides by it. When he takes a wrong decision he takes, he is abide by it. When he takes a wrong decision, there will be no other head to correct it. This is another deficiency of trading concern.

Partnership Firms

The need for partnership form of organization arose from the limitation of sole-proprietorship. In sole-proprietorship, the financial resources and managerial skills were limited; one man could not supervise all the business activities personally. Moreover risk, bearing capacity of an individual was also limited. When business activities started expanding, the need for more funds arose. More persons were required for supervising different functions. It was at this stage that a need for associating more persons arose. So more persons were associated to form groups to carry on business. These persons brought into the business their financial resources and are also helpful in business administration.

Meaning of Partnership Firms

A partnership is an association of two or more persons to carry on, as co-owners, a business and to share its profits and losses. The partnership may come into existence either as a result of the expansion of the sole-trading concern or by means of an agreement between two or more persons desirous of forming a partnership. When the business expands in size, the proprietor finds it difficult to manage the business and is forced to take more outsiders who will not only provide additional capital but also assist him in managing the business on sound lines. Sometimes, the nature of business demands large amount of capital, effective supervision and greater specialization. It is ideal form of organization for the enterprise requiring moderate amount of capital and diversified managerial talent. This form is not suitable for a business resuming big capital an expert managerial personnel.

Definition

Section 4 of the *Partnership Act 1952*, "The relation between persons who have agreed to share profits of a business carried on by all or any one of them acting for all". According to the act, there must be two or more persons having contractual relationship. It is not necessary that the business shoul[illegible] managed by all the partners but any one or more partners can run the business on behalf by all the persons. Any partner acting on behalf of other partner can bind the firm to third parties. So there is an implied authority on behalf of other partners.

Nature/Characteristics/ Features of Partnership Firm

1. **Association of Two or More Persons:** In partnership firm as discussed earlier there must be at least two persons. Partnership is the outcome of a contract, so there must be two or more persons.

The persons becoming partners must be competent to enter into a contract. Minors cannot form a partnership firms they are incompetent to enter into a contract.

2. **Contractual Relation:** The persons joining the partnership enter into a contract for running a business. According to Partnership Act, the relation of partnership arises from the contract and not from status. The contract may be oral or written but in practice written agreement is made because it helps to settle disputes if they arise later on.

3. **Earning of Profits:** The purpose of the business should be to make profits and distribute them among partners. If a work is done for charity purposes or to serve the society it will not be called partnership. So, the motive of the business should be to earn profits. It doesn't mean that there will not be loses but the emotive should be the earning of profits.

4. **Existence of Business:** Partnership can only be for some kind of business. The term "Business" includes any trade, profession or occupation. By business we mean all activities concerning production, distribution and rendering of services for the purpose of earning profits. If the work is related to social service, we do not call it a business and hence, no partnership.

5. **Implied Authority:** There is implied authority that any partner can act on behalf of the firm. The business will be bound by the acts of partners.

6. **Unlimited Liability:** As the case of sole-trade business liability of the partners of a firm is unlimited. In case some obligation arises then not only the partnership assets but also the private property of the partners can be taken for the payment of liabilities of the firm to the third parties.

7. **Principal and Agent Relationship:** In partnership the relationship of principal and agent exists. It is not necessary that all partners should work in the business. Any one or more partners can act on behalf or other partners. Each partner is thereby an agent and can hence bind the firm through his activities and thereby bind other partners too.

8. **Utmost Good Faith:** The very basis of the partnership business is good faith and mutual trust. Every partner should act honestly and give proper accounts to other partner. The partnership cannot run if there is suspicion among other partners. It is very important that the partners should act as trustees and for the common good of all. Distrust and suspicion among partners may lead to the failure of many firms.

9. **Restriction to Transfer of Shares:** No partner can sell or transfer his shares to anybody else without the consent of the other partners. In case any partner does not want to continue in the partnership, he can give a notice for dissolution of firm.

10. **Common Management :** Every partner has right to take part in the running of the business. It is not necessary for all partners to participate in the day-to-day activities of the business but they are entitled to participate. Even if partnership business is run by some partners, the consent of all other partners is necessary for taking important decisions.

11. **Partners and Partnership are one:** A partnership firm has no separate entity from the partners. A firm is only a name to the collective name of partners. No firm can exist without partners. The rights and liabilities of partners are the rights and liabilities of the firm. Partners have implied authority to bind the firm for their acts.

12. **Capital Contribution:** The partners contribute to the capital of the firm. It is not necessary to

have capital in profit sharing ratio. A partner can be admitted to the firm even without contribution of capital. It is not essential that the partners should contribute to the firm's capital.

13. **Protection of Minority Interest:** All important decisions are generally taken by consensus. It ensures protection of those who may not agree to the majority view point. A partner may even ask for the dissolution of partnership if he feels aggrieved.

14. **Continuity:** There is no true limit for the continuity of a partnership firm. It goes on up to the time the partners want it to go. Any misunderstanding among partners, death or insolvency of a partner may dissolve the partnership. Dissolution of partnership does not necessarily mean dissolution of the firm. The remaining partners may continue the firm after meeting the claims of the outgoing partner.

Hindu Undivided Family [H.U.F]

Another form of business organization is Joint Hindu Family or Undivided Hindu Family. From the time immemorial, in India, the family business is carried on in the form of "Hindu Undivided Family" firm (HUF). This business has the feature of sole trading concern. An individual carries on the business on behalf of the firm. The business comes into being by the operation of law. HUF or Joint Hindu Family (JHF) will be set up by a male member of the family and carried on by the male members of the family. In the whole of India (except in Bengal and Assam where Dayabhaga system of Hindu law is operating) Mitakshara system is in operation. According to this system, male members inherit the ancestral property successively fro three generations. In this manner, son, grandson, and the great grand son become joint owners of the ancestral property. The business is managed by the senior member of the family called "Karta". Other members who are called coparceners have no right to participate in the management. If any misappropriation is caused by the Karta which results in a loss to the firm, he has to make good of such loss. The liability of the Karta is unlimited. HUF can be dissolved by mutual agreement of all co-parceners.

On the basis of the school of Hindu Law, joint Hindu Family is considered under two heads:

(i) Mitakshara

(ii) Dayabhaga

Characteristics /Nature/ Features of the Hindu Undivided

1. **Governed by Hindu Law:** The control and management of the joint Hindu family firm is done according to the uncodified and codified Hindu Law. The uncodified Hindu Law consists of two schools Mitakshara and Dayabhaga. In the same way rights and duties of its members are governed by uncodified Hindu Law.

2. **Membership by Birth:** The membership of the family can be acquired only by birth. Whosoever is born in the family becomes a member. Unlike other business an outsider cannot be admitted to its membership, because adoption is considered to be replantation in the family by which a person is being adopted. Marriage with the male member also confers membership. This is by the virtue of the fact that they are married to the person who is having membership by birth. These are the only two exceptions by which membership is acquired other than birth.

3. **Management:** The family affairs are managed by the senior most male member of the family known as 'karta' or 'manager'. The powers of the management are unlimited. He may manage or

mismanage, it cannot be questioned by any member. He can discriminate between the members but cannot deny maintenance or use of property. But the management is more effective due to the natural love and affection with members of the family.

4. **Limited Liabilities of Others:** All the members in a Joint Hindu Family have limited liability to the extent of property which is jointly held by the family. The self-acquired property of any member cannot be taken in order to satisfy the loans taken by the family. It is only the Joint Family property which is liable for satisfying debts. However Karta is also personally liable for the loans taken on promissory note.

5. **Continuity:** As it is already been discussed in the introduction, the death in the family doesn't bring the joint family firm to an end. It continues forever. There is no limit to its membership number also.

6. **Minor is also a member:** In partnership firm minor cannot become a partner. This is an important feature of this business organization that a person from its very birth becomes the member.

7. **Accounts:** As discussed earlier accounts are maintained by karta but this is not obligatory on his part. He is not accountable to any member and no member can ask what are the profits and losses of a transaction.

8. **Implied Authority of Karta:** There is an implied authority in favor of karta to contract debts and pledge the credit and property of the family for ordinary purposes of family business. These are binding on the entire family. No other member is having such authority.

Advantages of Hindu Undivided Family

- ***Centralized Management*** : The management of a Hindu joint family firm is centralized in the hands of one man known as "karta". He being the eldest and most experienced person gives a much disciplined management. Karta takes all decisions and gets them implemented with management. Karta takes all decisions and gets them implemented with the help of other members. He may be managing rightly or wrongly. No other member interferes in his management.

- ***Utmost Secrecy*** : The business requires secrecy of facts regarding it. As in Joint Hindu Family firm only the karta is to manage the entire show. He can do it with utmost secrecy which no other business can maintain; he can keep a thing secret even with the members of the firm.

- ***Quick Decision*** : In Joint Stock Company, it takes a long time to take a decision. A quick decision is of great advantage. Sometimes a very profitable venture is lost due to lack of decision. In joint family firm, as karta is the only decision maker, he can take a very quick decision. It is further advantageous the decision is final and unchallengeable.

- ***Credit Facilities*** : For every business money is required. In joint Hindu family firm the credit facilities are more. One reason for this is that the liability of karta is unlimited. There is also a pious obligation on the part of the sons of the karta to satisfy even the unsatisfied debts raised by him during his lifetime. Moreover, karta has personal relation with others and hence it becomes helpful to raise funds.

  Working according to capacity : Unlike other business organization the work assigned to the members according to their capacity. A physically handicapped or a partly disabled member may be assigned a little work or no work at all. This will not disentitle him of his various needs and the benefits which are being given to other members. A person who is physically strong may be assigned work of physical nature. Infants are not required to work at all even though they are the members of such firm.

- ***Natural love between members :*** There may be a contractual force or the temptations of profits which is between the members of a business organization. But in Joint Hindu Family Firm, it is the natural love and affection which the members are having for each other. Due to this, they are ignoring the shortcomings of each other and help to run the business more smoothly and efficiently.
- ***Economy :*** In a business, for its success, economy is a must. It is well balanced and maintained in Joint Hindu Family firm. The family is concerned with profits as they are to form the part of joint family property. Karta spends money with great caution and economy. This is also due to the constantly hanging sword of partition of family on the neck of karta.
- ***Limited Liability :*** The liability of all the members of the family firm is limited to their undivided shares in the property of the family. However, karta's liabilities are unlimited. This is also great advantage to Joint Hindu Family firm.

Dis-advantages/Limitations of Hindu Undivided Family

- ***No reward for efficiency :*** All the members of the family are provided with basic needs and other facilities. The persons who work more efficiently and dedicatedly are not rewarded for their work. So efficient workers are also tempted to work less. It encourages laziness on the part of family members. The members try to avoid work.
- ***Limited Capital :*** The investments are limited only up to the resources of one family. There may not be sufficient funds to meet business requirements or expansion. This is great disadvantage these days, when big industries are being encouraged.
- ***Limited Managerial Skill :*** Only the eldest make member of the family is to manage the family business. He is performing all the functions of the management. He may not be well conversant with the knowledge of business skill and other problems of the business management. In spite of this he is managing and continuous to mange the business of joint Hindu family firm.
- ***Suspicion :*** The Karta is empowered with vast power of secrecy and he can keep a thing Secret even from its members. But there is no restriction on him that he cannot disclose anything to any person with whom he is having more love. This gives birth to suspicion among the members themselves which can be disastrous to Joint Hindu Family Firm.

Distinction Between Partnership and Joint Hindu Firm

- ***Governance***: Partnership firm is governed by the Indian Partnership Act where as Joint Hindu Family Firm is governed by the two schools – (i) Mitakshara and (ii) Devabhaga
- ***Creation***: The partnership firm is created by mutual agreement between the partners which may be written or oral. Their relationship is contractual whereas for the creation of Joint Hindu Family firm no such contract is required.
- ***Number of Members***: In partnership firm the maximum number of members is fixed. It is ten in

case of banking firm and twenty in case of other type of partnership firm, but in case of Joint Hindu Family Concern there is not such maximum limit fixed for the number of members.

- ***Admission***: A new partner can be admitted to Partnership only with the due consent of other partners,whereas in case of Joint Hindu Family concern the birth of the person to the family itself brings him in folds. However, one can also be admitted by adoption or by marriage to the male member of the family.
- ***Position of Minor***: A minor can become the partner in case of a partnership firm to the extent of benefits of the firm and that to with consent among all the other members. But in Joint Hindu Family firm there is no such restriction and a child, as soon as he is born, becomes the active member.
- ***Management***: Every partner can take active part in the management of Partnership firm whereas in Joint Hindu Family firm he power to manage is centralized in the hands of Karta.
- ***Accounts***: Accounts are to be properly maintained and any partner can inspect the accounts at any time in case of Partnership firm, but in case of Joint Hindu Family concern karta is not under any obligation to maintain accounts. No member can even ask fro account details from the karta.
- ***Easy Dissolution***: The partnership firm can be dissolved on insolvency, lunacy, or death of a partner where as in case of Joint Hindu Family concern will not be dissolved on insolvency, lunacy, or death of a member. Only partition can bring it to an end.
- ***Registration***: Registration is not compulsory and advisable for a Partnership firm to enable it to enforce a claim against outsider. But in case of Joint Hindu Family concern it is not necessary at all.

Joint Stock Company

Prior to the Industrial Revolution there was no use of plant and machinery to produce goods. The production at that time was on a very small scale and the manufacturing activity was carried on in cottages. Craftsmen were producing the goods on a small scale market and the market was limited. Only luxury goods were produced for foreign market. That too on small scale. Hence only, sole trading concerns and partnership firms were the forms of business that were operating.

However, the limitations of sole-proprietorship and partnership forms of ownership gave birth to joint stock company form of organization. Two important limitations of earlier forms of organization were inadequacy of funds and unlimited liability. The capacity of sole-trader to provide funds for business is limited. Even in partnership where two or more persons join and combine their funds, the limitation of funds is felt. The demand for funds in business increased with the expansion and development of the trade and industry. The earlier forms of organization could not meet the ever increasing demands for funds of business. The other limitation which hampered the growth of business was the unlimited liability of the owners. The liability of proprietors was the unlimited liability of owners. The liability of proprietors was not limited to only the amounts invested in business. Their private properties could also be used to meet business liabilities. The factor of unlimited liability discouraged people to invest more even if they had the capacity to do so. The joint stock company form of organization provides an answer to difficulties faced by earlier form of organization provides an answer to the difficulties faced by earlier forms. The liability of members is limited and the participation of large number of persons help in raising more funds under joint stock company form of organization.

Definitions

A company is "Associations of many persons who contribute money or money's worth to a common stock and employ it in some trade or business, and who share the profit and loss arising there form." – ***James Stephen***

"A corporation is an artificial being, invisible, intangible and existing only in contemplation of the law. Being a mere creation of law, it possesses only the properties which the charter of its creation confers upon it either expressly or incidental to its very existence. " – ***Chief Justice Marshall***

Characteristics of the Joint Stock Company

1. ***Association of Persons:*** A company is an association of persons joining hands with the common motive. A private limited company must have at least two persons and a public limited company must have at least seven members to get registered. Furthermore, the number of shareholders should not exceed 50 in private companies but there is no limitation of maximum number in case of public limited company.

2. ***Independent Legal Entity:*** The company is created under law. It has a separate entity apart from its members. A company acts independently of its members. The company is not bound by the acts of its members and members do not act as agents of the company. A person can own its shares and can be its creditor too. The life of the company is independent of the lives of its members. The company can sue and get sued by its own name.

3. ***Limited Liability:*** The liability of its shareholders is limited to the values of its shares they have purchased. In case the company incurs huge balance on their shares. The company being a separate legal entity can incur debts in its own name and the shareholders will not be personally liable for that. However, shareholders of a limited company have unlimited liability. The liability of members of a company limited by guarantee is limited to the guaranteed amount.

4. ***Common Seal:*** A company being an artificial person cannot put its signature. The law requires every company to have a seal and get its name engraved on it. The seal of the company is affixed on all important documents or contracts as a token of signature. The directors must witness the affixation of the seal.

5. ***Transferability of Shares:*** The shares of a company can be transferred by its members. Whenever the members want to dispose off the shares, they can do so by following the procedure devised for this purpose. Under Articles of Association the company can out certain restrictions on the transfer of shares but it cannot altogether stop it. However, private companies can put more restrictions on transferability of shares, virtually making it zero.

6. ***Separation of Ownership of Management:*** The shareholders of a company are widely scattered. A shareholder may like to invest money but may not be interested in its management. The companies are managed by Board of Directors. The Ownership and management are in two separate hands. The shareholders do not get any right to participate in company management. The right to manage company affairs is vested in the directors who are elected representatives of shareholders.

7. ***Perpetual Existence:*** The company has a permanent existence. The shareholders may come or may go out but the company will go but the company will go forever. The continuity of the company is not affected by death, lunacy or insolvency of the shareholders. The company can be

wound up only by the operation of law. The shares of the company may change different hands but the continuity of the company is not affected.

8. ***Corporate Finance:*** A joint stock company, generally, raises large amounts of funds. The capital is divided into shares of small denominations. A large number of persons purchase shares and contribute to the capital of the company. Since there is no limit on number of maximum members in public companies, large amounts of sources can be raised from persons in different walks of life.
9. ***Centralized and Delegated Management:*** A Joint Stock Company is an autonomous and self-governed body. The shareholders being large in number cannot look after the day-to-day activities of the company. They elect Board of Directors in general body meeting for managing the company. All policies of the company are decided by a majority vote. All important decisions are taken in a democratic way. The centralized management and democratic functioning brings a unity of action.
10. ***Publication of Accounts:*** A Joint Stock Company is required to file annual statements with the registrar of companies at the end of a financial year. The annual statement is available for inspection in the office of Registrar.

Trusts

A trust is an obligation annexed to the ownership of property and arising out of a confidence reposed and accepted by the owner, or declared and accepted by him, for the benefit of another, or of another and the owner. The person who reposes or declares the confidence is called the 'author of trust'; Person who accepts the confidence is called 'Trustee'; the person for whose benefit the confidence is accepted is called the 'Beneficiary'. The subject-matter of the trust is called 'Trust Property or Trust Money'.

In the words of ***Prof. Keeton***, "A trust is the relationship which arises whenever a person is called the trustee is compelled in Equity to hold property, whether real or personal, and whether by legal or equitable title, for the benefit of persons or for some object permitted by law, in such a way that the real benefit of the property accrues not to the trustee, but to the beneficiaries or other objects of the trust".

Clubs and Associations

Meaning of Clubs

A club is an association of persons to possess a building as a common resort for the members, like a club house or the house occupied by the club itself. No members of a club are liable to pay any money beyond the subscription required by the rules to be paid so long as he remains a member.

The formation off club and its control, management provision for elections and providing facilities to the members and other related things are left to the discretion of the members forming a club. Clubs are subject to certain legal restrictions and duties. Clubs provide a variety of facilities such as accommodation, food etc. at confessional rates to its members. However most of the clubs are meant for the high income groups and the elite as membership fees are exorbitant. Some of the clubs carry on antisocial activities within its premises.

Meaning of Associations

Associations are voluntary organizations which are formed to protect or further the interests of members. The associations pursue common interests of the members through actions. Besides social organizations, there are organizations for protecting the business interests of members also. Different type of business units forms their own associations for furthering their interests. The member units do not loss this identity while becoming the members of these associations. The decisions of the associations are not binding on the members and they also have a freedom to withdraw their membership. In the context of business, associations can take the form of Trade Associations. Trade Unions, Chambers of Commerce and Informal Agreements. These organization, though related to business, do not undertake any type of business. These associations are merely to protect the interests of members and take up the issues of members with different authorities.

1. Trade Associations

A Trade and Industrial Association may be described as a voluntary association of business units operating in the same field for the promotion of their common economic interests. It is a non-profit organization and does not lose their common economic interests. It is non profit organization and does not enter into any business transactions. The member units of such associations do not lose their separate entity and the association does not interfere in their internal functioning in anyway. The main object of the associations is to protect the common interests of combining units. The working of trade association is similar to that of ordinary company form of organization. The representatives of member units elect Board of Directors to supervise management of the association. The office-bearers retire at the annual general meeting and can seek re-election.

A trade association may or may not have the share capital. Of it does not have the share capital, its financial requirements are met by subscription fees. A trade association prepares its own Memorandum and Articles of Association or by-laws for regulating it. The documents contain the powers and duties of the office bearers.

The examples of trade associations in India are Bombay Mill Owners' Association, Ahemdabad Textile Mill Owners' Association, Bengal Silk and Art Silk Mill Owners' Association. Calcutta Trade Association, Madras Trade Association and so on. These associations are established to look after the interests of their members. They aim at encouraging friendly communication among members.

Nature/Feature/Characteristics of Trade

1. The membership of trade association is voluntary.
2. The associations are formed by persons engaged in similar branch of trade and industry.
3. These associations are not profit earning bodies.
4. The associations are generally named after the nature of trade or industry conducted by members.
5. The members are free to carry on their business as they like. The associations do not interfere in the working of units.

Advantages of Trade Associations

These associations serve the interests of members in a number of ways. The following are some of the advantages of trade associations.

i. The association arrange a number of facilities for members which otherwise may not be possible for individual members.

ii. The problems faced by the member units are taken up with local or state authorities. The focal point associations take up the problems of infrastructural facilities with the authorities. The delays in supplying controlled raw materials are taken up with appropriate authorities.

iii. The associations create a sense of co-operation among traders and industrialists. They sit together and discuss their difficulties. This forum helps them to adopt uniform policies also.

iv. They also help members in avoiding cut-throat competition and avoid losses. Sometimes the prices are fixed, sometimes production quotas are fixed etc. though these decisions cannot be forced on the members but still such things are followed because this serves the interests of members.

v. The associations also try to settle the disputes among members and save them from litigation etc.

2. Trade Unions

According to the Indian Trade Union Act, a Trade Union is "a combination formed for the purpose of regulating the relations between workmen and employers, or between workmen and workmen, or between employers and employees or for imposing restrictive conditions on the conduct of any trade or business." In general, the term 'trade union' is understood to mean a union or an association of workers formed for looking after their interests. There can also be trade unions of employers. These Unions are registered under the Trade Union Act.

3. Chambers of Commerce

A Chamber of commerce is an association of persons engaged in commerce, trade and industry for protecting their interests and promoting their common causes. The merchants, manufacturers, bankers and others come together to form chambers so that they are able to raise those issues which affect all of them. As in case of workers they form trade unions, similarly in the case of businessmen they form chambers of commerce, trade, industry etc. these are the unions which work for the uplift of their business and try to protect their interests.

The chamber of commerce may be local, national, international. Bombay Chamber of Commerce, Bengal Chamber of Commerce, Madras Chamber of Commerce, are the examples of Local chamber. The Indian Chamber of commerce is an example if National Chamber. The London Chamber of Commerce is the example for International Chamber. The local chamber of commerce deals with the local problems associated to trade.

Need for Chambers of Commerce

There are many problem's faced by trade and industry. These may require them to be brought to the notice of government authorities. The problems may relate to certain laws, taxation policies, controls etc. The following may be few reasons for chambers:

1. **Government Interference:** The laissez-faire days are gone now. Government is taking active interest in the working of trade, commerce and industry. There are various government regulations which have a direct influence on the working of business houses. From the registration or start of a unit up to the sale of products, there are number of rules and regulations devised for the business. The excessive interference of government into economic activities of trade has necessitated the formation of chambers so that business viewpoint is put before the authorities.
2. **Specialized Services:** The present day business requires information about trade and industry. The business units require information about Trade and Industry. The business units require information about business opportunities at different places. It may not be possible for every unit to collect this information. The chambers collect every type of information about business and then pass it on to the members. So the chamber provides special services to the members.
3. **For Developing Business:** The chambers are also required for the development of business. There may be business opportunities at different opportunities. Unless otherwise these opportunities are known to the businessmen, these may not be exploited. So the chambers are necessary even for the development of business.
4. **Development of Trade Unions:** There is generally a conflict between the workers and the capitalists. The workers have organized themselves into various trade unions. They have increased their bargaining power by organizing themselves. The capitalists have organized themselves in the chamber of commerce

Advantages/ Merits/ Benefits of Chambers

1. The chambers provide every type of trade information to the traders at their door steps. They issue pamphlets and periodicals which contain trade information. The help the traders to find out the manufacturers of various products.
2. The chambers give suggestions to businessman about the expansion and diversion of their units. They suggest about the opportunities available in different areas. The businessman can take appropriate decisions in view of information and suggestions provided by the chambers.
3. The chambers bring together various businessmen under their banner. This gives strength to the business community. The chambers act as mouth-piece of trade and industry.
4. The chambers help the government by providing reactions of trade and industry to various regulations and laws framed by it. The government can make changes in laws etc. the chambers of their own too give advice to the government and suggest measures for the development of trade and industry.
5. The chambers also provide commerce education and have research facilities for the benefit of members.

Models of BGS Relationships

Interactions among business, government, and society are infinite and their meaning is open to interpretation. Faced with this complexity, many people use simple models to impose order and meaning on what they observe. These models are like prisms, each having a different refractive quality, each giving the holder a different view of the world. Depending on the model (or prism) used, a person will think differently about the scope of business power in society, criteria for managerial decisions, the extent of corporate responsibility, the ethical duties of managers, and the need for regulation. The following four models are basic alternatives for seeing the BGS relationship. As abstractions they oversimplify reality and magnify central issues. Each model can be both descriptive and prescriptive; that is, it can be both an explanation of how the BGS relationship does work and, in addition, an ideal about how it should work.

1. The Market Capitalism Model

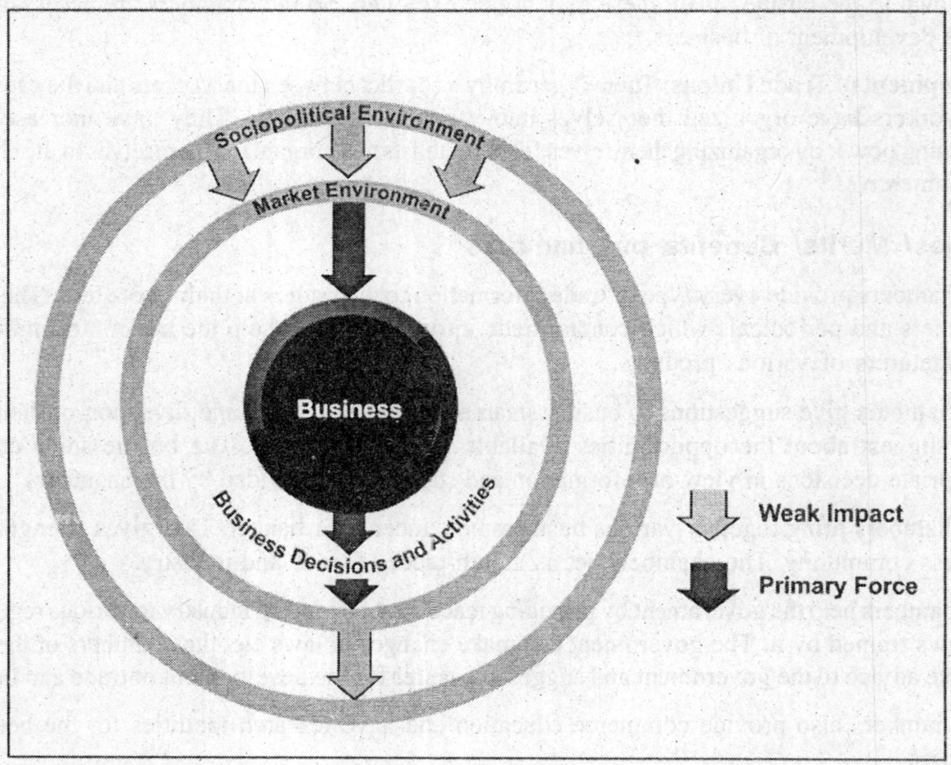

a. Business operates within a market environment.

b. Primarily responding to economic forces.

c. Sheltered from direct impact of social and political forces.

d. Business is substantially sheltered from the direct impact of socio political forces and focuses on the primary economic forces.

e. Market environment is shaped by business operations and by social and political pressures.

f. The market is a buffer between business units and non-market forces.

g. "Classic Capitalism": most economic activity is carried on by private firms in competitive markets.

h. It is based on the assumption of Laissez-faire (the government should let us alone).

i. Individuals have the freedom to pursue self-interest and therefore individuals are motivated by the desire to make money.

j. Assumes that individuals can own property and are free to risk investments.

Key Implications:

- Business interacts directly with market environment and is partly insulated from government and social environment.
- Business (managers) concentrates exclusively on market goals, i.e. profitability and expansion.
- Market performance is the only yardstick of business contribution to societal goals and efficiency is the superior value.
- Government, not business, has primary responsibility for solving social problems; government institutions are designed to monitor and adjust nonmarket environment of business.
- Business should not be subject to government regulation which undermines efficiency.
- Business executives should accept social values as given and not attempt to influence them.
- Support-the model is dominant in the thinking of a majority of managers in business, especially in small firms.

Model Origins:

Historically people produced for subsistence.

1700s people start to produce for trade.

Market economy reshaped human life.

Emerges when people move beyond subsistence production to production.

For trade: Adam Smith's, "The Wealth of Nations".

Capitalism and the "invisible hand".

Market's pricing mechanism reconciled supply & demand making commodities cheaper, better, and more available

Greater good for society when businesses compete freely

Managerial capitalism (early 1900s)

Market economy in which dominant businesses are large firms run by salaried managers, not smaller firms run by owners.

Model Assumptions:

Government interference is slight or "laissez-faire"

Government, not business, should correct social problems

Managers focus on profit and efficiency

Individuals can own property and freely risk investments

Markets convert selfish competition into broad social benefits

Informed consumers making rational decisions

Moral restraint of business

Many producers and consumers

Market Capitalism Model Perspective Conclusions:

Government regulation should be limited

Proper measure of corporate performance is profit

Ethical duty of management is to promote the interests of shareholders

Model Critics:

Creates prosperity only at the cost of rising inequality

Markets erode virtue

Greed

Ruthlessness

Profit motive encourages plundering of the earth

2. The Dominance Model

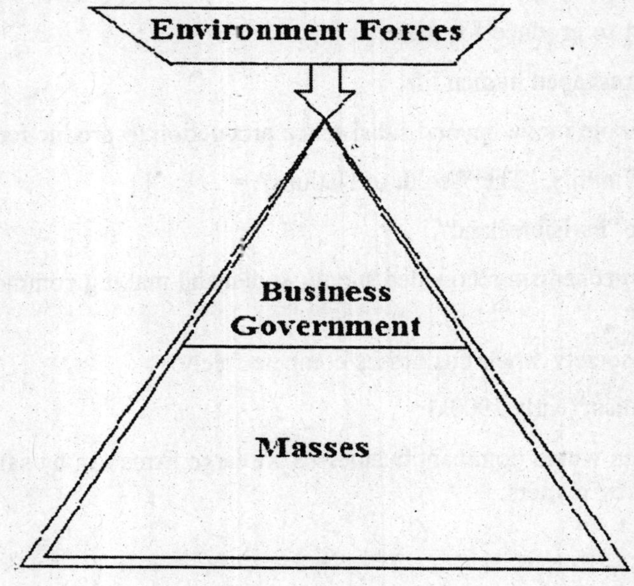

Implications:

Began in 1870s.

Resulted in reform movement of populism.

President, Union Pacific "could buy Congress".

Railroad magnate, Vanderbilt "The public be damned!

Rise of unionization of railroads and added government regulation.

Business and government dominate the great mass of people, which results in the enrichment of a few at the expense of many.

Populist reform movement opposed the dominance model. Marxism emerged in Europe about the same time.

Most accurate in the 1800s, but is being resurrected due to the fear of transnational corporations in a global context.

Business abuses the power as its size and wealth confer in many ways.

Corporate asset concentration creates monopoly or oligopoly in markets that reduces competition and harms consumers.

The idea that concentration of economic power results in abuse arose in response to the awesome economic growth of the nineteenth century.

Proper measure of corporate performance is profit

Ethical duty of management is to promote the interests of shareholders.

Perspectives of Dominance Model:

The view that business is the most powerful institution in society, because of its control of wealth. This power is held to be inadequately checked and therefore excessive.

A merger wave between 1895 and 1904 concentrated economic growth.

The public viewed these huge firms as colossal monuments to greed.

In the twentieth century, corporations continued to grow in size, but the marked rise in asset concentration slowed and leveled off.

Today the number of transnational firms and the scale of their activity have grown, however the largest global firms do not show signs of concentrating international assets.

Elite dominance: Beliefs that there are a small number of individuals who, by virtue of wealth and position, control the nation.

The Power Elite by C. Wright Mills is the modern impetus for this theory.

Power elite

A small group of individuals in control of the economy, government and the military.

Model Critics:

Creates prosperity only at the cost of rising inequality

Markets erode virtue

Greed

Ruthlessness

Profit motive encourages plundering of the earth

3. The Countervailing Forces Model

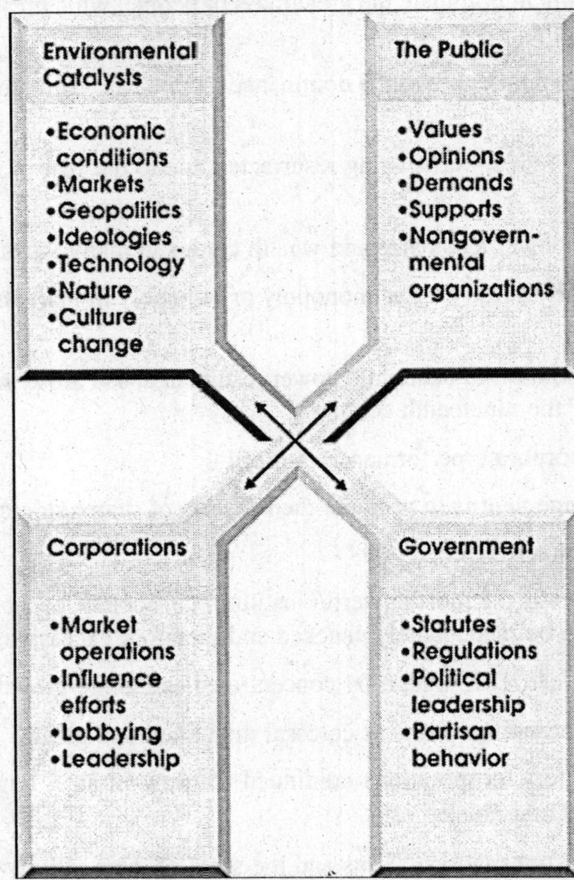

The Canadian-born, Berkeley-trained John Kenneth Galbraith has been considered by many as the "Last American Institutionalist". As a result, Galbraith has remained something of a renegade in modern economics - and his work has been nothing if not provocative. In the 1950s, he presented economics with two tracts that needled the mainstream:

a) One developing a theory of price control (which arose out of his wartime experience in the Office of Price Administration) which he argued for as an anti-inflation policy (1952);

b) The second, American Capitalism (1952), which argued that American post-war success arose not out of "getting the prices right" in an orthodox sense, but rather of "getting the prices wrong" and allowing industrial concentration to develop. It is a formula for growth because it enables technical innovation which might otherwise not been done. However, it can only be regarded as successful provided there is a "countervailing power" against potential abuse in the form of trade unions, supplier and consumer organizations and government regulation.

Many have since argued the formula for East Asian success. Later in the century it was based precisely on this combination of oligopolistic power and "countervailing" institutions.

Countervailing forces model conclusions:

Business is deeply integrated into an open society and must respond to many forces, both economic and noneconomic. Business is a major initiator of change in society through its interaction with government, its production and marketing activities, and its use of new technologies. Broad public support of business depends on its adjustment to multiple social, political, and economic forces. BGS relationships continuously evolve as changes take place in the main ideas, institutions and processes of society.

4. The Stakeholder Model

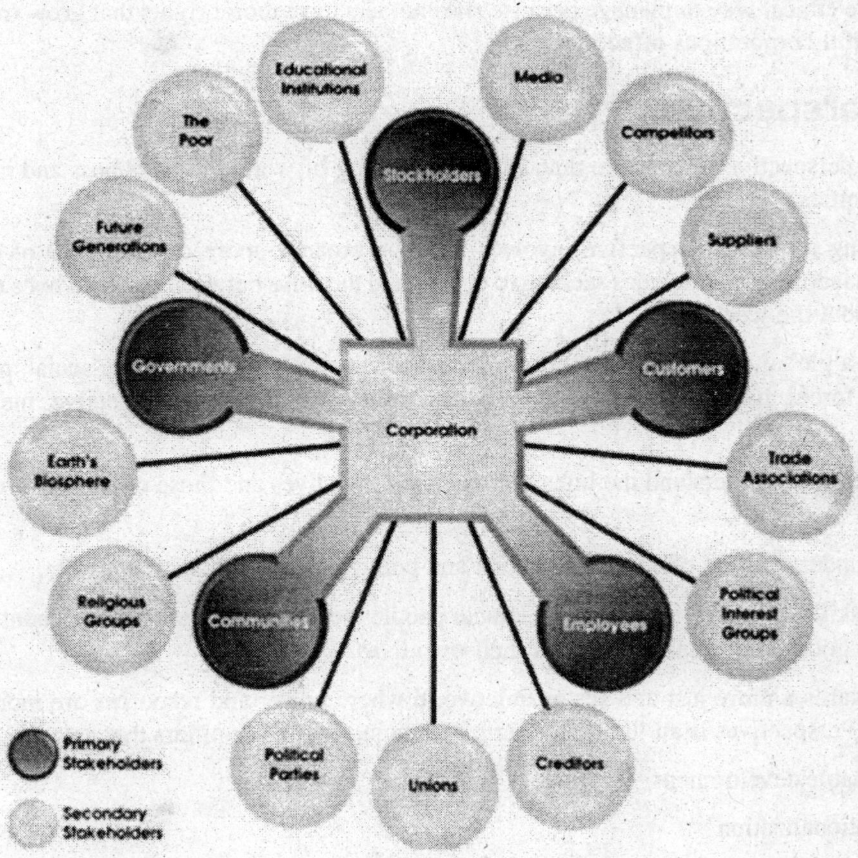

Stakeholders are those whom the corporation benefits or burdens by its actions and those who benefit or burden the firm with their actions:

(i) Primary stakeholders

(ii) Secondary stakeholders

(iii) Debate about how to identify who is a stakeholder.

(iv) Stakeholder model is an ethical theory of management in which the welfare of each stakeholder must be considered as an end.

1. **Criticism of the stakeholder model:**

   a) It is not a realistic assessment of the power relationships between the corporation and other entities.

   b) There is no single, clear and objective measure to evaluate the combined ethical/economic performance of a firm.

2. **Advocacy for the stakeholder model:**

   a) A corporation that embraces stakeholders performs better.

   b) It is the ethical way to manage because stakeholders have moral rights that grow from the way powerful corporations affect them.

Global Perspective of BGS

A global perspective is far more than an understanding of worldwide business and international career opportunities.

Developing a global perspective involves taking a broader, more critical view of experience, knowledge and learning and includes seeking to understand the links between our own lives and those of people throughout the world.

To adopt a global perspective, we need to enhance our understanding of the social, political and environmental forces that shape our existence. Thus, 'developing a global perspective' means that we aim to:

(i) Enable people to understand the links between their own lives and those of people throughout the world.

(ii) Increase understanding of economic, social and political forces which shapes life.

(iii) Develop skills, attitudes and values to enable people working together to bring about change for 'common good' and to take control of their own lives.

Work towards a more just and sustainable world where power and resources are more equitably shared. Global Perspectives is an 'umbrella' term embracing four main pillars that are:

a) Sustainable development

b) Internationalization

c) Global issues

d) Global processes.

e) Each pillar contributes to the development of global citizens.

The broadly encompassing definition of Sustainable Development is "Development that meets the needs of the present without compromising the ability of future generations to meet their own needs".

A global perspective emphasizes 'human values' but not at the expense of ignoring the need for sustainable development and environmental issues.

An understanding of sustainable development is part of the knowledge required of the global citizen who will also comprehend the potential impact of local activity on the global and vice versa, with regard to such things as pollution, climate change and exploitation of natural resources. Adopting a global perspective requires that:

a) Actions which secure more sustainable development are pursued.

b) Actions which are not sustainable are challenged.

c) Change is sought to ensure that development does not compromise the quality of life for future generations.

People around the globe are more connected to each other than ever before. Information and money too flow more quickly than ever before. Goods and services produced in one part of the world are increasingly available in all parts of the world. International communication is commonplace. This phenomenon has been titled "globalization." The era of globalization is fast becoming the preferred term for describing the current times. Because we are thoughtful people concerned about world affairs, our job is to pick up "globalization," examine it from all sides, dissect it, figure out what makes it tick, and then nurture and promote the good parts and mitigate or slow down the negetive parts. While it is homogenizing cultures, it is also enabling people to share their unique individuality farther and wider. Globalization has dangers and an ugly darker side. But it can also bring tremendous opportunities and benefits. Just as capitalism requires a net-work of governing systems to keep it from devouring societies, globalization requires vigilance and the rule of law. The term "globalization" was first coined in the 1980s, but the concept stretches back decades, even centuries, if you count the trading empires built by Spain, Portugal, Britain, and Holland. Some would say the world was as globalized 100 years ago as it is today, with international trade and migration. But the 1930s depression had a lasting impact to that. Nation-states drawback into their shells on realizing that international markets could deliver untold misery in the form of poverty and unemployment. The resolve of Western states to build and strengthen international ties in the aftermath of World War II laid the groundwork for today's globalization. It has brought diminishing national borders and the fusing of individual markets. The falloff protectionist barriers has stimulated free movement of capital and paved the way for companies to set up several bases around the world. The rise of the Internet and recent advances in telecommunications has boosted the already surging train. For consumers and avowed capitalists, this is largely a good thing. Vigorous trade has made for greater spending, rising living standards, and a growth in international trade. And that is just the tip of it. Supporters of globalization say it has promoted information exchange which led to a greater understanding of other cultures, and allowed democracy to triumph over autocracy.

For now, global capitalism is ascendant. It brings unprecedented wealth creation and new material comforts. But it also imposes burdens on human rights and the environment, challenges diversity of values, and creates conflict with those who are fed upon in the lively predation or who stand aloof from the free market consensus. A fitting perspective on the BGS relationship must, therefore, be global.

Historical Perspective of BGS

The BGS relationship is a stream of events, of which only one part exists today. Historical perspective is important for many reasons. It helps us see that today's BGS relationship is not like that of other eras; that current ideas and institutions are not the only alternative; that historical forces are irrepressible; that corporations both cause and adapt to change; that our era is not unique in undergoing rapid change; and that we are shaping the future now. When appropriate, we examine the antecedents of current arrangements.

Review Questions

Conceptual Type

1. What is a business?
2. What do you mean by government?
3. What do you mean by society?

Analytical Type

1. Explain importance of BGS to managers.
2. Explain the characteristics of business.
3. Explain model of BGS relationship.
4. Discuss assumptions of market capitalism model.
5. Discuss implications of dominance model.
6. Discuss stakeholder model.
7. Discuss BGS in historical perspectives.

Descriptive Type

1. Explain nature of the business.
2. What are the objectives of business?
3. Discuss market capitalism model with key implications.
4. Discuss dominance model in detail.
5. Write note on: countervailing forces model.
6. Explain BGS in global perspectives.
7. What are the responsibilities of government towards business and business towards government?

*****

Module-2

The Dynamic Environment

Syllabus

Historical forces changing the Business environment – Key environments of Business – Power dimensions of Business – Theoretical perspective – Sociological perspective.

Introduction

Business Environment means the environment that affects business, be it external or internal. Managers must understand the impact of these forces on the business. This understanding of the business environment help managers to react effectively to changes in the environment and make better decisions. The environmental factors also help organizations to plan for the future.

Any business manager must understand the environment to be able to make better decisions. The environment that affects business can be classified based on different contexts. The environment may be based on economic and non economic factors. The economic factors constitute the monetary and fiscal policy, the industrial policy, the price trends, the nature of the economic development etc. The non economic factors are the political and legal system, the socio cultural aspects and the educational system. The economic factors influence the non-economic factors and the non economic factors have an influence on the economic factors.

A business manager has to consider the economic environment to decide the price of a product, the financial environment helps to understand the means of financing available for the company and the legal environment is essential while framing the policies of the organization.

The term business environment is composed of two words 'Business' and 'Environment'. In simple terms, the state in which a person remains busy is known as Business. The word Business in its economic sense means human activities like production, extraction or purchase or sales of goods that are performed for earning profits.

On the other hand, the word 'Environment' refers to the aspects of surroundings. Therefore, Business Environment may be defined as a set of conditions-social, legal, economical, political or institutional that are uncontrollable in nature and affects the functioning of organization.

The environment is the surrounding. It could be a physical element; physical environment that includes the built environment, natural environment; air conditions, water, land, atmosphere etc. or it could be human environment - people surrounding the item or thing. This is also known as the social environment and includes elements like the spiritual environment, emotional environment, home, family etc. Business Environment is a set of conditions Social, Legal, Economical, Political or Institutional that are uncontrollable in nature and affects the functioning of organization.

Meaning of Environment

Environment is the sum of all living and non-living things that surround an organism or group of organisms. Environment includes all elements, factors and conditions that have some impact on the growth and development of certain organism. Environment includes both biotic and abiotic factors that have influence on observed organism.

Scope of the Environment

1. *Totality of external forces:* Business environment is the sum total of all things external to business firms and as such it is aggregated in nature.

2. *Specific and general forces:* Business environment includes both specific and general forces. Specific forces such as investors, customers, competitors and suppliers affect individual enterprises directly and immediately in their day-to-day working. General forces such as social, political, legal

and technological conditions have impact on all business enterprises and thus may affect an individual firm only indirectly.

3. ***Dynamic nature:*** Business environment is dynamic and it keeps on changing whether in terms of technological improvement, shifts in consumer preferences or entry of new competitor in the market.

4. ***Uncertainty:*** Business environment is largely uncertain as it is very difficult to predict future happenings, especially when environment changes are taking place too frequently as in the case of information technology or fashion industries.

5. ***Relativity:*** Business environment is a relative concept since it differs from country to country and even region to region. Political conditions in the USA, for instance, differ from those in China or Pakistan. Similarly, demand for sarees may be fairly high in India whereas it may be almost non-existent in France.

6. ***Strategies and policies:*** Helps an organization to form its broad strategies and long term policies.

7. ***Competitor's analysis:*** Enables an organization to analyse its competitor's strategy and thereby formulate effective competitive strategies.

8. ***Dynamism:*** Knowledge about changing environment will keep the organization dynamic in its approach.

9. ***Impact:*** Enables the organizations to foresee the impact of socio- economic changes at the national and international level on its stability.

10. ***Adjustment:*** As a result of the study, executives are able to adjust to the prevailing conditions and thus influence the environment to make it congenial to carry out business.

Environmental Analysis

Environmental analysis refers to the evaluation of the possible or probable effects of external forces and conditions on an organization's survival and growth strategies.

Environmental analysis is the use of analytical chemistry and other techniques to study the environment. The purpose of this is commonly to monitor and study levels of pollutants in the atmosphere, rivers and other specific settings.

Benefits of Environmental Analysis

The benefits of environmental analysis can be summarized as follows:

i) ***Identification of Strength:*** The analysis of the internal environment helps to identify strength of the firm. For instance, if the company has good personal policies in respect of promotion, transfer, training, etc. than it can indicates strength of the firm in respect of personal policies. This strength can be identified through the job satisfaction and performance of the employees. After identifying the strengths the firm must try to consolidate its strengths by further improvement in its existing plans & policies.

ii) ***Identification of Weakness:*** The analysis of the internal environment indicates not only strengths but also the weakness of the firm. A firm may be strong in certain areas; where as it may be weak in some other areas. The firm should identify sue weakness so as to correct them as early as possible.

iii) ***Identification of Opportunities:*** An analysis of the external environment helps the business firm to identify the opportunities in the market. The business firm should make every possible effort to grab the opportunities as and when they come.

iv) ***Identification of Threats:*** Business may be subject to threats from competitors and others. Therefore environmental analysis helps to identify threats from the environment identification of threats at an earlier date is always beneficial to the firm as it helps to defuse the same.

v) ***Exploitation of Business Opportunities:*** Environment opens new opportunities for the expansion of business activities. Study of environment is necessary in order to discover and exploit such opportunities fully.

vi) ***Keeping Business Enterprise Alert:*** Environment study is needed as it keeps the business unit alert in its approach and activities. In the absence of environmental changes, the business activities will be dull and lifeless. The problems & prospects of business can be understood properly through the study of business environment. This enables an enterprise to face the problems with confidence and secure the maximum benefits of business opportunities available.

vii) ***Keeping Business Flexible and Dynamic:*** Study of business environment is needed for keeping business flexible and dynamic as per the changes in the environmental forces. This will enable the development of business organization.

viii) ***Understanding Future Problems and Prospects:*** The study of business environment enables to understand future problems and prospects of business in advance. This enables business organizations to face the problems boldly and also take the benefit of favorable situation.

ix) ***Making Business Socially Acceptable:*** Environment study enables businessmen to expand the business and also make it acceptable to different social groups. Business organizations can make positive contribution for maintaining ecological balance by studying social environment.

x) ***Ensures Optimum Utilization of Resources:*** The study of business environment is needed as it ensures optimum use of resources available. For this, the study of economic and technological environment is useful. Such study enables organization to take full benefit of government policies, concessions provided, and technological developments and so on.

xi) ***Ensures Survival and Growth:*** Business environment inform about suitable changes to be affected in business policies. This helps the business organizations to grow and prosper.

xii) ***Maintaining adaptability to changes:*** Business environment guides the business organization about socio-economic changes & the organization must accordingly adapt this change. This enables the business organization to survive for a longer period.

Process of Environmental Analysis

The various stages of environmental analysis process are as follows:

Stage 1: Identification of relevant environmental variables

All environmental variables do not have the same relevance to all the industries. A variable that is relevant to one industry may not be relevant for another. It is essential to identify the critical environmental variables and to predict their future trends.

Stage 2: Collection of Information

This involves identification of sources of information, determination of the types of information to be collected, selection of methods of data collection etc.

Stage 3: Forecasting

Decision making requires a future orientation. Forecasting is concerned with developing projections of the direction, scope and intensity of environmental change.

Stage 4: Monitoring

The characteristics of the variables or their trends may undergo changes. New variables may emerge as critical or the relevance of certain variables may decline. It is necessary to monitor such changes. Some time it is necessary to re-collection of information and re-forecasting.

Environmental Factors

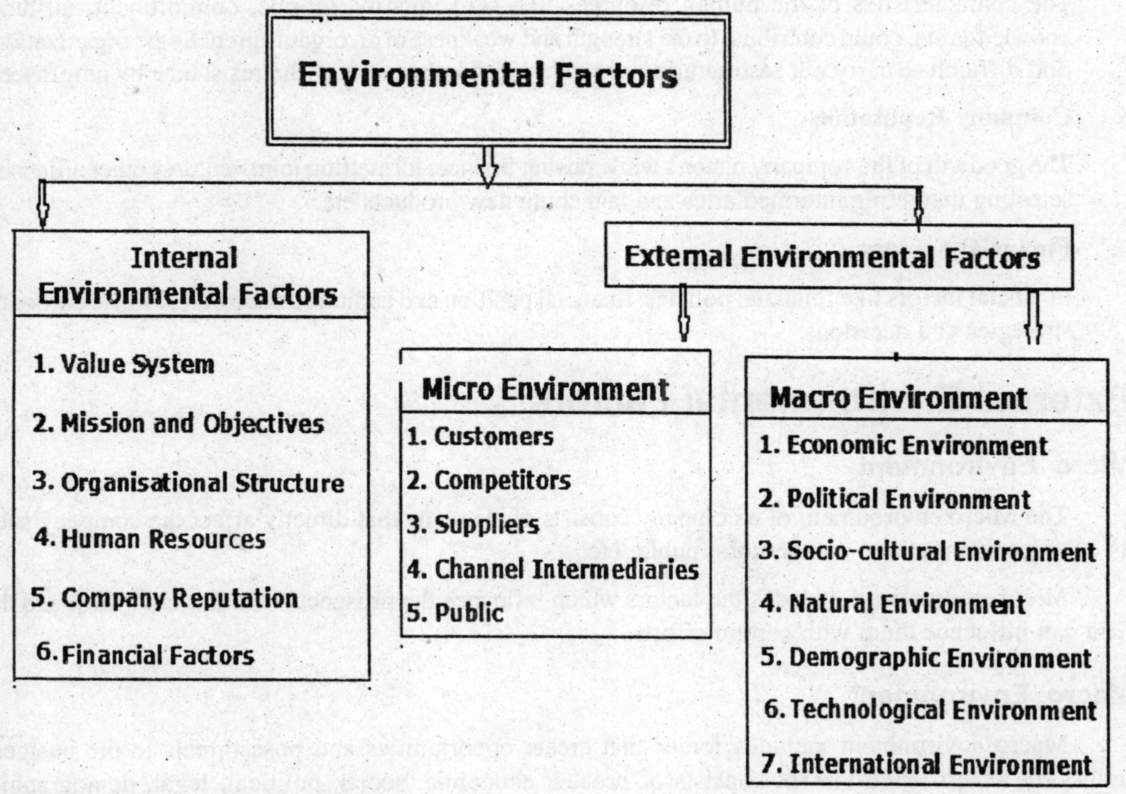

Internal Environmental Factors

Internal environment factors can be divided as follows:

1. **Value System**

   The value system of the founders, Board of directors, managers, workers of the organization has important bearing on the strategies of an organization.

2. **Mission and Objectives**

   Firms philosophies, priorities, development, policies are guided by the mission and objectives of the organization. Mission and objectives are the first steps in the development of an organization.

   Mission statement of the HUL, "Unilever's mission is to add vitality to life. We meet everyday needs for nutrition, hygiene, and personal cares with brands that help people feel good, look good and get more out of life."

3. **Organisational Structure**

   Organisational hierarchy is the authority which flows from top to bottom. Some management structures and styles delay decision making process and while others facilitate quick decision making.

4. **Human Resources**

   The characteristics of the human resources like skill, quality, morale, commitment, attitude, knowledge etc. could contribute to the strength and weakness of an organisation. Some organizations find difficult to carry out restructuring or modernization because of the resistance by employees.

5. **Company Reputation**

   The goodwill of the company matters while raising finance, formatting joint ventures other alliances, selecting marketing intermediaries and launching new products etc

6. **Financial Factors**

   Financial factors like financial policies, financial position and capital structure etc. affects corporate strategies and decisions.

External Environmental Factors

Micro Environment

The Micro environment of a company consists of elements that directly affect the company such as customers, suppliers, competitors, public etc.

Micro environment includes the factors which influence the prospects of a particular firm and the firm can influence them with certain efforts.

Macro Environment

Macro environment includes forces that create opportunities and pose threats to the business units. The macro environment consists of broader economic, social, political, legal, demographic, technological and natural setting within which the industry and business units are placed.

Micro Environment (In details)

The Micro environment of a company consists of elements that directly affect the company such as customers, suppliers, competitors, public etc.

Micro environment includes the factors which influence the prospects of a particular firm; the firm can influence them with certain efforts. They are as follows:

1. Customers

The type and the nature of the customers influence the rate of growth of any firm if the customers belong to an affluent section of the community; who are very particular about the quality of the commodity. The firm has to be very particular about choosing the inputs and transforming them into the output. The cost factor is subsidiary if the firm is dealing with such customers. If the customers are more common, the quality of the commodity is less important than the cost of production. The customers want the commodity at a lower price so the firm will have to be conscious about the cost in purchasing the inputs, in employment of labour, in packing and such other factors influencing the cost.

2. Competitors

In modern age an absolute monopoly is a very rare thing. Most of the firms have to work in some type of competition such as monopolistic competition or oligopoly. A firm has to be particular about the intensity of the competition. If the competition is severe the firm will have to be very particular about keeping the costs at the lowest level so that it can sell the commodity at a competitive price. If the firm is working in monopolistic competition it has to spend substantial amounts of money on marketing the commodity. The firm has to spend on advertisement, promotions the product through brand ambassadors undertaking sports and cultural programmes etc.

If the firm is working under oligopoly, There is inter-dependence of the firms. Therefore a firm has to think of the possible reactions of competitors before taking any action.

Now a days the non price competition has become more prominent than price competition. Instead of selling the commodity at a lower price the firms prefer to offer other incentives to the buyers so that they are attracted to the product. The other incentives are in the form of gifts, providing some complementary commodities, a longer period of guarantee home delivery, after sales service etc.

3. Suppliers

The quality of the commodity and the cost of production are considerably influenced by the supplies of the inputs. If the inputs are supplied at economical prices, are of standard quality and if the supply is uninterrupted and timely the firm can produce a standard quality of a commodity and sell it at reasonable prices. Often the firms employ more than one supplier so as to ensure an uninterrupted supply of inputs. Some firms setup their own firms / units for producing or supplying the inputs required. That is helpful in ensuring an uninterrupted supply of inputs at proper time and at proper prices.

If the supplies of inputs are regular, consistent and reliable there is no need to keep a larger quantity in stock. The working capital required will be less since the interest on working capital will be less. Interest is a part of the cost of production. If the firm economizes on interest payments it can bring down the cost of production and sell the commodity at a lower price

4. Channel Intermediaries

They refer to the different levels in the chain from the production unit to the final customer. The chain incorporates the stockist, the wholesalers, the distributors, the retailer etc. If there is a high level of efficiency maintained at every part of the chain the commodity can reach the final consumer in good condition and at a reasonable price. So the firm has to select and maintain efficient intermediaries. The firm has to offer them proper terms.

5. Public

Public is any group that has actual or potential interest in the business. The prospects of a firm depend upon the society in which it has to work and sell its products. In a homogenous society the job of the firm is easy. The people have almost the same habits, likes and dislikes, values and ethical norms. In a heterogeneous society the job of the firm is difficult. A particular product may be acceptable to a particular section of the society but not acceptable to some other sections. In a country like India a firm has to consider all sections of the community such as the religious sections, the caste, the sect, language, region etc.

Macro Environment (In details)

Macro environment includes forces that create opportunities and pose threats to the business units. The macro environment consists of broader economic, social, political, legal, demographic, technological and natural setting within which the industry and business units are placed.

The various macro environmental factors-

A business and its forces in its micro environment operate in larger macro environment of forces that shape opportunities and pose threats to the business. It refers to the major external and uncontrollable factors that influence an organization's decision making and affect its performance and strategies. The important environmental factors are; (1) Economic Environment (2) Political and Governmental Environment (3) Socio-cultural Environment (4) Natural Environment (5) Demographic Environment (6) Technological Environment (7) International Environment.

1. Economic Environment

Economic environment consists of economic factors that influence the business in a country. These factors include gross national product, corporate profits, inflation rate, employment, balance of payments, interest rates consumer income etc. In a developing country, low income may be the reason for very low demand for a product.

Economic environment of business has reference to the broad characteristics of the economic system in which the business operates. The business sector has economic relation with the government, capital market; household sector and global sector. These sectors together influence the trends and structure of the economy. The form and functioning of the economy vary widely. The important external factors that affect the economic environment of a business are:

(i) ***Economic Conditions:*** The general economic conditions prevailing in the country viz. national income, per capita income, economic resources, distribution of income and assets, economic development etc. are important determinants of the business strategies. Business cycles and economic growth of the economy are important factors defining the economic environment.

(ii) ***The Economic system:*** The economic system operating in the country also affects the business enterprise to a very great extent. The economic system of a country may be capitalist, socialist, communist or mixed.

(iii) ***Economic Policies:*** The government decides the economic environment of business through budgets, industrial regulations, economic planning, import and export regulations, business laws, industrial policy, control on prices and wages, trade and transport policies, the size of the national income, demand and supply of various goods etc.

(iv) ***Economic Growth:*** The stage of economic growth of the economy has direct impact on the business strategies. Increased economic growth rate and increase in consumption expenditure, lower the general pressure within an industry and offers more opportunities then threats.

(v) ***The rate of interest:*** The rate of interest affects the demand for the products in the economy, particularly when general goods are to be purchased through borrowed finance. Low interest rate provides opportunities to the industries to expand whereas rising interest rates pose a threat to such institutions.

(vi) ***Currency Exchange:*** Current exchange rates have direct impact on the business environment. When the rupee was devalued in 1991, it was to make Indian products cheaper in the world market and consequently boost India's exports.

2. Political Environment

Political environment refers to the influence exerted by the three political institutions which are; Legislature, Executive, Judiciary etc. The legislature decides on a particular course of action. Government is the executive and its job to implement whatever was decided by the parliament. The judiciary has ensure that both the legislature and executive function in acordance with public interest and within the boundaries of constitution. Legal and political environment provides a framework within the business is to function and its existence depends on the success with which it can face the various challenges constructed out of political and legal framework.

The government, in every country, regulates the business according to its defined priorities. Legal system of a country is framed by the government. The laws which are passed by the government for business operation is called legal environment.

3. Socio-Cultural Environment

Socio-cultural environment is relating to the social and cultural practices, beliefs and traditions within a particular society. It consists of language and organizations, business custom practices etc.

Changes in social trends can impact on the demand for a firm's products and the availability and willingness of individuals to work. Social class and caste of a person goes a long way in deciding the business activities in relation to its production and marketing activities. Tradition, customs and social attitudes have changed the attitude and beliefs of the persons which have their effect on organizational environment. Class and caste are influencing the purchasing pattern. Socio-cultural environment may include expectations of the society from business, attitudes of society towards business and its management, views towards achievement of work, views towards structure, responsibility and organizational positions, views towards customs, traditional and conventional, class structure and labour mobility and level of education.

4. Natural Environment

Environmental factors include weather and climate change. Changes in temperature can impact on many industries including farming, tourism and insurance. With major climate changes occurring due to global warming and with greater environmental awareness this external factor is becoming a significant issue for firms to consider. The growing desire to protect the environment is having an impact on many industries such as the travel and transportation industries. For example, more taxes being placed on air travel and the success of hybrid cars and the general move towards more environmentally friendly products and processes is affecting demand patterns and creating business opportunities.

The natural environment encompasses all living and non-living things occurring naturally on Earth or some region thereof. The natural environment is contrasted with the built environment, which comprises the areas and components that are strongly influenced by humans. A geographical area is regarded as a natural environment.

5. Demographic Environment

Demographic factor include size, growth rate, age composition, sex composition etc. of population, Family size, economic stratification of population, educational level, caste, religion etc. All these demographic factors are relevant to business. These factors affect the demand for goods and services. High population growth rate indicates an enormous increase in labour supply. Population with varied tastes, preferences, beliefs, temperaments etc. gives rise to differing demand pattern and calls for different marketing strategies.

6. Technological Environment

Technological environment refers to the external factors in technology that impact business operations. Changes in technology affect how a company will do business. A business may have to dramatically change their operating strategy as a result of changes in the technological environment.

In order to survive in today's competitive world, a business has to adopt technological changes from time to time. New technologies create new products and new processes. Technology can reduce costs, improve quality and lead to innovation. These developments can benefit consumers as well as the organizations providing the products. MP3 players, computer games, online gambling and high definition TVs are all new markets created by technological advances. Online shopping, bar coding and computer aided design are all improvements to the way we do business as a result of better technology.

7. International Environment

A final component of the general environment is actions of other countries or group of countries that affect the organization. Governments may act to reserve a portion of their industries for domestic firms, or may subsidize particular types of businesses to make them more competitive in the international market. Another environmental factor which is fast emerging as the force to reckon with is the international environment. Implications of global or international environment are; (i) Due to liberalization, Indian companies are forced to view business issues from the global perspective. (ii) Safe and protected markets are no longer exits. World is becoming small in size due to advanced means of transport and communication facilities. (iii) Learning of foreign languages is must for every business manager. (iv) Acquiring familiarity with foreign currencies is also must. (v) Facing political and legal uncertainties is inevitable.

Business Environment

Meaning of Business Environment

The term business environment is composed of two words 'Business' and 'Environment'. In simple terms, the state in which a person remains busy is known as business. The word Business in its economic sense means human activities like production, extraction or purchase or sales of goods that are performed for earning profits.

Business environment is an environment in which business is conducted. Business environment encompasses all those factors that affect a company's operations; including customers, competitors, suppliers, distributors, industry trends, substitutes, regulations, government activities, the economy, demographics, social and cultural factors, innovations, and technological developments.

Business Environment is the combination of internal and external factors that influence a company's operating situation. The business environment can include factors such as: clients and suppliers; its competition and owners; improvements in technology; laws and government activities; and market, social and economic trends.

Environment of a business means the external forces influencing the business decisions. They can be forces of economic; social, political and technological factors. These factors are outside the control of the business.

A business environment is an environment in which business is conducted. An example of a business environment is a business office, such as an insurance office because they conduct the business of selling insurance to people.

Characteristics of Business Environment

Characteristics of business environment are as follows:

1. Business environment is compound in nature.
2. Business environment is constantly changing process.
3. Business environment is different for different business units.
4. It has both long term and short term impact.
5. Unlimited influence of external environment factors.
6. It is very uncertain.
7. Inter-related components.
8. It includes both internal and external environment.

Features of Business Environment

The main features of business environment are as follows:

1. ***Totality of external forces:*** Business environment is the sum total of all things external to business firms and, as such, is aggregated in nature.

2. ***Specific and general forces:*** Business environment includes both specific and general forces. Specific forces (such as investors, customers, competitors and suppliers) affect individual enterprises directly and immediately in their day-to-day working. General forces (such as social, political, legal and technological conditions) have impact on all business enterprises and thus may affect an individual firm only indirectly.

3. ***Dynamic nature:*** Business environment is dynamic in that it keeps on changing whether in terms of technological improvement, shifts in consumer preferences or entry of new competition in the market.

4. ***Uncertainty:*** Business environment is largely uncertain as it is very difficult to predict future happenings, especially when environment changes are taking place too frequently as in the case of information technology or fashion industries.

5. ***Relativity:*** Business environment is a relative concept since it differs from country to country and even region to region. Political conditions in the USA, for instance, differ from those in India, China or Pakistan. Similarly, demand for Sarees may be fairly high in India whereas it may be almost non-existent in France.

Importance of Business Environment

An analysis of business environment helps to identify strength, weakness, opportunities and threats. Analysis is very necessary for the survival and growth of the business enterprise. The importance of business environment is briefly explained below:

(1) ***Identification of Strength:*** The analysis of the internal environment helps to identify strength of the firm. For instance, if the company has good personnel policies in respect of promotion, transfer, training, etc then it can indicates strength of the firm in respect of personnel policies. This strength can be identified through job satisfaction and performance of the employees. After identifying the strengths the firm must try to consolidate its strengths by further improvement in its existing plans and policies.

(2) ***Identification of Weakness:*** The analysis of the internal environment indicates not only strengths but also the weakness of the firm. A firm may be strong in certain areas; where as it may be weak in some other areas. The firm should identify such weakness so as to correct them as early as possible.

(3) ***Identification of Opportunities:*** An analysis of the external environment helps the business firm to identify the opportunities in the market. The business firm should make every possible effort to grab the opportunities as and when they come.

(4) ***Identification of Threats:*** Business may be subjected to threats from competitors and others. Therefore environmental analysis helps to identify threats from the environment. Identification of threats at an earlier stage is always beneficial to the firm as it helps to defuse the same.

(5) ***Exploitation of Business Opportunities:*** Environment opens new opportunities for the expansion of business activities. Study of environment is necessary in order to discover and exploit such opportunities fully.

(6) ***Keeping Business Enterprise Alert:*** Environment study is needed as it keeps the business unit alert in its approach and activities. In the absence of environmental changes, the business activities will

be dull and lifeless. The problems and prospects of business can be understood properly through the study of business environment. This enables an enterprise to face the problems with confidence and secure the maximum benefits of business opportunities available.

(7) ***Keeping Business Flexible and Dynamic:*** Study of business environment is needed for keeping business flexible and dynamic as per the changes in the environmental forces. This will enable the development of business organization.

(8) ***Understanding Future Problems and Prospects:*** The study of business environment enables to understand future problems and prospects of business in advance. This enables business organizations to face the problems boldly and also take the benefit of favorable situation.

(9) ***Making Business Socially Acceptable:*** Environment study enables businessmen to expand the business and also make it acceptable to different social groups. Business organizations can make positive contribution for maintaining ecological balance by studying social environment.

(10) ***Ensures Optimum Utilization of Resources:*** The study of business environment is needed as it ensures optimum use of resources available. For this, the study of economic and technological environment is useful. Such study enables organization to take full benefit of government policies, concessions provided, and technological developments and so on.

(11) ***Ensures Survival and Growth:*** Business environment inform about suitable changes which affects business policies. This helps the business organizations to grow and prosper.

(12) ***Maintaining adaptability to changes:*** Business environment guides the business organization about socio-economic changes and the organization must accordingly adapt these changes. This enables the business organization to survive for a longer period.

Goals of the Business Environment

Following are main goals of business environment:

1. **Knowledge of Information**

   By studying the business environment, we can know the changes of business. This information is very useful for any business. Every businessman should aware current environment of business. With this, he can think the future of his business in such environment.

2. **Basis of Decisions**

   One of the main goals of the business environment is that it can provide all the information which is needed for taking good decisions. Suppose, you completed your internal business environment study. With this study, you can take decision relating to purchase, sale, salary and price because you know your competitor, you know your suppliers and you know your customers.

3. **Helpful in making of Policies**

   For making good business policies, we need to know and scan business through business environment.

4. **Technological Planning**

   Today, technology is changing very fast. So, you have to study technological environment. With this, you can make better technological planning of the business.

5. **Survive in the Business**

   Sometime industry may face recession. Production may be unlimited but sales will be limited. Only that business will survive who estimate this entire situation in advance through business environment study.

The Company and its Environment

The manager's job cannot be accomplished in a vacuum within the organization. There are a number of factors both internal and external which jointly affect managerial decision-making. It is therefore very important for the manager to understand and evaluate the impact of the business environment due to the following reasons:

1. Businesses may face problems due to restrictive business environment which may be because of rigid government laws e.g. no polluting industry can ever be located within a 50 Km radius of the Taj Mahal , state of competition etc.
2. The present and future viability of an enterprise is impacted by the environment. For e.g. no TV manufacturer can be expected to survive by making only the traditional cathode-ray tube television sets when consumer preference has clearly shifted to plasma and LCD television sets.
3. The cost of capital and the cost of borrowing – the two key financial drivers of any enterprise are impacted by the external environment. For e.g. the ability of a business to fund its expansion plan by raising money from the stock markets depends on the prevalent public mood towards investment in stock markets.
4. The availability of all key inputs like skilled labour, trained managers, raw materials, electricity, transportation, fuel etc., is a factor of the business environment.
5. Increasing public awareness of the negative aspects of certain industries like hand woven carpets pesticides (damage to environment in the form of chemical residues in groundwater), plastic bags (choking of sewer lines) have resulted in the slow decline of some industries.
6. Finally, the environment offers the opportunities for growth and profits. For e.g. when the insurance and the aviation industries were thrown open to the private sector, the new entrant could easily build on the expectations of the public.

Historical Forces Changing the Business Environment

There are basically five historical forces which have influenced management thinking and practice:

Social forces: The aspects of culture that guide and influence relationships among people. Need to consider social contracts

Political forces: The influence of politics depends on the structure of the organization.

Economic forces: Forces that affect the availability production and distribution of resources.

Other forces are legal and technological

Among the various constituents of business environment discussed above briefly, we will focus on the following constituents and discuss them in greater detail. The constituents now elaborated are: Economic environment, political environment and cultural environment.

Effects of the Political Environment on Business Organizations

The political environment in a country affects business organizations and could introduce a risk factor that could cause them to suffer loss. The political environment could change as a result of the actions and policies of governments at all levels, from the local level to the federal level. Businesses need to be prepared to deal with the fallouts of government policies.

Impact on the Economy

The political environment in a country affects its economic environment. The economic environment, in turn, affects the performance of a business organization. In the United States, for instance, there are significant differences in democratic and republican policies. This has implications for factors such as taxes and government spending, which in turn affect the country's economy. A higher level of government spending tends to stimulate the economy, for instance.

Changes in Regulation

Governments could change their rules and regulations, and this could have an effect on a business. For instance, after the accounting scandals of the early twenty-first century, the United States Securities and Exchange Commission became more focused on corporate compliance and the government introduced the Sarbanes-Oxley compliance regulations of 2002. This was a response to the social environment that called for such change to make public companies more accountable.

Political Stability

Particularly for businesses that operate internationally a lack of political stability in any country has an effect on its operations. A hostile takeover could overthrow a government, for instance. This could lead to rioting and looting and general disorder in the environment. All this disrupts the operations of a business. Such disruptions have occurred in Sri Lanka, which went through a protracted civil war, and in Egypt and Syria, which have been subject to disturbances as people agitate for certain rights.

Mitigation of Risk

One way to manage political risk is to buy political risk insurance. Organizations that have international operations use this type of insurance to mitigate their risk exposure as a result of political instability. There are indices that provide an idea of the risk exposure an organization has in certain countries. For instance, an index of economic freedom ranks countries based on how political interference impacts business decisions in each country.

Dimensions of Business Environment

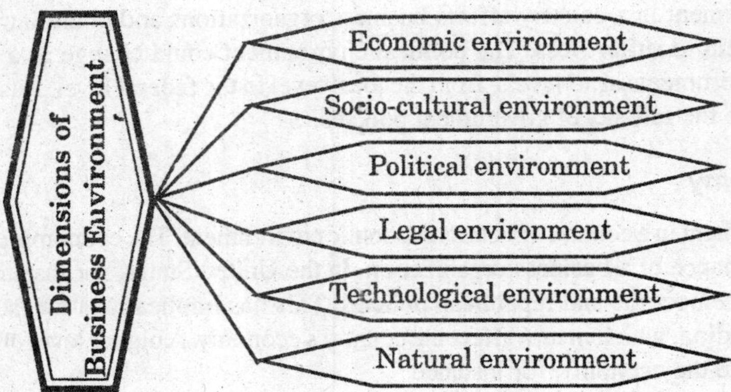

The several dimensions of business environment are given below:

a. Economic environment

Economic environment consists of economic factors that influence the business in a country. These factors include gross national product, corporate profits, inflation rate, employment, balance of payments, interest rates consumer income etc. In a developing country, the low income may be the reason for the very low demand for a product.

b. Socio-cultural environment

Socio-cultural environment is related to the social and cultural practices, beliefs and traditions within a particular society. It consists of language, aesthetics, education, religion& superstitions, attitudes, values, material culture, technology, social groups & organizations, business custom practices etc.

c. Political environment

The political environment is the state, government and its institutions and legislations and the public and private stakeholders who operate and interact with or influence that system. The stability of the political environment and government will impact on the prioritization of mental health policy in relation to other policies, the funding available to mental health and the time frames in which policies and programmes can be realized.

d. Legal environment

The government, in every country, regulates the business according to its defined priorities. Legal system of a country is framed by the government. The laws which are passed by the government for business operation is called legal environment.

e. Technological environment

Technological environment refers to the external factors in technology that impact business operations. Changes in technology affect how a company will do business. A business may have to dramatically change their operating strategy as a result of changes in the technological environment.

f. Natural Environment

The natural environment encompasses all living and non-living things occurring naturally on Earth or some region thereof. The natural environment is contrasted with the built environment, which comprises the areas and components that are strongly influenced by humans. A geographical area is regarded as a natural environment.

Dimensions of Business Environment (In details)

Economic Environment

Economic environment consists of economic factors that influence the business in a country. These factors include gross national product, corporate profits, inflation rate, employment, balance of payments, interest rates consumer income etc.

In a developing country, the low income may be the reason for the very low demand for a product. The sale of a product for which the demand is income elastic naturally increases with an increase in income. But a firm is unable to increase the purchasing power of the people to generate a higher demand for its product. Hence, it may have to reduce the price of the product to increase the sales. The reduction in the cost of production may have to be effected to facilitate price reduction. It may even be necessary to invent or develop a new low-cost product to suit the low-income market. Thus Colgate designed a simple, hand-driven, inexpensive washing machine for low-income buyers in less developed countries. Similarly, the National Cash Register Company took an innovative step backward by developing a crank-operated cash register that would sell at half the cost of a modern cash register and this was well received in a number of developing countries.

In countries where investment and income are steadily and rapidly rising, business prospects are generally bright, and further investments are encouraged. There are a number of economists and businessmen who feel that the developed countries are no longer worthwhile propositions for investment because these economies have reached more or less saturation levels in certain respects.

In developed economies, replacement demand accounts for a considerable part of the total demand for many consumer durables whereas the replacement demand is negligible in the developing economies. The economic policy of the government, needless to say, has a very great impact on business. Some types or categories of business are favorably affected by government policy, some adversely affected, while it is neutral in respect of others. For example, a restrictive import policy, or a policy of protecting the home industries, may greatly help the import-competing industries. Similarly, an industry that falls within the priority sector in terms of the government policy may get a number of incentives and other positive support from the government, whereas those industries which are regarded as inessential may have the odds against them.

In India, the government's concern about the concentration of economic power restricted the role of the large industrial houses and foreign concerns to the core sector, the heavy investment sector, the export sector and backward regions. The monetary and fiscal policies, by the incentives and disincentives they offer and by their neutrality, also affect the business in different ways. An industrial undertaking may be able to take advantage of external economies by locating itself in a large city; but the Government of India's policy was to discourage industrial location in such places and constrain or persuade industries undertaking, a backward area location may have many disadvantages. However, the incentives available for units located in these backward areas many compensate them for these disadvantages, at least to some extent. According to the industrial policy of the Government of India until July 1991, the development of 17 of the most important industries was reserved for the state. In the development of another 12 major industries, the state was to play a dominant role. In the remaining industries, co-operative enterprises, joint sector enterprises and small scale units were to get preferential treatment over large entrepreneurs in the private sector. The government policy, thus limited the scope of private business. However, the new policy ushered in since July 1991 has wide opened many of the industries for the private sector.

The scope of international business depends, to a large extent, on the economic system. At one end, there are the free market economies or capitalist economies, and at the other end are the centrally planned economies or communist countries. In between these two are the mixed economies. Within the mixed economic system itself, there are wide variations.

The freedom of private enterprise is the greatest in the free market economy, which is characterized by the following assumptions:

(i) The factors of production (labor, land, capital) are privately owned, and production occurs at the initiative of the private enterprise.

(ii) Income is received in monetary form by the sale of services of the factors of production and from the profits of the private enterprise.

(iii) Members of the free market economy have freedom of choice in so far as consumption, occupation, savings and investment are concerned.

(iv) The free market economy is not planned controlled or regulated by the government. The government satisfies community or collective wants, but does not compete with private firms, nor does it tell the people where to work or what to produce.

Meaning of Economic Environment

Economic environment refers to that entire economic factor which has a bearing functioning of the business unit. Business depends on the economic environment for all the needed inputs. It also depends on the economic environment to sell the finished goods.

Components of the Economic Environment

The economic environment comprises of:

(i) ***Income and wealth:*** Income in an economy is measured by GDP, GNP and per capita income. High values of these factors show a progressive economic environment.

(ii) ***Employment levels:*** High employment represents a positive picture of the economy. However, there are many forms of unemployment, including partial employment and disguised unemployment.

(iii) ***Productivity:*** This is the output generated from a given amount of inputs. High levels of productivity support the economic environment.

Importance of Economic Environment

The competent and successful management must be capable of adapting to the economic environment. The knowledge of the economic environment helps in:

i) ***Capitalizing early opportunities:*** Environment friendly enterprise is the first movers to avail of the existing opportunities of resources to grab the market. These enterprises do not loose emerging opportunities to their competitors. For example: Asian pains have been losing their market to Good lass Nerolac because of their failure to match their technology with Cathodic Electro Deposition (CED) technology, which helped the competitor to grab the opportunity of meeting 90% paint requirement of Maruti Udyog.

ii) ***Activating management to changing needs:*** The knowledge of environmental changes sensitizes the management to make strategy to cope with the emerging problems. For example: The turmoil in the USSR resulted in the loss of market to many companies like Hoechst. In order to meet the situation Hoechst divested its manufacturing facility in favors of IPCA Laboratories Ltd.

iii) ***Image building:*** Environmental understanding by the management builds image of the company in the minds of the people. They feel that the company is sensitive and responsive to their needs and problems. For example: G. E is said to be image conscious. It divested its computer and air-conditioning business because they could not attain 1st or 2nd position in the business as per their policy. Now they are snickering to out sourcing in India, aircraft engineering, plastic etc.

iv) ***Basis of strategy:*** Strategists can gather qualitative information regarding business environment and utilizing them in formulating effective plants. For example: ITC Hotels foresaw bright opportunities in the travel and tourism industry and started building hotels in India and abroad.

v) ***Intellectual stimulation:*** Knowledge of environment changes provides intellectual stimulation to planners and decision-making authorities. They can do it by paying more attention to people by listening to their problems and suggestion. They can also eliminate procedure complexities in a visible way. The drastic and dynamic steps will definitely keep the company better placed.

vi) ***Continuous learning:*** Environmental scanning provides continuing broad based learning to be executives. Reliance adopted the policy of decentralization and empowered their managers to close the deal themselves even regarding price. In 1993 managers were require to chat with the proprietress on alternate days for 15 minutes. The process made them so competent that now the managers are required to chat only three times in a month. It shows that continuous learning made the managers competent to take independent decision.

Impact of Economic Environment on Business

Any business organization has one goal, to maximize profit. The process of maximizing revenue is simple. Evaluate need for customers, and provide appropriate provide, within top quality and quantity. There are nevertheless many factors which affect this simple operation. These elements are often categorized as macro as well as mini, internal and external, technical as well as non-technical. All the same, the actual product sales, production and procurement of the business organizations, straight or not directly depends upon these types of elements. Therefore, you will find which entrepreneurs carefully analyze and ponder upon the economic elements impacting business companies. The impact of economic environment on business considers the following concepts:

i) Demand and offer

The need and offer are two primary elements that affect the working associated with a business design. The need is the will as well as capability of shoppers to buy a specific item and the provide may be the ability of the company to provide for the need for customers. It should be mentioned that all the standards which are included in this list are inter-connected. You may even study need and supply analysis.

ii) Marginal and Complete Power

Utility may be the quantity of fulfillment, that's produced by consumers from consumption of goods. This so happens that whenever continuous and successive use of units of the same goods, the fulfillment that's experienced by consumer begins decreasing. This often results into short term or even long-term fall of sales. Some organizations get ready for the actual launch of some other brand name before the fall in power and sales is experienced. The actual release of new brand, helps to ensure that the actual revenue pattern from the company does not drop. Decreasing power is among the exterior elements affecting business. You may even read more on diminishing minor utility.

iii) Cash as well as Finance

Financial allows for financial and financial policies which impact company as well as the clients from the business. Money in circulation dictates the having to pay power or rather the demand of the actual customers and also the financial facility dictates the borrowing capability of people along with the business.

iv) Financial Development and growth

Financial development dictates the quantity of finances that the society in particular is actually earning as well as improvement signifies the amount of money that's being spent in to channels associated with long-term up-gradation. Amongst all the financial elements affecting business environment, improvement is an essential one, since the company needs to focus on the actual need for a good economically dynamic society.

v) Income and Employment

An additional very important facet of the economic climate that impacts the significant from the business may be the degree of work as well as rate of earnings. The actual for each capita income as well as density of work determines the speed of need, denseness associated with need and also the purchasing power of those.

vi) Common Price Level

An additional very important facet of the actual economy, which impacts the business, is the general price levels from the goods which additionally modify the product sales from the business. Expenses of recyclable, having to pay power of individuals, price of production and finally, cost of transport are a few of the important components that determine the general cost level and also, the actual product sales from the firm.

vii) Industry Cycles

Industry series are the changing expenses of products as well as commodities within an economic climate. Increase, stability, a continual and drop are some of the important series which modify the costs away all goods for example uncooked materials, credit score, last products, and so on. Trade cycles additionally often modify the general cost degree.

Factors of Economic Environment

1. **Growth strategy**

   Growth strategy is a strategy based on investing in companies and sectors which are growing faster than their peers. The benefits are usually in the form of capital gains rather than dividends.

2. **Economic system**

   An economic system is the combination of the various agencies, entities that provide the economic structure that defines the social community. The economics system involves production, allocation of economic inputs, and distribution of economic outputs, Landlords and land availability, households, Capitalists, Banks and Government. It is a set of institutions and their various social relations.

3. **Economic planning**

   Economic planning refers to any directing or planning of economic activity outside the mechanisms of the market, in an attempt to achieve specific economic or social outcomes. Planning is an economic mechanism for resource allocation and decision-making in contrast with the market mechanism. Most economies are mixed economies, incorporating elements of market mechanisms and planning for distributing inputs and outputs.

4. **Industry**

   As per Section 2(j) of Industrial Disputes Act, 1947 "Industry" means any systematic activity carried on by co-operation between an employer and his workmen (whether such workmen are employed by such employer directly or by or through any agency, including a contractor) for the production, supply or distribution of goods or services with a view to satisfy human wants or wishes.

5. **Agriculture**

   Agriculture is the cultivation of animals, plants, fungi, and other life forms for food, fiber, and other products used to sustain life. Agriculture was the key development in the rise of sedentary human civilization, whereby farming of domesticated species created food surpluses that nurtured the development of civilization. The study of agriculture is known as agricultural science. Agriculture generally speaking refers to human activities, although it is also observed in certain species of ant and termite.

6. **Infrastructure**

   Infrastructure is basic physical and organizational structures needed for the operation of a society or enterprise or the services and facilities necessary for an economy to function. It can be generally defined as the set of interconnected structural elements that provide framework supporting an entire structure of development. It is an important term for judging a country or region's development.

7. **Financial and fiscal factor**

   Financial factors consider the income statement is a simple and straightforward report on the proposed business's cash-generating ability. It is a score card on the financial performance of your business that reflects when sales is made and when expenses are incurred. It draws information from the various financial models developed earlier such as revenue, expenses, capital and cost of goods. Fiscal policy is the use of government expenditure and revenue collection (taxation) to influence the economy. Fiscal policy can be contrasted with the other main type of macroeconomic policy, monetary policy, which attempts to stabilize the economy by controlling interest rates and spending.

8. **Removal of regional imbalance**

Government had appointed a Fact Finding Committee (FFC) in August, 1983 under the Chairmanship of Dr. V.M. Dandekar for studying the problem of imbalance between different regions of the State to identify regional backlog on the basis of such a study and to suggest measures for removal of the regional backlog including long term measures to avoid such regional imbalance in the future.

9. **Price and distribution control**

During the ongoing post-communist economic transitions, the relative well-being of many people is changing rapidly, and governments are not well positioned to accurately measure individual living standards. Under such circumstances, continued price controls over basic consumer goods within the state sector, and the associated queuing, can form a serviceable device for targeting poor people for subsidies.

10. **Economic reforms**

India was a latecomer to economic reforms, embarking on the process in earnest only in 1991, in the wake of an exceptionally severe balance of payments crisis. The need for a policy shift had become evident much earlier, as many countries in East Asia achieved high growth and poverty reduction through policies which emphasized greater export orientation and encouragement of the private sector.

11. **Per capita and national income**

Per capita income or income per person is a measure of mean income within an economic aggregate, such as a country or city. It is calculated by taking a measure of all sources of income in the aggregate (such as GDP or Gross National Income) and dividing it by the total population. It does not attempt to reflect the distribution of income or wealth.

Growth Strategy

The growth strategy of a company needs to be studied in the long term perspective. The companies cannot grow overnight. They need a context in which they grow. This context comes from the existing customer base, the present size of operations, the technology and the manufacturing/ service facilities at its disposal. Growth can be expected to have a commensurately larger or bigger manufacturing/service facilities or asset base, purchase of more materials, producing more, hiring more employees, incurring larger overheads. The company pursuing growth may aspire to increase its income, serve larger customer base, expand its operations and generally embark on increased business activities. Needless to say, all this would call for additional funds and resources. Economic activity as a whole is benefited by the active acquisition and divestiture marketplace, which allows young companies to be bought and mature companies to adapt to changing circumstances.

It is interesting to view the growth path of some Indian companies or Business Groups like Reliance Group, Tata Group, ITC Group, Sahara group, the IT leaders like Wipro, Infosys etc. These companies have followed the growth path that has taken various routes. These routes can be organic or in organic or a judicious mix of both.

Tata Steel and Corus on January 31, 2007, Tata Steel Limited, one of the leading steel producers in India, acquired the Anglo Dutch steel producer Corus Group for US$ 12.11 billion. Corus was 2.5 times bigger company than TATA. It took nine rounds for Tata to acquire Corus. In the first bid Tata had closed the deal at US $ 7.6 billion and later it ended up by paying US $ 12.11 billion, making it an expensive turnover. This acquisition was the biggest overseas acquisition by an Indian company. Tata Steel emerged as the fifth largest steel producer in the world. After acquisition Tata benefited itself from Corus: i) Distribution network of Europe, ii) Expertise in steel making for automobiles. In return Corus benefit itself from Tata Steel's expertise in low cost manufacturing of steel.

Types of Growth Strategies

The various types of growth strategy are as follows:

1. Merger and Acquisition

Merger is the combination of two or more existing companies. All assets, liabilities and the stock of one company stand transferred to Transferee Company in consideration of payment in the form of:

i) Equity shares in the transferee company,

ii) Debentures in the transferee company,

iii) Cash, or

iv) A mix of the above modes.

Acquisition is a deal when one company takes over another company and buyer becomes sole proprietor. At times takeover occurs when the target company does not want to be purchased. However with better offering of prices shareholder are attracted by acquire. In legal terms, the target company ceases to survive. The buyer swallows the company and the buyer's stock continues to be traded. Unlike mergers which are friendly, acquisitions can be friendly and unfriendly.

The process of mergers and acquisitions has gained substantial importance in today's corporate world. This process is extensively used for restructuring the business organizations. In India, the concept of mergers and acquisitions was initiated by the government bodies. Some well known financial organizations also took the necessary initiatives to restructure the corporate sector of India by adopting the mergers and acquisitions policies. The Indian economic reform since 1991 has opened up a whole lot of challenges both in the domestic and international spheres. The increased competition in the global market has prompted the Indian companies to go for mergers and acquisitions as an important strategic choice. The trends of mergers and acquisitions in India have changed over the years. The immediate effects of the mergers and acquisitions have also been diverse across the various sectors of the Indian economy.

Among the different Indian sectors that have resorted to mergers and acquisitions in recent times, telecom, finance, FMCG, construction materials, automobile industry and steel industry are worth mentioning. With the increasing number of Indian companies opting for mergers and acquisitions, India is now one of the leading nations in the world in terms of mergers and acquisitions.

Objectives of Acquiring

i) To reduce competition.

ii) To increase growth rate & capture a greater market share

iii) To improve value of organization's stock.

iv) To acquire a needed resource quickly.

v) To take advantage of synergy.

vi) To acquire resources to stabilize operations.

vii) To achieve economies of scale.

2. Joint Venture

A joint venture (JV) is a business agreement in which parties agrees to develop, for a finite time, a new entity and new assets by contributing equity. They exercise control over the enterprise and consequently share revenues, expenses and assets. There are other types of companies such as JV limited by guarantee, joint ventures limited by guarantee with partners holding shares.

India has an open philosophy on capital markets, and it closely parallels its English peers in operation. The Bombay Stock Exchange (BSE) has close to 5,000 listed shares, and trades in several thousand more, making it the largest stock exchange in the world. The National Stock Exchange is the other exchange at present. English is one of the preferred languages of the market, and its policies are first announced in English. The Indian people are skilled and entrepreneurial by nature as evident in world markets, but in India, less than 1% of its billion populations at present that is, only 11 million people representing 3% of households invest in the market.

Joint Venture in India

Joint Venture Maruti Udyog Ltd. & Suzuki Motor Corp. Maruti Suzuki is one of India's leading automobile manufacturers and the market leader in the car segment, both in terms of volume of vehicles sold and revenue earned. Until recently, 18.28% of the company was owned by the Indian government, and 54.2% by Suzuki of Japan. The Indian government held an initial public offering of 25% of the company in June 2003. As of May 10, 2007, Govt. of India sold its complete share to Indian financial institutions. With this, Govt. of India no longer has stake in Maruti Udyog. During 2007-08, Maruti Suzuki sold 764,842 cars, of which 53,024 were exported. In all, over six million Maruti cars are on Indian roads since the first car was rolled out on December 14, 1983.

3. Strategic Alliance

A Strategic Alliance is a relationship between two or more parties to pursue a set of agreed upon goals or to meet a critical business need while remaining independent organizations. This form of cooperation lies between M & A and organic growth. Strategic alliance is a form of affiliation that involves mutual sharing of resources or "partnering" to improve efficiency. In strategic alliances, the focus is on "sharing" of resources rather than seeking change in control. Equity investment in each other's company is not any focus.

Types of Strategic Alliances

i) Cross-Promotional Alliance

Cross promotion Alliances are one of the more common types of alliances. Companies promoting each other with the use of discounts, coupons, specials, shared advertising space or in-store promotions. Exceptionally efficient is reducing costs of advertising. Example: Business Class flights offering a free AOL disk with peanuts.

ii) Strategic Alliances for Co-Branding

Co-branding strategy involves two companies putting their name on a common product. At the very least, co-branding offers twice the exposure and market impact opposed to traditional single brand advertising. Ex: Mattel and McDonalds offering toys that produce McDonald's hamburgers and Fries.

iii) Strategic Alliances to Serve National Customers

Serving National customers is often too costly or too difficult for a firm to handle by themselves. To create an alliance to serve national customers, companies share information, sales accounts and materials with the other members. This also allows for a more consistent customer satisfaction that otherwise wouldn't be available. Trust is a very important factor for an alliance to succeed, especially when the scope of the alliance is national or global. Example: Canvas Awnings drawing together with several other fabricators to meet the needs of clients all over the U.S. by dividing the country into 5 regions, which allows them to service the national need for awnings.

iv) Industry-specific Geographical Strategic Alliances

Industry-specific Geographical Strategic Alliances focuses on a specific industry in a certain geographical area. These businesses are general within very close proximity to one another and can satisfy all the needs of their customers in one phone call or visit. Example: The Minnesota Connection: Services the Direct Marketing Industry, alliance involving Telemarketing, Plastic, Printing, Envelope, Letter shop, and Listing Services.

v) Community-based Alliances

Community-based Alliances involves working together with other companies to create some community benefit that essentially differentiates your organization from your competitors in the eyes of your customers. Community-Based Alliances are typically a form of advertising, although they allow different companies to come together for the benefit of the community, and the resulting networking and friendships are a priceless benefit for the companies involved.

Example: Investors Advantage Corporation holding an Economic Forum in Westlake Village, California. By providing high-profile speakers and representatives from many companies, the forum benefits the citizens and customers and also provides the companies involved with exceptional advertising and name recognition as well as the ability to attract new customers in attendance.

vi) Alliances with Competitors to Open New Markets

Often time's foreign or new markets have some characteristic that makes them unserviceable for an organization. Examples are markets that are too large, too far away, too different, undeveloped, and so on. Forming alliances with competitors is a viable solution is many cases when these issues are at large. By working together with the competition, organizations are able to increase output, lower costs of distribution and provide advertising and marketing that make the penetration of the market much easier that it would be if they were to go at it alone.

Example: La Tapatia Tortilleria and El Aguillea Tortillas formed a strategic alliance to open the new market of California to fresh tortillas. Neither of the companies had the production ability to service the market alone, but together they were able to capture a huge market and become very successful.

Reasons for Strategic Alliances

i) **Market entry:** A strategic alliance can ease entry into a foreign market. E.g.: strategic alliance between British Airways and American Airlines.

ii) **Share risk & expenses:** Firms involved can share risks. E.g.: In early 1990's film manufacturers Kodak and Fuji joined with camera manufacturers Nikon, Canon, and Minolta to create cameras and film for advanced Photo System.

iii) **Synergistic Effects of Shared Knowledge and Expertise:** It helps a firm gain knowledge and expertise Skills+ brand + market knowledge+ assets= synergizing effect e. g. : For example, in the early 1990s, Motorola initiated an alliance among various partners, including Raytheon, Lockheed Martin, China Great Wall, and Nippon Iridium, to develop and build a global satellite-based communications network.

Growth Strategy Matrix

The growth of business through mergers & acquisition may be structured in variety of ways, including, purchase of an asset, stock purchase or a merger. The structure of the deal shall be determined by a variety of factors like accounting, business, legal, and tax considerations. For legal and tax purposes, the 'merger' is defined under appropriate laws. In any case, growth through merger and acquisition shall be of our interest. In merger, the assets and liabilities of two separate companies are combined to form a single business entity. Commonly, the term acquisition is used when a larger firm absorbs a smaller firm and the term 'merger' is used when the combination is portrayed to be between equals or near equals. In a merger of companies that are approximate equals, the transaction may be settled by payment of case upfront, also referred to as all-cash deal. In the alternative, the shareholders of the target firm may be paid partly in cash and partly by issue of shares in the acquiring firm. The deal may be entirely a non-cash one in that the acquirer only issues shares in certain ratio to the shareholders of the target form.

Market Development

Market development is the name given to a growth strategy where the business seeks to sell its existing products into new markets.

There are many possible ways of approaching this strategy, including:

- New geographical markets; for example exporting the product to a new country
- New product dimensions or packaging: for example
- New distribution channels
- Different pricing policies to attract different customers or create new market segments..

Product Development

Product development is the name given to a growth strategy where a business aims to introduce new products into existing markets. This strategy may require the development of new competencies and requires the business to develop modified products which can appeal to existing markets.

Diversification

Diversification is the name given to the growth strategy where a business markets new products in new markets. This is an inherently more risk strategy because the business is moving into markets in which it has little or no experience. For a business to adopt a diversification strategy, therefore, it must have a clear idea about what it expects to gain from the strategy and an honest assessment of the risks.

Economic System

An Economic System of a nation or a country may be defined as a framework of rules, goals and incentives that controls economic relations among people in a society. It also helps in providing framework for answering the basic economic questions. Different countries of a world have different economic systems and the prevailing economic system in a country affect the business units to a large extent.

Types of Economic system

Economic systems of a nation can be of any one of the following type:

(a) Capitalism

The economic system in which business units or factors of production are privately owned and governed is called Capitalism. The profit earning is the sole aim of the business units. Government of that country does not interfere in the economic activities of the country. It is also known as free market economy. All the decisions relating to the economic activities are privately taken. Examples of Capitalistic Economy: England, Japan, America etc.

Capitalism is variously defined by sources. There is no consensus on the definition nor on how the term should be used as a historical category. There is general agreement that capitalism is an economic system that includes private ownership of the means of production, creation of goods or services for profit or income, the accumulation of capital, competitive markets, voluntary exchange, and wage labor. The designation is applied to a variety of historical cases, varying in time, geography, politics and culture. There is general agreement that capitalism became dominant in the Western world following the demise of feudalism.

Economists, political economists and historians have taken different perspectives on the analysis of capitalism. Economists usually emphasize the degree that government does not have control over markets (laissez faire), and on property rights. Most political economists emphasize private property, power relations, wage labor, class and emphasize capitalism as a unique historical formation. Capitalism is generally viewed as encouraging economic growth. The extent to which different markets are free, as well as the rules defining private property, is a matter of politics and policy, and many states have what are termed mixed economies. A number of political ideologies have emerged in support of various types of capitalism, the most prominent being economic liberalism.

Benefits of Capitalism

i) *Capitalism encourages competition:* Since goods and services are freely traded in the open market with each seller setting his/her price, competition is bound to occur and this results in monopoly and cartels being removed.

ii) *Capitalism encourages trade:* As business is conducted in open markets, traders Endeavour to avail a variety of goods and services thereby increasing trade opportunities.

iii) *Employment:* Capitalism provides employment opportunities for a people in form of labour.

iv) *Development of skills:* Capitalism results in a variety of goods and services in the market place. This affords a people to specialize in an area that they feel they can perform better.

v) *Investment:* Capitalism provides room for investment opportunities as those with the capital seek ways to put their capital in use to make profits.

vi) *Organization:* Capitalism encourages self-organization. As competition levels rise, traders are bound to organize themselves and set a reasonable pricing method that benefits them all.

(b) Socialism

Under socialism economic system, all the economic activities of the country are controlled and regulated by the Government in the interest of the public. The first country to adopt this concept was Soviet Russia.

A socialist economic system would consist of an organization of production to directly satisfy economic demands and human needs, so that goods and services would be produced directly for use instead of for private profit driven by the accumulation of capital, and accounting would be based on physical quantities, a common physical magnitude, or a direct measure of labour-time. Distribution of output would be based on the principle of individual contribution.

As a political movement, socialism includes a diverse array of political philosophies, ranging from reformism to revolutionary socialism. Proponents of state socialism advocate for the nationalization of the means of production, distribution and exchange as a strategy for implementing socialism. Social democrats advocate redistributive taxation in the form of social welfare and government regulation of capital within the framework of a market economy. In contrast, anarchism and libertarian socialism propose direct worker's control of the means of production and oppose the use of state power to achieve such an arrangement, opposing both parliamentary politics and state ownership over the means of production.

Modern socialism originated from an 18th-century intellectual and working class political movement that criticized the effects of industrialization and private property on society. In the early 19th-century, "socialism" referred to any concern for the social problems of capitalism regardless of the solution. However, by the late 19th-century, "socialism" had come to signify opposition to capitalism and advocacy for an alternative system based on some form of social ownership. Utopian socialists such as Robert Owen (1771–1858) tried to found self-sustaining communes by secession from a capitalist society. Socialists inspired by the Soviet model of economic development, such as Marxist-Leninists, have advocated the creation of centrally planned economies directed by a single-party state that owns the means of production.

The two main forms of Socialism are:

i) ***Democratic Socialism:*** All the economic activities are controlled and regulated by the government but the people have the freedom of choice of occupation and consumption.

ii) ***Totalitarian Socialism:*** This form is also known as Communism. Under this, people are obliged to work under the directions of Government.

Benefits of Socialism

i) Socialism provides the government with control of virtually all functions of a society. It can be used to provide all citizens with their survival needs, creating a stable social environment as long as production of those needs meets the demand for them and absolute power over the economy does not corrupt the government that has it.

ii) People who cannot participate economically (due to mental disabilities, age, or poor health) are still valued and cared for as long as the government is more compassionate than the family (who would be empowered and responsible under free enterprise).

iii) When their basic needs are provided whether they work or not, there is opportunity for citizens to explore non-economically-productive pursuits, such as pure science, math and the arts or drugs, sexual promiscuity and television.

(c) Mixed Economy

The economic system in which both public and private sectors co-exist is known as Mixed Economy. Some factors of production are privately owned and some are owned by Government. There exists freedom of choice of occupation and consumption. Both private and public sectors play key roles in the development of the country.

The basic plan of the mixed economy is that the means of production are mainly under private ownership; that markets remain the dominant form of economic coordination; and that profit-seeking enterprises and the accumulation of capital would remain the fundamental driving force behind economic activity. However, the government would wield considerable indirect influence over the economy through fiscal and monetary policies designed to counteract economic downturns and capitalism's tendency toward financial crises and unemployment, along with playing a role in interventions that promote social welfare. Subsequently, some mixed economies have expanded in scope to include a role for indicative economic planning and/or large public enterprise sectors.

There is not one single definition for a mixed economy, but the definitions always involve a degree of private economic freedom mixed with a degree of government regulation of markets. The relative strength or weakness of each component in the national economy can vary greatly between countries. Economies ranging from the United States to Cuba have been termed mixed economies. The term is also used to describe the economies of countries which are referred to as welfare states, such as Norway and Sweden. Governments in mixed economies often provide environmental protection, maintenance of employment standards, a standardized welfare system, and maintenance of competition. As an economic ideal, mixed economies are supported by people of various political persuasions, typically centre-left and centre-right, such as social democrats or Christian democrats. Supporters view mixed economies as a compromise between state socialism and laissez-faire capitalism that is superior in net effect to either of those.

Elements of Mixed Economy

The elements of a mixed economy have been demonstrated to include a variety of freedoms:

i) To possess means of production (farms, factories, stores, etc.)

ii) To participate in managerial decisions (cooperative and participatory economics)

iii) To travel (needed to transport all the items in commerce, to make deals in person, for workers and owners to go to where needed)

iv) To buy (items for personal use, for resale; buy whole enterprises to make the organization that creates wealth a form of wealth itself)

v) To sell (same as buy)

vi) To hire (to create organizations that create wealth)

vii) To fire (to maintain organizations that create wealth)

viii) To organize (private enterprise for profit, labor unions, workers' and professional associations, non-profit groups, religions, etc.)

ix) To communicate (free speech, newspapers, books, advertisements, make deals, create business partners, create markets)

x) To protest peacefully (marches, petitions, sue the government, make laws friendly to profit making and workers alike, remove pointless inefficiencies to maximize wealth creation)

Benefits of Mixed Economy

There are numerous advantages of a mixed economy:

i) ***Provides fair competition:*** The presence of private enterprise ensures that there is fair competition in the market and the quality of products and services are not compromised.

ii) ***Market prices are well regulated:*** The government with its regulatory bodies ensures that the market price does not go beyond its actual price.

iii) ***Optimum utilization of national resources:*** In a mixed economy, the resources are utilized efficiently as both government and private enterprises are utilizing them.

iv) ***People are given more power:*** The general people have more say when it comes to the quality and the prices of products and services.

v) ***It does not allow monopoly at all:*** Barring a few sectors, a mixed economy does not allow any monopoly as both government and private enterprises enter every sector for business.

Economic Policies

Economic Policies affects the different business units in different ways. It may or may not have favorable effect on a business unit. The Government may grant subsidies to one business or decrease the rates of excise or custom duty or the government may increase the rates of custom duty and excise duty, tax rates for another business. All the business enterprises frame their policies keeping in view the prevailing economic policies.

Different Economic Policies

Important economic policies of a country are as follows:

i) ***Monetary Policy:*** The policy formulated by the central bank of a country to control the supply and the cost of money (rate of interest), in order to attain some specified objectives is known as Monetary Policy.

ii) ***Fiscal Policy:*** It may be termed as budgetary policy. It is related with the income and expenditure of a country. Fiscal Policy works as an instrument in economic and social growth of a country. It is framed by the government of a country and it deals with taxation, government expenditure, borrowings, deficit financing and management of public debts in an economy.

iii) ***Foreign Trade Policy:*** It also affects the different business units differently. E.g. if restrictive import policy has been adopted by the government then it will prevent the domestic business units from foreign competition and if the liberal import policy has been adopted by the government then it will affect the domestic products in other way.

iv) ***Foreign Investment Policy:*** The policy related to the investment by the foreigners in a country is known as Foreign Investment Policy. If the government has adopted liberal investment policy then it will lead to more inflow of foreign capital in the country which ultimately results in more industrialization and growth in the country.

v) ***Industrial Policy:*** Industrial policy of a country promotes and regulates the industrialization in the country. It is framed by government. The government from time to time issues principals and guidelines under the industrial policy of the country.

Industry

India is fourteenth in the world in factory output. The manufacturing sector in addition to mine, quarrying, electricity and gas together account for 27.6% of the GDP and employ 17% of the total workforce. Economic reforms introduced after 1991 brought foreign competition, led to privatization of certain public sector industries, opened up sectors hitherto reserved for the public sector and led to an expansion in the production of fast-moving consumer goods. In recent years, Indian cities have continued to liberalize, but excessive and burdensome business regulations remain a problem in some cities, like Kochi and Kolkata.

Post-liberalization, the Indian private sector, which was usually run by oligopolies of old family firms and required political connections to prosper was faced with foreign competition, including the threat of cheaper Chinese imports. It has since handled the change by squeezing costs, revamping management, focusing on designing new products and relying on low labour costs and technology.

Global/International Economic Environment

The role of international economic environment is increasing day by day. If any business enterprise is involved in foreign trade, then it is influenced by not only its own country economic environment but also the economic environment of the country from/to which it is importing or exporting goods. There are various rules and guidelines for these trades which are issued by many organizations like World Bank, WTO, and United Nations etc.

International economics is concerned with the effects upon economic activity of international differences in productive resources and consumer preferences and the institutions that affect them. It seeks to explain the patterns and consequences of transactions and interactions between the inhabitants of different countries, including trade, investment and migration.

International trade is the exchange of capital, goods, and services across international borders or territories. In most countries, such trade represents a significant share of Gross Domestic Product (GDP). While international trade has been present throughout much of history, it's economic, social, and political importance has been on the rise in recent centuries. Industrialization, advanced transportation, globalization, multinational corporations and outsourcing are all having a major impact on the international trade system. Increasing international trade is crucial to the continuance of globalization.

The economic theory of international trade differs from the remainder of economic theory mainly because of the comparatively limited international mobility of the capital and labour. In that respect, it would appear to differ in degree rather than in principle from the trade between remote regions in one country.

Thus the methodology of international trade economics differs little from that of the remainder of economics. However, the direction of academic research on the subject has been influenced by the fact that governments have often sought to impose restrictions upon international trade, and the motive for the development of trade theory has often been a wish to determine the consequences of such restrictions. The branch of trade theory which is conventionally categorized as "classical" consists mainly of the application of deductive logic, originating with Ricardo's Theory of Comparative Advantage and developing into a range of theorems that depend for their practical value upon the realism of their postulates. "Modern" trade theory, on the other hand, depends mainly upon empirical analysis.

Economic globalization takes many forms. It may involve trade between individuals or businesses in one country with those of another. Globalization of this sort is as old as recorded history. Ancient coastal tribes traded with those in the mountains and deserts, each gaining prized goods they could not otherwise have enjoyed. Today, we take for granted the fact that much of what we consume or use originated elsewhere, often in a strange foreign land.

Businesses may decide to produce their products not only at home but also in other countries, either to evade the tariffs or quotas of countries where they wish of sells their products, or to cut their costs of production by hiring cheaper labour. Then globalization involves the bundling together of financial capital, technology, and other strategic inputs in order to transfer them as direct foreign investment in another country. Direct investment implies control over the assets transferred abroad. Foreign investments that don't involve control are called foreign portfolio equity investments. They are more likely to be made by financial institutions or investors like pension funds, insurance companies or investment trusts, which are interested only in a return on their investments commensurate with the risks they are taking. If returns fall or risks rise, portfolio investment is much less dependable than direct investment as a source of longer-term finance for a country's development.

The activities of transnational corporations are a still deeper form of globalization. They coordinate their activities with many entities throughout the world, producing in many places with complex networks of production and finance. This form of globalization has recently been named "alliance capitalism," in order to stress the growing importance of strategic alliances between business entities, as businesses search for ways to protect their competitive advantages and global market positions.

Governments also compete for economic advantage globally. They often support private research and development activities, finance worker retraining, protect the environment, and promote inter-firm alliances. When governments decide it is in their interest to cooperate rather than compete, they may form supranational organizations, like the International Monetary Fund (IMF) and the World Trade Organization (WTO), or less formal regional bodies, in order to achieve shared objectives, e.g., stable macroeconomic conditions, more growth through trade, or "market-friendly" economies.

Globalization of economic activity describes the process of merging between domestic economies, businesses and societies. The phrase relates to economic activity that indicates that globalization involves the participation of companies and corporations actively contributing to the integration of international businesses. The features of the globalization of economic activity include an international development of trade, production, investments and flow of workforce.

International trade relates to the exchange of capital and goods in the global market. It is an essential component of the globalization of economic activity as business acts on an international level mainly to ensure benefiting from participation in the global trade system. Imports and exports are the aspects of international trade countries and corporations producing more than they can consume focus on exporting goods to countries which demand production. For example, a report by the European Central Bank indicates that through the satisfaction of foreign demand, countries like China and India have massively expanded their economies. These destinations are now a major focus for businesses looking to buy goods and import them in countries that require production, such as the U.S. and the E.U.

International production in the global economy or exported production as many economic scholars refer the term to is the occurrence where businesses start producing their goods in countries with cheaper labor and more relaxed tax systems. This allows big companies to produce more and pay less for the labor and the country housing their production facilities and activities. For example, the German car industry giants, as indicated by Turkish economist Lale Duruiz, have already exported their production in Turkey, benefiting from the economic treaty of the country with the E.U. for free movement of goods. Thus, the German producers pay no import fees when delivering their production in Europe and save up from labor costs and taxation.

Investing on an international level allows companies and financial organizations to participate in projects in different areas in the world depending on profitability and market situation. For example, where financial organizations from the developed world seek to expand their influence on an international level, they would offer to invest in the developing economies to either have a share in the production or to receive a fixed interest upon the investment they have made. This has happened in the relationships between United Arab Emirates and the United States as described by the U.A.E - U.S. Business Council. When first started investing in the developing Arab Union in the late 1990s, the U.S. input $540 million in investments. Seven years later, the U.S. investments had already grown by 724 percent, thus turning the Emirates into one of the most successful destinations American financial institutions have ever participated in. This increase in the investment value has contributed to the development of stronger ties between the countries and stable trade relations between businesses from both sides.

The globalization of economic activity includes the integration of people willing to work in foreign economies. The most advanced example of such integration is the European Union every citizen of the Union is allowed to participate and exercise a profession in all the member states of the organization through a freedom of movement legislation.

Economic Legislations

Besides the above policies, Governments of different countries frame various legislations which regulates and control the business. In India there are 20 essential economic laws, listed here in chronological order. They form the overall legal framework of the Indian business environment.

- **The Indian Contract Act (1872):** Established the framework within which contracts can be executed and enforced.
- **Negotiable Instruments Act (1881):** Set rules for promissory notes, bills of exchange, and checks.
- **Workmen's Compensation Act (1923):** Set the compensation to be paid by employers to injured workers.
- **Sale of Goods Act (1930):** A mercantile law that complemented the Contract Act (see above).
- **Payment of Wages Act (1936):** Established a minimum monthly salary for industrial and factory workers.
- **Industrial Disputes Act (1947):** Provided for the investigation and settlement of industrial disputes.
- **Minimum Wages Act (1948):** Fixed minimum pay rates for certain jobs.
- **Factories Act (1948):** Regulated labor in factories.
- **Employees Provident Fund and Miscellaneous Provisions Act (1952):** Established provident funds, family pensions, and other monetary benefits for factory employees.
- **Maternity Benefits Act (1961):** Regulated post-childbirth time off for female employees.
- **Payment of Bonus Act (1965):** Regulated bonus payments to be made to certain categories of employees on the basis of production, profit, or productivity.
- **Monopolies and Restrictive Trade Practices Act (1969):** Established rules to prevent unfair concentrations of economic power.
- **Indian Patents Act (1970):** Set rules for patent protection in India.
- **Payment of Gratuity Act (1972):** Provided for payment of gratuities to Indian employees in certain industries.
- **Copyright Act (1975):** Helped establish copyright protection in India.
- **Arbitration and Conciliation Act (1996):** Set up to govern arbitration issues.
- **Geographical Indications of Goods Act (1999):** Provided legal protection for goods originated in a particular area or region within India (examples include Darjeeling tea and Basmati rice).
- **Trademarks Act (1999):** Helped establish trademark protection in India.
- **Designs Act (2000):** Helped establish protection of designs.
- **Competition Act (2002):** Provided for the establishment of a commission that promotes competition, protects consumers, and ensures freedom of trade.

Socio-Cultural Environment

Social environment describes the characteristics of the society in which the organization exists. Literacy rate, customs, values, beliefs, life-style, demographic features and mobility of population are part of the social environment. It is important for managers to notice the direction in which the society is moving and formulate progressive policies according to the changing social scenario.

The socio-cultural fabric is an important environmental factor that should be analyzed while formulating business strategies. The cost of ignoring the customs, traditions, taboos, tastes and preferences, etc., of people could be very high. The buying and consumption habits of the people, their language, beliefs and values, customs and traditions, tastes and preferences, education are all factors that affect business. For a business to be successful, its strategy should be the one that is appropriate in the socio-cultural environment. The marketing mix will have to be so designed as best to suit the environmental characteristics of the market. In Thailand, Helene Curtis switched to black shampoo because Thai women felt that it made their hair look glossier. Nestle, a Swiss multinational company, today brews more than forty varieties of instant coffee to satisfy different national tastes. Even when people of different cultures use the same basic product, the mode of consumption, conditions of use, purpose of use or the perceptions of the product attributes may vary so much so that the product attributes method of presentation, positioning, or method of promoting the product may have to be varied to suit the characteristics of different markets. For example, the two most important foreign markets for Indian shrimp are the U.S and Japan. The product attributes for the success of the product in these two markets differ. In the U.S. market, correct weight and bacteriological factors are more important rather than eye appeal, colour, and uniformity of size and arrangement of the shrimp which are very important in Japan. Similarly, the mode of consumption of tuna, another seafood export from India, differs between the U.S. and European countries. Tuna fish sandwiches, an American favourite which accounts for about 80 per cent of American tuna consumption, have little appeal in high tuna consumption European countries where people eat it right from the can. A very interesting example is that of the Vicks Vaporub, the popular pain balm, which is used as a mosquito repellant in some of the tropical areas. The differences in languages sometimes pose a serious problem, even necessitating a change in the brand name. Preett was, perhaps, a good brand name in India, but it did not suit in the overseas market; and hence it was appropriate to adopt 'Prestige' for the overseas markets. Chevrolet's brand name 'Nova' in Spanish means "it doesn't go". In Japanese, General Motors' "Body by Fisher" translates as corpse by Fisher".

The values and beliefs associated with colour vary significantly between different cultures. Blue, considered feminine and warm in Holland, and is regarded as masculine and cold in Sweden. Green is a favourite colour in the Muslim world; but in Malaysia, it is associated with illness. White indicates death and mourning in China and Korea; but in some countries, it expresses happiness and is the colour of the wedding dress of the bride. Red is a popular colour in the communist countries; but many African countries have a national distaste for red colour.

Social inertia and associated factors come in the way of the promotion of certain products, services or ideas. We come across such social stigmas in the marketing of family planning ideas, use of bio-gas for cooking, etc. In such circumstances, the success of marketing depends, to a very large extent, on the success in changing social attitudes or value systems. There are also a number of demographic factors, such as the age, and sex composition of population, family size, habitat, religion, etc., which influence the business.

While dealing with the social environment, we must also consider the social environment of the business which encompasses its social responsibility and the alertness or vigilance of the consumers and of society at large. The societal environment has assumed great importance in recent years. As Barker observes, business traditionally has been held responsible for quantities for the supply of goods and jobs, for costs, prices, wages, hours of works, and for standards of living. Today, however, business is being asked to take a responsibility for the quality of life in our society. The expectation is that business- in addition to its traditional accountability for economic performance and results will concern itself with the health of the society that it will come up with the cures for the ills that currently beset us and, indeed, will find ways of anticipating and preventing future problems in these areas.

As Stern succinctly points out, the more educated the society becomes, the more interdependent it becomes, and the more discretionary the use of its resources, the more marketing will become enmeshed in social issues. Marketing personnel are at interface between company and society. In this position, they have the responsibility not merely for designing a competitive marketing strategy, but for sensitizing business to the social, as well as the product demand of society.

Humans essentially create their own cultural and social environment. Customs, practices and traditions for survival and development are passed down from one generation to the next. In this way, the members of a particular society become conditioned to accept certain "truths" about life around them. The increasingly competitive international business environment calls upon exporters to tailor or adapt their business approach to the culture and traditions of specific foreign markets. The inability or unwillingness to do so could become a serious obstacle to success.

The task of adjusting to a new cultural environment is probably one of the biggest challenges of export marketing. Export marketing attempts are frequently unsuccessful because the marketer either consciously or unconsciously - makes decisions or evaluations from a frame of reference that is acceptable to his/her own culture but unacceptable in a foreign environment. Therefore, business practices which are successful in one group of countries may be entirely inappropriate in another group of countries. For example, the Marlboro Company took its famous lone cowboy advertisement to Hong Kong in the early 1960's. However, the image of the cowboy riding off in the distance by himself led the Chinese to wonder what he had done wrong.

Meaning of Social Environment

Social environment of business means all factors which affects business socially. Every business works in a society, so societies' different factors like family, educational institutions and religion affects business.

Main elements of Societies and its effect on Business

1. ***Family:*** Family is basic part of society from the birth of a person and up to death, he lives in family so personal decision of buying and selling of goods are affects from family. In the culture of a family, it may happen that parent does not allow using any product, then sale of such product will decrease, so businessman must analyze different family's needs. Many occasion of family like marriage of any family member, can increase the demand of goods.
2. ***Educational institutions:*** Educational institutions are also main part of societies. They provide good knowledge, education, awareness, thinking what should students buy or not to buy. Suppose

if a student is habitual to drink the tea and if his teacher advice him that this is harmful to his health after his guidance students can avoid drinking tea after this the sale of tea will decrease.

3. ***Religion:*** Like family and education institution, religion is also affects the business socially. Religion means the system in which group of persons trust in God. They believe that there is one supernatural power in this earth and its name is God. Different religions have different principles, rules and regulations in which they sacrifice to use some products and to eat some food, in Hindu religion, they never use leather products. They affect the sale of leather industries. So, businessman must analyze the targeted audience and after listening their religious thoughts, he should produce the goods.

Meaning of Culture

According to Mitchell, "Culture is a set of learned core values, beliefs, standards, knowledge morals, laws and behaviors shared by individuals and societies determination how an individual acts, feel, and views oneself and others".

Meaning of Cultural Environment

The cultural environment refers to the institutions and other forces that affect the basic values, behaviors, and preferences of the society-all of which have an effect on consumer marketing decisions.

Meaning of Socio-cultural Environment

Socio-cultural Environment refers to the sum of all learned attitudes and behaviours that influence how a person thinks and behaves. For example, the way a person dresses, or feels about the need to express their individuality, is largely selected from a set of options available in that person's socio-cultural environment.

Factors of the Socio-cultural environment

There are a number of factors that you will need to consider:

i) Language

Language is central to the expression of culture. Within each cultural group, the use of words reflects the life-style, attitudes and many of the customs of that group. Language is not only a key to understanding the group; it is the principal way of communicating within it. A language usually defines the parameters of a particular culture. Thus if several languages are spoken within the borders of a country, that country is seen to have as many cultures. In Canada, for instance, both English and French are spoken; in Belgium, French and Flemish; while in South Africa there are 11 official languages with a number of other African languages also spoken by the population. In addition, there are often variations within a language - different dialects, accents, pronunciations and terminology may distinguish one cultural group from another, e.g. English-speaking South Africans, the British, Americans and Australians.

ii) Material culture

Material culture relates to the way in which a society organizes and views its economic activities. It includes the techniques and know-how used in the creation of goods and services, the manner in which the people of the society use their capabilities, and the resulting benefits. When one refers to an 'industrialized' or a 'developing' nation, one is really referring to a material culture.

The material culture of a particular market will affect the nature and extent of demand for a product. Whereas a luxury item, such as a sophisticated piece of computer hardware, may have a ready market in a country such as France, demand for it may be non-existent in a developing country which is hampered by inadequate facilities and/or foreign exchange shortages. The material culture of a country may also necessitate modifications to the product. Electrical appliances, for example, may have to be adapted to cater for differences in voltage levels. To illustrate this: the United States operates under a system of 110V in contrast to South Africa's 220V. Alternatively, weights and measurements may have to be converted to those applicable in the importing country.

Material culture can also have a significant effect on the proposed marketing and distribution strategies. While highways and rail transport are the principal means of moving goods within the United States, rivers and canals are used extensively in certain European countries. If the company is planning to develop a manufacturing operation in a foreign market, aspects such as the supply of raw materials, power, transportation and financing need to be investigated.

iii) Aesthetics

A culture's aesthetics refer to its ideas concerning good taste and beauty as expressed in the fine arts - music, art, drama and dance - and in the appreciation of colour and form. Insensitivity to aesthetic values can not only lead to ineffective advertising and package design for products, it can also offend prospective customers.

iv) Social organization

Social organization refers to the ways in which people relate to one another, form groups and organize their activities, teach acceptable behaviour and govern themselves. It thus comprises the social, educational and political systems of a society.

The exporter's ability to communicate depends to some extent, on the educational level of the foreign market. If the consumers are largely illiterate, advertising materials or package labels may have to be adapted to the needs of the market. In this regard, however, a company marketing baby food in a certain African country put the picture of a smiling child on the outside of the jar. The local resident assuming there were preserved babies inside avoided the product! In addition, there are unspoken signals which identify cultural differences, from certain taboos to less obvious practices like the time taken to answer a letter. In some societies, for instance, an important issue is dealt with immediately; in others, promptness is taken as a sign that the matter is regarded as unimportant, the time taken corresponding with the gravity of the issue.

In a culture where great importance is attached to the family unit, promotional efforts should be directed at the family rather than the individual. The size of the family unit differs from one culture to another. It can range from the nuclear family, i.e. mother, father, and children, to the extended family which includes many relatives and whose role is to provide protection, support and economic security to its members. In the extended family, characteristic of developing countries, consumption decision-making takes place in a larger unit and purchasing power patterns may be different from those evident in western cultures.

In any society, certain occupations carry more prestige, social status and monetary reward than others. In India, for example, there is a strong reluctance amongst people with university education to perform 'menial' tasks using their hands, even answering the telephone. In many countries, including France, Italy and Singapore, financial independence is considered essential for occupation-related prestige. In Japan, however, the majority of university-educated professionals tend to prefer working for large multinational firms than for themselves. Social organization is also evidenced in the operation of the class system, e.g. the Hindu caste system and the grouping of society members according to age, sex, political orientation, etc.

v) Religious beliefs, attitudes, values, space and time

Religious system refers to the spiritual side of a culture or its approach to the supernatural. Western culture is accepted as having been largely influenced by the Judeo-Christian traditions, while Eastern or Oriental cultures have been strongly influenced by Buddhism, Confucianism, Taoism and Hinduism. Although very few religions influence business activities directly, the impact of religion on human value systems and decision-making is significant. Thus, religion exerts a considerable influence on people's actions and outlook on life, as well as on the products they buy. In certain part of the world, such as Latin America, the influence of religion extends even beyond the individual or family and is manifested in a whole community's deep involvement in, and devotion to, the church.

A society's religious belief system is often dependent on its stage of human or economic development. Primitive tribesmen tend to be superstitious about life in general while people in technologically advanced cultures seem to have dismissed the notion of traditional religious worship and practice in favour of a more scientific approach to life and death.

The failure to consider specialized aspects of local religions has created a number of difficulties for firms. Companies have encountered problems in Asia when they incorporated a picture of a Buddha in their promotions. Religious ties are strong in this area, and the use of local religious symbols in advertising is strongly resented - especially when words are deliberately or even accidentally printed across the picture of a Buddha. One company was nearly burned to the ground when it ignorantly tried such a strategy. The seemingly minor incident led to a major international political conflict remembered for years.

Attitudes are psychological states that predispose people to behave in certain ways. Attitudes may relate, for example, to work, wealth, achievement, change, the role of women in the economy, etc.

Western cultures, for example, value individualism and promote the importance of autonomy and personal achievement needs. In contrast, in many eastern and developing countries, there is a strong sense of collectivism and the importance of social and security needs. For instance, the Hindu religion imparts a type of work ethic that considers work central to one's life but maintains that it must be performed as a service to others, not for one's own personal achievement.

Stereotypes are sets of attitudes in which one attributes qualities or characteristics to a person on the basis of the group to which that person belongs. An international business person's tendency to judge others by his or her personal and cultural standards instead of attempting to understand others in the context of their unique historical, political, economic and social backgrounds could, for example, be termed an undesirable attitude.

Values are judgements regarding what is valuable or important in life, and they vary greatly from one culture to another. People who are operating at a survival level will value food, shelter and clothing. Those with high security needs, on the other hand, may value job security, status, money, etc. From its value system, a culture sets norms, i.e. acceptable standards of behaviour.

Pepsodent reportedly tried to sell its toothpaste in regions of south-east Asia through a promotion which stressed that the toothpaste helped enhance white teeth. In this area, where some local people deliberately chewed betel nut in order to achieve the social prestige of darkly stained teeth, such an ad was understandably less than effective. The slogan "wonder where the yellow went" was also viewed by many as a racial slur.

The **concept of space** is different wherever one goes. In western corporate culture, the size and location of an executive's office is usually determined by his level of seniority in the company. The locality and size of an Arab business executive's office, on the other hand, are a poor indication of the person's importance.

Conversation distance between two people is learned early in life - almost completely unconsciously. A western business executive, conditioned to operating within a certain amount of personal space, may feel uncomfortable or alarmed at the closeness and physical contact displayed in the Middle East or Latin America, for example.

Time also has a different meaning in each country. Western cultures tend to perceive time in terms of past, present and future. They are orientated towards the future and in the process of preparing for it, they save, waste, make up or spend time. In South Africa, giving a person a deadline is a way of indicating the degree of urgency or relative importance of the work. In the Middle East, however, time does not usually include schedules and timetables. The time required to get something accomplished depends on the relationship. With South Africans, the more important an event is, the earlier it is planned, which is why last minute invitations are often regarded as an insult. In planning future events with Arab businesspersons, it is often advisable to keep the lead time to a week or less, because other factors may intervene and take precedence.

Some time ago, an American lost a major contract in Greece because he did not appreciate the Greek concept of time. The Greek executive could not understand the American's insistence on setting time limits on the length of their business meetings - he and his colleagues were prepared to spend as much time in discussion as they felt was necessary. The American also insisted that the senior managers involved in the transaction be responsible only for working out the general principles of the deal, with the actual details being left to subordinates. Suspicious that this represented a lack of commitment on the part of the American, the Greek called off the deal.

Many factors continuously produce cultural changes in a society - new technology, population shifts, availability of scarce resources and changing values regarding the role of education or women. Culture is thus dynamic, and exporters, particularly those involved in international travel and marketing, need to regularly assess what new products and service needs have been created, who the potential buyers and users are, and how best to reach them.

Impact of Socio-cultural Environment in Business

The relationship among business, culture and society involves a two-way interaction. Although we tend to think of business as operating according to a distinctive instrumental rationality of profit-and-loss and the 'bottom line' it is also influenced by the social-cultural setting in which it is embedded. At the same time business affects the wider culture and society profoundly. The impact of socio-cultural environment in business can be summarized as follows:

a) In estimating the demand for a product the consumer behaviour and their consumption pattern are to be understood apart from their purchasing power. Some latent needs of people, if understood properly, can be converted into demand. For example some products sold in sachets get good response due to the convenience and low cost.

b) The product features are designed by understanding the cultural background of consumers. The tastes and preference differ due to this aspect. For instances, products containing vegetable fats than animal fats are preferred by some groups, natural ingredients than chemical or artificial goods, are preferred by somebody, the food-stuffs also vary consumed by different groups.

c) The sales promotion techniques based on the understanding of cultural values of people usually become successful. The appeals are selected best suited to the attitude of people. We could see a number or advertisements based on the affection and importance of family relationships.

d) In developing human relations with workers, suppliers, middlemen and the public, it is necessary to understand the culture and mental make-ups of those people. For example workers in different regions behave differently. If this is understood conflicts with workers may be reduced.

e) The trade practices and services are designed based on the customs and habits of the people. This includes holidays, (Fridays, instead of Sundays in Muslim areas) working hours, consumer service, sales retail-outlets, demonstrations etc.

f) In introducing varieties, improvements and innovations in products, care should be taken to understand the social characteristics of people. Many products in cosmetics failed in Indian markets. We can also quote the hesitated acceptance of electric appliances and gas stoves in rural markets.

g) The general attitude of people towards consumption, savings and investment patterns also affect the overall business growth. Indian people usually don't prefer 'use and throw' goods. They prefer investing in gold than in shares and bonds.

h) Business is an activity undertaken by people whose values and attitudes are shaped by the culture and society of which they are a part. To some extent the roles we perform in business are quite discrete from other aspects of our lives and require that we adopt different behaviours and personas. However there is not, of course, a complete separation between 'work' and 'life'. We carry values and attitudes shaped by the wider culture and society into our roles as managers, employees and consumers.

i) It can be argued that capitalist business owes its historical origins and development in part to non-economic factors. Max Weber argued that the 'spirit of capitalism', or ethos of capitalist business, with its emphasis on accumulating wealth, can be traced to religious belief the 'Protestant ethic'. This religious belief encouraged the reinvestment of wealth in business rather than the pursuit of a life of luxury, thus fuelling economic growth and dynamism. A version of this theory persists today in the idea that economic success depends on the prevalence of a 'work ethic' in society which sees work as a morally desirable activity.

j) There may be concern that wearing a religious symbol may cause offence to others (customers or colleagues) of a different faith or none. An employer may want to keep religious conflicts out of the workplace or avoid putting off customers. If the policy was designed to protect the company's image and to attract customers, it seems to have back-fired on both counts.

k) Values are the terms on which we interact with business have a profound influence on our lives. Work is a central aspect of our lives and the vast majority of employees work in the private sector. We also depend very largely on the private sector to supply the goods and services we consume on a daily basis. It is not surprising, then, that business has major impacts on culture and society.

l) The culture industries make up a significant part of business activity, reflecting the shift from manufacturing to service industries in the wealthy economies. Culture has become increasingly big business as a growing share of consumer expenditure is dedicated to 'life-style' purchases rather than material necessities. This can be seen in the growth of the wide range of businesses concerned with leisure and tourism.

Cross Culture

Cross culture means the interaction of people from different backgrounds in the business world. Cross culture is a vital issue in international business, as the success of international trade depends upon the smooth interaction of employees from different cultures and regions. A growing number of companies are consequently devoting substantial resources toward training their employees to interact effectively with those of companies in other cultures in an effort to foment a positive cross-cultural experience.

Cross culture can be experienced by an employee who is transferred to a location in another country. The employee must learn the language and culture of those around him, and vice-versa. This can be more difficult if this person is acting in a managerial capacity; someone in this position who cannot effectively communicate with or understand their employees' actions can lose their credibility. In an ever-expanding global economy, cross culture and adaptability will continue to be important factors in the business world.

Cross Cultural Environment

Globalization, the expansion of intercontinental trade, technological advances and the increase in the number of companies dealing on the international stage have brought about a dramatic change in the frequency, context and means by which people from different cultural backgrounds interact. Within companies there are many facets in which cultural differences manifest. Some key areas which cross cultural consultants deal with include, but are not exclusive to, the following:

i) ***Cross Cultural HR:*** HR covers a wide range of business critical areas that need cross cultural analysis. Consultants may offer advice on a number of areas including recruitment, relocation, international assignments, staff retention and training programmes.

ii) ***Cross Cultural Team-Building:*** In order to have a well functioning business unit within a company, communication is critical. Cross cultural consultants will provide tools and methods to promote staff integration, reduce cross cultural conflicts and build team spirit. This is essentially done through highlighting differences and building on strengths to ensure they are used positively.

iii) ***Cross Cultural Synergy:*** International mergers, acquisitions and joint-ventures require people from different cultural backgrounds to harmonize in order to succeed. Cross cultural consultants counsel on group mechanics, communication styles, norms, values and integration processes.

iv) ***Cross Cultural Awareness Training:*** Working with colleagues, customers or clients from different cultural backgrounds, with different religions, values and etiquettes can occasionally lead to problems. Cross cultural awareness training is usually a generic introduction into a culture, country, region or religion. The aim is to equip the trainee with the adequate knowledge to deal comfortably with people from different cultures, avoiding misunderstandings and mistakes.

v) ***Cross Cultural Training for Expatriate Relocation:*** Staff that travel overseas need to understand the cultural basics of the host country or region. Knowledge of the country's history, culture, laws, traditions, business practices and social etiquettes all help to minimize the impact of culture shock and hence smooth their transition overseas.

vi) ***Cross Cultural Negotiations:*** Equipped with their knowledge of the two or more cultures that can be meeting around the negotiation table, a cross cultural consultant advises on areas such as negotiation strategies, styles, planning, closure and etiquette in order to increase the chance of a successful outcome, free from misunderstandings, suspicions and general cross cultural communication breakdown.

vii) ***Cross Cultural PR Consultancy:*** Brand image, public relations and advertising are all areas companies must be careful of when moving out of the national context. Tastes and values change dramatically from continent to continent. It is crucial to understand whether the brand name, image or advertising campaign is culturally applicable in the target country. Cross cultural consultants examine words, images, pictures, colours and symbols to ensure they fit well with the target culture.

viii) ***Cross Cultural Language Training:*** Language training is an area where little investment is made by companies, but where the business advantages are great. Linguistic knowledge goes a long way in bridging cultural gaps and smoothing lines of communication. Cross cultural consultancies provide language training to business staff, moulding their learning to the business environment in which they work.

Political Environment

Political environment comprises political stability and the policies of the government. Ideological inclination of political parties, personal interest on politicians, influence of party forums etc. create political environment. For example, Bangalore established itself as the most important IT centre of India mainly because of political support.

Political and government environment has close relationship with the economic system and economic policy. For example, the communist countries had a centrally planned economic system. In most countries, apart from those laws that control investment and related matters, there are a number of laws that regulate the conduct of the business. These laws cover such matters as standards of products, packaging, promotion etc.

In many countries, with a view to protecting consumer interests, regulations have become stronger. Regulations to protect the purity of the environment and preserve the ecological balance have assumed great importance in many countries. Some governments specify certain standards for the products to be marketed in the country; some even prohibit the marketing of certain products. In most nations, promotional activities are subject to various types of controls. Media advertising is not permitted in Libya. Several European countries restrain the use of children in commercial advertisements. In a number of countries, including India, the advertisement of alcoholic liquor is prohibited. Advertisements, including packaging, of cigarettes must carry the statutory warning that "cigarette smoking is injurious to health". Similarly, advertisements of baby food must necessarily inform the potential buyer that breast-feeding in the best. In countries like Germany, product comparison advertisements and the use of superlatives like 'best' or 'excellent' in advertisements is not allowed In the United States, the Federal Trade Commission is empowered to require a company to provide the quality, performance or comparative prices of its products.

There are a host of statutory controls on business in India. If the MRTP companies wanted to expand their business substantially, they had to convince the government that such expansion was in the public interest. Indeed, the Government in India has an all-pervasive and predominantly restrictive influence over various aspects of business, e.g, industrial licensing which decides location, capacity and process; import licensing for machinery and materials; size and price of capital issue; loan finance; pricing; managerial remuneration; expansion plans; distribution restrictions and a host of other enactments. Therefore, a considerable part of attention of a Chief Executive and his senior colleagues has to be devoted to a continuous dialogue with various government agencies to ensure growth and profitability within the framework of controls and restraints.

Many countries today have laws to regulate competition in the public interest. Elimination of unfair competition and dilution of monopoly power are the important objectives of these regulations. In India, the monopolistic undertakings, dominants undertakings and large industrial houses are subject to number of regulations which prevent the concentration of economic power to the common detriment. The MRTP Act also controls monopolistic, restrictive and unfair trade practices which are prejudicial to public interest. Such regulations brighten the prospects of small and new firms. They also increase the scope of some of the existing firms to venture into new areas of business. The special privileges available to the small scale sector have also contributed to the phenomenal success of the Nirma.

Certain changes in government policies such as the industrial policy, fiscal policy, tariff policy etc. may have profound impact on business. Some policy developments create opportunities as well as threats. In other words, a development which brightens the prospects of some enterprises may pose a threat to some others. For example, the industrial policy liberalizations in India, particularly around the mid-eighties have opened up new opportunities and threats. They have provided a lot of opportunities to a large number of enterprises to diversify and to make their product mix better. But they have also given rise to serious threat to many existing products by way of increased competitions; many seller's markets have given way to buyer's markets. Even products which were seldom advertised have come to be promoted very heavily. This battle for the market has provided a splendid opportunity for the advertising industry. Advertising billing has been increasing substantially. That an estimated cost savings of about Rs. 200 crores per year have accrued to the Reliance Industries as a result of the changes in duties on some of the material inputs used by them is just an indication of the tremendous impact the fiscal and tariff policies can have on the business.

The Constitution in general establishes the mastery of the people under the leadership of the Communist Party, of which the highest representation is the Politburo and the Party Secretary General. The power of the people is to be exercised through the National Assembly at the central level and the People's Councils at different local levels.

The National Assembly is the supreme representative and legislative body and determines both domestic and foreign policy. It is elected by universal suffrage. The National Assembly in turn elects and may remove from office the President, Vice-President, Chairman of the National Assembly, Vice-chairman of National Assembly, members of the Standing Committee of the National Assembly, the Prime Minister, the Chief Justice of the People's Supreme Court and the Head of the Supreme People's Procuracy. In addition, the National Assembly has the responsibility of sanctioning the Prime Minister's selection of Deputy Prime Ministers and Ministers.

The National Assembly is also responsible for approving the organization of the Government and its agencies, and is the supreme law making body. The duration of the National Assembly is 5 years and elections are held two months prior to the expiry of its term. The Standing Committee possesses the power to manage the day-to-day affairs of the National Assembly when it is not in session and during this time the Standing Committee assumes all its powers, including the law making power on matters entrusted to it by the National Assembly. The Head of State is the President. He is elected by the National Assembly and represents the Nation internally and externally.

The highest executive body in Vietnam is the Government, formerly known as the Council of Ministers. It is charged generally with the management of the economy and the state. It is made up of the Prime Minister, Deputy Prime Ministers, Ministers and the Chairmen of the various State Committees and the Governor of the State Bank. Individual ministries and organizations equivalent to ministries aid the Prime Minister in the administration of the Country within the specific fields in which they have jurisdiction. The deputy prime ministers and the ministers are selected by the Prime Minister but must be approved by the National Assembly. With the exception of the Prime Minister, the members of the Government do not have to be members of the National Assembly. Decisions on major issues must be taken on a majority basis.

The court and prosecution systems in Vietnam have a structure similar to the administrative system. In the central level, the Supreme People's Court is the highest juridical body in Vietnam and the Chief Justice is elected by the National Assembly for the term of the National Assembly. The Supreme People's Procuracy has the highest power on prosecution in Vietnam and the Head is also elected by the National Assembly for the term of the National Assembly. In local levels, these bodies occur at the levels of city/ province and district.

The political environment in which the firm operates (or plan to operate) will have a significant impact on a company's international marketing activities. The greater the level of involvement in a foreign markets, the greater the need to monitor the political climate of the countries business is conducted. Changes in government often result in changes in policy and attitudes towards foreign business. Bearing in mind that a foreign company operates in a host country at the discretion of the government concerned, the government can either encourage foreign activities by offering attractive opportunities for investment and trade, or discourage its activities by imposing restrictions such as import quotas, etc. An exporter that is continuously aware of shifts in government attitude will be able to adapt export marketing strategies accordingly.

Nearly all governments today play active roles in their countries' economies. Although evident to a greater or lesser extent in most countries, government ownership of economic activities is still prevalent in the former centrally planned economies, as well as in certain developing countries which lack a sufficiently well developed private sector to support a free market system.

The implications of government ownership to a company marketing abroad might be that certain sectors of the foreign market are the exclusive preserve of government enterprise or that the company is obliged to sell directly to a state trading organization. In either case, the company's influence on the market is greatly reduced. Similarly, if an exporter is seeking to establish a subsidiary in a country where there is a high degree of state influence over the factors of production, the investor should bear in mind that marketing activities in the country concerned may be restricted and that the so-called controllable elements of the marketing mix will be less controllable.

Primary concern to an exporter should be the stability of the target country's political environment. A loss of confidence in this respect could lead to a company having to reduce its operations in the market or to withdraw from the market altogether. One of the surest indicators of political instability is a frequent change in regime. Although a change in government need not be accompanied by violence, it often heralds a change in policy towards business, particularly international business. Such a development could impact harshly on a firms long-term international marketing programme.

Reflected in a government's attitudes and policies towards foreign business are its ideas about how best to promote national interest in the light of the country's economic and political resources and objectives. Foreign products and investment seen to be vital to the growth and development of the economy often receive favourable treatment from the government in the form of reduced tax, exemption from quotas, etc. On the other hand, products considered by a government to be non-essential, undesirable, or a threat to local industry are frequently subjected to a variety of import restrictions such as quotas and tariffs. It is also important to be aware of the nature of the relationship between South Africa and the foreign target market. This was a major consideration during South Africa's political isolation. Fortunately, South Africa's international relations have normalized and today South Africa is viewed very favourably, from a political perspective, by the rest of the world. The political environment is connected to the international business environment through the concept of political risk.

Meaning of Political Environment

Political environment means the set of activities of the government which include plans, policies, programs and controls which directly or indirectly involve with the business.

Political Risk

Political risk can be defined as the impact of political change on the export firm's operations and decision-making process.

Political risk is determined differently for different companies, as not all of them will be equally affected by political changes. For example, industries requiring heavy capital investment are generally considered to be more vulnerable to political risk than those requiring less capital investment. Vulnerability stems from the extent of capital invested in the export market, e.g. capital-intensive extracting or energy-related businesses operating in the foreign market are more vulnerable than manufacturing companies exporting from a South African base.

Political risk is of a macro nature when politically inspired environmental changes affect all foreign investment. It is of a micro nature when the environmental changes are intended to affect only selected fields of business activity or foreign firms with specific characteristics.

When business is conducted in developing countries, the risks of greatest concern are civil disorder, war and expropriation. When business is conducted in industrialized countries, labour disruptions and price controls are generally seen to pose the greatest threats to a company's profitability.

All organizations do business abroad should be aware of the fact that what they do could be the object of some political action. Hence, they need to recognize that their success or failure could depend on how well they cope with political decisions, and how well they anticipate changes in political attitudes and policies.

Impact of Political Environment on doing Business in India

As in any part of the world, political influence is highly essential to start a business in India. Especially if you are planning to start a multibillion business, some sort of political patronage is an absolute necessity. Not only for safeguarding the interest of the company but even to begin the process of getting the required sanctions, one requires hold in the high echelons of politics and administrative circles.

Indian society is highly plural. It is the biggest democracy in the world with multi party political system. In population, India is second to China, with nearly 1200 million people. This is the most important consumer market in the world. It is a fast developing world. India is the third largest economy in the world and second fast growing economy in Asia. It has the tremendous potential of development with huge intellectual human force. With all these advantages and the huge market potential, world super entrepreneurs are looking for business establishments in India. With the overcrowded population and the millions of hard working and qualified personals, India offers a very cheap work force to the world. Many have realized the business potential in India, started exploring the unique opportunities of investments.

During the last couple of decades, India has opened its market to world. It has absolutely become an open global market. Banking sector, Insurance sector and all fields of industrial and business are now open for multinational investment. Of course there are many obstructions to cross. And mostly all issues can overcome and establish business if you have the political patronage.

India has a plural political system. With numerous political parties, national level and state level, it is very difficult to get a consensus among all parties for starting any business. Also these political parties have patronage of many factors, caste, creed and ideologies.

Political Institutions

Fundamental Rights

The Fundamental Rights, embodied in Part III of the Constitution, guarantee civil rights to all Indians, and prevent the State from encroaching on individual liberty while simultaneously placing upon it an obligation to protect the citizens' rights from encroachment by society. Seven fundamental rights were originally provided by the Constitution:

1. Right to Equality

The Right to Equality is one of the chief guarantees of the Constitution. It is embodied in Articles 14–16, which collectively encompass the general principles of equality before law and non-discrimination and Articles 17–18 which collectively further the philosophy of social equality. Article 14 guarantees equality before law as well as equal protection of the law to all persons within the territory of India. This includes the equal subjection of all persons to the authority of law, as well as equal treatment of persons in similar circumstances. The latter permits the State to classify persons for legitimate purposes, provided there is a reasonable basis for the same, meaning that the classification is required to be non-arbitrary.

based on a method of intelligible differentiation among those sought to be classified, as well as have a rational relation to the object sought to be achieved by the classification.

2. Right to Freedom

The Right to Freedom is covered in Articles 19–22, with the view of guaranteeing individual rights that were considered vital by the framers of the Constitution, and these Articles also include certain restrictions that may be imposed by the State on individual liberty under specified conditions. Article 19 guarantees six freedoms in the nature of civil rights, which are available only to citizens of India. These include the freedom of speech and expression, freedom of assembly, freedom of association without arms, freedom of movement throughout the territory of India, freedom to reside and settle in any part of the country of India and the freedom to practice any profession. All these freedoms are subject to reasonable restrictions that may impose on them by the State, listed under Article 19 itself. The grounds for imposing these restrictions vary according to the freedom sought to be restricted, and include national security, public order, decency and morality, contempt of court, incitement to offences, and defamation. The State is also empowered, in the interests of the general public to nationalize any trade, industry or service to the exclusion of the citizens.

3. Right against Exploitation

The Right against Exploitation, contained in Articles 23–24, lays down certain provisions to prevent exploitation of the weaker sections of the society by individuals or the State. Article 23 provides prohibits human trafficking, making it an offence punishable by law, and also prohibits forced labour or any act of compelling a person to work without wages where he was legally entitled not to work or to receive remuneration for it. However, it permits the State to impose compulsory service for public purposes, including conscription and community service. The Bonded Labour system (Abolition) Act, 1976, has been enacted by Parliament to give effect to this Article. Article 24 prohibits the employment of children below the age of 14 years in factories, mines and other hazardous jobs. Parliament has enacted the Child Labour (Prohibition and Regulation) Act, 1986, providing regulations for the abolition of, and penalties for employing, child labour, as well as provisions for rehabilitation of former child labourers.

4. Right to Freedom of Religion

The Right to Freedom of Religion, covered in Articles 25–28, provides religious freedom to all citizens and ensures a secular State in India. According to the Constitution, there is no official State religion, and the State is required to treat all religions impartially and neutrally. Article 25 guarantees all persons the freedom of conscience and the right to preach practice and propagate any religion of their choice. This right is, however, subject to public order, morality and health, and the power of the State to take measures for social welfare and reform. The right to propagate, however, does not include the right to convert another individual, since it would amount to an infringement of the other's right to freedom of conscience. Article 26 guarantees all religious denominations and sects, subject to public order, morality and health, to manage their own affairs in matters of religion, set up institutions of their own for charitable or religious purposes, and own, acquire and manage property in accordance with law. These provisions do not derogate from the State's power to acquire property belonging to a religious denomination. The State is also empowered to regulate any economic, political or other secular activity associated with religious practice.

5. Cultural and Educational Rights

The Cultural and Educational rights, given in Articles 29 and 30, are measures to protect the rights of cultural, linguistic and religious minorities, by enabling them to conserve their heritage and protecting them against discrimination. Article 29 grants any section of citizens having a distinct language, script culture of its own, the right to conserve and develop the same, and thus safeguards the rights of minorities by preventing the State from imposing any external culture on them. It also prohibits discrimination against any citizen for admission into any educational institutions maintained or aided by the State, on the grounds only of religion, race, caste, language or any of them. However, this is subject to reservation of a reasonable number of seats by the State for socially and educationally backward classes, as well as reservation of up to 50 percent of seats in any educational institution run by a minority community for citizens belonging to that community.

Article 30 confers upon all religious and linguistic minorities the right to set up and administer educational institutions of their choice in order to preserve and develop their own culture, and prohibits the State, while granting aid, from discriminating against any institution on the basis of the fact that it is administered by a religious or cultural minority. The term "minority", while not defined in the Constitution, has been interpreted by the Supreme Court to mean any community which numerically forms less than 50% of the population of the state in which it seeks to avail the right under Article 30. In order to claim the right, it is essential that the educational institution must have been established as well as administered by a religious or linguistic minority.

6. Right to Property

The Constitution originally provided for the right to property under Articles 19 and 31. Article 19 guaranteed to all citizens the right to acquire, hold and dispose of property. Article 31 provided that "no person shall be deprived of his property save by authority of law." It also provided that compensation would be paid to a person whose property has been taken for public purposes.

The provisions relating to the right to property were changed a number of times. The Forty-Forth Amendment of 1978 deleted the right to property from the list of fundamental rights. A new provision, Article 300-A, was added to the constitution which provided that "no person shall be deprived of his property save by authority of law". Thus if a legislature makes a law depriving a person of his property, there would be no obligation on the part of the State to pay anything as compensation. The aggrieved person shall have no right to move the court under Article 32. Thus, the right to property is no longer a fundamental right, though it is still a constitutional right. If the government appears to have acted unfairly, the action can be challenged in a court of law by citizens.

7. Right to Constitutional Remedies

The Right to Constitutional Remedies empowers citizens to approach the Supreme Court of India to seek enforcement, or protection against infringement, of their Fundamental Rights. Article 32 provides a guaranteed remedy, in the form of a Fundamental Right itself, for enforcement of all the other Fundamental Rights, and the Supreme Court is designated as the protector of these rights by the Constitution. The Supreme Court has been empowered to issue writs, namely habeas corpus, mandamus, prohibition, certiorari and quo warranto, for the enforcement of the Fundamental Rights, while the High Courts have been empowered under Article 226 – which is not a Fundamental Right in itself – to issue these prerogative writs even in cases not involving the violation of Fundamental Rights. The Supreme

Court has the jurisdiction to enforce the Fundamental Rights even against private bodies, and in case of any violation, award compensation as well to the affected individual. Exercise of jurisdiction by the Supreme Court can also be suo motu or on the basis of a public interest litigation. This right cannot be suspended, except under the provisions of Article 359 when a state of emergency is declared.

Laws inconsistent with or in derogation of the fundamental rights

(1) All laws in force in the territory of India immediately before the commencement of this Constitution, in so far as they are inconsistent with the provisions of this Part, shall, to the extent of such inconsistency, be void.

(2) The State shall not make any law which takes away or abridges the rights conferred by this Part and any law made in contravention of this clause shall, to the extent of the contravention, be void.

(3) In this article, unless the context otherwise requires.

(a) "Law" includes any Ordinance, order, bye-law, rule, regulation, notification, custom or usage having in the territory of India the force of law.

(b) "laws in force" includes laws passed or made by a Legislature or other competent authority in the territory of India before the commencement of this Constitution and not previously repealed, notwithstanding that any such law or any part thereof may not be then in operation either at all or in particular areas.

(4) Nothing in this article shall apply to any amendment of this Constitution made under article 368.

imperfect.

Legal Environment

Legal environment consists of legislation that is passed by the parliament and state legislatures. Examples of such legislation specifically aimed at business operations include the Trade mark Act 1969, Essential Commodities Act 1955, Standards of Weights and Measures Act 1969 and Consumer Protection Act 196.

The legal environment facing businesses operating internationally is not simply a scaled-up version of domestic law. Businesses are faced with legal rules derived from multiple sources, and enforced by bodies with fragmented and overlapping jurisdictions. Research in the Department of Commercial Law in these areas currently encompasses:

i) ***Private trade law:*** For example, types of international sale contract, mechanisms for payment and security, the insurance of goods in transit, conflicts between the laws of different trading countries, contracts for the international carriage of goods by sea, and dispute resolution.

ii) ***International trade and investment law:*** The national and international rules that facilitate economic integration between countries, including the World Trade Organization and regional and bilateral trade and investment agreements.

iii) ***International competition law:*** Analysis of the legal and policy issues associated with the control of restrictive business practices and anti-competitive mergers in international markets.

iv) ***International finance law and securities regulation:*** The global governance of securities and financial markets and the consequences for, and strategies open to, the New Zealand legislature.

Meaning of Legal Environment

The legal environment of a business refers to the relevant laws and regulations under which the business operates. Legal environment includes factors that provide rules, and penalties for violations, designed to protect society and consumers from unfair business practices and to protect businesses from unfair competitive practices. It assures uniform application of the laws by regulating the behavior and interactions of individuals against each other.

Needs for Legal Environment

i) Legal Environment maintain status quo in society ensuring stability and security of social order, enable individuals, maximum of freedom to assert themselves and determine the sphere within which the existence and activity of each individual will be secure and free.

ii) The principle of law provides uniformity and certainty to the administration of justice.

iii) The existence of fixed principles of law avoids the dangers of arbitrary, biased and dishonest decisions.

iv) The fixed principles of law protect administrators of justice from the errors of individual judgment.

Importance of Legal Environment

Legal environment is important because it incorporates the following lows:

i) ***Laws on Production or Sales:*** The production or sale of certain goods is prohibited, or at least severely restricted in many countries. This includes, among others, selling of dangerous drugs, guns and explosives, for instance. Aerosol cans containing CFCs, which are harmful to the environment, or more specifically, the ozone layer, are banned and no longer produced.

ii) ***Consumer Protection:*** Most countries have laws ensuring customers are being treated fairly by businesses. This includes the act regulating weights and measurements, ensuring that goods sold actually are the weight or size they are sold at, and the Trade Description Act, making misleading descriptions of products illegal.

Other laws include the Consumer Credit Act, ensuring consumers are aware of loan durations, interest rates etc when taking out a loan, as well as receiving copies of credit agreements, and the Sale of Goods Act, making it illegal to sell faulty or damaged goods. The return of goods and refunds, etc, is also governed by laws.

iii) ***Employee Protection:*** Laws to protect employees include laws against unfair discrimination based on race, color, religion, sex, or age; laws against unfair dismissal and sexual or other harassment; health and safety laws and laws regulating minimum wages. Many countries make written contracts between employer and employees mandatory.

iv) ***Tax and Financial Laws:*** These laws vary between countries, but generally regulate accountancy practices, interest rates on loans, taxes etc. Businesses are expected to provide sufficient documentation of income and expenditure, for instance.

Indian Legal Environment

Indian legal environment consists of the followings:

a) The Courts

Though India has a quasi-federal structure, the judiciary is unified. Broadly, there is a three tier structure. First, each administrative district (there are over 600 districts) is headed by a District Court. Then each State has a High Court. Since some States share the same High Court, there are 21 High Courts in India.

At the apex is the Supreme Court of India situated at New Delhi. The various High Courts can have very diverse characteristics. For instance, the High Court for the small State of Sikkim has strength of only two Judges, whereas the High Court for the State of Uttar Pradesh has about 100 Judges. The Supreme Court of India has about 25 Judges who sit in several divisions of varying strengths. Matters of fundamental significance are decided by a bench comprising of 5 Judges. Besides the broad three tier structure there are various specialized tribunals the more prominent ones being the Company Law Board; Monopolies and Restrictive Trade Practices Commission; Consumer Protection Forum; Debts Recovery Tribunal; Tax Tribunal. These Tribunals function under the supervisory jurisdiction of the High Court where they may be situated, though many of them (like the Monopolies Commission) allow an appeal directly to the Supreme Court.

b) Judiciary

The Indian judiciary is known for its independence and extensive powers. The High Court or the Supreme Court in exercise of their constitutionally conferred writ jurisdiction is empowered strike down legislation on the ground of unconstitutionality. They can and fairly routinely intervene with executive action as well on the ground of unreasonableness or unfairness or arbitrariness in State action.

Indeed Courts can even strike down an amendment to the Constitution on the ground that it violates the basic structure of the Constitution. Besides, the High Courts and the Supreme Court have adapted an activist mantle, which goes under the name of Public Interest Litigation, where under they can intervene with governmental policies if it may adversely impact the public at large or the public interest is such that it requires Court intervention.

c) The Bar

India has a unified all India Bar which means that an advocate enrolled with any State Bar can practice and appear in any court in the length and breadth of the country, including the Supreme Court of India.

Foreign lawyers are not permitted to appear in courts and the entry of foreign law firms into India (for non – court matters) has not yet been permitted though it is currently being debated and considered. However, they can appear in arbitrations.

d) Court Practice and Procedure

The influence of the British Judicial System which India imbibed continues in significant aspects. The official language for court proceedings in the High Court & the Supreme Court is English. Lawyers don a gown and a band as part of their uniform and address Judges as – "My Lord".

The procedural law of the land as well as most commercial and corporate laws is modeled on English laws. English case law is regularly referred to and relied upon in courts.

There is great emphasis on oral arguments. Almost all matters are heard extensively in open Court. Advocates are seldom restrained in oral arguments and complex hearings may well take days of arguments to conclude. Specialization is relatively a new phenomenon and most lawyers have a wide-ranging practice.

Technological Environment

Technological environment includes the level of technology available in a country. It also indicates the pace of research and development and progress made in introducing modern technology in production. Technology provides capital intensive but cost effective alternative to traditional labor intensive methods. In a competitive business environment technology is the key to development.

Technological Environment is a systematic application of scientific knowledge to practical task is known as technology. Everyday there has been vast changes in products, services, life-styles and living conditions, these changes must be analyzed by every business unit and should adapt these changes. Business prospects depend also on the availability of certain physical facilities. Some products, like many consumer durables, have certain use facility characteristics. The sale of television sets, for example, is limited by the extent of the coverage of the telecasting. Similarly, the demand for refrigerators and other electrical appliances is affected by the extent of electrification and the reliability of power supply. The demand for LPG gas stoves is affected by the rate of growth of gas connections.

Technological factors sometimes pose problems. A firm, which is unable to cope with the technological changes, may not survive. Further, the differing technological environment of different markets or countries may call for product modifications. For example, many appliances and instruments in the U.S.A. are designed for 110 volts but this needs to be converted into 240 volts in countries which have that power system. Technological developments may increase the demand for some existing products. For example, voltage stabilizers help increase the sale of electrical appliances in markets characterized by frequent voltage fluctuations I power supply. However, the introduction of TV's, Fridges etc, within built voltage stabilizer adversely affects the demand for voltage stabilizers.

Advances in the technologies of food processing and preservation, packaging etc., have facilitated product improvements and introduction of new products and have considerably improved the marketability of products. The television has added a new dimension to product promotion. The advent of TV and VCP/VCR has, however, adversely affected the cinema theatres. The fast changes in technologies also create problems for enterprises as they render plants and products obsolete quickly. Product-market-technology matrix generally has a much shorter life today than in the past. It is particularly so in the international marketing context. It may be interesting to note that almost half of Hindustan Lever's 1980 export business did not exist in 1987. In fact, as much as a third of the company's 1987 turnover was from products and markets, which were under three years of age.

Meaning of Technology

Technology refers to the method or technique for converting inputs to outputs in accomplishing a specific task. Thus, the terms 'method' and 'technique' refer not only to the knowledge but also to the skills and the means for accomplishing a task. It is the application of scientific knowledge for practical purposes. Technology is the usage and knowledge of tools, techniques, crafts, systems or methods of organization.

Definition of Technology

J.K. Galbraith defined technology as: "A systematic application of scientific or other organized knowledge to practical tasks".

Importance of Technology

Technology plays a vital role in business. Over the years businesses have become dependent on technology so much so that if we were to take away that technology virtually all business operations around the globe would come to a grinding halt. Almost all businesses and industries around the world are using computers ranging from the most basic to the most complex of operations.

Technology played a key role in the growth of commerce and trade around the world. It is true that we have been doing business since time immemorial, long before there were computers; starting from the simple concept of barter trade when the concept of a currency was not yet introduced but trade and commerce was still slow up until the point when the computer revolution changed everything. Almost all businesses are dependent on technology on all levels from research and development, production and all the way to delivery. Small to large scale enterprises depend on computers to help them with their business needs ranging from Point of Sales systems, information management systems capable of handling all kinds of information such as employee profile, client profile, accounting and tracking, automation systems for use in large scale production of commodities, package sorting, assembly lines, all the way to marketing and communications. It doesn't end there, all these commodities also need to be transported by sea, land, and air. Just to transport your commodities by land already requires the use of multiple systems to allow for fast, efficient and safe transportation of commodities.

Without this technology the idea of globalization wouldn't have become a reality. Now all enterprises have the potential to go international through the use of the internet. If your business has a website, that marketing tool will allow your business to reach clients across thousands of miles with just a click of a button. This would not be possible without the internet. Technology allowed businesses to grow and expand in ways never thought possible.

The role that technology plays for the business sector cannot be taken for granted. If we were to take away that technology trade and commerce around the world will come to a standstill and the global economy would collapse. It is nearly impossible for one to conduct business without the aid of technology in one form or another. Almost every aspect of business is heavily influenced by technology. Technology has become very important that it has become a huge industry itself from computer hardware manufacturing, to software design and development, and robotics. Technology has become a billion dollar industry for a number of individuals.

Benefits of Technology in Business

The days when the Chief Information Officer (CIO) took implementation decisions and passed the responsibility down the line are passed. Today, the CIO is an individual who possesses business as well as technical skills, understands the new IT issues facing a business, and drives the IT changes from the top down. This is a clear indicator of the benefits businesses are enjoying through the implementation of technology. Today technology is an integral part of any business right from the purchase of computers and software to the implementation of network and security tools. This helps businesses to: i) Remain up-to-date, ii) Drive business forward iii) Sustain and survive competition.

Benefits of Technology in Communication

From hand-held computers to touch phones, technological advancements in the field of communication are endless. The means and the modes of communication are unlimited. Some of the benefits of technological advancements in the field of communication are:

i) ***Speed:*** time is no longer a constraint in communication.

ii) ***Clarity:*** With megapixel images and video, and high fidelity audio systems clarity in communication has become a never-before experience.

iii) ***Proximity:*** Technological advancements have made the world a smaller place to live in.

iv) ***Dissemination:*** whether spreading information, broadcasting news, or sharing knowledge, technology has made it faster, easier, and smarter.

Benefits of Technology in Education

Technological advancements in the field of education are fast evolving. Today, e-learning is a familiar and popular term. Some of the benefits of technology in this field are:

i) ***Personalized learning experience:*** Learners are able to take control and manage their own learning. They set their own goals, manage the process and content of learning, and communicate with peers.

ii) ***Immediate response:*** Most e-learning programs provide immediate feedbacks on learner assessments. Similarly there are features such as chat, discussion boards, e-libraries, etc that allow clarifications at a faster pace than in traditional classrooms.

iii) ***Self-paced:*** Learners can chart courses at their own pace. This ensures higher levels of motivation both in terms of completing the course as well as in performance.

iv) ***Greater access:*** Technological advancements have opened education to learners with learning disabilities and in remote locations.

Benefits of Technology in Healthcare

The marriage between medicine and technology has reshaped healthcare and revolutionized the medical profession. Some of the major benefits are:

i) ***Secure environment:*** Technology allows physicians and patients to interact in a secure and comfortable environment to discuss sensitive issues.

ii) ***Flexibility:*** Physicians can answer routine and less critical queries at a convenient time.

iii) ***Cost- and time-saving:*** Physicians can follow-up, provide advice, and re-direct patients to resources on the Internet. This saves cost and time by reducing office visits.

iv) ***Medical devices:*** Medical aids allow patients to continue recovery at home reducing their hospital stay.

v) ***Vulnerable population:*** Technology aids the very young, elderly, and patients with complex birth defects, chronic illnesses, and disabled children by alleviating their problems so that they can continue living in their homes.

Features of Technology

The main features of technology are as follows:

i) Technology continuously keeps changing. The time gap between idea and implementation is falling rapidly and the time between introduction and peak production is shortening considerably.

ii) Effects of technology are widespread and are reaching beyond the immediate point of technological impact.

iii) Technology is self-reinforcing. "Technology feeds on itself. Technology makes more technology possible". It acts as a multiplier to its own faster development.

iv) Technology has evolved and transformed our lives and society. Overall, it has brought about tremendous growth and benefit to mankind.

Definition of Innovation

Innovation maybe defined as "the technical, industrial and commercial steps which lead to the marketing of new manufactured products and to commercial use of new technical process and equipment".

Technological innovation refers to the increase in knowledge, the improvement in skills, or the discovery of a new or improved means that extends people's ability to achieve a given task.

Meaning of Technological Environment

Technological environment refers to the firm's external environment in which changes in technology affect the firm's marketing effort. The changing technological environment may pose threats or present opportunities.

Social benefits of Technological Environment

Today technology pervades almost all aspects of our daily life from shopping, banking, making travel arrangements to university admissions. Some of the social benefits are:

i) ***Convenience:*** Provides a great deal of convenience in expediting personal and business transactions be it shopping, banking, or simply paying bills.

ii) ***Speed:*** From sending gifts to making payments everything gets a done with a few clicks.

iii) ***Communication:*** The world is a smaller place and technology allows everyone to keep in touch with their families and friends at a more affordable cost.

iv) ***Accuracy:*** Technology has reduced errors in mundane and monotonous chores, saving time and cost.

v) ***Development:*** Technology has brought about development in many fields such as medicine, government, business, education, etc.

Steps for Technological Development in India

After Independence India had basic problems like poverty, unemployment and development of India. Indian Govt. has taken many following steps for technological development:

1. ***Establishment of technological and research institute:*** Indian govt. has established 500 technological institutes for providing education to Indian students. It has also established 1080 research institutes. In these institutes major names like space research centre, medical research centre and agricultural research centre have developed India technically.
2. ***Positive Technical policy:*** India has strong and positive technical policy for technological development. This policy opens door to import technology from foreign countries for increasing agricultural and industrial developments.
3. ***High Growth Rate of Information Technology in India:*** In India, IT sector is developing with 35% growth rate, India is second country after China who is using internet at large scale for e-commerce, e-education and e-accounting.
4. ***Incentive for promoting Technology in India:*** Indian Govt. has given 100% income tax exemption for expenses incurred in research of technology in India. State financial corporation is uplifting domestic technology by supporting finance to domestic Industries.

Transfer of Technology

Transfer of Technology is the process of sharing of skills, knowledge, technologies, methods of manufacturing, samples of manufacturing and facilities among governments and other institutions. It ensures the scientific and technological developments which are accessible to a wider range of users who can then further develop and exploit the technology into new products, processes, applications, materials or services.

Transfer Pricing

Transfer pricing refers to the pricing of contributions (assets, tangible and intangible, services, and funds) transferred within an organization. For example, goods from the production division may be sold to the marketing division, or goods from a parent company may be sold to a foreign subsidiary. Since the prices are set within an organization, the typical market mechanisms that establish prices for such transactions between third parties may not apply.

Transfer Pricing Concept

The price charged between related parties for goods, services, intangibles, loans as well as cost sharing agreements are considered to fall within the broad purview of transfer pricing.

Transfer pricing is fast developing into one of the most important and complex tax issues that modern businesses are faced with today. With transfer pricing being seen more and more as an essential part of business planning and strategy, taxation authorities worldwide are investigating transfer-pricing arrangements with increased vigour. Similar imperatives seem to be on their way in India as well.

The choice of the transfer price will affect the allocation of the total profit among the parts of the company. This is a major concern for fiscal authorities who worry that multi-national entities may set transfer prices on cross-border transactions to reduce taxable profits in their jurisdiction. This has led to the rise of transfer pricing regulations and enforcement, making transfer pricing a major tax compliance issue for multi-national companies.

For tax purposes, revenue authorities would expect arm's length pricing on all transactions whether they are between related (i.e., having a common thread of ownership or control) or unrelated parties. An arm's length price is the price that would be charged between two parties acting independently, each trying to get the best deal. While this is a simple statement of principle, its implication has been a subject of considerable interpretation.

Transfer Prices

A transfer price refers to the price used for intra-company transfers, i.e., transfers between segments of a company. The term transfer pricing normally means pricing transfers between divisions, but could be used in any situation where the output of one segment (e.g., department, operation, process) becomes the input for another segment within the same company.

Objectives of Transfer Prices

The overall objective is to establish a transfer price that will motivate effort and goal congruence. There are at least three underlying objectives:

1. To aid in Evaluating Division Performance, i.e., investment centers or profit centers. If the divisions are treated as investment centers, then Return on Investment (ROI) and Residual Income (RI) are the relevant measurements. For profit centers, contribution margin, segment margin, or net income would be a more appropriate measurement.
2. To maintain Division Autonomy. Since autonomy means decentralization and freedom to make decisions, it is also an ingredient in motivating effort. Remember, however, that effort and goal congruence are different. Managers may exert considerable effort in pursuing their own goals that conflict with the goals of the firm. Central office interference in a transfer-pricing dispute will affect autonomy and effort. The dilemma is that goal congruent behavior may not be obtained with or without interference.
3. To provide the buying segment with the information necessary for the make or buy question. Intra-company profits included in a transfer price make it impossible for the buying division to answer the make or buy question.

Natural Environment

Natural Environment includes natural resources, weather, climatic conditions, port facilities, topographical factors such as soil, sea, rivers, rainfall etc. Every business unit must look for these factors before choosing the location for their business. Geographical and ecological factors, such as natural resource endowments, weather and climatic conditions, topographical factors, location aspects in the global context, port facilities, etc., are all relevant to business.

Differences in geographical conditions between markets may sometimes call for changes in the marketing mix. Geographical and ecological factors also influence the location of certain industries. For example, industries with high material index tend to be located near the raw material sources. Climatic and weather conditions affect the location of certain industries like the cotton textile industry. Topographical factors may, affect the demand pattern. For example, in hilly areas with a difficult terrain, jeeps may be in greater demand than cars. Ecological factors have recently assumed great importance. The depletion of natural resources, environmental pollution and the disturbance of the ecological balance has caused great concern. Government policies aimed at the preservation of environmental purity and ecological balance, conservation of non-replenish resources, etc., have resulted in additional responsibilities and problems for business, and some of these have the effect of increasing the cost of production and marketing.

The Earth's crust, or lithosphere, is the outermost solid surface of the planet and is chemically and mechanically different from underlying mantle. It has been generated largely by igneous processes in which magma (molten rock) cools and solidifies to form solid rock. Beneath the lithosphere lies the mantle which is heated by the decay of radioactive elements. The mantle though solid is in a state of rich convection. This convection process causes the lithospheric plates to move, albeit slowly. The resulting process is known as plate tectonics. Volcanoes result primarily from the melting of sub-ducted crust material or of rising mantle at mid-ocean ridges and mantle plumes.

Meaning of Natural Environment

A natural environment is an environment that encompasses all living and non-living things occurring naturally on Earth or some region thereof. The concept of the natural environment can be distinguished by components:

i) Complete ecological units that function as natural systems without massive human intervention, including all vegetation, microorganisms, soil, rocks, atmosphere and natural phenomena that occur within their boundaries.

ii) Universal natural resources and physical phenomena that lack clear-cut boundaries, such as air, water, and climate, as well as energy, radiation, electric charge, and magnetism, not originating from human activity.

Elements of Natural Environment

a) Water on Earth

An ocean is a major body of saline water, and a component of the hydrosphere. Approximately 71% of the Earth's surface (an area of some 362 million square kilometers) is covered by ocean, a continuous body of water that is customarily divided into several principal oceans and smaller seas. More than half of this area is over 3,000 meters (9,800 ft) deep. Average oceanic salinity is around 35 parts per thousand (3.5%). Though generally recognized as several 'separate' oceans, these waters comprise one global, interconnected body of salt water often referred to as the World Ocean or global ocean. This concept of a global ocean as a continuous body of water with relatively free interchange among its parts is of fundamental importance to oceanography. The major oceanic divisions are defined in part by the continents, various archipelagos, and other criteria: these divisions are (in descending order of size) the Pacific Ocean, the Atlantic Ocean, the Indian Ocean, the Southern Ocean and the Arctic Ocean.

A river is a natural watercourse, usually freshwater, flowing toward an ocean, a lake, a sea or another river. In a few cases, a river simply flows into the ground or dries up completely before reaching another body of water. Small rivers may also be termed by several other names, including stream, creek and brook. In the United States a river is generally classified as a watercourse more than 60 feet (18 metres) wide. The water in a river is usually in a channel, made up of a stream bed between banks. In larger rivers there is also a wider floodplain shaped by waters over-topping the channel. Flood plains may be very wide in relation to the size of the river channel. Rivers are a part of the hydrological cycle. Water within a river is generally collected from precipitation through surface runoff, groundwater recharge, springs, and the release of water stored in glaciers and snow packs.

A stream is a flowing body of water with a current, confined within a bed and stream banks. Streams play an important corridor role in connecting fragmented habitats and thus in conserving biodiversity. The study of streams and waterways in general is known as surface hydrology. Types of streams include creeks, tributaries, which do not reach an ocean and connect with another stream or river, brooks, which are typically small streams and sometimes sourced from a spring or seep and tidal inlets.

A lake is a terrain feature, a body of water that is localized to the bottom of basin. A body of water is considered a lake when it is inland, is not part of a ocean, is larger and deeper than a pond, and is fed by a river.

Natural lakes on Earth are generally found in mountainous areas, rift zones, and areas with ongoing or recent glaciation. Other lakes are found in endorheic basins or along the courses of mature rivers. In some parts of the world, there are many lakes because of chaotic drainage patterns left over from the last Ice Age. All lakes are temporary over geologic time scales, as they will slowly fill in with sediments or spill out of the basin containing them.

b) Atmosphere, Climate and Weather

Atmospheric gases scatter blue light more than other wavelengths, creating a blue halo when seen from space. The atmosphere of the Earth serves as a key factor in sustaining the planetary ecosystem. The thin layer of gases that envelops the Earth is held in place by the planet's gravity. Dry air consists of 78% nitrogen, 21% oxygen, 1% argon and other inert gases, such as carbon dioxide. The remaining gases are often referred to as trace gases, among which are the greenhouse gases such as water vapor, carbon dioxide, methane, nitrous oxide, and ozone. Filtered air includes trace amounts of many other chemical compounds. Air also contains a variable amount of water vapor and suspensions of water droplets and ice crystals seen as clouds. Many natural substances may be present in tiny amounts in an unfiltered air sample, including dust, pollen and spores, sea spray, volcanic ash, and meteoroids. Various industrial pollutants also may be present, such as chlorine (elementary or in compounds), fluorine compounds, elemental mercury, and sulphur compounds such as sulphur dioxide.

The ozone layer of the Earth's atmosphere plays an important role in depleting the amount of ultraviolet (UV) radiation that reaches the surface. As DNA is readily damaged by UV light, this serves to protect life at the surface. The atmosphere also retains heat during the night, thereby reducing the daily temperature extremes.

c) Effects of global warming

The potential dangers of global warming are being increasingly studied by a wide global consortium of scientists. These scientists are increasingly concerned about the potential long-term effects of global warming on our natural environment and on the planet. Of particular concern is how climate change and global warming caused by anthropogenic, or human-made releases of greenhouse gases, most notably carbon dioxide, can act interactively, and have adverse effects upon the planet, its natural environment and humans' existence. Efforts have been increasingly focused on the mitigation of greenhouse gases that are causing climatic changes, on developing adaptative strategies to global warming, to assist humans, animal and plant species, ecosystems, regions and nations in adjusting to the effects of global warming.

A significantly profound challenge is to identify the natural environmental dynamics in contrast to environmental changes not within natural variances. A common solution is to adapt a static view neglecting natural variances to exist. Methodologically, this view could be defended when looking at processes which change slowly and short time series, while the problem arrives when fast processes turns essential in the object of the study.

d) Ecosystems

An ecosystem (also called as environment) is a natural unit consisting of all plants, animals and micro-organisms (biotic factors) in an area functioning together with all of the non-living physical (abiotic) factors of the environment.

Central to the ecosystem concept does the idea that living organisms are continually engaged in a highly interrelated set of relationships with every other element constitute the environment in which they exist. Eugene Odum, one of the founders of the science of ecology, stated: "Any unit that includes all of the organisms in a given area interacting with the physical environment so that a flow of energy leads to clearly defined trophic structure, biotic diversity, and material cycles (i.e. exchange of materials between living and nonliving parts) within the system is an ecosystem."

The human ecosystem concept is then grounded in the deconstruction of the human/nature dichotomy, and the emergent premise that all species are ecologically integrated with each other, as well as with the abiotic constituents of their biotope.

A greater number or variety of species or biological diversity of an ecosystem may contribute to greater resilience of an ecosystem, because there are more species present at a location to respond to change and thus "absorb" or reduce its effects. This reduces the effect before the ecosystem's structure is fundamentally changed to a different state. This is not universally the case and there is no proven relationship between the species diversity of an ecosystem and its ability to provide goods and services on a sustainable level.

The term ecosystem can also pertain to human-made environments, such as human ecosystems and human-influenced ecosystems, and can describe any situation where there is relationship between living organisms and their environment. Fewer areas on the surface of the earth today exist free from human contact, although some genuine wilderness areas continue to exist without any forms of human intervention.

India's Business Environment

India's business environment has improved considerably after the initiation of economic reforms in early 1990s. Domestic and foreign investors are finding it easier to do business after the reforms, which are aimed at reorientation of the centrally-controlled economy to a market-oriented one in order to foster greater efficiency and growth. This is being done by introducing greater competition in the economy through progressive internal deregulation accompanied by foreign direct investment and trade liberalization. However, the turmoil which surfaced in the US financial system has also adversely hit the Indian economy. Compared to other emerging economies, India has several strengths that can help mitigate the adverse effects of the global economic crisis. In spite of the global meltdown, Indian economy offers ample opportunities for business, both to the domestic and foreign entrepreneurs. This work contains 21 research papers dealing with various aspects of current business scenario in India, and it examines the economic policies of India's government.

International Business in India looks really lucrative and every passing day, it is coming up with only more possibilities. The growth in the international business sector in India is more than 7% annually. There is scope for more improvement if only the relations with the neighboring countries are stabilized. The mind-blowing performance of the stock market in India has gathered all the more attention. India definitely stands as an opportune place to explore business possibilities, with its high-skilled manpower and budding middle class segment.

With the diverse cultural setup, it is advisable not to formulate a uniform business strategy in India. Different parts of the country are well-known for its different traits. The eastern part of India is known as the 'Land of the intellectuals', whereas the southern part is known for its 'technology acumen'. On the other hand, the western part is known as the 'commercial-capital of the country', with the northern part being the 'hub of political power'. With such diversities in all the four segments of the country, international business opportunity in India is surely huge.

Sectors having potential for International business in India:

1. Information Technology and Electronics Hardware.
2. Telecommunication.
3. Pharmaceuticals and Biotechnology.
4. R&D.
5. Banking, Financial Institutions and Insurance & Pensions.
6. Capital Market.
7. Chemicals and Hydrocarbons.
8. Infrastructure.
9. Agriculture and Food Processing.
10. Retailing.
11. Logistics.
12. Manufacturing.
13. Power and Non-conventional Energy.

Sectors like Health, Education, Housing, Resource Conservation & Management Group, Water Resources, Environment, Rural Development, Small and Medium Enterprises (SME) and Urban Development are still not tapped properly and thus the huge scope should be exploited. To foster the international business scenario in India, bodies like CII, FICCI and the various Chambers of Commerce, have a host of services like:

i) These bodies work closely with the Government and the different business promotion organizations to infuse more business development in India.

ii) They help to build strong relationships with the different international business organizations and the multinational corporations.

iii) These bodies help to identify the bilateral business co-operation potential and thereafter make apt policy recommendations to the different overseas Governments.

iv) With opportunities huge, the International Business trend in India is mind boggling. India International Business community along with the domestic business community is striving towards a steady path to be the Knowledge Capital of the world.

Globalization of Indian Business Environment

India's economic integration with the rest of the world was very limited because of the restrictive economic policies followed until 1991. Indian firms confined themselves, by and large, to the home market. Foreign investment by Indian firms was very insignificant. With the new economic policy ushered in 1991, there has, however, been a change. Globalization has in fact become a buzz-word with Indian firms now, and many are expanding their overseas business by different strategies.

Factors favouring Globalization in Indian Business Environment

i) ***Human Resources:*** Apart from the low cost of labour, there are several other aspects of human resources to India's favour. India has one of the largest pools of scientific and technical manpower. The number of management graduates is also surging. It is widely recognized that given the right environment, Indian scientists and technical personnel can do excellently. Similarly, although the labour productivity in India is generally low, given the right environment it will be good. While several countries are facing labour shortage and may face diminishing labour supply, India presents the opposite picture. Cheap labour has particular attraction for several industries.

ii) ***Wide Base:*** India has a very broad resource and industrial base which can support a variety of business.

iii) ***Growing Entrepreneurship:*** Many of the established industries are planning to go international in a big way. Added to this is the considerable growth or new and dynamic entrepreneurs who could make a significant contribution to the globalization of Indian business.

iv) ***Growing Domestic Market:*** The growing domestic market enables the Indian companies to consolidate their position and to gain more strength to make foray into the foreign market or to expand their foreign business.

v) ***Niche Markets:*** There are many marketing opportunities abroad present in the form of market niches.

vi) ***Expanding Markets:*** The growing population and disposable income and the resultant expanding internal market provide enormous business opportunities.

vii) ***Transnational of World Economy:*** Transnational of the world economy. i.e., the integration of the national economies into a single world economy as evinced by the growing interdependence and globalization of markets is an external factor encouraging globalization of India Business.

viii) ***NRIs:*** The large number of non-resident Indians who are resourceful – in terms of capital, skill, experience, exposure, ideas etc. is an assed which can contribute to the globalization of Indian Business. The contribution of the overseas Chinese to the recent impressive industrial development of China may be noted here.

ix) ***Economic Liberalization:*** The economic liberalization in India is an encouraging factor of globalization. The relicensing of industries, removal of restrictions on growth, opening up of industries earlier reserved for the public sector, import liberalizations, liberalization of policy towards foreign capital and technology etc., could encourage globalization of Indian Business.

x) **Competition:** The growing competition, both from within the country and abroad, provokes many Indian companies to look to foreign markets seriously to improve their competitive position and to increase the business.

Obstacles to Globalization in Indian Business Environment

i) ***Government policy and procedures:*** Government policy and procedures in India are among the most complex, confusing and cumbersome in the world. Even after the much publicized liberalization, they do not present a very conducive situation. One prerequisite for success in globalization is swift and efficient action. Government policy and the bureaucratic culture in India in this respect are not that encouraging.

ii) ***High Cost:*** High cost of many vital inputs and other factors like raw materials and intermediates, power, finance infrastructural facilities like port etc., tend to reduce the international competitiveness of the Indian Business.

iii) ***Poor Infrastructure:*** Infrastructure in India is generally inadequate and inefficient and therefore very costly. This is a serious problem affecting the growth as well as competitiveness.

iv) ***Obsolescence:*** The technology employed, mode and style of operations etc., are, in general, obsolete and these seriously affect the competitiveness.

v) ***Resistance to Change:*** There are several socio-political factors which resist change and this comes in the way of modernization, rationalization and efficiency improvement. Technological modernization is resisted due to fear of unemployment. The extent of excess labour employed by the Indian industry is alarming. Because of this labour productivity is very low and this in some cases more than offsets the advantages of cheap labour.

vi) ***Poor Quality Image:*** Due to various reasons, the quality of many India products is poor. Even when the quality is good, the poor quality image India has becomes a handicap.

vii) ***Supply Problems:*** Due to various reasons like low production capacity, shortages of raw materials and infrastructures like power and port facilities, Indian companies in many instances are not able to accept large orders or to keep up delivery schedules.

viii) ***Small Size:*** Because of the small size and the low level of resources, in many cases Indian firms are not able to compete with the giants of other countries. Even the largest of the Indian companies are small compared to the multinational giants.

ix) ***Lack of Experience:*** The general lack of experience in managing international business is another important problem.

x) ***Limited R&D and Marketing Research:*** Marketing Research and R&D in other areas are vital inputs of development of international business. However, these are poor in Indian Business. Expenditure on R&D in India is less than one per cent of GNP while it is two to three per cent in most of the developed countries.

xi) ***Growing Competition:*** The competition is growing not only from the firs in the developed countries but also from the developing country firms. Indeed, the growing competition from the developing country firms is a serious challenge to India's international business.

xii) ***Trade Barriers:*** Although the tariff barriers to trade have been progressively reduced thanks to the GATT/WTO, the non-tariff barriers have been increasing, particularly in the developed countries. Further, the trading blocs like the NAFTA, EC etc., could also adversely affect India's business.

Review Questions

Conceptual Type

1. Give the meaning of business.
2. What is environment?
3. What is environmental analysis?
4. Give the meaning of business environment.
5. What do you mean by dynamic environment?
6. What is internal and external environment?
7. What is economic environment?
8. What is non-economic environment?
9. What is democracy?
10. Define global environment and its components.

Analytical Type

1. Discuss the goals of the business environment.
2. Describe the economic environment as it prevails today in our country.
3. How does business effect natural environment?
4. Explain briefly how socio-cultural environment affects business.
5. What are the salient features of technological environment?
6. Explain key environment of business.
7. Discuss various power dimensions of business.
8. Discuss the impact of socio-cultural environment in business.
9. What is the impact of politcal environment on business? Explain.

Descriptive Type

1. Explain in details the Environmental Factors.
2. Explain the dimensions of Business Environment.
3. Explain various components of the Economic Environment.
4. Discuss various factors of Economic Environment.
5. Discuss various types of Economic system.
6. Discuss various steps for technological development in India.
7. What is the impact of natural environment on business? Explain.
8. Explain the environmental factors that affect a business.
9. Explain the meaning and scope of business environment.
10. What is economic environment? Explain the economic factors that affect the economy.
11. Explain in detail economic and non-economic factors of environment influencing business planning.
12. Explain the technological factors which influence business on the economy.
13. Discuss the historical forces changing the business environment.

*****

Module-3

Corporate Governance

Syllabus

Introduction, Definition, Market model and control model, OECD on corporate governance, A historical perspective of corporate governance, Issues in corporate governance, relevance of corporate governance, need and importance of corporate governance, benefits of good corporate governance, the concept of corporate, the concept of governance, theoretical basis for corporate governance, obligation to society, obligation to investors, obligation to employees, obligation to customers, managerial obligation, Indian cases.

Introduction

Corporate governance is a dynamic aspect of business. The term 'governance' derives from the Latin Gubernare, meaning 'to steer', usually applying to the steering of a ship. There were several frauds and scams in the corporate history. It was felt that the system for regulation is not satisfactory. These regulations should penalize the wrong doers, while those who adhere the rules and regulations, should be motivated by the market forces. There were several changes brought out by governments, insistence of mutual funds and large institutional investors, that corporate they invested in adopt better governance practices and in formation of several committees to study the issues in depth and make recommendations, codes and guidelines on Corporate Governance that are to be put in practice. Companies around the world are realizing that better corporate governance adds considerable value to their operational performance

Corporate governance refers to the set of systems, principles and processes by which a company is governed. They provide the guidelines as to how the company can be directed or controlled such that it can fulfill its goals and objectives in a manner that adds to the value of the company and is also beneficial for all stakeholders in the long run. Stakeholders in this case would include everyone ranging from the Board of Directors, management, shareholders to customers, employees and society. The management of the company hence assumes the role of a trustee for all the others.

Corporate Governance refers to the way a corporation is governed. It is the technique by which companies are directed and managed. It means carrying the business as per the stakeholders' desires. It is actually conducted by the board of Directors and the concerned committees for the company's stakeholder's benefit. It is all about balancing individual and societal goals, as well as, economic and social goals. Corporate governance is the interaction between various participants in shaping corporation's performance and the way it is proceeding towards. The relationship between the owners and the managers in an organization must be healthy and there should be no conflict between the two. The owners must see that individual's actual performance is according to the standard performance. These dimensions of corporate governance should not be overlooked.

It also deals with determining ways to take effective strategic decisions. It gives ultimate authority and complete responsibility to the Board of Directors. In today's market- oriented economy, the need for corporate governance arises. Also, efficiency as well as globalization are significant factors urging corporate governance. Corporate governance is essential to develop added value to the stakeholders.

Corporate Governance ensures transparency which ensures strong and balanced economic development. This also ensures that the interests of all shareholders are safeguarded. It ensures that all shareholders fully exercise their rights and that the organization fully recognizes their rights. Corporate Governance has a broad scope. It includes both social and institutional aspects. Corporate Governance encourages a trustworthy, moral, as well as ethical environment.

Thus, corporate governance is "the system by which companies are directed and controlled". It involves regulatory and market mechanisms, and the roles and relationships between a company's management, its board, its shareholders and other stakeholders, and the goals for which the corporation is governed.

Meaning of Corporate Governance

Corporate governance refers to the relationship that exists between the different participants and defining the direction and performance of a corporate firm. The CEO, board of directors and the shareholders are the main actors in corporate governance. The other actors who influence governance in corporations are the staff, suppliers, creditors, customers and the community. In other words Corporate governance is a systematic process by which companies are directed and controlled to enhance their wealth generating capacity.

Corporate governance refers to the rules, procedures, and administration of the firm's contracts with its shareholders, creditors, employees, suppliers, customers, and sovereign governments. Governance is legally vested with the Board of Directors who have a fiduciary duty to serve the interests of the corporation rather than their own interests or those of the firm's management.

In a narrow sense, corporate governance involves a set of relationships amongst the company's management, its Board of Directors, its shareholders, its auditors and other stakeholders. These relationships, which involve various rules and incentives, provide the structure through which the objectives of the company are set and the means of attaining these objectives as well as monitoring performance are determined. Thus, the key aspects of good corporate governance include transparency of corporate structures and operations the accountability of managers and the boards to shareholders; and corporate responsibility towards stakeholders.

While corporate governance essentially lays down the framework for creating long-term trust between companies and the external providers of capital, it would be wrong to think that the importance of corporate governance lies solely in better access of finance.

Companies around the world are realizing that better corporate governance adds considerable value to their operational performance:

- It improves strategic thinking at the top by inducting independent directors who bring a wealth of experience, and a host of new ideas.
- It rationalizes the management and monitoring of risk that a firm faces globally.
- It limits the liability of top management and directors, by carefully articulating the decision making process.
- It assures the integrity of financial reports.
- It has long term reputational effects among key stakeholders, both internally and externally.

In a broader sense, however, good corporate governance- the extent to which companies are run in an open and honest manner is important for overall market confidence, the efficiency of capital allocation, the growth and development of countries industrial bases and ultimately the nations overall wealth and welfare.

Corporate governance means framework of rules and practices by which a board of directors ensures accountability, fairness, and transparency in a company's relationship with its all stakeholders

The corporate governance framework consists of:

(i) Explicit and implicit contracts between the company and the stakeholders for distribution of responsibilities, rights and rewards.

(ii) Procedures for reconciling the conflicting interests of stakeholders in accordance with their duties, privileges and roles.

(iii) Procedures for proper supervision, control, and information-flows to serve as a system of checks-and-balances.

Corporate governance involves a set of relationships between a company's management, its board, its shareholders and other stakeholders. Corporate governance also provides the structure through which the objectives of the company are set and the means of attaining those objectives and monitoring performance are determined.

Corporate governance consists of two elements:

The long term relationship which has to deal with checks and balances, incentives for manager and communications between management and investors.

The transactional relationship which involves dealing with disclosure and authority.

The main mechanisms for understanding corporate governance are the following:

1. The market for corporate control (i.e. a hostile takeover market and the market for partial control).
2. Large shareholder and creditor monitoring.
3. Internal control mechanisms, i.e. the board of directors, non-executive committees and the design of executive compensation contracts.
4. External mechanisms, i.e. product-market competition, external auditors and the regulatory framework of the corporate-law regime and stock exchange.

Definitions

Corporate governance can be viewed as a set of arrangements internal to the corporation that define the relationship between the owners and managers of the corporation.

Monks and Minow (2001), Corporate governance is the relationship among various participants in determining the direction and performance of corporations. The primary participants are (i) the shareholders, (ii) the management, and (iii) the board of directors.

World Bank (1999), World Bank defines corporate governance from the two different perspectives. From the standpoint of a corporation, the emphasis is put on the relations between the owners, management board and other stakeholders (the employees, customers, suppliers, investors and communities). Major significance in corporate governance is given to the board of directors and its ability to attain long-term sustained value by balancing these interests. From a public policy perspective, corporate governance refers to providing for the survival, growth and development of the company and at the same times its accountability in the exercise of power and control over companies. The role of public policy is to discipline companies and, at the same time, to stimulate them to minimize differences between private and social interests.

OECD (1999), "Corporate governance is the system by which business corporations are directed and controlled. The corporate governance structure specifies the distribution of rights and responsibilities among different participants in the corporation, such as the board, managers, shareholders and other stakeholders, and spells out the rules and procedures for making decisions on corporate affairs. By doing this, it also provides the structure through which the company objectives are set, and the means of attaining those objectives and monitoring performance."

The OECD also offers a broader definition: "Corporate governance refers to the private and public institutions, including laws, regulations and accepted business practices, which together govern the relationship, in a market economy, between corporate managers and entrepreneurs ('corporate insiders') on one hand, and those who invest resources in corporations, on the other."

OECD (2001), Another perspective in defining corporate governance is called path dependence. Central to the idea of path dependence is that initial historical conditions matter in determining the corporate governance structures that are prevalent today. A national system of corporate governance evolves in order to exploit the advantages of the corporate form of organization while mitigating concomitant agency costs in a manner consistent with a country's history and legal, political, and social traditions Therefore, a nation's system of corporate governance can be seen as an institutional matrix that structures the relations among owners, boards, and top managers, and determines the goals pursued by the corporation. The nature of this institutional matrix is one of the principal determinants of the economic vitality of a society (Davis, Useem, 2000). In order to understand the problem of corporate governance it is most important to stress that it is, first of all, dependent on the political system of any country and the country's historical and cultural characteristics.

Concept of Corporate and Governance

Corporate is a business or entity which has separate legal personality, with limited liability or unlimited liability for its members or shareholders, who buy and sell their shares/stocks depending on the performance of the board of directors.

Corporations are the most common form of business organization, and one which is chartered by a state and given many legal rights as an entity separate from its owners. This form of business is characterized by the limited liability of its owners, the issuance of shares of easily transferable stock, and existence as a going concern. The process of becoming a corporation, called incorporation, gives the company separate legal standing from its owners and protects those owners from being personally liable in the event that the company is sued. Incorporation also provides companies with a more flexible way to manage their ownership structure. In addition, there are different tax implications for corporations, although these can be both advantageous and disadvantageous. In these respects, corporations differ from sole proprietorship and limited partnership.

Governance is the act of governing. It relates to decisions that define expectations, grant power, or verify performance. It consists of either a separate process or part of decision-making or leadership processes. In modern nation-states, these processes and systems are typically administered by a government. When discussing governance in particular organizations, the quality of governance within the organization is often compared to a standard of good governance. In the case of a business or of a non-profit organization, governance relates to consistent management, cohesive policies, guidance, processes and decision-rights for a given area of responsibility. For example, managing at a corporate level might involve evolving policies on privacy, on internal investment, and on the use of data.

Governance is the exercise of political, economic and administrative authority to manage a nation's affairs. It is the complex mechanisms, processes and institutions through which citizens and groups articulate their interests, exercise their legal rights and obligations, and mediate their differences.

-UNDP

"Governance is the manner in which power is exercised in the management of a country's social and economic resources for development. Governance means the way those with power use that power." ***- ADB***

Governance is "the traditions and institutions by which authority in a country is exercised for the common good. This includes (i) the process by which those in authority are selected, monitored and replaced, (ii) the capacity of the government to effectively manage its resources and implement sound policies, and (iii) the respect of citizens and the state for the institutions that govern economic and social interactions among them". ***- World Bank***

Corporate Governance may be defined as a set of systems, processes and principles which ensure that a company is governed in the best interest of all stakeholders. It is the system by which companies are directed and controlled. It is about promoting corporate fairness, transparency and accountability. In other words, 'good corporate governance' is simply 'good business'. It ensures:

- Adequate disclosures and effective decision making to achieve corporate objectives;
- Transparency in business transactions,
- Statutory and legal compliances,
- Protection of shareholder interests,
- Commitment to values and ethical conduct of business.

In other words, corporate governance is the acceptance by management of the inalienable rights of shareholders as the true owners of the corporation and of their own role as trustees on behalf of the shareholders. It deals with conducting the affairs of a company such that there is fairness to all stakeholders and that its actions benefit the greatest number of stakeholders. In this regard, the management needs to prevent asymmetry of benefits between various sections of shareholders, especially between the owner-managers and the rest of the shareholders.

It is about commitment to values, about ethical business conduct and about making a distinction between personal and corporate funds in the management of a company. Ethical dilemmas arise from conflicting interests of the parties involved. In this regard, managers make decisions based on a set of principles influenced by the values, context and culture of the organization. Ethical leadership is good for business as the organization is seen to conduct its business in line with the expectations of all stakeholders.

The aim of "Good Corporate Governance" is to ensure commitment of the board in managing the company in a transparent manner for maximizing long-term value of the company for its shareholders and all other partners. It integrates all the participants involved in a process, which is economic, and at the same time social.

The fundamental objective of corporate governance is to enhance shareholders' value and protect the interests of other stakeholders by improving the corporate performance and accountability. Hence it harmonizes the need for a company to strike a balance at all times between the need to enhance shareholders' wealth whilst not in any way being detrimental to the interests of the other stakeholders in the company. Further, its objective is to generate an environment of trust and confidence amongst those having competing and conflicting interests.

It is integral to the very existence of a company and strengthens investor's confidence by ensuring company's commitment to higher growth and profits. Broadly, it seeks to achieve the following objectives:

- A properly structured board capable of taking independent and objective decisions is in place at the helm of affairs;
- The board should be balance with regards to the representation of adequate number of non-executive and independent directors who will take care of their interests and well-being of all the stakeholders;
- The board adopts transparent procedures and practices and arrives at decisions on the strength of adequate information;
- The board has an effective machinery to subserve the concerns of stakeholders;
- The board keeps the shareholders informed of relevant developments impacting the company;
- The board effectively and regularly monitors the functioning of the management team;
- The board remains in effective to control the affairs of the company at all times.

Significance and Importance of Corporate Governance

The significance and importance of corporate governance is listed below:

1. ***Changing Ownership Structure:*** In recent years, the ownership structure of companies has changed a lot. Public financial institutions, mutual funds, etc. are the single largest shareholder in most of the large companies. So, they have effective control on the management of the companies. They force the management to use corporate governance. That is, they put pressure on the management to become more efficient, transparent, accountable, etc. The also ask the management to make consumer-friendly policies, to protect all social groups and to protect the environment. So, the changing ownership structure has resulted in corporate governance.
2. ***Importance of Social Responsibility:*** Today, social responsibility is given a lot of importance. The Board of Directors have to protect the rights of the customers, employees, shareholders, suppliers, local communities, etc. This is possible only if they use corporate governance.
3. ***Growing Number of Scams:*** In recent years, many scams, frauds and corrupt practices have taken place. Misuse and misappropriation of public money are happening everyday in India and worldwide. It is happening in the stock market, banks, financial institutions, companies and government offices. In order to avoid these scams and financial irregularities, many companies have started corporate governance.
4. ***Indifference on the part of Shareholders:*** In general, shareholders are inactive in the management of their companies. They only attend the annual general meeting. Postal ballot is still absent in India. Proxies are not allowed to speak in the meetings. Shareholders associations are not strong.

Therefore, directors misuse their power for their own benefits. So, there is a need for corporate governance to protect all the stakeholders of the company.

6. ***Globalisation:*** Today most big companies are selling their goods in the global market. So, they have to attract foreign investor and foreign customers. They also have to follow foreign rules and regulations. All this requires corporate governance. Without corporate governance, it is impossible to enter, survive and succeed in the global market.

7. ***Takeovers and Mergers:*** Today, there are many takeovers and mergers in the business world. Corporate governance is required to protect the interest of all the parties during takeovers and mergers.

8. ***SEBI:*** SEBI has made corporate governance compulsory for certain companies. This is done to protect the interest of the investors and other stakeholders.

Benefits of Corporate Governance

- Good corporate governance ensures corporate success and economic growth.
- Strong corporate governance maintains investors' confidence, as a result of which, company can raise capital efficiently and effectively.
- It lowers the capital cost.
- There is a positive impact on the share price.
- It provides proper inducement to the owners as well as managers to achieve objectives that are in interests of the shareholders and the organization.
- Good corporate governance also minimizes wastages, corruption, risks and mismanagement.
- It helps in brand formation and its development.
- It ensures an organization to manage in a manner that fits the best interests of all.

Corporate Governance and the Economy

Good corporate governance practices should make firms more profitable and productive, in turn contributing to the overall health of the economy. However, the evidence for a causal relationship between corporate governance and either firm performance or stock returns is sketchy and conflicting.

The absence of a causal relationship between governance practices and stock returns perhaps should not be surprising. Public companies provide substantial and ever increasing disclosures with regard to their governance practices. As a result, assuming the capital markets are efficient, those practices should be fully impounded by stock market prices. Only a change in a firm's governance practices-for good or it should result in the cumulative abnormal returns that stock prices studies would identify.

As for operating performance, there is some evidence that firms with weak corporate governance have lower operating results. One recent study, for example, found a correlation between governance characteristics and operating ROA. This evidence is consistent with the hypothesis that weak governance constraints on agency costs permit managers to shirk and otherwise engage in value-reducing activities.

Cumulated across all the firms, weak governance thus should be a drag on the economy as a whole.

Why is it important?

Fundamentally, there is a level of confidence that is associated with a company that is known to have good corporate governance. The presence of an active group of independent directors on the board contributes a great deal towards ensuring confidence in the market. Corporate governance is known to be one of the criteria that foreign institutional investors are increasingly depending on then for deciding on which companies to invest in. It is also known to have a positive influence on the share price of the company. Having a clean image on the corporate governance front could also make it easier for companies to source capital at more reasonable costs. Unfortunately, corporate governance often becomes the center of discussion only after the exposure of a large scam.

Why was it in the news recently?

Corporate governance has most recently been debated after the corporate fraud by Satyam founder and chairman Ramalinga Raju. In fact, trouble started brewing at Satyam around December 16th when Satyam announced its decision to buy stakes in Maytas Properties and Infrastructure for $1.3 billion. The deal was soon called off owing to major discontentment on the part of shareholders and plummeting share-price. However, in what has been seen as one of the largest corporate frauds in India, Raju confessed that the profits in the Satyam books had been inflated and that the cash reserve with the company was minimal. Ironically, Satyam had received the Golden Peacock Global Award for Excellence in Corporate Governance in September 2008 but was stripped of it soon after Raju's confession.

Market Model and Control Model

Two models of Corporate Governance are:

1. Market Model or Outsider (shareholders) model
2. Control Model or Insider (stakeholders) model

1. Market Model or Outsider (shareholders) model

Mathematical representation of the interactions among various participants, economic forces, and choices made. There are hundreds or even thousands of market models that attempt to explain or predict the behavior of one or more aspects of a market. In the context of the securities market, for example, one model would try to express how the return on a particular portfolio can be maximized.

Main Stakeholders

- Shareholders
- Employees
- Management
- Customers
- Creditors (i.e. Banks)
- Suppliers

- Local Communities
- Others

Characteristics:

- A priority to market regulation.
- The owners of firms tend to have a transitory interest in the firm.
- The absence of close relationships between shareholders and management.
- The existence of an active `market for corporate control-takeovers, particularly hostile ones.
- The primacy of shareholder rights over those of other organizational groups.

2. Control Model or Insider (stakeholders) model

- The priority to stakeholders control
- The owners of firms tend to have an enduring interest in the company
- They often hold positions on the Board of Directors or other senior managerial positions
- The relationships between management and shareholders are close and stable
- There is little by way of a market for corporate control
- the existence of formal rights for employees to influence key managerial decisions

Insider model in Eurasian countries:

- The mass privatization with favourable conditions for employees has created prerequisites for the insider model of corporate governance
- The exist a tendency that the employees' shares pass to other holders is also present but not so sharp
- Particularity for some countries there are the high concentration of share's capital at the management
- Nevertheless, employees continue to play important role as shareholders in Armenia, Azerbaijan, Georgia, Kazakhstan, Kyrgyzstan, Moldova, Ukraine and Uzbekistan.

International private initiative in CG:

- The role of employees in corporate governance has an important place in widespread corporate governance guidelines and codes of conduct for example, in Corporate Governance Forum Principles (1998), Bosh Report, General Motors Board Guidelines, Dey Report and others (Holly J. Gregory, International comparison of board "Best practices" in developed markets, 1999)
- As said in Corporate Governance Forum Principles: "Without stable cooperation between employees and management, shareholders' value will never be maximized"

OECD on Corporate Governance

Corporate governance is based on principles such as conducting the business with all integrity and fairness, being transparent with regard to all transactions, making all the necessary disclosures and decisions, complying with all the laws of the land, accountability and responsibility towards the stakeholders and commitment to conduct the business in an ethical manner. Another point which is highlighted in the SEBI report on corporate governance is the need for those in control to be able to distinguish between what are personal and corporate funds while managing a company.

- ***Rights and equitable treatment of shareholders:*** Organizations should respect the rights of shareholders and help shareholders to exercise those rights. They can help shareholders exercise their rights by openly and effectively communicating information and by encouraging shareholders to participate in general meetings.
- ***Interests of other stakeholders:*** Organizations should recognize that they have legal, contractual, social, and market driven obligations to non-shareholder stakeholders, including employees, investors, creditors, suppliers, local communities, customers, and policy makers.
- ***Role and responsibilities of the board:*** The board needs sufficient relevant skills and understanding to review and challenge management performance. It also needs adequate size and appropriate levels of independence and commitment
- ***Integrity and ethical behavior:*** Integrity should be a fundamental requirement in choosing corporate officers and board members. Organizations should develop a code of conduct for their directors and executives that promotes ethical and responsible decision making.
- ***Disclosure and transparency:*** Organizations should clarify and make publicly known the roles and responsibilities of board and management to provide stakeholders with a level of accountability. They should also implement procedures to independently verify and safeguard the integrity of the company's financial reporting. Disclosure of material matters concerning the organization should be timely and balanced to ensure that all investors have access to clear, factual information

A Historical Perspective of Corporate Governance

The seeds of modern corporate governance were probably sown by the Watergate scandal in the United States. The global movement for better corporate governance progressed in fits and starts from the mid-1980s up to 1997. There were the odd country-level initiatives such as the Cadbury Committee Report in the United Kingdom (1992) or the recommendations of the National Association of Corporate Directors of the US (1995). It would be fair to say, however, that such initiatives were few and far between. And while there were the occasional international conferences on the desirability of good corporate governance, most companies-both global and Indian knew little of what the phrase meant, and cared even less for its implications. More recently, the first major stimulus for corporate governance reforms came after the South-East and East Asian crisis of 1997-98. This was no classical Latin American debt crisis. Here were fiscally responsible, healthy, rapidly growing, export-driven economies going into crippling financial crises. Gradually, governments, multilateral institutions, banks as well as companies began to understand that the devil lay in the institutional, micro-economic details-the nitty-gritty of transactions between companies, banks, financial institutions and capital markets; the design of corporate laws, bankruptcy procedures and practices; the structure of ownership and crony capitalism; sharp stock market practices; poor boards of directors showing scant regard to fiduciary responsibility; poor disclosures and transparency; and inadequate accounting and auditing standards.

Suddenly, 'corporate governance' came out of dusty academic closets and moved to centre stage. Barring Japan and possibly Indonesia, countries in Asia recovered remarkably fast. By the year 2001, Thailand, Malaysia and Korea were on the upswing and on course to regain their historical growth rates. With such rapid recovery, corporate governance issues were in the danger of being relegated to the back stage once again. There were projects to be executed, under valued assets to be bought, and profits to be made. International investors were again showing bluishness. In such a milieu, there seemed no urgent need to impose concepts like better accounting practices, greater disclosure, and independent board oversight. Corporate governance once again settled into a phase of extended inactivity.

India's experience was somewhat different from this Asian scheme of things. First, unlike South-East and East Asia, the corporate governance movement did not occur due to a national or region-wide macro-economic and financial collapse. Indeed, the Asian crisis barely touched India.

Secondly, unlike other Asian countries, the initial drive for better corporate governance and disclosure, perhaps as a result of the 1992 stock market 'scam', and the onset of international competition consequent on the liberalization of economy that began in 1990, came from all-India industry and business associations and in the Department of Company Affairs.

Thirdly, it is fair to say that, since April 2001, listed companies in India are required to follow some of the most stringent guidelines for corporate governance throughout Asia and which rank among some of the best in the world.

Even so, there is scope for improvement. For one, while India may have excellent rules and regulations, regulatory authorities are inadequately staffed and lack of sufficient number of skilled people. This has led to less than credible enforcement. Delays in courts compound this problem. India has had its fair share of corporate scams and stock market scandals that has shaken investor confidence. Much can be done to improve the situation.

Just as the global corporate governance movement was going into a bit of hibernation, there came the Enron debacle of 2001, followed by other scandals involving large US companies such as WorldCom, Qwest, Global Crossing and the exposure of lack of auditing that eventually led to the collapse of Andersen. After having shaken the foundations of the business world, that too in the stronghold of capitalism, these scandals have triggered another more vigorous phase of reforms in corporate governance, accounting practices and disclosures – this time more comprehensively than ever before.

As a US-based expert recently put it, "Enron and WorldCom have done more to further the cause of corporate transparency and governance in less than one year, than what activists could do in the last twenty."

In June 2002, less than a year from the date when Enron filed for bankruptcy, the US Congress introduced in record time the Sarbanes-Oxley Bill. This piece of legislation (popularly called SOX) brought with it fundamental changes in virtually every area of corporate governance – and particularly in auditor independence, conflicts of interest, corporate responsibility and enhanced financial disclosures. The SOX Act was signed into law by the US President on 30 July 2002. While the US Securities and Exchanges Commission (SEC) is yet to formalize most of the rules under various provisions of the Act, and despite there being rumbles of protest in the corporate world against some of the more draconian measures in the new law, it is fair to predict that the SOX Act will do more to change the contours of board structure, auditing, financial reporting and corporate disclosure than any other previous law in US history.

Although India has been fortunate in not having to go through the pains of massive corporate failures such as Enron and WorldCom, it has not been found wanting in its desire to further improve corporate governance standards. On 21 August 2002, the Department of Company Affairs (DCA) under the Ministry of Finance and Company Affairs appointed this Committee to examine various corporate governance issues.

Issues in Corporate Governance

Major issues in corporate governance reports have included the role of board, the quality of financial reporting and auditing, directors' remuneration, risk management and corporate social responsibility. In order to clear the above statement we need to expand on these issues in later articles but for now let's examine the major areas that have been affected by the corporate governance.

Duties of Directors

The corporate governance reports have aimed to build on the directors' duties as defined in statutory and case law duties of directors. These include the fiduciary duties to act in the best interests of the company, use their powers for a purpose, avoid conflicts of interest and exercise a duty of care.

Composition and Balance of the Board

A feature of many corporate governance scandals has been boards dominated by a single senior executive or small 'cabinet of kitchen' with other member of board who are working just as a robot toy. It is possible that a single person may bypass the board directions to meet his own personal interests. The report on the UK Guinness case suggested that the Earnest Saunders' chief executive paid himself a reward of £ 3 million without the consent of other directors.

In the case where the organization is not dominated by a single person, there may be other problem in the composition of board of directors. The organization may be run by a minority group revolve around CEO or CFO and recruitment and appointments may be done by personal recommendations rather than formal system. So in order to run a smooth business a board must be balanced in sense of talents, skills, and competence from numerous specialism related to the organization's situation and also in terms of age.

Remuneration and Reward of Directors

Directors being paid excessive bonuses and salaries have been identified as significant corporate abuses for a large number of years. It is, however, unavoidable that the corporate governance codes have been targeted this significant issue.

Reliability of Financial Reporting and External Auditors

Financial reporting and auditing issue are seen more critical to corporate governance by the investors because of their main consideration in ensuring management accountability. It is the reason that they have been must debated and the focus of serious litigation. Whilst considering the corporate governance debate only on reporting and accounting issues is insufficient, the greater regulation of practices such as off-balance sheet financing has directed to greater transparency and reduction in risks faced by investors.

The necessary questioning may not be carried out by external auditor from senior management because the auditors may have threat of loosing audit assignment. In the same way internal auditor may not ask an alien question to senior member because their employment matters are determined by the CFO. But generally the external auditors become the reason of corporate collapse, for instance in the case of Barlow Clowes that was poorly focused and planned audit failed to determine the illegal usage of monies from clients.

Board's Responsibility for Risk Management and Internal Control

If the board does not arrange the regular meetings in order to consider the organizational activities systematically then it means that the board is not meeting their responsibilities. But can occur when the board is not provided by full information to properly oversight on business activities. All this mess results in the poor system that makes them unable to report and measure the risks associated with business.

Shareholders' Rights and Responsibilities

Shareholders' role and rights is a subject of particular importance. They should be informed about all those information that are material to them because these information may influence their amount of investment. They should also be given the right to vote on policies affecting the governance of organization.

Corporate Social Responsibility and Business Ethics

The lack of mutual decision and sense of responsibility for businesses and stakeholders has unavoidably turned out the business ethics and social responsibility a significant part of corporate governance debate.

Relevance of Corporate Governance

Corporate governance (CG) is a set of systems, principles and processes, about how companies are directed and controlled. It regulates the way boards manage the running of a company by its executives; and how board members are accountable to shareholders and the company. This has a direct influence on company's attitude, accountability and responsibility, towards all stakeholders, including employees, shareholders, and customers alike. Superior CG plays a fundamental role in strengthening the integrity and efficiency of financial markets. Inadequate corporate governance however undermines a company's potential and at worst leads to financial difficulties and even may result in fraud. Well-governed companies usually outperform other companies and are able to attract new investors whose support can help to finance further growth.

To ensure transparency in corporate arena, good principles of CG focus generally on publicly traded companies with the view to help governments improve the legal, institutional and regulatory framework that relate to CG. Additionally, they provide practical guidance and suggestions for relevant entities such as stock exchanges, investors, corporations, and other entities that play a part in the process of developing good corporate governance.

Experiences derived from advanced and emerging economies have demonstrated that no single framework for CG is adequate for all markets, as rules and regulations vary greatly from one country to another, so the internationally recognized principles are not authoritarian or compulsory, but rather made as recommendations that each country can amend to suit their traditions and market conditions.

Whilst corporate regulations may lead in part to improve governance, which is mainly about how companies are directed and controlled, the prime responsibility for superior governance ought to lie within the company rather than outside it. For example, the balance sheet is the result of structural and strategic decisions and activities across the organization, from stock options to risk management, from the board of directors' composition to the decentralization of decision-making process.

Crafting and introducing into practice effective CG policies are important, but encouraging the right culture is paramount. Senior executives need to set the agenda not least in ensuring that board members feel at ease to participate in open and worthwhile discussion. However, not all board members need to be finance or risk experts however. The primary task for the board is to understand and approve both the risk appetite of a particular company at any particular stage in its evolution and the processes that are in place to monitor risk.

Considering the inverse relationship between innovation and conservatism, governance and growth, a good CG can bring benefits to companies but may impede growth. For example, strict CG policies may negatively impact mergers and acquisitions deals as a result of the lengthening of due-diligence procedures, and compromise leadership's ability to make prompt and effective decisions.

Fundamentally, there is a level of confidence that is associated with a company that is known to have good CG. Transparent company's governance policies are crucial, as long as information is made readily available to investors and shareholders. Beyond this, the market can deal with the rest, designating an appropriate risk premium to companies that have no or too few independent directors or too aggressive compensation policy, or cutting the costs of capital for companies that adhere to conservative accounting policies.

CG is known to be one of the criteria that foreign institutional investors are increasingly depending on when deciding on which companies to invest in. As far as corporate transparency is concerned, too few companies are genuinely transparent in the Middle East, thus the regional leadership, board of directors as well as CEO's, are encouraged to voluntarily design good CG, that addresses the managements' concerns over government regulation and strict internal procedures and how it could adversely impact their ability to manage their business effectively. Investors, board members, and CEO's have to recognize the need for trade-off between enhancing corporate reputation and delivering growth.

Theoretical basis for Corporate Governance

Corporate Governance involves the processes, structures and mechanisms by which the affairs of the company are directed and managed in such a way that the long-term shareholder value is increased through enhanced corporate performance and accountability of managers.

The fundamental theoretical basis of corporate governance is agency costs. In a limited liability company structure a large number of investors provide the risk capital. They are called shareholders, the deemed owners of the company. They delegate the power to manage the company to board of directors. The board delegates the same to managers while retaining its role to monitor and control the executive management. Shareholders are viewed as the principal and the manager as their agents and this relationship is described as 'principal-agent relationship'. The shareholders, of a widely held firm, practically do not have any control over the managers. They are only informed of the financial results on a periodical basis while the managers controls the firms' assets. This structure provides an opportunity to the managers to expropriate shareholders' wealth and misappropriate the funds by way of transfer of money as loans to his own companies, or sale of the company assets to themselves at a lesser price or pay themselves more perks. The divergence of interest between the owners and the managers, due to the separation of ownership from control, results in the agency costs. The diffused nature of corporate ownership, which is characterized by a large number of small shareholders aggravate the costs further.

But the core of corporate governance is ethical conduct of business. Unless the corporations adopt and demonstrate ethical conduct and act in the best interest of its various stakeholders namely customers, employees, investors, vendor partners, government and society, they will not be able to succeed. In the short run, they may concentrate on their narrow business objectives, sometimes detrimental to the interests of stakeholders in general, but in the long run; they can ascertain growth only by caring for broader societal concerns as about labor, environment, social welfare etc.

Most of the countries around the world are showing much concern for the Corporate Governance issues due to many parallel developments. The intensifying global competition, rapid technological changes, the world-wide waves of privatization for the past two decades, the pension fund reforms, the growth of private savings, the takeover wave of the 1980s, the deregulation and integration of capital markets, the 1997 East Asian Crisis and the series of recent corporate failures and accounting scandals in U.S. and the rest of the world validated the need for good governance.

The developments around the world and the series of scams like Harshad Mehta scam, M.S. Shoes scam, Reliance share switching scandal and the recent Satyam scam stunned the Indian economy also and drawn its attention towards the governance problems of Indian corporate sector. To overcome the agency problem and improve the corporate governance many committees have been constituted around the world and in India too. They have laid down number of policy guidelines and legislations for good corporate governance. But the never-ending scams and scandals and governance problems all over the world witness that just formulation of laws is not enough rather their effective enforcement need to be ensured. The meaningful implementation of rules and regulations require the change in basic mind-set of corporate sector.

Till date, the focus of corporate governance reforms has been on the quality, independence and responsibilities of the board of directors and its major committees and performance of the management. But a very pertinent phenomenon, institutional investor activism also deserve adequate attention of the policy makers and regulatory bodies. By virtue of their large stock holdings, they have the opportunity, resources, and the ability to monitor discipline and influence managers, which can force them to focus more on corporate performance and corporate governance.

Although the role that the institutional investors can play in the corporate governance system of a company is a controversial question and a subject of continuing debate. While some believe that the institutional investors must interfere in the corporate governance system of a company, others believe that these investors have other investment objectives to follow. The group of observers against the institutional investor activism argue that the investment objectives and the compensation system in the institutional investing companies often discourage their active participation in the corporate governance system of the companies. Institutional investors are answerable to their investors the way the companies (in which they have invested) are answerable to their shareholders. And the shareholders do invest their funds with the institutional investors expecting higher returns. The primary responsibility of the institutional investors is therefore to invest the money of the investors in companies, which are expected to generate the maximum possible return rather than in companies with good corporate governance records. The other apprehension shown by these observers is free-rider problem. Only few institutions involve in active monitoring and hence, bear the monitoring cost while all of them get the benefit.

While the other group strongly believes that if the corporate governance system in the companies has to succeed then the institutional investors must play an active role in the entire process. If they become dissatisfied with the performance of management, they can voice their dissatisfaction or sell their shares. Both actions will have significant impact over the corporate management provided the size of the shareholder is substantial and also retained for a considerable time period. They have certainly an edge over the other types of shareholders, even more, if they are also the lending institutions. Therefore, their role does not limit to acquire the vital information from management rather, to disseminate the same to the other shareholders.

The apprehensions shown by the group of experts against the institutional investor activism do not undermine its importance. As though the main focus of institutional investors should always be on attaining their own business objectives, investing in the companies, which generate maximum returns irrespective of their governance practices. But if the companies with good governance practices generate more returns to the companies with poor governance practices then the argument does not hold good. Similarly, the free-rider problem is also sub-sided if the active institutional investors are able to generate super-normal returns for their own investors.

Therefore the role of institutional investors has been widely recognized all over the world in the recent era. Most of the reports on Corporate Governance have also emphasized the role that the institutional investors should play in the entire system. For instance, the Cadbury Committee (1992), Greenbury Report (1995) and Hampel Report (1998) in UK, Japan Corporate Governance Committee, (2001) in Japan and CII report on Corporate Governance (1998) and SEBI committee Report (1999) etc. have duly recognized that because of their large ownership stakes, it is their moral responsibility to use their professional competence and voting power more constructively to improve the corporate governance practices.

Obligation to Society

Corporate social responsibility (CSR), also known as corporate responsibility, corporate citizenship, responsible business, sustainable responsible business (SRB), or corporate social performance, is a form of corporate self-regulation integrated into a business model. Ideally, CSR policy would function as a built-in, self-regulating mechanism whereby business would monitor and ensure its support to law, ethical standards, and international norms. Consequently, business would embrace responsibility for the impact of its activities on the environment, consumers, employees, communities, stakeholders and all other members of the public sphere. Furthermore, CSR-focused businesses would pro-actively promote the public interest by encouraging community growth and development, and voluntarily eliminating practices that harm the public sphere, regardless of legality. Essentially, CSR is the deliberate inclusion of public interest into corporate decision-making, and the honoring of a triple bottom line: people, planet, profit.

The practice of CSR is much debated and criticized. Proponents argue that there is a strong business case for CSR, in that corporations benefit in multiple ways by operating with a perspective broader and longer than their own immediate, short-term profits. Critics argue that CSR distracts from the fundamental economic role of business others argue that it is nothing more than superficial window-dressing others yet argue that it is an attempt to pre-empt the role of governments as a watchdog over powerful multinational corporations. Corpcrate Social Responsibility has been redefined throughout the years. However, it essentially is titled to aid to an organization's mission as well as a guide to what the company stands for and will uphold to its consumers.

Development business ethics is one of the forms of applied ethics that examines ethical principles and moral or ethical problems that can arise in a business environment.

In the increasingly conscience-focused marketplaces of the 21st century, the demand for more ethical business processes and actions is increasing. Simultaneously, pressure is applied on industry to improve business ethics through new public initiatives and laws.

Business ethics can be both a normative and a descriptive discipline. As a corporate practice and a career specialization, the field is primarily normative. Corporate governance refers to the relationship that exists between the different participants and defining the direction and performance of a corporate firm. The CEO, board of directors and the shareholders are the main actors in corporate governance. The other actors who influence governance in corporations are the staff, suppliers, creditors, customers and the community. In other words Corporate governance is a systematic process by which companies are directed and controlled to enhance their wealth generating capacity. The range and quantity of business ethical issues reflects the degree to which business is perceived to be at odds with non-economic social values.

The term "CSR" came into common use in the early 1970s, after many multinational corporations formed, although it was seldom abbreviated. The term stakeholder, meaning those on whom an organization's activities have an impact, was used to describe corporate owners beyond shareholders as a result of an influential book by R Freeman in 1984.

Potential business benefits

The scale and nature of the benefits of CSR for an organization can vary depending on the nature of the enterprise, and are difficult to quantify, though there is a large body of literature exhorting business to adopt measures beyond financial ones. Orlitzky, Schmidt, and Rynes found a correlation between social/environmental performance and financial performance. However, businesses may not be looking at short-run financial returns when developing their CSR strategy.

The definition of CSR used within an organization can vary from the strict "stakeholder impacts" definition used by many CSR advocates and will often include charitable efforts and volunteering. CSR may be based within the human resources, business development or public relations departments of an organization, or may be given a separate unit reporting to the CEO or in some cases directly to the board. Some companies may implement CSR-type values without a clearly defined team or program.

The business case for CSR within a company will likely rest on one or more of these arguments:

Human resources

A CSR program can be an aid to recruitment and retention, particularly within the competitive graduate student market. Potential recruits often ask about a firm's CSR policy during an interview, and having a comprehensive policy can be added advantage. CSR can also help improve the perception of a company among its staff, particularly when staff can become involved through payroll giving, fund raising activities or community volunteering. Consider also Corporate Social Entrepreneurship, whereby CSR can also be driven by employees' personal values, in addition to the more obvious economic and governmental drivers.

Risk management

Managing risk is a central part of many corporate strategies. Reputations that take decades to build up can be ruined in hours through incidents such as corruption scandals or environmental accidents. These can also draw unwanted attention from regulators, courts, governments and media. Building a genuine culture of 'doing the right thing' within a corporation can offset these risks.

Brand differentiation

In crowded marketplaces, companies strive for a unique selling proposition that can separate them from the competition in the minds of consumers. CSR can play a role in building customer loyalty based on distinctive ethical values. Several major brands, such as The Co-operative Group, The Body Shop and American Appare are built on ethical values. Business service organizations can benefit too from building a reputation for integrity and best practice.

License to operate

Corporations are keen to avoid interference in their business through taxation or regulations. By taking substantive voluntary steps, they can persuade governments and the wider public that they are considering issues such as health and safety, diversity, or the environment seriously as good corporate citizens with respect to labour standards and impacts on the environment.

Stakeholder priorities

Increasingly, corporations are motivated to become more socially responsible because their most important stakeholders expect them to understand and address the social and community issues that are relevant to them. Understanding the causes are important to employees as it is usually the first priority because of the many interrelated business benefits that can be derived from increased employee engagement. Key external stakeholders include customers, consumers, investors communities in the areas where the corporation operates its facilities, regulators, academics, and the media.

Obligations to Investors

The principles for responsible investment:

- Address ESG issues in investment policy statements.
- Support development of ESG-related tools, metrics and analysis.
- Assess the capabilities of internal investment managers to incorporate ESG issues.
- Assess the capabilities of external investment managers to incorporate ESG issues.
- Ask investment service providers such as financial analysts, consultants, brokers, research firms, or rating companies to integrate ESG factors into evolving research and analysis.
- Encourage academic and other research on this theme.
- Advocate ESG training for investment professionals.

Obligation to Employees, Customers and Managerial Obligation

1. Code of Conduct

- Awareness of the areas of ethical risk;
- Honest and ethical conduct, including the ethical handling of actual or apparent conflicts of interest between personal and professional relationships;
- A culture of honesty and accountability;
- Full, fair, accurate, timely, and understandable disclosure in reports and documents that the company files or submits to regulators and in other public communications made by the company;
- Compliance with applicable governmental laws, rules, regulations and company policies; and
- Pompt internal reporting to an appropriate person of violations of the code.

2. Compliance with Law

The company expects all directors, officers and employees to comply with all applicable laws, rules and regulations and to be able to recognize potential liabilities, seeking legal advice where appropriate.

In particular, all directors, officers and employees shall comply with laws, rules and regulations prohibiting insider trading. Insider trading is both unethical and illegal and will be dealt with decisively.

The company expects all directors, officers and employees to comply with this Code and all other Company policies.

Directors, officers and employees must not only comply with the requirements of applicable laws, rules, regulations, policies and this Code, they must ensure that their actions do not give the appearance of violating this code or indicate a casual attitude towards compliance with laws, rules, regulations, policies and this code.

If there are any doubts as to whether a course of action is proper or about the application or interpretation of any legal requirement, directors, officers and employees should discuss it with the company's secretary.

3. Disclosure of Information

It is the company's policy to make full, timely and complete disclosure of important information concerning its activities

Except as required by law, the Company will not disclose confidential information, which includes all non-public information that might be of use to competitors or harmful to the Company or its customers, if disclosed. Confidential information is not to be disclosed by any director, officer or employee unless such disclosure is properly authorized or legally mandated. Questions regarding the appropriateness of disclosing particular information should be discussed with the Secretary.

4. Accounting Records and Practices

The Company's books and records will reflect all Company transactions in an accurate and timely manner . In particular, all funds and assets will be properly recorded.

5. Prohibited payments

Directors, officers and employees are prohibited from paying or accepting any bribe, kickback or any other unlawful payment or benefit to secure any concession, contract or any other favourable treatment. Directors, officers and employees will report any such attempted actions in accordance with Clause 14 of this code.

6. Fair dealing

Each director, officer and employee shall endeavour to deal fairly with the Company's customers, suppliers, competitors and employees. No director, officer and employee is permitted to take unfair advantage of anyone through manipulation, concealment, abuse of privileged information, misrepresentation of material facts, or any other unfair-dealing practice.

7. Conflicts of Interest

A conflict of interest occurs when an individual's private interest interferes in any way – or even appears to interfere-with the interests of the company as a whole. A conflict situation can arise when a director, officer or employee takes actions or has interests that may make it difficult to perform his / her Company work objectively and effectively. Conflicts of interest also arise when a director, officer or employee, or a member of his/her family, receives improper personal benefits as a result of his / her position in the company. Loans to, or guarantees of obligations of, such persons are of special concern.

Conflicts of interest are prohibited. Every director, officer and employee must avoid any conflict of interest. Every director, officer and employee shall disclose all circumstances that constitute an actual or apparent conflict of interest. Disclosure shall be made, in the case of directors and officers, to the board of directors, and in the case of employees, to the CEO. When in doubt about whether a conflict of interest exists, directors, officers and employees should discuss the issue with the Secretary.

Directors, officers or employees who find themselves in a conflict of interest must abstain from voting or taking any other action that may impact the outcome of the activity or business transaction in question. Full disclosure enables directors, officers and employees to resolve unclear situations and gives an opportunity to dispose of or appropriately address conflicts of interest before any difficulty arises. However, if the board of directors determines that a potential conflict cannot be cured, the individual will resign from the board, if a director, or from their position with the Company, if an officer or employee.

8. Corporate Opportunities

Directors, officers and employees are prohibited from: (a) taking for themselves personally opportunities that are discovered through the use of corporate property, information or position; (b) using corporate property, information of position for personal gain; and (c) competing with the company. Directors, officers and employees owe a duty to the Company to advance its legitimate interests when the opportunity to do so arises.

9. Use of Company Property

The company assets must not be misappropriated for personal use by directors, officers or employees.

Directors, officers and employees shall protect the company's assets and ensure their efficient use. Theft, carelessness and waste have a direct impact on the company's profitability. All Company assets should be used for legitimate business purposes.

10. Safety and Environmental Protection

Safety and environmental protection are fundamental values of the company and every director, officer and employee has a role in ensuring the company's operations to comply with safety and environmental legislation and standards.

Each director, officer and employee is responsible for taking all prudent precautions in every activity to ensure both personal safety and the safety of others.

11. Fundamental Rights

The company is committed to providing all employees a workplace that respects their basic human rights. Each director, officer and employee at the company has the right to work in an environment that is free from discrimination and harassment, including sexual harassment. Every director, officer and employee is responsible for taking all reasonable precautions not to demonstrate behaviour that can be reasonably construed as discrimination or harassment.

The company will take every incident of harassment or discrimination very seriously and any director, officer or employee who is found to have engaged in conduct constituting discrimination or harassment will be disciplined and, in appropriate circumstances, dismissed or removed from office.

The company encourages reporting of all incidents of discrimination and harassment. Every employee has the right to pursue a complaint without reprisal, retaliation or threat of either, for doing so.

12. Responsibility

Each director, officer and employee must be familiar with and adhere to the provisions of this Code and to the standards set out in the applicable policies of the company.

Failure to adhere to this code may lead to disciplinary action, including dismissal or removal from office in appropriate circumstances.

13. Where to Seek Clarification

Directors and officers should refer questions relating to this Code or its application to a particular situation to the Secretary. Employees should refer questions relating to this Code or its application to a particular situation to their immediate manager. If the issue is one which the employee feels unable to discuss with his / her immediate manager then the matter should be discussed with the Secretary.

All disclosure to the Secretary shall be kept strictly confidential unless, in the sole opinion of the Secretary, the matter disclosed constitutes an actual or potential threat of serious harm to the Company, to another director, officer or employee of the Company or to the general public.

14. Reporting Breaches of this Code

Save for the CEO all directors and officers are required to report breaches of this Code, including violations of laws, rules, regulations or Company policies, to the CEO or if they feel unable to discuss this with the CEO then to the chairman. The CEO is required to report breaches of this code, including violations of laws, rules, regulations or company policies, to the chairman or if he / she feels unable to discuss this with the chairman then to the board of directors.

Employees are required to report breaches of this code, including violations of laws, rules, regulations or company policies, to their immediate supervisor or if they feel unable to discuss this with their immediate supervisor then to the CEO or the chairman.

15. Waivers from Code

In extraordinary circumstances and where it is clearly in the company's best interest to do so, the company may waive compliance with a requirement under this code for a director, officer or employee conditions may be attached to this waiver.

The director, officer or employee to whom a waiver is granted accepts that public disclosure of the granting of any such waiver may be required by applicable securities laws, regulations, policies or guidelines.

Indian Cases

Case study: 1

Several years ago, when his fortune was a mere several hundred million dollars, a weekly magazine labeled Bill Gates as 'America's richest nerd.' In 1992, at age 36, he had passed Donald Trump, Ross Perot and others to be listed as America's wealthiest person by Forbes magazine; the value of his holdings had grown to an estimated $ 6.3 billion. How did the free enterprise system help him to attain such phenomenal wealth?

After graduating from high school in Seattle in 1973, Gates went to Harvard. While there, he learned that the personal computer [PC] was in the development stage. He dropped out of school and threw himself completely into designing an operating system [the program that coordinates the hardware and software of the computer] for the PC. His system, [S - DOS the Microsoft Disk Opening System] was so good that IBM agreed to use it in their line of, personal computers. With IBM setting the industry standard, other computer manufacturers quickly adopted MS DOS as well. Today it is estimated that more than 80 per cent of all personal computers in the world use this system: Gate's firm, Microsoft, Inc., makes money on every computer sold with MS-DOS as the operating system.' In the 1992, the firm recorded $2.8 billion in revenue and $ 708 million in net profit. It ranks third in size in the industry, behind IBM and Hewlett - Packard. Gate's personal holdings of some 90 million shares of common stock represent about 33 per cent ownership share of the company.

Microsoft also produces programs for word processing, spreadsheets, and a variety of other applications. One of Gate's latest ventures has been to purchase the electronic reproduction rights to thousands of art and photographic works from museums and libraries around the world. These will be used as a part of his plan for interactive home entertainment systems.

With extremely hard work, a creative mind, and a willingness to take risks, Gates has demonstrated how the market rewards the successful entrepreneur. He was able to produce what consumers wanted at a price they were willing to pay the result was that both and they are better off ! This is the essence of free market economic system.

From the above case study, it would be clear how a pro-active, imaginative and innovative entrepreneur can, carry the business with him. Though a school drop out. Gates has climbed the pinnacle of business world, merely by his ability to anticipate the changes, in the personal computer industry.

Failure to read the business environment and initiate appropriate steps to protect the business, can lead to a serious threat to existence itself. This would-be clsar from the following case on Maruti Udyog of India and Doordarshan.

Case study: 2

MARUTI UDYOG LTD.,

When Indian car market was opened for new private players, Maruti Udyog limited, which had till then enjoyed an enviable position in the market, suddenly faced severe market erosion. Even though Maruti is the market leader and has the largest range of products, cheaper cars, good service network and better cost structures, it has been steadily losing its market share for the last three years and the valuation of the company has halved in 4 years time from Rs. 80 bn in 1996 to Rs. 40 bn in 2000.

A Marjti udyog rival: What MUL did to Premier Automobiles and Hindustan motors is now being done lo it.

Empire under siege

Jagdish Khattar, MD MUL was a man in trouble. He was facing what was the biggest setback ever for the company. With all strategies backfiring, he seemed to be fighting a losing battle.

Problems were aplenty - the Maruti 800 segment was facing demand - erosion, Zen and its arch-rival Santro were very close in terms of volumes, Esteem was losing ground, Baleno, Wagon R and Alto were yet to prove themselves, while Gypsy was snugly ensconced in its niche.Despite the fact the fact that MUL had the biggest range of products, the cheapest cars in the market and a service network and cost structures that were better than anyone else, it had steadily lost market share - down from 82.62 percent in 1998 to 52 per cent in 2000. With the impending disinvestments, [Government's. policy of disinvestments in Public sector units includes MUEL also along with other profit making PSUs.] MD was facing flak from the government as well. With market share declining, MUL's valuation had also come down drastically. While it was valued at Rs. 80 bn in 1996, by December, 2000, the figure had touched Rs. 40 bn.

The building blocks

MUL was the largest car manufacturer in India with a market share of over 52 per cent. It was a joint sector corporation set up by the government of India and Suzuki Motor Corporation, Japan. MUL was incorporated in 1981 to take over the assets of the erstwhile MUL set up in June 1971 and wound up by a High Court order in 1978. The assets of MUL were then acquired buy the Government under MUL Acquisition and Transfer of Undertakings Act, 1980. In 1982, the Government signed a joint venture agreement with Suzuki of Japan. Suzuki's stake increased from 26 to 40% in 1987, and to 50.25% in 1992. The company was a significant exporter with exports to over 50 countries.

The company manufactured passenger cars at its factor in Gurgaon, Haryana, with an installed capacity of 350,000 vehicles. The first product, Maruti 800 was launched in 1984, followed by the all-terrain vehicle Gypsy in 1985. Over the years. MUL expanded its portfolio with the launch of the Maruti 1000 [1990]; the Zen and the Esteem [1993]; Zen Diesel [1998]p Baleno, Wagon R and the Alto.

MUL was known for its 'value for money pricing' strategy, which had been made possible due to the high levels of indigenization of its vehicles. While the Maruti 800, Zen, Esteem, and Omni were indigenized to the extent of over 90%, the Gypsy was indigenized to the extent of 82% and the Alto to the extent of 76%. The company had a network of about 375 vendors and had several joint ventures with some of them to source its raw material requirements.

Much ado about nothing?

As the Indian automobile market moved from monopoly to free competition, market share comparisons from the old era seemed to have lost relevance. The alarm over MUL's declining market share somehow did not seem fully justified. In its heyday, huge waiting lists for its products ensured that Maruti's market share was directly linked to the supply side of the equation. In other words, if MUL had an 80% share of the market, that was also its share of the total industry capacity. By the late 1990's, things changed radically with over 12 car manufacturers having a presence in the country, with a total capacity of about 1,250,000 cars, of which MUL produced about 400,000 [33%]. Khattar commented tell me, if we have market share of 50% out of a capacity that is 33% [of the industry], are we doing badly? Why don't you ask the others who together have a capacity of 800,000, but cannot match our sales? All said and done, MUL was still the leader in early -2001. It still had its early mover advantages. Provided Khattar plays his cards right, MUL can still rule the roost for years to come. Whether this will happen for real, is a question too early to be answered.

Review Questions

Conceptual Type

1. What is corporate governance?
2. Give the underlying principles of Corporate Governance
3. Explain the need for Corporate Governance?

Analytical Type

1. Explain market model of Corporate Governance.
2. Explain control model of Corporate Governance.
3. Discuss OECD on Corporate Governance.
4. Explain various issues of accountability in C.G.
5. Discuss relevance of corporate governance.
6. Justify corporate governance as a dimension of ethical decision making with reasons.
7. What are the principal constituents of corporate governance?
8. What are benefits of good corporate governance?
9. Write note on: corporate.
10. Give the concept of Governance.
11. Write note on: obligation to society.
12. What are the obligations to the investors?

Descriptive Type

1. State the objectives of corporate governance.
2. Explain various models of Corporate Governance.
3. Explain Corporate Governance in historical perspective.
4. Explain various issues in corporate governance.
5. Explain need and importance of corporate governance.
6. What are the requirements for a good corporate governance?
7. Explain the Code on Corporate Governance 2008.
8. Explain theoretical basis for corporate governance.
9. Discuss various obligations to employees, customers and managerial obligations.

*****

Module-4

Public Policies

Syllabus

The role of public policies in governing business, Government and public policy, classification of public policy, areas of public policy, need for public policy in business, levels of public policy, elements of public policy, the corporation and public policy, framing of public policy, business and politics levels of involvement, business, government, society and media relationship 35 government regulations in business, justification of regulation, types of regulation, problems of regulation.

Introduction

Public policy is an attempt by a government to address a public issue by instituting laws, regulations, decisions, or actions pertinent to the problem at hand. Numerous issues can be addressed by public policy including crime, education, foreign policy, health, and social welfare. While public policies are most common in the United States, several other countries, such as those in the United Kingdom, implement them as well. The process of creating a new public policy typically follows three steps: agenda-setting, option-formulation, and implementation. The time-line for a new policy to be put in place can range from weeks to several years, depending on the situation. Public policies can also be made by leaders of religious and cultural institutions for the benefit of the congregation and participants, and the term can also refer to a type of academic study that covers topics such as sociology, economics, and policy analysis. Once governments have been created they must govern; the process of governing concerns the formulation and implementation of public policies.

Public Policy

Public Policy is basically a set of rules and regulations set forth that the public is expected to adhere to. Public laws are a classic example of public policy in the legality sense, while the laws of society are those that are unwritten but are still expected to be followed in public.

Public policy means courses of action, regulatory measures, laws and funding priorities concerning a given topic promulgated by a governmental entity or its representatives.

Public policy is a course of action adopted and pursued by a government.

Public policy is a purposive and consistent course of action produced as a response to a perceived problem of a constituency, formulated by a specific political process and adopted, implemented, and enforced by a public agency.

Public: It comprises domain of human activity which is regarded as requiring governmental interventions or common action. A domain of life which is not private or purely individual but held in common.

Policy: a purposive course of action taken or adopted by those in power in pursuit of certain goals and objectives.

- Public policy is "whatever governments choose to do or not to do".
- The term public policy always refers to the actions of the government and the intentions that determine those actions.
- Public policy is the outcome of struggle in government over who gets what.
- Public policy consists of political decisions for implementing programs to achieve societal goals.
- Public policy is sum of government activities, whether acting directly or through agents, as it has an influence on the life of citizens.
- A public policy is a deliberate plan of actions of the government to guide decisions and achieve rational outcomes.
- Public policy can be generally defined as the course of action or inaction taken by governmental entities with regard to a particular issue or set of issues.

Categories of Public Policies

1. ***Substantive and Procedural Policies:*** This is the classification of public policies with respect to the time of execution. While the former is the policy the government is executing, doing, done or executed, the latter is in the pipeline or going to be done.

2. ***Distributive, Regulatory, Self-regulatory, and Re-distributive Policies:*** This is the division of public policies with respect to allocation and control. Distributive policies concern the allocation of services and benefits of public resources to various segments of the economy. Regulatory policies imposes restrictions or limitations on the ways and manners the individuals and group of individuals and firms could behave an economy. Self-regulatory policies are the policies similar to regulatory policies but each unions or bodies supervised themselves. Re-distributive policies are the policies that allocate resources among the already divided sections of the society for example the haves and the have-nots through different government program.

3. ***Material and Symbollc Policies:*** This is the categorisation of public policies with respect to the tangibility of power and or assets involved. Material policies are the policies that involve tangible assets or substantive powers to the beneficiaries or disadvantaged people in the economy. Symbolic Policies are the policies that attached little or are yet to attach tangible assets or substantive powers to the beneficiaries or disadvantaged people in the economy. It includes policy on patriotism, peace, social justice, etc. for instance burning of the National Flag of a nation which indicates hatred for that nation. Also passing stool and smoking at public places which are forbidden on health ground.

4. ***Policies involving Public Goods and Private Goods:*** Public goods are collectively owned, divisible and non-excludable, so the policy is that they must be provided for everybody in the economy. Example of public goods is defense. Private goods are the goods that are privately owned, indivisible and excludable. For example: food, book, clothes, houses, motor vehicles etc.

5. ***Liberal and Conservative Policies:*** This is the specification of policies with respect to freedom and ability to influence or change policies. Liberal Policies are the policies that are easily amenable. For example social policies on equality, movement of people, employment, etc. conservative policies are the policies that are rigid or difficult to change. Examples of conservative policies are rigid constitutions and military decrees.

Relevance of Public Policy

- Scientific understanding
- Improves our knowledge of society
- Linkages between social and economic conditions
- Response of political system to those conditions
- Professional advice

Application of knowledge to the solution of practical problems:

- Policy recommendations- To inform political discussion, advance the level of political awareness and improve the quality of public policy.

The Policy-Making Process

The policy-making process is sequential in most respects. It evolves along the following lines: From the initial issue identification and agenda setting, policies are formulated, then policies are adopted. There will be attempts to implement the policy and then finally there will be an effort to examine the results of the policy implementation.

Getting on the agenda can be a difficult process. First an issue needs to be identified as a problem that deserves serious attention from the government. Some theorize that all issues that are recognized as deserving of public attention get on a systematic agenda and issues that are being seriously considered by the policy makers make it onto another agenda, the institutional agenda. Policies that make it to the institutional agenda are much more likely to find their way into legislation. Issues that make it onto the institutional agenda are often advocated by powerful interest groups, supported by the bureaucracy, or propelled by a public crisis.

Once a decision has been made to do something about the issue, alternative policy solutions need to be compared and a decision needs to be made about what sort of solution will be supported. The resulting policy must be acceptable to both the legislators and the public there by this process of building support is called policy legitimation. Once the policy is determined, the implementation process begins. However, few can predict what might go wrong with a new public policy and so the process of policy evaluation is crucial, so that policy makers can determine if the outcome was what they expected.

Policies are developed within a context of public opinion, policy history, ideological conflict, budgetary constraints-resulting in bargaining and trade-offs. Many believe that the creation of policy occurs as a rational process in which issues and problems are identified and approached in a very rational sequence, with the ultimate result being the development of the most appropriate policies. Others believe that the process is more incremental, meaning that policy makers make small policy changes and then adjust policies to reflect the knowledge gained from problems in implementation.

Economic Policy

Economic policy is of vital importance as it affects Americans and citizens of other countries. Much of economic policy deals with the tools that the government uses to manage the economy and solve economic problems. Tools can be divided into several categories. The general category of fiscal policy refers to the use of changes in tax rate and levels of government spending to influence economic productivity. The use of these tools in a systematic fashion is called Keynesian economics. Monetary policy is more closely associated with the work of Milton Friedman and uses the manipulation of the money supply and interest rates as a tool to affect inflation rates. Presidents also have other tools at their disposal such as lowering tariffs and the removal of other types of trade restrictions. Additionally, they can loosen regulatory controls by the government and increase taxes. In view of the burgeoning federal deficits and the federal debt, President Clinton raised taxes and stimulated economic prosperity with relatively low interest rates and removal of trade restrictions. As a result America for a time enjoyed economic prosperity and budget surpluses rather than deficits. Clinton was helped in this endeavor by technological advances and a very conservative Congress. However, an economic turndown began in 2000 and continued into 2001. The attacks of September 11 accelerated this decline. The administration of George W. Bush responded with tax cuts. The Federal Reserve Board cut interest rates. But as the economic recovery grew at the start of 2004, The Federal Reserve Board raised interest rates in response to concerns about increasing inflation. By August of 2005, short term rates were at 3.5 percent and were expected to continue to rise.

Social Welfare Policy

The notion that the government is responsible for the welfare of its citizens is a relatively new idea. Social welfare policy is implemented through many programs designed to improve health, education, housing, employment, and the retirement years. Programs that promote the welfare of citizens are newer in the U.S. than in Europe. The U.S. has a tradition of individualism, and a suspicion of government held off programs designed as "safety nets." With the advent of the Great Depression, the attitudes of Americans changed somewhat and President Roosevelt was able to implement many new programs to prevent economic disaster at the national and individual level. However, we still do not have universal health coverage, which most European democracies provide for their citizens, and the U.S. has a much smaller public welfare system. Welfare systems can be designed to prevent poverty, to alleviate poverty, to punish poverty (with very minimal programs), to cure poverty (trying to eliminate the causes of poverty), or to force individuals to work for government assistance in a form of "incomes approach."

This act fundamentally changed welfare in this country, moving responsibility for welfare programs from the national to the state governments, giving block grants to states to help finance the programs, instituting lifetime limits on total benefits, and requiring work within a two-year period. Americans were unhappy with the welfare system and supported this fundamental change. As a result, welfare rolls decreased significantly and perhaps due to the economic prosperity, poverty did not increase. Even the economic recession of 2000-02 did not increase welfare rolls, although they did decrease at a slower rate.

Public Policy Process

When new public policies are created, there are generally three key things involved in the process: the problem, the player, and the policy. The problem is the issue that needs to be addressed, the player is the individual or group that is influential in forming a plan to address the problem in question, and the policy is the finalized course of action decided upon by the government. Typically the general public will make the government aware of an issue through writing letters and e-mail, or making phone calls, to local government leaders; the issue is then brought forward during government meetings and the process for creating new public policies begins.

The rational model for the public policy-making process can typically be divided into three steps: agenda-setting, option-formulation, and implementation. Within the agenda-setting stage, the agencies and government officials meet to discuss the problem at hand. In the second stage, option-formulation, alternative solutions are considered and final decisions are made regarding the best policy. Consequently, the decided policy is implemented during the final stage; in most cases, once public policies are in place, they are widely open to interpretation by non-governmental players, including those in the private sector. Implied within this model is the fact that the needs of the society are a priority for the players involved in the policy-making process also it is believed that the government will follow through on all decisions made by the final policy.

Unfortunately, those who frame the issue to be addressed by policy often exert an enormous amount of influence over the entire process through their personalities, personal interests, political affiliations, and so on. The bias is extenuated by the players involved. The final outcome of the process, as well as its implementation, is therefore not as effective as that which could result from a purely rational process. Overall, however, public policy continues to be a vital tool in addressing social concerns.

In 1993, due to ineffective health care policies, the Clinton administration in the US sought to implement a policy that would bring about a national health care system. As part of the policies being considered, the US federal government would protect the health care consumer's rights, consumers would be able to form alliances to obtain better healthcare prices, and caregivers would be required to provide fair healthcare packages. Players involved in the policy-making process included lobbying groups and politicians. While some changes were made to healthcare provisions by legislators, the policies advocated by the Clinton administration were not put into effect as result of political differences.

In 2010, US president Barack Obama signed the Affordable Care Act into law; this health care reform and public policy is meant to offer all American citizens health insurance that is easier to afford. The policy implemented several changes in health care that no longer allow health insurance companies to deny coverage to children with pre-existing conditions, nor can they drop coverage when insurance carries become ill. Several years elapsed before the policy was finally passed, and the final stages of the policy are planned to be put in place in 2014.

As an Academic Study

The study of public policy began in 1922, when Charles Merriam, a political scientist, sought to build a link between political theory and its application to reality. Most studies of public policyfocus on areas that apply to problems within government management, administration, and operations; some of these topics include economics, program evaluation, sociology, political economy, and public management. Most college degrees on this topic are offered only as master's or doctorate degrees, and the course of study may vary between universities.

Public Policy Management

Public policy management is the process of working to formulate and influence public policy from the outside. This is a process mainly unique to democratic forms of government, where those in power must answer to a constituency base. While public policy management may not be successful in all cases, those companies and organizations that have a plan are more apt to see positive results for their causes.

A great deal of money may be put into public policy management because so much is at stake. Often, non-profit organizations, and even for-profit companies researching new products, may depend on government grants or other government funding. If not, these companies may try to influence regulatory rules or other barriers in order to make it easier for them to do business. That involves making their views known to a group of legislators.

Before going to legislators, organizations often take the time to come up with a public policy management strategy, which may be the most difficult part of the process. Often, companies may even hire consultants to help them devise a strategy to fit with their particular situation. This policy may be discussed and voted on by an executive team or the board of directors before being implemented.

Most strategies involving public policy management include a multi-pronged effort specifically focused on the legislative and regulatory processes. This means having provisions for monitoring and tracking legislation for changes in rules or laws, researching issues to determine how legislation could affect a person or thing, lobbying in order to make views heard, and possibly even the formation of a political action committee. A comprehensive public policy management strategy could also include meetings and event planning, program management, and strategy formulation.

Some portions of the plan will likely take more time and money than others. For example, lobbying efforts, while they may be done over the phone, by letter or e-mail, often take place in person. This requires transporting individuals to a state or national capital, and paying for time and expenses while there so that they can make a case. Some companies also hire professional lobbyists for this reason.

Public Policy Administration

Public policy administration is the implementation and management of governmental policies, based on expert analysis and the resolution of specific issues that generally have a far-reaching impact on the citizens who live under the government in question. Politicians and policy analysts formulate public policy at the national, regional, and local levels. Citizens are often active players who have an influence on public policy decisions that could be beneficial to their special interests. As a result, public policy administration is, from time to time, seen as a humanistic endeavor.

A rational approach can also be taken when it comes to public policy administration. One example of this can be seen in the United States in 1980s, while President Reagan was in the White House, and later during the first decade of the 21st century, under the George W. Bush administration. With a rational approach, public policy administrators attempt to implement and sustain policy in such a way that it promotes private business and governmental bureaucracy. It might be debated that policies implemented under those presidencies were not actually "public," in the true sense of the word, as they largely ignored the issues of the average man or woman on the street, and especially the poor, who have typically relied heavily on government programs like Medicaid and food stamps. As an example, President Bush went to great lengths to try to get the American public, and policy analysts, to agree with the privatization of Social Security system.

Since the 19th century, public administration theorists have fluctuated between the advocacy of rational and humanistic systems for the formulation and administration of policy. In a seminal article entitled The Study of Administration, published in 1887, future US president Woodrow Wilson advanced ways in which policy framers could best serve citizens, based on scientific managerial practices. He advocated keeping politics and administration as independent areas, since he considered administration to be more of a scientific endeavor.

In fact, public policies are decisions that have been reached through analysis of data, and implemented, ostensibly for the good of the people living under governments, by public policy administrations. Political science, however, has always been considered one of the social sciences, which means it can be affected by human contingencies. While all social scientists use scientific methods, such as the compilation of quantifiable data to reach or replicate certain conclusions, it is possible that, besides the citizens, the key players in public policy administration-the analysts and decision makers-are never really unbiased or neutral in actual practice.

Government and Public Policy

A policy is typically described as a principle or rule to guide decisions and achieve rational outcomes. The term is not normally used to denote what is actually done, this is normally referred to as either procedure or protocol. Policies are generally adopted by the Board of or senior governance body within an organization whereas procedures or protocols would be developed and adopted by senior executive officers. Policies can assist in both subjective and objective decision making. Policies to assist in subjective decision making would usually assist senior management with decisions that must consider the relative merits of a number of factors before making decisions and as a result are often hard to objectively test e.g. work-life balance policy. In contrast policies to assist in objective decision making are usually operational in nature and can be objectively tested e.g. password policy.

A Policy can be considered as a "Statement of Intent" or a "Commitment". For that reason at least, the decision-makers can be held accountable for their "Policy".

The term may apply to government, private sector organizations and groups, and individuals. Presidential executive orders, corporate privacy policies, and parliamentary rules of order are all examples of policy. Policy differs from rules or law. While law can compel or prohibit behaviors policy merely guides actions toward those that are most likely to achieve a desired outcome.

Policy or policy study may also refer to the process of making important organizational decisions, including the identification of different alternatives such as programs or spending priorities, and choosing among them on the basis of the impact they will have. Policies can be understood as political, management, financial, and administrative mechanisms arranged to reach explicit goals. In public corporate finance, a critical accounting policy is a policy for a firm/company or an industry which is considered to have a notably high subjective element, and that has a material impact on the financial statements.

Shaping public policy is a complex and multifaceted process that involves the interplay of numerous individuals and interest groups competing and collaborating to influence policy makers to act in a particular way. These individuals and groups use a variety of tactics and tools to advance their aims, including advocating their positions publicly, attempting to educate supporters and opponents, and mobilizing allies on a particular issue.

As an academic discipline

As an academic discipline, public policy brings in elements of many social science fields and concepts, including economics, sociology, political, program evaluation, policy analysis, and public management, all as applied to problems of governmental administration, management, and operations. At the same time, the study of public policy is distinct from political science or economics, in its focus on the application of theory to practice. While the majority of public policy degrees are master's and doctoral degrees, several universities also offer undergraduate education in public policy.

Classification of Public Policy

Policy addresses the intent of the organization, whether government, business, professional, or voluntary. Policy is intended to affect the 'real' world, by guiding the decisions that are made. Whether they are formally written or not, most organizations have identified policies. Policies may be classified in many different ways.

Distributive policies

Distributive policies extend goods and services to members of an organization, as well as distributing the costs of the goods/services amongst the members of the organization. Examples include government policies that impact spending for welfare, public education, highways, and public safety, or a professional organization's benefits plan.

Regulatory policies

Regulatory policies, or mandates, limit the discretion of individuals and agencies, or otherwise compel certain types of behavior. These policies are generally thought to be best applied when good behavior can be easily defined and bad behavior can be easily regulated and punished through fines or sanctions. An example of a fairly successful public regulatory policy is that of a speed limit.

Constituent policies

Constituent policies create executive power entities, or deal with laws. Constituent policies also deal with fiscal policy in some circumstances.

Miscellaneous policies

Policies are dynamic they are not just static lists of goals or laws. Policy blueprints have to be implemented, often with unexpected results. Social policies are what happens 'on the ground' when they are implemented, as well as what happens at the decision making or legislative stage.

When the term policy is used, it may also refer to:

- Official government policy.
- Broad ideas and goals in political manifestos and pamphlets.
- A company or organization's policy on a particular topic. For example, the equal opportunity policy of a company shows that the company aims to treat all its staff equally.

The actions the organization actually takes may often vary significantly from stated policy. This difference is sometimes caused by political compromise over policy, while in other situations it is caused by lack of policy implementation and enforcement. Implementing policy may have unexpected results, stemming from a policy whose reach extends further than the problem it was originally crafted to address. Additionally, unpredictable results may arise from selective or idiosyncratic enforcement of policy.

Types of policy analysis include:

- Causal
- Deterministic
- Index
- Memory less
- Opportunistic
- Stationary

Types of Public Policy

1. Defense Policy

Defense policy is public policy dealing with international security and the military. It comprises the measures and initiatives that governments do or do not take in relation to decision-making and strategic goals, such as when and how to commit national armed forces.

It is used to ensure retention of independence in national development, and alleviation of hardships imposed from hostile and aggressive external actors.

Purpose of Defense Policy

Defence policy identifies threats of hostility and aggression based on intelligence analysis, and defines military scope of national security, defence alliances, combat readiness, military organisation of national forces and their use of military technology.

The national defence policy defines the national defence strategy, the "when" of committing national armed forces. The national defence policy also defines the strategic posture, the "how", towards any possible threats to national territory, its society, environment, and economy, and defines options available to deal with such threats. The more options a defence policy provides to the government, the better it is considered in its formulation. Strategic posture in turn defines the military doctrine of the armed forces. This doctrine may include confronting threats to national interests located outside of the national territory such as shipping lanes. The defence strategy and military doctrine are developed though strategic policy and capability development processes.

Development of Defense policy

A defence policy is created through the defence policy process of making important organisational decisions, including the identification of priorities and different alternatives such as defence personnel and technology programs or budget priorities, and choosing among them on the basis of the impact they will have on the overall national development. Defence policies can be understood as political, management, financial, administrative and executable mechanisms arranged to reach explicit military goals and objectives.

Applications of Defense policy

Defence policy addresses the achievement of its military goals and objectives by making explicit statements about the desired capability in: combat readiness, military organization, political-military relationships the role of the armed forces, command and control, military intelligence and counterintelligence, defence diplomacy, defence capability in terms of block obsolescence, professionalism and training, recruiting, social change in the military, standing forces, military reserve forces, and conscriptions. Defence policy differs from rules of engagement determine when, where, and how military force is be used by formations and units.

2. Domestic Policy

Domestic policy is an area of public policy which concerns, laws, government programs, and administrative decisions which are directly related to all issues and activity within a nation's borders. It differs from foreign policy, which refers to the ways a government advances its interests in world politics. Domestic policy covers a wide range of areas, including business, education, energy, health care, law enforcement, money and taxes, natural resources, social welfare, and personal rights and freedoms.

Domestic policy decisions usually reflect a nation's history and experience, its social and economic conditions, the needs and priorities of its people, and the nature of its government. Domestic policy is a frequent source of disagreement among people of different backgrounds and philosophies. People who hold conservative beliefs, for instance, will likely stress order, security, and traditional values in domestic policy. People who hold more liberal beliefs, on the other hand, will likely emphasize equality and government efforts to help the needy.

Issues of Defense Policy

Many broad domestic policy issues are similar for nearly all countries of the world. For example, all governments are expected to provide education, law and order, and other basic services for their citizens. However, the specific goals and objectives of domestic policy vary depending on each nation's needs and capabilities. Most wealthy democracies, for instance, spend substantial sums of money on domestic programs. Many poorer countries have difficulty devoting resources to such essential areas as education and health care.

Many domestic policy debates concern the appropriate level of government involvement in economic and social affairs. Traditionally, conservatives believe that the government should not play a major role in regulating business and managing the economy. Most conservatives also believe that government action cannot solve the problems of poverty and economic inequality. Most liberals, however, support government programs that seek to provide economic security, ease human suffering, and reduce inequality. Many liberals also believe that the government should regulate businesses to ensure safe and fair working conditions and to limit environmental pollution.

Certain domestic policy issues are especially controversial among people of different cultures, religions, and personal beliefs. Examples of such issues include abortion rights, the rights of homosexuals, the role of religion in public life, and the place of cultural diversity in education and employment.

Shaping and Implementing

A nation's form of government largely determines how its domestic policy is formed and implemented. Under authoritarian governments, a ruling group may pursue its domestic policy goals without the input or consent of the people being governed. But in democratic societies, the will of the people has a much greater influence.

In a democracy, the formal design of domestic policy is chiefly the responsibility of elected leaders, lawmaking bodies, and specialized government agencies. But a number of other factors also play a role in the process. Voters, for instance, determine which individuals and political parties have the power to determine policy. The mass media distribute information about domestic issues and influence the beliefs and opinions of the people. Lobbyists, activist groups, and other organizations also work to influence policy through a variety of methods. Such methods may include monetary donations, promises of support, advertising campaigns, or demonstrations and protests.

The effectiveness of domestic policy depends on the government bureaucracy that puts laws and programs into action. In some cases, bureaucracies act slowly or inefficiently, or fail to apply policies as they were originally intended. Domestic policy may also face challenges in the courts. In many countries, courts have the power of judicial review, which allows them to strike down any legislative or executive action that they find in violation of the nation's constitution.

3. Economic Policy

Economic policy refers to the actions that governments take in the economic field. It covers the systems for setting interest rates and government budget as well as the market, national, and many other areas of government interventions into the economy. Such policies are often influenced by international institutions like the International Monetary Fund or World Bank as well as political beliefs and the consequent policies of parties.

Types of Economic Policy

Almost any aspect of government has an economic aspect and so many terms are used. A few example of types of economic policy include:

- Macroeconomic stabilization policy tries to keep the money supply growing, but not so quick that it results in excessive inflation.
- Trade policy refers to tariffs, trade agreements and the international institutions that govern them.
- Policies designed to create economic growth
- Policies related to development economics,
- Redistribution of income, property, or wealth
- Regulation
- Anti-trust
- Industrial policy
- Technology-based economic development policy.

4. Education Policy

Education policy refers to the collection of laws and rules that govern the operation of education systems. Education occurs in many forms for many purposes through many institutions. Examples include early childhood education, kindergarten through to 12th grade, two and four year colleges or universities, graduate and professional education, adult education and job training. Therefore, education policy can directly affect the education people engage in at all ages.

Examples of areas subject to debate in education policy, specifically from the field of schools, include school size, class size, school choice, school privatization, tracking, teacher education and certification, teacher pay, teaching methods, curricular content, graduation requirements, school infrastructure investment, and the values that schools are expected to uphold and model.

Education policy analysis is the scholarly study of education policy. It seeks to answer questions about the purpose of education, the objectives that it is designed to attain, the methods for attaining them and the tools for measuring their success or failure. Research intended to inform education policy is carried out in a wide variety of institutions and in many academic disciplines. Important researchers are affiliated with departments of psychology, economics, sociology, and human development, in addition to schools and departments of education or public policy.

5. Energy Policy

Energy policy is the manner in which a given entity has decided to address issues of energy development including energy, distribution and consumption. The attributes of energy policy may include legislation, international treaties, incentives to investment, guidelines for energy conservation, taxation and other public policy techniques. The energy policy of India is characterized by trades between four major drivers:

- Rapidly growing economy with a need for dependable and reliable supply of electricity, gas, and petroleum products.
- Increasing household incomes, with a need for affordable and adequate supply of electricity, and clean cooking fuels.
- Limited domestic reserves of fossil fuels, and the need to import a vast fraction of the gas, crude oil, and petroleum product requirements, and recently the need to import coal as well.
- Indoor, urban and regional environmental impacts, necessitating the need for the adoption of cleaner fuels and cleaner technologies.

6. Environmental Policy

Environmental policy is any action deliberately taken to manage human activities with a view to prevent, reduce, or mitigate harmful effects on nature and natural resources, and ensuring that man-made changes to the environment do not have harmful effects on humans.

Definition

It is useful to consider that environmental policy comprises two major terms: environment and policy. Environment primarily refers to the ecological dimension but can also take account of social dimension (quality of life) and an economic dimension (resource management). Policy can be defined as a "course of action or principle adopted or proposed by a government, party, business or individual". Thus, environmental policy focuses on problems arising from human impact on the environment, which retracts onto human society by having a impact on human values such as good health or the 'clean and green' environment.

Environmental issues generally addressed by environmental policy include air and water pollution, waste management, ecosystem management, biodiversity protection, and the protection of natural resources, wildlife and endangered species. Relatively recently, environmental policy has also attended to the communication of environmental issues.

Rationale

The rationale for governmental involvement in the environment is market failure in the form of externalities, including the free rider problem and the tragedy of the commons. An example of an externality is a factory that engages in water pollution in a river. The cost of such action is paid by society-at-large, when they must clean the water before drinking it and is external to the costs of the factory. The free rider problem is when the private marginal cost of taking action to protect the environment is greater than the private marginal benefit, but the social marginal cost is less than the social marginal benefit. The tragedy of the commons is the problem that, because no one person owns the commons, each individual has an incentive to utilize common resources as much as possible. Without governmental involvement, the commons is overused. Examples of tragedies of the common are overfishing and overgrazing.

Instruments, Problems, and Issues

Environmental policy instruments are tools used by governments to implement their environmental policies. Governments may use a number of different types of instruments. For example, economic incentives and market-based instruments such as taxes and tax exemptions, tradable permits, and fees can be very effective to encourage compliance with environmental policy.

Voluntary measures, such as bilateral agreements negotiated between the government and private firms and commitments made by firms independent of government pressure, are other instruments used in environmental policy. Another instrument is the implementation of greener public purchasing programs.

Often, several instruments are combined in an instrument mix formulated to address a certain environmental problem. Since environmental issues often have many different aspects, several policy instruments may be needed to adequately address each one. Furthermore, instrument mixes may allow firms greater flexibility in finding ways to comply with government policy while reducing the uncertainty in the cost of doing so. However, instrument mixes must be carefully formulated so that the individual measures within them do not undermine each other or create a rigid and cost-ineffective compliance framework. Also, overlapping instruments lead to unnecessary administrative costs, making implementation of environmental policies more costly than necessary.

7. Foreign Policy

A country's foreign policy, also called the foreign relations policy, consists of self-interest strategies chosen by the state to safeguard its national interests and to achieve its goals within international relations milieu. The approaches are strategically employed to interact with other countries. In recent times, due to the deepening level of globalization and transnational activities, the states will also have to interact with non-state actors. The aforementioned interaction is evaluated and monitored in attempts to maximize benefits of multilateral international cooperation. Since the national interests are paramount, foreign policies are designed by the government through high-level decision making processes. National interests accomplishment can occur as a result of peaceful cooperation with other nations, or through exploitation. Usually, creating foreign policy is the job of the head of government and the foreign minister.

The sub-discipline that specializes in relations is known as foreign policy analysis . FPA contributes to overall communication between nations. A country's international policy, called the international relations policy, consists of strategies chosen by the state to safeguard its national interests and to achieve its goals in international relations. The approaches are strategically employed to interact with other countries. In recent times, due to the deepening level of globalization and transnational activities, the states will also have to interact with non-state actors. The aforementioned interaction is evaluated and monitored in attempts to maximize benefits of multilateral international cooperation. Since the national interests are paramount, foreign policies are designed by the government through high-level decision making processes. National interests accomplishment can occur as a result of peaceful cooperation with other nations, or through exploitation, usually creating foreign policy is the job of the head of government and the foreign minister.

8. Health Policy

Health policy can be defined as the "decisions, plans, and actions that are undertaken to achieve specific health care goals within a society." According to the World Health Organization, an explicit health policy can achieve several things: it defines a vision for the future; it outlines priorities and the expected roles of different groups; and it builds consensus and informs people.

There are many categories of health policies, including personal health care policy, pharmaceutical policy, and policies related to public health such as vaccination policy, tobacco control policy or breast feeding promotion policy. They may cover topics of financing and delivery of health care, access to care, quality of care, and health equity.

There are also many topics in the politics and evidence that can influence the decision of a government, private sector business or other group to adopt a specific policy. Evidence-based policy relies on the use of science and rigorous studies such as randomized controlled trials to identify programs and practices capable of improving policy relevant outcomes. Most political debates surround personal health care policies, especially those that seek to reform health care delivery, and can typically be categorized as either philosophical or economic. Philosophical debates center around questions about individual rights, ethics and government authority, while economic topics include how to maximize the efficiency of health care delivery and minimize costs.

The modern concept of health care involves access to medical professionals from various fields as well as medical technology, such as medications and surgical equipment's. It also involves access to the latest information and evidence from research, including medical research and health services research.

In many countries it is left to the individual to gain access to health care goods and services by paying for them directly as out-of-pocket expenses, and to private sector players in the medical and pharmaceutical industries to develop research. Planning and production of health human resources is distributed among labour market participants.

Other countries have an explicit policy to ensure and support access for all of its citizens, to fund health research, and to plan for adequate numbers, distribution and quality of health workers to meet health care goals. Many governments around the world have established universal health care, which takes the burden of health care expenses off of private businesses or individuals through pooling of financial risk. There are a variety of arguments for and against universal health care and related health policies. Health care is an important part of health systems and therefore it often accounts for one of the largest areas of spending for both governments and individuals all over the world. For example, medical debt is now a leading cause of personal bankruptcy in the United States.

Need and Features of Business Policy

Business Policy defines the scope or spheres within which decisions can be taken by the subordinates in an organization. It permits the lower level management to deal with the problems and issues without consulting top level management every time for decisions. Business policies are the guidelines developed by an organization to govern its actions. They define the limits within which decisions must be made. Business policy also deals with acquisition of resources with which organizational goals can be achieved. Business policy is the study of the roles and responsibilities of top level management, the significant issues affecting organizational success and the decisions affecting organization in long-run.

Features of Business Policy

An effective business policy must have following features:

- ***Specific:*** Policy should be specific/definite. If it is uncertain, then the implementation will become difficult.
- ***Clear:*** Policy must be unambiguous. It should avoid use of jargons and connotations. There should be no misunderstandings in following the policy.
- ***Reliable/Uniform:*** Policy must be uniform enough so that it can be efficiently followed by the subordinates.
- ***Appropriate:*** Policy should be appropriate to the present organizational goal.
- ***Simple:*** A policy should be simple and easily understood by all in the organization.
- ***Inclusive/Comprehensive:*** In order to have a wide scope, a policy must be comprehensive.
- ***Flexible:*** Policy should be flexible in operation/application. This does not imply that a policy should be altered always, but it should be wide in scope so as to ensure that the line managers use them in repetitive/routine scenarios.
- ***Stable:*** Policy should be stable else it will lead to indecisiveness and uncertainty in minds of those who look into it for guidance.

Difference between Policy and Strategy

- The term "policy" should not be considered as synonymous to the term "strategy". The difference between policy and strategy can be summarized as follows-
- Policy is a blueprint of the organizational activities which are repetitive/routine in nature. While strategy is concerned with those organizational decisions which have not been dealt/faced before in same form.
- Policy formulation is responsibility of top level management. While strategy formulation is basically done by middle level management.
- Policy deals with routine/daily activities essential for effective and efficient running of an organization. While strategy deals with strategic decisions.
- Policy is concerned with both thought and actions. While strategy is concerned mostly with action.
- A policy is what is, or what is not done. While a strategy is the methodology used to achieve a target as prescribed by a policy.

Elements of Public Policy

A public policy is an action by a government that affects public welfare. It Includes:

- Laws

- Rules and regulations (FDA)
- Programs (welfare, Medicare) and practices
- Specific policy changes
- At international, national, state, and local levels

Examples:

- Health and safety
- Poverty and welfare (Medicare/Medicaid)
- Crime (gun control)
- Education (no child left behind)
- Transportation (gas mileage for cars, air bags)
- Environment (Kyoto protocol, global warming)
- Foreign Policy (Iraq)

Corporate and Public Policy

In addition to being a socially responsible firm, a firm's social responsiveness is also of interest. Generally, companies react to issues after they have been brought to light. Critics argue that this kind of responsiveness does not do much, and that instead, corporations should have policies in place that identify their views on issues and willingness to stand behind those views. This is known as corporate public policy.

Corporations are increasingly considering the stakeholder model of social responsibility. The debate is how expansive the list of stakeholders should be and the corporation's duties to those stakeholders. Satisfying only primary stakeholders is not enough.

Public Policy

Public policy is the process by which society recognizes and manages its problems and goals. Businesses, like society, must also be aware of, react to, and take part in this process. Companies should develop and follow public policy.

Planning and Implementing Corporate Public Policy

The adoption of a corporate public policy agenda generally involves five steps. The first step is to constantly scan the environment to predict how social trends will change and to be ready with policies regarding the trend. The second step is to assess organizational assets, meaning that once social trends have been identified, the company must figure out how it can address that trend and whether it has the ability to do so with its current assets. The third step is to set the policy. Top-level management must devote the time to review steps 1 and 2 to set a policy. The fourth step is to implement the policy by appointing an officer or committee to achieve this goal. The fifth step is to measure the results of the public policy to see whether the policy is a success or if adjustments must be made.

Framing of Public Policy

Public policy is created by legislation. It is generally defined as principles or standards regarded by legislature, or the courts, as being of fundamental concern to the state and the whole of society. Public policy is based on the principle, "a person should not be allowed to do anything that would tend to injure or damage the public at large. "Public policies are regulatory measures that can apply to the government, the private sector, organizations/groups, etc.

I. What is Public Policy?

Public Policy is what governments decide. These decisions are codified in the form of laws, of executive agreements, orders, and actions, and of Supreme Court decisions. It consists of established rules, procedures and practices.

Policies are not necessarily the same as laws. Rather it is more a matter of how the laws are implemented. For example, the law may state that the speed limit is 55 miles per hour. If, however, the state police never stop anyone unless their speed exceeds 65 miles per hour, then public policy is really 65 miles per hour because no penalty is imposed as long as drivers stay under the speed.

II. How is Public Policy Formed?

Policy is formulated with active involvement on the part of interest groups whose members do not seek election. These groups bring together leaders and experts to define and discuss a problem and to reach consensus on policies addressing the problem. Some groups will lobby on a particular issue while others will provide research and training on issues. The Brooking Institute, the Heritage Foundation, the American Enterprise Institute and the Committee on Economic Development are some of the more notable of the privately funded groups who actively seek to influence public policy in the United States.

III. Terms

Interest group. An organized group with shared interests that works on behalf of a particular cause in order to influence the government to adopt certain policies or measures without its members seeking to be elected. Also called pressure group.

Lobbyist a person acting on her own or with corporate backing to achieve the goals of an interest group is called a lobbyist. The term lobbyist also has an official definition whereby lobbyists are required to register and disclose information about such efforts. The term advocacy group or interest group can be used even for groups that are not officially registered as lobbying concerns.

Political Action Group ("PAC"). A private group organized to elect or defeat government officials in order to promote legislation supporting its interests. Federal laws limit the amount that federal PACs can contribute to other organizations, for example, $5,000 per candidate per election and $15,000 per political party per year.

Public policy think tank. An organization that sponsors research on specific problems and/or provides advice and ideas on how to improve government policies or create alternatives. Public policy think tanks are typically closely involved with the academic and scholarly world (especially at universities) where many of the ideas that change politics are generated.

Iron Triangle. A tight policy-making circle resulting from a close alliance and mutually beneficial relationship between the legislature, government agencies, and special interest groups

Levels of Public Policy

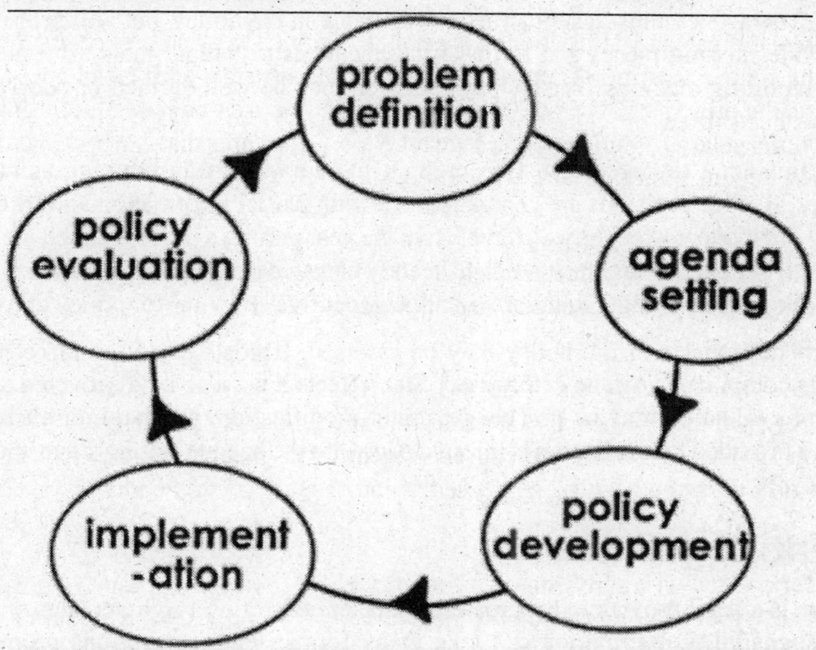

The policy cycle has thus been cast as steps that display the sequential flow depicted by Jones's approach to public policy:

1. ***Agenda setting:*** Problems are defined and issues are raised. Gate keepers filter out those which well be given attention by either the executive or the legislative branches.

2. ***Formulation:*** Analysis and politics determines how the agenda item is translated into an authoritative decision: a law, rule or regulation, administrative order, or resolution. There are two steps in policy formulation:

   (i) Alternative policy proposals are put forth, claiming rationality and technical analysis within the process. Policy analysts bring these alternatives to the attention of political decision makers with their recommendations.

   (ii) The policy prescription is chosen among the alternatives, including the no-action option. This is usually accomplished by building the support of a majority. What is produced here is a binding decision or series of decisions by elected or appointed officials who are not necessarily experts but who are presumably accountable to the public.

3. ***Implementation:*** The authorized policy must be administered and enforced by an agency of government. The agency must take instructions as stated in the policy, but will probably be called upon to provide missing pieces and to make judgments as to intent, goals, timetables, program design, and reporting methods. The agency's mission may be well defined or poorly understood, but the action has shifted.

4. ***Budgeting:*** Financial resources must be brought to bear within an ongoing annual stream of budget cycles. Budget decisions are generally made with partial information and by changes from year to year which are only slightly different from the year before, a process called incrementalism. In recent years, budget constraints have significantly elevated budget considerations in importance within the policy cycle. Budget items are highly competitive and vital for policy delivery.

5. ***Evaluation:*** The impacts of the policy may be assessed. If goals exist, the effectiveness of the policy and its components can be determined. Side-effects must also be discovered and reckoned. The output of evaluation may be no change, minor modification. overhaul, or even termination. The feedback provided by evaluation is injected back into the agenda setting stage, thus closing the loop of the cycle.

Government Regulation

A regulation is a legal provision that creates, limits, or constrains a right, creates or limits a duty, or allocates a responsibility. Regulation can take many forms: legal restrictions promulgated by a government authority, contractual obligations that bind many parties, self-regulation by an industry such as through a trade association, social regulation, co-regulation, or market regulation. One can consider regulation as actions of conduct imposing sanctions, such as a fine, to the extent permitted by the law of the land.

Regulation mandated by a state attempts to produce outcomes which might not otherwise occur, produce or prevent outcomes in different places to what might otherwise occur, or produce or prevent outcomes in different time scales than would otherwise occur. In this way, regulations can be seen as implementation artifacts of policy statements. Common examples of regulation include controls on market entries, prices, wages, development approvals, pollution effects, employment for certain people in certain industries, standards of production for certain goods, the military forces and services. The economics of imposing or removing regulations relating to markets is analysed in regulatory economics.

Reasons for Regulation

Regulations, like any other form of coercive action, have costs as well as benefits. Efficient regulations can be defined as those where total benefits exceed total costs.

Regulations can be justified for a variety of reasons, including:

- Market failures - regulation due to inefficiency. Intervention due to a classical economics argument to market failure.
- Risk of monopoly
- Collective action, or public good
- Inadequate information

- Unseen externalities
- Collective desires - regulation about collective desires or considered judgments on the part of a significant segment of society
- Diverse experiences - regulation with a view of eliminating or enhancing opportunities for the formation of diverse preferences and beliefs
- Social subordination - regulation aimed to increase or reduce social subordination of various social groups
- Endogenous preferences - regulation's purpose is to affect the development of certain preferences on an aggregate level
- Irreversibility - regulation that deals with the problem of irreversibility – the problem in which a certain type of conduct from current generations results in outcomes from which future generations may not recover from at all.
- Professional conduct - the regulation of members of professional bodies, either acting under statutory or contractual powers.
- Interest group transfers - regulation that results from efforts by self-interest groups to redistribute wealth in their favor, which may be disguised as one or more of the justifications above.

Government Controls and Regulations

Since independence, Government of India introduced a number of controls and regulations so as to lead the country on the path of progress. Originally these controls and regulations were considered to be a part of development strategy. But subsequently, they emerged as the need of the society. While the 1948 Industrial policy resolution did not lay much emphasis on the controls and regulations, in 1951 the government brought in the Industrial Development and Regulations Act. This Act made licensing a part of industrial development. The objectives of licensing were stated as:

- Facilitate desired pattern of industrial development.
- Provide for development of backward regions.
- To encourage broad based ownership of industries.
- To prevent concentration of power in the hands of a few.
- To offer protective environment for the small scale industries.
- To regulate inflow of foreign capital and technology.
- To provide for the use of appropriate technology.
- To eliminate industrial pollution.
- To encourage more of exports and adopt import substitution measures.
- To ensure conservation of foreign exchange resources and to ensure proper allocation of the exchange resources.
- To achieve high growth in employment opportunities.

With the above objectives, the government passed the Act. Consequent to this Act, the following categories of industries were required to obtain license:

- New undertaking
- Manufacture of new article
- Expansion of existing capacity substantially
- Continuation of certain category of business in certain areas
- Changing the location of the industry

This licensing policy continued for a long time till 1991 Industrial policy adopted the policy of liberalization. The licensing policy has resulted in a number of malpractices among the large industrial houses. This was brought to light by the Dutt Committee report in 1967 The revelations of the Dutt committee led to the enactment of Monopolies and Restrictive Trade Practices Act in 1970. In 1991, the government changed the contents of the Licensing policy and the important provisions are spelt out hereunder.

Industrial Licencing Policy

To achieve the objectives of the strategy of the industrial sector in the 90's a number of changes in the system of industrial approvals have been brought about. The domestic producers will be able to withstand the competition in the country as well as abroad only through procedural reforms. Hence, the role of government will be changed from that of exercising control to one of providing help and guidance. Changes in the policy towards public sector in the last few years have clearly indicated that private sector enterprises will be allowed to compete in many areas hitherto earmarked for public sector. Consequently, the new policy has completely reclassified the Indian industries as below:

Eight industries have been completely reserved for the public sector. They are: (i) Arms and ammunition and allied items of defence equipment, defence aircraft and warships, (ii) atomic energy, (iii) coal and lignite, (iv) mineral oils, (v) mining of iron ore, manganese ore, chrome ore, gypsum, sulphur, gold and diamond, (vi) mining of copper, lead, zinc, tin, molybdenum and wolfram, (vii). Mineral specified in Schedule to the Atomic Energy Order, 1953 and (viii) railway transport.

Eighteen industries have been listed as industries which require compulsory licensing. However, this provision would not apply in respect of the small scale units taking up the manufacture of any of the items reserved for exclusive manufacturing in small scale sector. Compulsory licensing would be required in the following industries:

i. Coal and lignite,

ii. Petroleum other than crude and its distillation products,

iii. Distillation and brewing of alcoholic drinks,

iv. Sugar,

v. Animal fats and oils,

vi. Cigars and cigarettes of tobacco and manufactured tobacco substitutes,

vii. Asbestos and asbestos based products,

viii. Plywood, decorative veneers and other wood based products such as particle board, medium density fibre board, block board,

ix. Raw" hides and skins, leather, chamois leather and patent leather,

x. Tanned or dressed fur skins,

xi. Motor cars,

xii. Paper and newsprint except bagasse based units,

xiii. Electronic aerospace and Defence equipment of all types,

xiv. Industrial explosives,

xv. Hazardous chemicals,

xvi. Drugs and pharmaceutical

xvii. Entertainment electronics and

xviii. White goods like domestic refrigerators.

As regards the provisions of the industrial licensing policy,

i) Industrial licensing has been completely abolished for all projects except for the industries classified above, i.e., the area reserved for public sector ,and the list of 18 industries and the areas reserved for small scale industries will continue.

ii) Public sector will continue to maintain monopoly in industries coming under the areas of security and strategic considerations.

iii) In projects where imported capital goods are required, automatic clearance will be given provided the foreign exchange availability is ensured through foreign equity. Or alternatively if the value of imported goods does 1101 exceed 25% of the total value of plant and equipment subject to the ceiling of Rs. 2 crores, automatic clearance will be given. However, this would come into effect only from April, 1992 in view of the current balance of payments position. In all the other cases, the prior approval and clearance from the Secretariat of Industrial approvals in the Department of Industrial development will be required.

iv) Except the list of industries requiring compulsory licensing, the other industries will not require any approval from the Central government for their location in ares other than cities of more than one million population. In cities with more than one million population, non-polluting industries like electronics, computer software and printing will be permitted outside 25 kms. of the periphery. If such cities require industrial re-generation policies will be made more flexible. However, the existing zoning and land use regulation and environmental legislation will continue to regulate industrial locations. All efforts will be made through incentives and other methods like infrastructural development, to disperse the industry to rural and backward areas.

v) New Broad banding facility will be provided to the existing units so as to enable them to produce any article without additional investment. The exemption from licensing will be applicable to all substantial expansion of existing units.

vi) The mandatory convertibility clause will no longer be applicable for term loans from the financial institutions for new projects.

vii) A very significant step is to abolish all the existing registration schemes.

viii) In case of substantial expansions and new projects, it is enough if the entrepreneurs file the information memorandum.

ix) The list of industries requiring compulsory licensing and industries for automatic approval of foreign technology agreements will be notified in the Indian Trade Classification (Harmonized system).

As a result of the wide changes in the Licensing policy, the government also brought about changes in the MRTP Act.

MRTP ACT

A major deviant of the new policy is in respect of the MRTP Act. The new policy aim at removing the unnecessary bureaucratic controls and allow the industries to breathe in an atmosphere of freedom. The efforts of the government in the past intervening in the investment decisions of the MRTP companies; have been proved to be counter-productive. Hence, the newly empowered MRTP Commission will enquire into complaints received from individual consumers or classes of consumers. The following is the essence of the provisions in the new policy regarding MRTP Act.

i. The limits of assets in respect of the MRTP companies and dominant undertakings have been removed and suitable amendment in the MRTP Act will be made in due course.

ii. The need to obtain the prior approval of the central government for establishing new units, expansion of existing units, merger, amalgamation and take over as well as appointment of Directors have all been removed.

iii. The MRTP Act will be used only for controlling and regulating monopolistic, restrictive and unfair tarde practices. As a follow-up the MRTP Commission will be authorized to inquire suo moto or complaints lodged by individual consumers or classes of consumers regarding monopolistic, restrictive and unfair trade practices.

iv. All the necessary amendments will be made in the MRTP Act to give more punitive and compensatory powers to the MRTP Commission.

Control of capital issues

Since independence, capital issues in India have gone through different types of control mechanism. Initially control of Stock exchanges was contemplated and accordingly Securities Contracts [Regulation] Act was passed in 1956. It aimed at centralization of control, regulation of the stock exchanges and the transactions entered therein, the avoidance of illegitimate and manipulative speculation and the protection of genuine investors, The Act applied to all transactions whether forward or ready and it prohibited or regulated factors, which facilitated speculation in stock exchanges. But the Act could not abolish forward trading which ultimately caused erratic behavior of the Stock exchange. The government basically depended on two institutions to control the capital market viz., the Controller of Capital Issues [CCI] and the Directorate of Stock Exchanges. CCI gave consent to the issue of non-government companies consisting of equity and preference shares, partly and fully convertible debentures, bonus shares and right shares. It also gave consent to the issue of bonds of public sector undertakings. But on the recommendations of the Narasimham committee, the government abolished the office of CCI and freed the primary capitol market from the government regulations.

The recommendations of Narasimham Committee – II on financial sector reforms

The main recommendations of the Narasimham committee are:

1. Phased reduction of Statutory Liquidity Ratio to 25 % over a period of five years.
2. Progressive reduction in Cash Reserve Ratio.
3. Phasing out of directed credit programs and redefinition of the priority sector.
4. Deregulation of interest rates so as to reflect emerging market conditions.
5. Stipulation of minimum capital adequacy ratio of 4% to risk weighted assets by March 1993, 8% by March 1996 and 8% by those banks having international operations by March, 1994.
6. Adoption of uniform accounting practices in regard to income recognition, asset classification and provisioning against bad and doubtful debts.
7. Imparting transparency to bank balance sheets and making full disclosures.
8. Setting up of special tribunals to speed up the process of recovery of loans.
9. Setting up of Asset Reconstruction Fund to lake over from banks a portion of their bad and doubtful advances at a discount.
10. Restructuring of the Banking system so as to have three or four large banks which could become international in character, 8 to 10 national banks and local banks confined to specific regions and rural banks including RRBs confining to rural areas.
11. Setting up one or more rural banking subsidiaries by public sector banks.
12. Permitting RRBs to engage in all types of Banking business.
13. Abolition of branch licensing.
14. Liberalising the policy with regard to allowing foreign banks to open offices in India.
15. Rationalisation of foreign operations of Indian banks.
16. Giving freedom to individual banks to recruit officers.
17. Inspection by supervisory authorities based essentially on the internal audit and inspection reports
18. Ending duality of control over Banking system by Banking division and RBI.
19. A separate authority for supervision of banks and financial institutions which would be a semi-autonomous body under RBI.
20. A revised procedure for selection of Chief Executives and Directors on Boards of Public Sector banks.
21. Segregation of direct lending functions of IDBI to a separate institution.
22. Obtaining resources from the market on competitive terms by DFIS.
23. Speedy liberalization of capital market by removing restrictions on premia dispensing with prior government approval etc.
24. Supervision of merchant banks, mutual funds, leasing companies, etc., by separate agency to be

set up by RBI and enactment of separate legislation providing appropriate framework for mutual funds and laying down prudential norms for such institutions.

After the abolition of CCI, the government set up the Securities and Exchange Board of India (SEBI) in 1988 which became a statutory body since 1992. SEBI has the following objectives:

- Regulating the business in stock markets and other securities market
- Registering and regulating the working of the stock brokers, sub-brokers, share transfer agents, bankers to an issue, trustees of trust deeds, registrars to an issue, merchant bankers, bankers to an issue, trustees of trust deeds, registrars to an issue, merchant bankers, underwriters, portfolio managers and other intermediaries associated with the securities market
- Registering and regulating the working of collective investment schemes including mutual funds
- Promoting and regulating the self regulatory organizations
- Prohibiting fraudulent and unfair trade practices relating to securities market
- Promoting investors education and training of intermediaries of Securities market
- Prohibiting inside trading in Securities
- Regulating substantial acquisition of shares and take over of companies
- Performing such functions and exercising such powers under the provisions of Capital Issues Control Act, 1947, and Securities Contract Regulation Act, 1956, as may be delegated to it by the Central government

Since its inception, SEBI has achieved the following: guidelines to suing companies, regulation of portfolio management services, regulation of mutual funds, action for delays in transfers and refunds, action for delays in transfers and refunds, issue of guidelines to protect investors, ensuring proper functioning of the Stock exchanges, regulation of foreign institutional investors and periodical review of the working of the capital market.

FOREIGN CAPITAL AND THE POLICY OF GOVERNMENT REGARDING THE USE OF FOREIGN CAPITAL

Foreign capital or investment has become significant part of sources of funding for various projects in every country. This source of funding has received the attention of both the government as well as the corporate sector that there has been increasing reliance on this source for planning and execution of projects by the government as well as the corporate sector. Foreign capital can come into a country in different forms. Let us first understand these forms of foreign capital before discussing the need for foreign capital.

Forms of foreign capital:

(a) Direct entrepreneurial investment: In this form of foreign capital, the foreign investors can start a company abroad mainly for the purpose of establishing its branches and subsidiaries in other countries. For instance an American business group may invest in a new project in India directly and start its own affiliate or branch or even a subsidiary. Sometimes, the investors abroad may participate in the stocks or share capital of Indian companies. Whenever the Indian companies go for public issue of shares or debentures, the foreign investors may respond by participating in such public issue. This is also called foreign capital. In the past external business group used to invest in new companies and that form of foreign capital used to flow much, but now-a-days participation in the equity or debenture of companies by foreign investors and non-resident Indians is becoming more predominant.

(b) Foreign collaboration: Foreign collaboration is another form of foreign capital. Under this a domestic company may join with the foreign company, mostly the reputed one in the industry, and start with the joint operation in India. Usually this type of effort is undertaken to get the state of the art or the latest technology available abroad in the Indian companies. Foreign collaboration may be only for technology or for funding or both. Accordingly we may have technical collaboration, financial collaboration or mixed collaboration. The collaboration may be between private parties or companies in the two countries, or the foreign company with Indian Government or between the foreign government and the Indian government.

(c) Inter-government loans: This type of foreign capital refers to the loans granted by the government of one country to that of the other for a specific purpose or for general economic reconstruction. For example under the Marshall plan, USA gave loans to various European governments to help them in the reconstruction of their war-shattered economies. The developed countries also grant loans and grants to the under developed countries to help them in economic development programme.

(d) Loans from international institutions: This source of foreign capital has emerged as a very important source in the recent years. Most of the developing countries get sizeable quantum of funds from this source. International institutions like International Monetary Fund (IMF), International Bank for Reconstruction and Development (IBRD), Asian Development Bank, Aid India Consortium, and others have all become very important providers of funds for developing countries. The role of IMF and IBRD in tiding over the balance of payment difficulties and execution of power and irrigation projects, cannot be exaggerated. The Asian Development, Bank has also been a major provider of funds for development in Indian case.

(e) External commercial borrowing: Another source of foreign capital is the borrowing in the capital market of other countries. This can be done either directly or indirectly by the government. In both ways, the inter-government understanding and political relationship apart from the domestic investment climate are all important. Such capital is normally used for international trade purposes and specifically for export credits. Agencies like US EXIM bank, Japanese EXIM bank, ECGC of UK, etc., are all playing vital role in this segment of foreign capital.

Need for Foreign Capital

No country can be self-sufficient today. Even developed countries have to depend on the developing countries for certain purposes and also for marketing their products. Further the specialisation in finance has become world wide, that every investor wants to maximise return on his investments and minimize the risk. This is applicable both to government investment as well as corporate and private investments. These are days of multi-national corporations and giants that closed economic system can no longer be realistic. In this situation, flow of capital from one country to another in different forms takes place for several reasons. From the view point of a country, there is a need to execute their plans for economic development. Specifically in Indian case, the need for foreign capital cannot be exaggerated. This could be explained in terms of the points given below:

(a) The availability of funds for execution of plans and achieve rapid economic development determine the objective of such plans. Domestic availability of funds, especially in the developing countries is becoming difficult with the government in these countries undertaking increasing responsibility for the welfare activities. Hence, these countries have to tap the source lying outside to get the funds required for their development purposes. In this respect the foreign capital should be attracted at any cost and in any form.

(b) Domestic investors and managers of funds available, may not have the required expertise or entrepreneurship in identifying the right and profitable avenues for investment. This may be due to lack of experience or inability to identify opportunities. When foreign capital is allowed to flow, the benefits of the experience of the foreign technicians, finance specialists, production specialists, marketing wizards, etc., are made available to the domestic ventures. This will improve the efficiency of the domestic projects which is directly benefitting the country. On this count foreign capital should be welcomed.

(c) One of the basic requirements for achieving rapid economic development is mobilizing savings. Savings depend upon income and income depends on the level of economic activity. Hence, any attempt to increase savings should start with attempts for increasing income which necessitates increasing investment If the domestic rate of savings and the purpose for which savings is used is unproductive, then efforts should be made to obtain the necessary investment from abroad. This would accelerate economic development leading to income generation and increased savings. Hence, in the process of economic development foreign capital becomes an essential ingredient.

(d) Foreign capital is necessary for one more reason. In every developing country, the economic development requires investment in certain projects relating to infrastructural development, basic industries, etc., which are long gestation projects, low income yielding, but accelerating economic development. No private investment or corporate investment in these projects will come about in the early stage of development either because the investors have no inclination or because the capital market in such a situation is not developed. But the government has to initiate development activities, for which foreign capital becomes essential. Once the 'economic engine' is activated, in due course, the economic development will start taking place. Until then foreign capital is needed.

(e) Foreign capital can be in different forms as has been already explained. Countries like India having high rate of savings, but low investment in productive projects, with large human force but with less employment opportunities, have to seek technical know-how and technology available abroad. These can be slightly modified to suit the domestic conditions so that the production can take place in large scale, cost can be minimized and employment opportunities can be generated in large scale. Further there are areas like atomic energy, automobile industry, management, marketing and others where we do not have the best of experts or expertise. The best available talent or technology available abroad can be imported so that we can improve our strength in these areas and become a force to reckon with. This will also help us to achieve higher level of economic development.

(f) One of the methods of achieving higher levels of development is through mutual co-operation with other countries through bi-lateral or multi-lateral agreements which provide excellent scope for transfer of technology, etc., between countries. Political wisdom warrants use of such agreements for mutual benefits which leads to flow of foreign capital from one country to another.

Problems of Foreign Capital

So far we have discussed the need for and role of foreign capital in Indian economic development. Let us now study the problems that are associated with the foreign capital.

1. The foreign investors are choosy in extending their funds to projects floated in our country. It is found that foreign capital flows easily towards the private sector projects but with a lot of hesitation to the projects of public sector. While there is justification for hesitant flow towards public sector, our government has been giving pride of place only to pubic sector in achieving rapid economic development Hence, it is clear that there is no lack of investment opportunities, but there is difference in ideology. Therefore, flow of foreign capital is not uniform to all sectors. This trend has to be observed so that corrective measures can be taken to attract more foreign capital to public sector projects.

2. Another serious problem of foreign capital is the domestic technology is simply duplicated due to over indulgence and dependence on external assistance. There are several areas where India has achieved excellence as in electronics industry, but there are collaborations with foreign products in this field. Such duplication is in no way beneficial to the country. This has to be corrected.

3. One more experience is that under the pretext of transferring technology, foreign countries simply Jump their obsolete technology in India. Apart from importing inappropriate technology, there are also situations when the technology not required is imported. Further, there are tie-up agreements with such imported technology which are unfavourable to India. But such agreements have been approved much against the interest of our domestic manufacturers and technologists.

4. Often me complaint about foreign capital is the restrictive conditions imposed by the exporting country. It may be relate to spares or technicians or repatriation of profits, etc. An increasing number of such agreements would only be against our own interest

5. Heavy remittance of profits, dividends, etc., is yet another problem under foreign capital. In Indian experience, there were cases when the inflow of foreign capital was less than the remittance of profits, the classic examples being ESSO and CALTEX, the two oil companies of US origin. Such remittances cause severe strain on our already strained balance of payments and foreign exchange reserve position. Even if the agreement provides for such remittances, the country cannot afford to lose the hard earned foreign exchange resources under this type of remittances.

6. One more consequence of foreign capital is that it causes serious balance of payments problem. When foreign capital in different forms is permitted, with the preference of the foreign investors, the private sector is able to attract more than the public sector. As a result the private sector indulges in importing heavily their requirements which results in heavy outflow of earned exchange reserves on the one hand and leads to balance of payments deficits on the other. Even if the government has to ultimately approve of such imports, yet the private sector is able to appease the officials through liaison officers and get the necessary approvals.

7. One of the essential conditions laid by the government while approving the foreign collaboration is that in due course there should be Indianisation of personnel. This policy is easily defeated in practice. In the past under the provisions of Foreign Exchange Regulations Act, every foreign multinational company is made to dilute their ownership to 74% and in case of branches of foreign companies their total holding should not exceed 40%. It is found that these foreign companies

have very high profitability, as in the case of Colgate Palmolive with 89% of profit rate, are able to very easily raise capital from the Indian capital market. Their shares are being quoted at very high rate that they raise the necessary funds easily. The shareholders of these companies indirectly support the company through political lobbying. The Indianisation of personnel is easily by-passed as these companies retain the powers to appoint their own Chairmen and Managing Directors. Obviously even with a holding of only 26% of the shares, these foreign companies have control over the companies easily by-passing the policy. Whenever the multinationals become Indian companies they stand to gain. So long they remain multinationals they are subjected to heavy taxes. But once our Indianisation of Personnel policy is invoked, these multinationals become Indian companies and pay less tax. Hence, our policy is in no way affecting the foreign companies, in tact, the policy is turning out to be unfavorable to India itself

Government Policy

Since independence, the government has been declaring its policy towards foreign capital of different types. The policy declared in April, 1949 has remained the main framework for the subsequent policies. The salient features of the 1949 policy are:

(i) Foreign capital will have the same treatment as given to domestic capital.

(ii) The investors will be allowed to remit the profits earned.

(iii) The ownership and control of the foreign companies should in due course be in the hands of Indians.

(iv) In case of take over of the undertaking, a fair and equitable compensation would be paid.

(v) In case a foreign company wants to have control for some time, the government may examine this in each individual case before giving permission.

This policy in nut shell means that there will be no discrimination against the foreign companies or their investments in India. This remained as the basic framework of foreign policy all through. With this policy, the government pursued its foreign policy making minor changes at times. Broadly we may refer to three phases through which our foreign policy relating to foreign capital and investments evolved. In the first phase which lasted from 1951 to 1965, the government was liberal in its attitude towards foreign capital. This included concessions and incentives to foreign capital which helped us to achieve industrial development. The second phase which started from 1965, is a period in which the government was very strict and imposed several restrictions and regulations. Once again in Phase III, starting from 1991, a liberal policy is introduced. The salient features of the latest policy towards foreign capital (1991 is given below:

Foreign Investments

Foreign investments carry with it the benefit of technology transfer, marketing expertise, modern managerial techniques and new possibilities for promotion of exports. As this requirement is felt in this world of industrial change and co-operation, the New Industrial Policy (NIP) has clearly contained the following provisions relating to foreign investments:

1. In high priority industries approval will be given for direct foreign investment upto 51% foreign equity and all the bottlenecks in this process will be removed. Clearance in such cases will be given

if the foreign equity covers the foreign exchange requirements for imported capital goods. The necessary amendments to the FERA will be made.

2. The general policies governing the domestic units in regard to import of components, raw materials and intermediate goods and payment of knowhow fees and royalties will also be applicable to the high priority industries in which foreign investment is limited to 51% However, the payment of royalty will be routed through the RBI to enable it to monitor the outflow of foreign exchange on payments are balanced by export earnings over period of time.

3. All the other foreign investments not included in the category 1 stated above will require prior clearance.

4. Trading companies primarily export oriented will also be permitted under the foreign equity proposals as indicated in 1 above. However, the provisions of his export-import policy applicable to the domestic units will also be applicable to such trading companies.

5. To encourage substantial inflow of foreign investment, a Special Empowered Board would be constituted. This Board would negotiate with the large international firms and approve direct foreign investment in select areas. This is expected to fetch foreign technology and open the industries in India to wider world market. Such investments will be subjected to favourable treatment based on the merits irrespective of the rules, regulations and procedures in practice.

As regards foreign technology agreement, a welcome change in the outlook of the government is the realization that the sophisticated technology from abroad can be brought in only through liberal and less restrictive procedures and policies. The interference of the government in this regard is to be reduced so as to enable the domestic industries in achieving a high rate of industrialization. As a result of this liberalization, automatic approval for technology agreements related to high priority industries will be made with respect to certain specific parameters. Other industries which can enter into such agreements without incurring the expenditure of foreign exchange will also be extended liberal treatment. The industrialists are left to themselves to decide and enter into foreign technology agreements depending upon the commercial viability of their enterprises. In due course this measure is expected to pave the way for exchange of superior technology from India with other countries. With the overall liberalization, the competition will be high and it is expected that industries will invest much more in research and development activities. Keeping in view all these expectations, the government has announced the following changes in regulation governing foreign technology agreement:

1. No prior permission is needed for hiring foreign technicians, foreign testing of indigenously developed technologies. Such activities involving payments will be governed by the guideline of the RBI and such payments can be made through blanket permits.

2. Automatic permission will be given for foreign technology agreements, relating to the high priority industries. The royalty payments through such agreements will be subjected to certain provisions. Up to the payment of Rs. 1 crore royalty will be at the rate of 5% for domestic sales and 8% for foreign sales or exports. However, the total royalty payment should not exceed 8% of the sales over a 10 year period from the date of agreement or 7 year period from the date of commencement of production.

3. In case of industries not covered in the high priority list automatic permission will be given for technology agreement provided it does not entail any foreign exchange payment commitment.

4. In all the other cases, the general procedures in practice will be adhered to and such industries will require specific approval.

Foreign assistance and Indian five year plans

In the Table given below we find that the external assistance is playing a vital role in the financing of our five year plans. Right from the I Five Year Plan, we find that in absolute terms the inflow of foreign assistance is very much on the increase. While it was a modest figure of Rs. 190 crores in the I Plan, it was Rs. 15,139 crores by VII Plan and during the VIII Plan it rose to nearly Rs. 28,700 crores. Hence, it is clear that the external assistance or foreign capital has become a major component of financing of Indian five year plans. In terms of percentage, the external assistance went up from a mere 9.6 in the I Plan to 28.2 in the III Plan, 35.9 during the Annual plans. From the IV Plan onwards, the percentage of external assistance declined from 13 to 8.2% during the VIII Plan, but this decline should not be misunderstood as declining importance of external assistance in the financing of our five year plans. The table given below will clarify this aspect

FOREIGN ASSISTANCE AND INDIAN FIVE YEAR PLANS

PLAN	AMOUNT (Rs.crores)	Percentage
FIRST	190	10
SECOND	1,090	24
THIRD	2,390	28
FOURTH	2,090	13
FIFTH	5,830	15
SIXTH	10,930	11
SEVENTH	15,139	8.4
EIGHTH	28,700	8.2

Policy on FDI

The government policies on Foreign Direct Investment [FDI] have been changing since 1991 - 92. Analysis of these policies would help to place in proper perspective the prospects and problems of FDI. This was also taken into consideration while suggesting methods of improving the inflows of FDI.

As apart of the structural adjustment policies introduced in the Indian economy by Government of India since July 1991, policies relating to foreign financial participation in Indian companies and those relating to foreign technology agreements have also undergone a radical charge. Briefly stated, three tiers for approving proposals for foreign direct investment in this country were introduced: (1) the Reserve Bank's automatic approval system; (2) Secretariat for Industrial Approvals for considering proposals within the general policy framework but outside the powers delegated to Reserve Bank; and (3) Foreign. Investment Promotion Board, specially created to invite, negotiate and facilitate substantial investment by international companies that would provide access to high technology and world markets.

The foreign investment policy was further liberalized during the period under review. Fully owned foreign enterprises will hence forth be allowed to set up giant power projects without the requirement to balance dividend payments with export earnings.

The general permission granted by the Reserve Bank under the provision of.: the Foreign Exchange Regulation Act, 1973 has brought the FERA companies (i.e. those having more than 40% foreign equity) on par with the Indian companies and thus provides a level playing field to all. The existing FERA companies have also been extended the facility of 51% equity. Also, the use of foreign brand names and trademarks on goods for sale within the country has been permitted. Significant amendments to the FERA for relaxing several of its restrictive provision have been contemplated.

The following measures were introduced in the recent period to further liberalise the foreign investment policy:

1. Except for 22 industries in the consumer goods sector, the earlier stipulation that dividend remittances of companies receiving approval under the foreign equity up to 51% scheme, must be balanced by export earnings over a period of 7 years, was scrapped in respect of all foreign direct investment (by non -NRIs) in June 1992. The measure was extended to investment by NRIs /Overseas Corporate Bodies (OCBs) in September 1992.

2. For the purpose of investment in oil refineries and development of discovered oil fields, foreign private equity participation to the extent of 26 per cent is considered as sufficient. For making investment in Indian companies, NRIs/OCBs have been granted automatic approval by the RBI to invest, with full repatriation benefits, up to 100% in the issue of capital or convertible debentures of a private/public limited company engaged in or proposing to engage in high priority industries, subject to certain conditions.

The existing scheme of 100% NRI investment in cent per cent export oriented units and also for the revival of sick units will continue cent per cent NRI participation in power generation has also been permitted. In the context of such revisions, the earlier 74% scheme has been discontinued.

The Government has set up a Bureau, officially known as the Interface for NRI Scientists and Technocrats (INRIST), that will bring NRI scientists and technocrats in contact with Indian industries which would benefit from the expertise of NRIs.

The Department of Industrial Development has set up an "investment promotion and project monitoring cell" popularly known as facilitation ceil, to provide pre and post investment services for different industrial approvals and respond to queries relating to various ministries / departments.

RBI has granted general permission to foreign citizens of Indian origin, whether resident in India or not, to acquire / hold and transfer by scale or inheritance, residential properties situated in India subject to certain stipulations.

General permission has been granted to Non-resident Indian citizens and foreign citizen of Indian origin to let out their residential properties acquired for their bonafide residential purpose but which on account of their residence abroad, are not required for their immediate residential purpose. The rental income or proceeds of any such income shall both be repatriable outside India at any time in future and such funds should be credited to the owner's Ordinary Non Resident Rupee account maintained with an authorized bank in India.

In order to simplify and remove regulations which hinder free flow of foreign capital in to India as also investment by Indian companies in joint venture overseas, restriction imposed on FERA companies (i.e, companies incorporated in India in which the non-resident interest is more than 40%) under sec 26 (7), 28, 29, and 31 of FREA, 1973 have all been removed as outlined below, there by placing them on par with other Indian companies in regard to their operations in India. FERA companies are now permitted.

a. To borrow money or accept deposits from persons resident in India.

b. To accept appointment as agent or technical or management advisers in India, of any person or company.

c. To allow their trademarks to be used by any person or company.

d. To carry on in India any activity of trading, commercial, or industrial nature except agricultural and plantation activity.

e. To acquire any undertaking in India carrying on any trade, commerce or industry or purchase the shares of any such company, and

f. To acquire, hold, transfer or dispose of by sale, mortgage, lease, gift, settlement or otherwise any improvable property in India.

Person of Indian nationality or origin and others (returning home after a minimum stay of immediate preceding 6 months abroad) have been granted general permission to bring into India as part of their baggage, gold, in any form, up to 5000 gms, provided duty is paid at the rate of Rs. 220 / per 100 gms. (earlier Rs, 450/- per 10 gms) in any convertible foreign currency (I).

As part of the continuing efforts to provide an investment friendly environment in India for foreign investors, the following policy initiative were undertaken during the year 1992-93.

(i) To keep pace with the ever expanding global technological revolution in the field of computers, an Electronic Hardware Technology Park (EHTP) scheme was set up allowing for 100% equity participation, duty free import of capital goods and a tax holiday i.e. exemption from corporate income tax for block of 5 years commencing from the date of the starting of commercial production.

(ii) In the new National mineral policy, the ceiling on foreign .equity participation in Indian companies engaged in mining activities was hiked to 50%. In the area of non-captive mines, equity participation of over 50% by foreign partners could be considered on a case by case basis.

(iii) Authorized dealers were delegated powers to allow remittance of dividend (including interim dividend) on equity/preference shares to non-resident shareholders of all Indian companies, as also those in which investments have been made by NRIs/OCBs under the 40% scheme or any other scheme with repatriation benefits.

(iv) NRIs were allowed to invest up to 100% on non-repatriation basis, in any partnership/proprietorship concern or in private/public limited companies (expect in agricultural/plantation activities) without seeking prior approvals of other RBI. However, OCBs are not permitted to invest-In proprietorship/ partnership concerns

In keeping with the objective of attracting funds from the NRIs in the form of deposit and foreign investment several steps were taken during the year 1993 -94, such inflows, even while adhering to considerations of cost effectiveness and dampening of volatility. Major policy initiatives undertaken during th : year were as follows:

(I) Deposits Under Foreign Currency Non Resident Account (FNCRA) scheme proved to be volatile during the payments crisis, of 1990-92. They were also relatively costly given the spread above international interest in the prescription of interest rates for these deposits as also the cost implicit in the provision of exchange guarantee for such deposits. In this regard, the Bank's Annual Report for 1992-93 had observed: "attempts have been made in the recent period to restructure the existing FCNRA scheme and to put in place new schemes which (a) reduce the reliance on the FCNRA scheme, (b) make exchange risk cover a commercial proposition, and (c) reduce volatile components of deposits under the existing FCNRA scheme." In pursuance of this objective deposits of four different maturities i.e. "6 months and above but less than one year", one year and above but less than two years" two years and above but less than three years," and three years only" were completely withdrawn effective from May 15,1993, Oct. 12,;993, Feb 15, 1994 and August 15, 1994 respectively. Furthermore, interest rates prescribed on FCNRA of various maturities were fine-tuned from time to time to secure alignment with movements in international interest rates. Interest rates on Non Resident (External) Rupee Accounts (NR (E) R) deposits were also revised downwards effective Oct 18,1994 while the interest rate on savings deposits was brought down from 5% to 4.5% those on term deposits are not allowed to exceed 8%.

(II) In consonance with the move toward full convertibility in the current account, the interest accruing on deposits under Non Resident (Non - Repatriable) Rupee Deposits (NR (NR) RD) was rendered eligible for repatriation effective from Oct 1, 1994. The principal amount under the scheme will continue to be non-repatriable

(III) The Foreign Currency Ordinary Non-repatriable (FCON) scheme, introduced in June J991, under which the principal as well as interest earned were not repatriable, was suspended with effect from August 20, 1994. Interest accruing on the existing FCON-scheme from the quarter beginning Oct 1, 1994 was however made eligible for repatriation.

(IV) With a considerable improvement in the external payments position and the level of reserves, it was considered necessary to follow a restrictive policy towards Foreign Currency Convertible Bonds (FCCBs) as they constitute a part of the country's external debt till their conversion in to equity. As per the fresh guidelines of the government (issued on May 11. 1994) for Euro issues, companies were allowed to issue FCCBS only on merits as a part of the external debt restructuring programme which was intended to lengthen maturity and soften terms.

(V) Under the automatic approval scheme for foreign investments, new guidelines were issued for determining issue price of preferential shares issued 10 foreign investors to increase their stakes up to 51% in the business of any Indian company engaged in the high priority industries shown in the Annex-Ill to the statement on industrial policy of July 24, 1991.

Consequent upon the abolition of the office of the Controller of Capital Issues (CCI) and subsequent guidelines issued by the Securities and Exchange Board of India (SEBI) on June 11 and 17,1992, existing companies wishing to raise foreign equity were to make the issue at a price decided by the shareholders in a special resolution. In certain proposal received from the existing companies for enhancement of foreign equity, however, the companies were found to be issuing foreign equities at a large discount to the market price, (set out in the last year's Report). This mismatch in the price of shares for investment and disinvestment could cause distortion in the inflows and outflows of foreign exchange under the head of foreign investment.

With the objective of preventing a few shareholders from getting substantial and undue enrichment and unearned gains, to ensure higher foreign equity flows, and to make both investment and dis-investments market-related, It was decided with effect from August 4, 1994 that preferential allotment of shares by companies must be at market related price applicable to all foreign investment proposals whether approved by the RBI or by the SIA / FIPB subject to the following, guidelines:

The issue price of shares under preferential allotment (other than allotment on rights basis), would have to be at the market value of the shares determined on the basis of their average price during the immediate preceding six months at the main listing center calculated on the monthly average of the high and low rates quoted for the shares at such centres. In the absence of a market price, however, (as in the case of Unlisted companies, Listed companies, where shares are not regularly traded, etc) the RBI would be guided by the net asset value and earnings per share.

(VI) Indian companies engaged in or proposing to engage in housing and real estate development, i.e. (1) development of serviced plots and construction of built-up residential premises, (2) real estate covering construction of residential and commercial premises including business centers and offices, (3) development of townships, (4) city and region level urban infrastructure facilities including roads and bridges, (5) manufacturing of building materials and (6) financing of housing development were allowed to issue shares/convertible debentures to NRIs up to 100% of the new issue on repatriation basis. Repatriation of original investment in such cases would be permitted by the RBI only after a lock in period of three years from the date of issues of shares/debentures.

The above facilities which were not available to OCBs, have now been extended to them on the same terms and conditions as applicable to NRIs

VII) NRIs/OCBs were so far permitted to invest in schemes of domestic Mutual Funds floated by public sector banks/financial institutions on non-repatriation basis. With a view to providing further incentives to NRIs/OCBs to invest in domestic Mutual Funds, they were permitted to invest on repatriation basis also. As a new policy measure, such investments were also permitted to be made through secondary market.

(VIII) Under the Oct 1993 guidelines for issue of bonds by Public Sector Undertaking (PSUs). Government have allowed PSUs to issue bonds under its public issues to NRIs / OCBs through prospectus by private placement with the facility of repatriation of both principal and interest on the bonds. No limit, however has been specified for NRI / OCB investments in such bonds.

(IX) Besides the various investment facilities extended to NRIs / OCBs on repatriation basis and under various non repatriable schemes, the NRIs / OCBs were permitted to make investment in partnership/ proprietorship concern, shares, debentures of Indian companies, Indian mutual funds floated by public sector banks/financial Institutions, deposits with Indian companies, real estate, etc. Neither the investment/deposit amount nor the income/interest thereon, was eligible for repatriation. Further, the investment/deposits held in India by Indian nationals who have become non-residents on account of their going abroad on employment/immigration, as well as income/interest earned on such investment / deposits was not allowed earlier to be repatriated abroad.

The income /interest on such investment / deposits are, however, now permitted to be repatriated in a phased manner over a period of three years, as indicated below:

(i) Income accruing during 1994-95 and thereafter to the extent of US Si000 per annum is remittable with immediate effect (b) income earned over and above US $1000 in a year would be allowed to be remitted as follows:-

One third of the annual income earned during the financial year 1994-95, (2) Two third of the annual income earned during 1995-96 and (3) the entire amount earned during 1996-97 and onwards Remittance of such income, However would be allowed only after the payments of tax as per the provision of the Income Tax Act (3).

With a view to opening more areas for investment by NRIs / OCBs RBI has decided to allow them to invest, on a repatriation basis, in all activities except agriculture and plantation activities, subject to certain conditions during 1994 -95. Accordingly, existing or new Indian companies (both private and public limited companies) engaged/proposing to engage in any activity including financial, hire purchase leasing, trading other services etc. (except agricultural/plantation activities) are allowed to issue equity shares/convertible debenture's on repatriation basis to NRIs/OCBs provided the aggregate allocation of shares/ convertible debentures qualifying for repatriation benefits to such non-residing investors does not exceed 24% of the new issue. Earlier NRIs and OCBs were permitted to invest on a repatriations basis in new issues of shares/convertible debentures made by companies engaged in industrial or manufacturing activities and also in certain other sectors such as hotels, hospitals, shipping development of computer software and oil exploration. It has also been decided to permit authorized dealers to grant loans to NRIs holding Indian passports for acquisition of a house / fiats for residential purpose against security of immovable property proposed to be acquired by them subject to certain conditions.

(ii) As a process of further liberalization , general permission has been granted to NRIs/OCBs to purchase the shares on repatriation basis of Public Sector Enterprise (PSES) dis-invested by Central Government subject to the condition that (a) the holding of share by a NRI or by an OCB, at any-time, does not exceed one percent of the paid-up capital of the PSE concerned, (b) the purchase consideration/bid money is received by way of remittance from abroad through normal banking channels.

(iii) NRIs resident in Nepal will be permitted hence forth to make investment in India provided the funds for the purpose are remitted in free foreign exchange through proper banking channels. Such investments will either be on repatriation or on non-repatriation basis depending on the terms and conditions applicable under the existing schemes under NRI investment.

(iv) In the context of on going economic liberalization, the policy and procedures governing approvals under the schemes for 100% Export Oriented Units (EOUS) and Export processing Zones (EPZs) were further revised. All proposals conforming to the parameters presented vide press note No 13 (1991) series dated Oct 9,1991, Department of Industrial Development, Ministry of Industry, shall receive automatic approval within two weeks from Secretariat of Industrial Approvals (SIA), Ministry of Industry (Department of Industrial Development) in the case of 100% EOUs and from the Developments Commissioners (DCs) concerned for units to be set up in EPZs. All other proposals which do not conform to the parameters for automatic approvals, shall be considered by the Board of Approvals (BOA) and disposed within 45 days from SIA.

(v) Under the National Telecom Policy, 1994 which enunciates the guidelines for the entry of private sector into Basic Telecom Services, joint venture between an Indian and a foreign company is allowed subject to a maximum of 49% equity participation from the latter.

(vi) It has been decided that foreign investment up to 51% and foreign technology agreements in the cast of bulk drugs, their intermediates and formulations thereof (except those produced by the use of recombinant DNA technology) will be granted automatic approval subject to the parameter of RBI.

Since the second half of 1993-94, the Indian economy has experienced surges in capital flows which took the forms of foreign investment flows both direct and portfolio, and inflows into various deposit schemes for non-resident Indians. With current account deficits remaining modest during 1993-94 and 1994-95, the policy response to the capital flows was accommodative and this enabled on unprecedented build up of international reserves. With the consequent attenuation of monetary targets threatening the objective of inflation control, the policy stance switched to one of throwing sand in the wheels in the second half of 1994-95. Various measures put in place were progressively tightened during the first half of 1995-96 in support of the conduct of monetary policy. With the widening of the current account deficit and the onset of volatility in the foreign exchange markets in the second half of 1995-96, the restrictive stance of policy was eased and a number of measures were taken to relax controls and allow for a larger inflow of foreign capital. As in the past, these measures were related to foreign investment flows and deposits by NRIs and the policy objective of attracting capital flows has been carried forward during the first half of 1996-97.

Policy changes in 1996 - 97 were: Under the Automatic route, the ceiling for lump sum payments of technical know-how fee was, increased from Rs.1 crore to US $ 2 million, effective Nov 5,1996. With a view to liberalizing the existing facility for investments by NRIs in India, it was decided to allow investments by NRIs to establish schools and colleges in India subject to certain regulations. With a view to expanding the coverage of investment proposals considered under the Automatic Approval Route effective Jan 17,1997, the Government announced the inclusion in Annexure III of the statement of Industrial Policy 1991 (i) 3 categories of industries / items relating to mining activities for foreign equity up to 50% (II) 13 additional categories of industries/items for foreign equity up to 51% and (III) 9 categories of industries / items for foreign equity up to 74%.

Foreign Direct Investment was allowed into sixteen non-banking financial services (merchant banking, underwriting, portfolio management services, investments advisory services, financial consultancy, stock brooking, asset management, venture capital, custodial services, factoring, credit refinance, credit rating, leasing and finance, housing finance, forex holding and credit card services) during the year 1997 98, through the Foreign Investment Promotion Board (FIPB) subject to guidelines relating to minimum capitalization norms, schedule of capitalization and domestic equity participation. In a major drive to simplify procedures for foreign direct investment under "automatic" route, the Reserve Bank dispensed with the need for its prior approval for such proposals. In order to simplify procedures further in respect to foreign direct investment cases already approved by the Government of India (SIA/FIPB), the Reserve Bank dispensed with requirement for its "in-principle" permission before receiving overseas investment or for issuing shares to foreign investors. Indian companies satisfying the conditions stipulated in the letter of approvals issued by SIA / FIPB could issue shares / securities to foreign investors and file one copy of the application together with required documents with the concerned Regional office of Reserve Bank within 30 days from the date of issue of shares. Expanding the scope of "automatic route" for foreign direct investments, the government of India approved 13 additional categories of industries / items under services sector for foreign equity participation up to 51% of the equity, three items relating to mining activity up to 50% foreign equity participation and nine categories of industries/activities up to 74% foreign equity participation.

As a part of liberalization process, Reserve Bank of India decided to permit foreign banks operating in India to remit their profits surplus to their head offices without the approvals of the Reserve Bank. The permission is subject to the banks complying with the provisions of Banking Regulation act, 1949.

Financial turmoil in the world economy, imposition of economic sanctions and sluggishness in domestic activity had some bearings on foreign investment during the year. The Union Budget, 1999-2000 announced the establishment of Foreign Investment Implementation Authority [FIIA] in order to rationalize and simplify approval and implementation procedures of foreign investment proposals. With a view to further facilitating inflows of foreign direct investment, expansion of automatic list of approvals and a more dynamic role for Foreign Investment Promotion Board were also announced.

Foreign investment recovered during 1999 - 2000 reflecting the stability of the domestic currency, broad-based industrial revival, easing of economic sanctions and return of orderliness in the financial markets coupled with strong stock market performance.

A number of policy initiatives were taken during the year to further facilitate inflows of foreign investment. In August 1999, a Foreign Investment, Implementation Authority (FIIA) was established for speedy conversion of approvals to actual flows. The Insurance Regulatory and Development Act (IRDA) was passed in December 1999 permitting foreign equity participation in domestic private insurance companies up to 26% of the paid-up capital. Moreover, investments in all sectors, except for small negative list, were placed, in February 2000, under automatic route for direct investments. Indian companies were allowed, subject to specified norms, to raise funds for investments through issue of ADRs / GDRs without prior government approval and up to 50% of these proceeds were allowed for acquisition of companies in overseas markets. Indian companies could acquire companies engaged in information technology and entertainment software, pharmaceuticals and bio - technology in the overseas market through stock - swap options up to $ 100 m on automatic basis or ten times the export earnings during the preceding financial year as reflected in the audited balance sheet, whichever is lower.

FDI is seen as a means to supplement domestic investment for achieving a higher level of economic growth and development. FDI benefits domestic industry as well as the Indian, consumers by providing opportunities for technological up-gradation, access to global managerial skills and practices, optimal utilization of human and natural resources, making Indian industry internationally competitive, opening up export markets, providing backward and forward linkages and access to international quality goods and services. Towards this end, the FDI policy has been constantly reviewed, and necessary steps have been taken to make India a most favourable destination for FDI. The major initiative taken to attract FDI during 2000 -2001 and 2001 - 2002 are as follows:

- In pursuance of Government's commitment to further facilitate Indian industry to engage unhindered in various activities, Government has permitted, except for a small negative list, access to the automatic route for FDI, whereby, foreign investors only need to inform the Reserve Bank of India within 30 days of bringing in their investment, and again within 30 days of issuing any shares.
- Non-Banking Financial Companies (NBFCs) may hold foreign equity up to 100% if these are holding companies.
- Foreign investors can set up 103% operating subsidiaries (without any restriction on number of subsidiaries) without the condition to disinvest a minimum of 25% of its equity to Indian entities, subject to brining in US $50 m out of which US $ 7.5 m to be brought upfront and the balance in 24 months. Joint venture operating NBFCs that have 75% or less than 75% foreign investment will also be allowed to set up subsidiaries for undertaking other Non Banking Financial Company activities, subject to the subsidiaries also complying with the applicable minimum capital inflow.

- FDI up to 49% from all sources is permitted in the private banking sector on the automatic route subject to conformity with RBI guidelines.
- In the process of liberalization of FDI policy, the following policy changes have been made:

  (i) 100% FDI permitted for B, to B e-commerce

  (ii) Condition of dividend balancing on 22 consumer items removed forthwith

  (iii) Removal of cap on foreign investment in the Power Sector

  (iv) 100% FDI permitted in oil-refining.
- Automatic Route is available to proposals in the Information and Technology Sector, even when the applicant company has a previous joint venture or technology transfer - agreement in the same field. Automatic Route of FDI up to 100% is allowed in all manufacturing activities in Special Economic Zones (SEZs), except for the following activities:

  (i) Arms and ammunition, explosives and allied items of defence equipment, defence aircraft and warships;

  (ii) Atomic substances;

  (iii) Narcotics and Psychotropic substances and hazardous chemicals;

  (iv) Distillation and brewing of alcoholic drinks;

  (v) Cigarettes/cigars and manufactured tobacco substitutes.
- FDI up to 100% is allowed with some conditions for the following activities in Telecom Sector:

  (i) ISPs not providing gateways (both for satellite and submarine cables);

  (ii) Infrastructure Providers providing dark fiber (IP Category I);

  (iii) Electronic Mail;

  (iv) Voice Mail.
- FDI up to 74% is permitted for the following telecom services subject to licensing and security requirements (proposals with beyond 49% shall require prior Government approval): (i) internet services providers with gateways; (ii) Radio Paging; and (iii) End-to-end bandwidth.
- Payment of royalty up to 2% on exports and 1% on domestic sales is allowed under automatic route on use of trademarks and brand name of the foreign collaborator without technology transfer. Payment of royalty up to 8% on exports and 5% on domestic sales by wholly owned subsidiaries to offshore parent companies is allowed under the automatic route without any restriction on the duration of royalty payments.
- Offshore Venture Capital Funds/Companies are allowed to invest in domestic venture capital undertakings as well as other companies through automatic route, subject only to SEBI regulations and sector specific caps on FDI.
- FDI up to 26% is eligible under Automatic Route in the Insurance sector, as prescribed in the Insurance Act, 1999, subject to their obtaining licence from Insurance Regulatory and Development Authority.

- FDI up to 100% is permitted in airports, with FDI above 74% requiring prior approval of the Government.
- FDI up to 100% is permitted with prior approval of the Government in courier services subject to existing laws and exclusion of activities relating to distribution of letters. FDI up to 100% is permitted with prior approval of the Government, for development of integrated township, including housing, commercial premises, hotels, resorts, city and regional level urban infrastructure facilities such as roads and bridges, mass rapid transit systems, and manufacture of building material in all metros, including associated commercial development of real estate. Development of land and providing allied infrastructure will form an integral part of township's development.
- FDI up to 100% is permitted on the automatic route in hotel and tourism sector and for Mass Rapid Transit Systems in all metropolitan cities, including associated commercial development of real estate. FDI up to 100% in drugs and Pharmaceuticals (excluding those, which attract compulsory licensing or produced by recombinant DNA technology and specific cell/tissue targeted formulations) placed on the automatic route.
- The Defence industry sector is opened up to 100 per cent for Indian private sector participation with FDI permitted up to 26 per cent, both subject to licensing.
- International Financial Institutions like Asian Development Bank, International Financial Corporation, Commonwealth Development Corporation, German Investment and Development Company (DEG) etc., are allowed to invest in domestic companies through the automatic route, subject to Securities and Exchange Board of India/Reserve Bank of India Guidelines and sector specific caps on FDI (10).

FDI policies for the year 1998 - 1999

Financial turmoil in the world economy, imposition of economic sanctions and sluggishness in domestic activity had some bearings on foreign investment during the year. The Union Budget, 1999 - 2000 announced the establishment of Foreign Investment Implementation Authority [FIIA] in order to rationalize and simplify approval and implementation procedures of foreign investment proposals. With a view to further facilitating inflows of foreign direct investment, expansion of automatic list of approvals and a more dynamic role for Foreign Investment Promotion Board were also announced.

FDI policies for the year 1999 - 2000

Foreign investment recovered during 1999 - 2000 reflecting the stability of the domestic currency, broad-based industrial revival, easing of economic sanctions and return of orderliness in the financial markets coupled with strong stock market performance.

A number of policy initiatives were taken during the year to further facilitate inflows of foreign investment. In August 1999, a Foreign Investment Implementation Authority (FIIA) was established for speedy conversion of approvals to actual flows. The Insurance Regulatory and Development Act (IRDA) was passed in December 1999 permitting foreign equity participation in domestic private insurance companies up to 26% of the paid up capital. Moreover, investments in all sectors, except for a small negative list, were placed, in February 2000, under automatic route for direct investments. Indian companies were allowed, subject to specified norms, to raise funds for investments through issue of ADRs/GDRs without prior government approval and up to 50% of these proceeds were allowed for acquisition of companies in overseas markets. Indian companies could acquire companies engaged in information technology and entertainment software, pharmaceuticals and bio-technology in the overseas market through stock - swap options up to $ 100 m on automatic basis or ten times the export earnings during the preceding financial year as reflected in the audited, balance sheet, whichever is lower.

FDI Policies For The Year 2000 - 2001

FDI is seen as a means to supplement domestic investment for achieving a higher level of economic growth and development FDI benefits domestic industry as well as the Indian consumers by providing opportunities for technological up-gradation, access to global managerial skills and practices, optimal utilization of human and natural resources, making Indian industry internationally competitive, opening up export markets, providing backward and forward linkages and access to international quality goods and services. Towards this end, the FDI policy has been constantly reviewed, and necessary steps have been taken to make India a most favourable destination for FDI.

The major initiative taken to attract FDI during 2000 -2001 and 2001 - 2002 are as follows:

- In pursuance of Government's commitment to further facilitate Indian industry to engage unhindered in various activities, Government has permitted, except for a small negative list, access to the automatic route for FDI, whereby, foreign investors only need to inform the Reserve Bank of India within 30 days of bringing in their investment, and again within 30 days of issuing any shares.
- Non-Banking Financial Companies (NBFCs) may hold foreign equity up 100% if these are holding companies.
- Foreign investors can set up 100% operating subsidiaries (without any restriction on number of subsidiaries) without the condition to disinvest a minimum of 25% of its equity to Indian entities, subject to bringing in US $50 m out of which US $ 7.5 m to be brought upfront and the balance in 24 months. Joint venture operating NBFCs that have 75% or less than 75% foreign investment will also be allowed to set up subsidiaries for undertaking other Non Banking Financial: Company activities, subject to the subsidiaries also complying with the 3, applicable minimum capital inflow.
- FDI up to 49% from all sources is permitted in the private banking sector on the automatic route subject to conformity with RBI guidelines.
- In the process of liberalization of FDI policy, the following policy changes have, been made:

  (i) 100% FDI permitted for B to B e-commerce

  (ii) Condition of dividend balancing on 22 consumer items removed forthwith

  (iii) Removal of cap on foreign investment in the Power Sector

  (iv) 100% FD permitted in oil-refining.
- Automatic Route is available to proposals in the Information and Technology Sector, even when the applicant company has a previous joint venture or technology transfer agreement in the same field. Automatic Route of FDI up to 100% is allowed in all manufacturing activities in Special Economic Zones (SEZs), except for the following activities:

  (v) Arms and ammunition, explosives and allied items of defence equipment, defence aircraft and warships;

(vi) Atomic substances; mi

(vii) Narcotics and Psychotropic substances and hazardous chemicals;

(viii) Distillation and brewing of alcoholic drinks;

(ix) Cigarettes/cigars and manufactured tobacco substitutes.

- FDI up to 100% is allowed with some conditions for the following activities in Telecom Sector:
- FDI up to 74% is permitted for the following telecom services subject to licensing and security requirements (proposals with beyond 49% shall require prior Government approval): (i) internet services providers with gateways; (ii) Radio Paging; and (iii) End-to-end bandwidth.
- Payment of royalty up to 2% on exports and 1% on domestic sales is allowed under automatic route on use of trademarks and brand name of the foreign collaborator without technology transfer. Payment of royalty up to 8% on exports and 5% on domestic sales by wholly owned subsidiaries lo offshore parent companies is allowed under the automatic route without any restriction on the duration of royalty payments.
- Offshore Venture Capital Funds/Companies are allowed to invest in domestic venture capital undertakings as well as other companies through automatic route, subject only to SEBI regulations and sector specific caps on FDI.
- FDI up to 26% is eligible under Automatic Route in the Insurance sector, as prescribed, in the Insurance Act, 1999, subject to their obtaining licence from Insurance Regulatory & Development Authority.
- FDI up to 100% is permitted in airports, with FDI above 74% requiring prior approval of the Government.
- FDI up to 100% is permitted with prior approval of the Government in courier services subject to existing -laws and exclusion of activities relating to distribution of letters, FDI up to 100% is permitted with prior approval of the Government, for development of integrated township, including housing, commercial premises, hotels, resorts, city and regional level urban infrastructure facilities such as roads and bridges, mass rapid transit systems, and manufacture of building material in all metres, including associated commercial development of real estate. Development of land and providing allied infrastructure will form an integral part of township's development.
- FDI up to 100% is permitted on the automatic route in hotel and tourism sector and for Mass Rapid Transit Systems in all metropolitan cities, including associated commercial development of real estate. FDI up to 100% in drugs and Pharmaceuticals (excluding those, which attract compulsory licensing or produced by recombinant DNA technology and specific cell/tissue targeted formulations) placed on the automatic route.
- The defence industry sector is opened up to 100 per cent for Indian private sector participation with FDI permitted up to 26 per cent, both subject to licensing.
- International Financial Institutions like Asian Development Bank, International Financial Corporation, Commonwealth Development Corporation, German Investment and Development Company (DEG) etc., are allowed to invest in I domestic companies through the automatic route, subject to Securities and Exchange Board of India / Reserve Bank of India Guidelines and sector specified caps on FDI.

Government Regulations in Business

Social, Technological, and Value Change

- National society
- Communal society
- Entitlements
- Quality of life

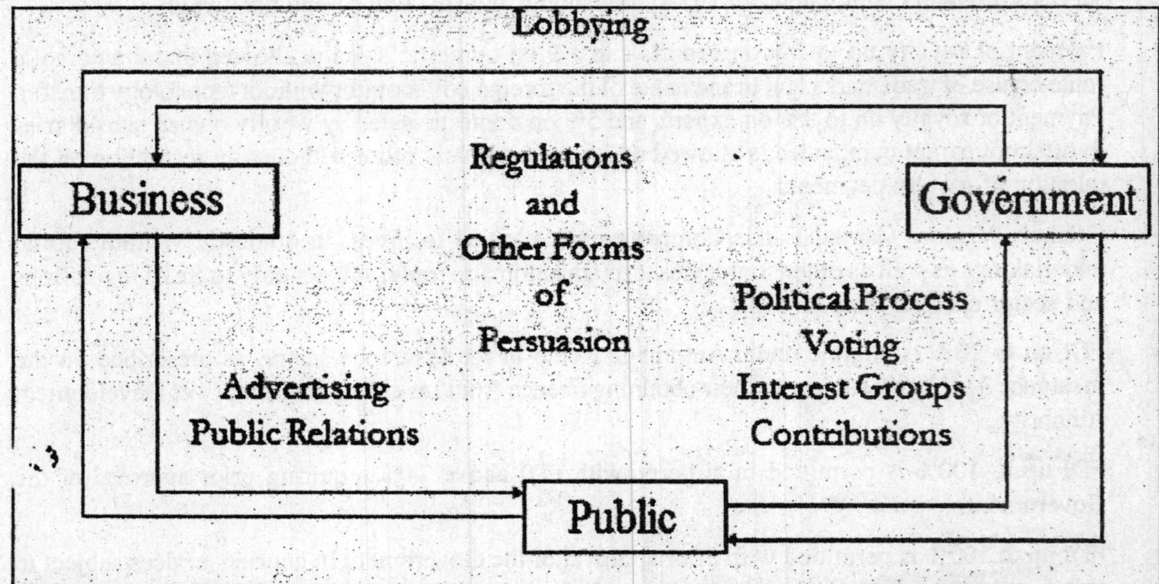

Interaction of Business, Government, and the Public

- Government/business relationship
- Public/government relationship
- Business/public relationship

Two Major Non regulatory Issues

- Industrial policy
- Privatization

Government's Non regulatory Influence on Business

Industrial Policy: Schools of Thought

- Accelerationists
- Adjusters
- Targeters

- Central planners
- Bankers

Industrial Policy

Pros

Decline of U.S. competitiveness

- Use by other nations
- Ad hoc system

Cons

- Reduces market efficiency
- Promotes political decisions
- Foreign success variable
- National attempts uncoordinated and irrational

Privatization

- Producing versus providing a service
- Privatization debate
  - Federalization of certain functions
- Airport security

Other Nonregulatory Influences

- Major employer
- Large purchaser
- Major influence
  - Subsidies
  - Transfer payments
- Major competitor
- Major lender
- Taxation
  - Monetary policy
  - Moral suasion

Factors to Consider Regarding Government Regulation

- Protection
- Scope

• Cost

Federal Regulatory Agency

1. Has decision-making authority
2. Establishes standards or guidelines conferring benefits and imposing restrictions on business conduct
3. Operates principally in the sphere of domestic business activity
4. Has its head and/or members appointed by the president (generally subject to Senate confirmation)
5. Has its legal procedures generally governed by the Administrative Procedures Act

Reasons for Regulation

• Controls natural monopolies
• Controls negative externalities
• Achieves social goals
• Other reasons
  – Controls excess profits
  – Controls excessive competition

Types of Regulation

• Economic regulation
  – Interstate Commerce Commission (ICC)
  – Civil Aeronautics Board (CAB)
  – Federal Communications Commission (FCC)
• Social regulation
  – Environmental Protection Agency (EPA)
  – Occupational Safety and Health Administration (OSHA)
  – Equal Employment Opportunity Commission (EEOC)

Benefits of Regulation

• Fair treatment of employees
• Safer working conditions
• Safer products
• Cleaner air and water

Costs of Regulation

• Direct costs
• Indirect costs

• Induced costs

– Effects

• Reduced innovation

• Reduced investment in plant and equipment

• Increased pressure on small business

Deregulation

Purpose & Dilemma

•Purpose

– Intended to increase competition with the expected benefits of greater efficiency, lower prices, and enhanced innovation.

• Dilemma

Must enhance competition without sacrificing applicable social regulations (e.g., health and safety requirements.

Review Questions

Conceptual Type

1. What do you mean by public policy?
2. What is substantive and procedural policy?
3. Give the meaning of self regulatory and redistributive policies.
4. Give the meaning of material and symbolic policies.
5. What is defense policy?
6. Give the meaning of domestic policy.
7. What is economic policy?
8. What is a government regulation?

Analytical Type

1. Explain various categories of public policy.
2. Discuss policy making process.
3. Write note on: Government and Public Policy.
4. Write short note on: Public policy administration.
5. Explain the various areas of public policy.
6. Explain need for public policy in business.
7. Write note on: Corporate and public policy.
8. Explain the framing of public policy.
9. Discuss the reasons for regulations.
10. Write note on: Justification of regulation.
11. State the problems of regulations.

Descriptive Type

1. Explain the role of public policies in governing business.
2. Explain the classification of public policy.
3. Discuss various levels of public policy.
4. Discuss elements of public policy.
5. Discuss political level of involvement business, government, society and media relationship government regulation in business.
6. Explain various types of regulations.

*****

Module-5

Environmental Concerns and Corporations

Syllabus

History of environmentalism, environmental preservation-role of stakeholders, international issues, sustainable development, costs and benefits of environmental regulation, industrial pollution, role of corporate in environmental management, waste management and pollution control, key strategies for prevention of pollution, environmental audit, Laws governing environment.

Introduction

In the developing world, many development projects have come under criticism for damaging, even when they are presented as helping it. Concerns have increased in line with the rising investment in the developing world.

In the late 1990s attention was drawn to a United Nations (U.N.) project to get corporate collaboration/sponsorship in development projects, supporting human rights and the environment, and being generally more responsible and accountable. However it fell under a lot of criticism for involving corporations that are known to have contributed or caused some of the more severe human rights and environment problems, allowing these companies to attempt to repair their tarnished image, while not actually tackling the problems.

In May 2002, the United Nations Environment Program (UNEP) released an extensive report saying that, "there was a growing gap between the efforts to reduce the impact of business and industry on nature and the worsening state of the planet" and that "this gap is due to the fact that only a small number of companies in each industry are actively integrating social and environmental factors into business decisions." One sharp example of environmental problems caused by multinational corporations is the drive to extract oil from Nigeria. As the previous link, from this site's section on Africa shows, corporations have even backed the military to harass, even kill, local people who continue to protest at the environmental and other problems the activities of the various oil companies have caused. Some local groups have become extreme themselves, kidnapping foreigners for example.

The interests of the various big polluters, such as the auto, mining, oil and chemical corporations influenced the Kyoto Global Climate Change Conference outcome.

And with biotechnology and genetically engineered food production, companies are accused of following a profit motive even as they promote the technology as a means to address world hunger. Environmental concerns also feature quite strongly on this issue.

With increased consumerism, there has been a rise in the number of environmental groups campaigning on various issues such as environmentally friendly products. To varying extents then, environmental concerns are issues that sometimes make the mainstream news. However, a cover story, of Down To Earth magazine from Delhi-based Centre for Science and Environment as an example, warns that the latest craze in green and ethical consumerism may just be another way for corporations to exploit people and make money by misrepresenting the facts. As another example of this, Earth Day Resources' annual Don't Be Fooled Awards highlight some of what they call the corporate "green washing" that goes on through advertising and lobbying campaigns. There are countless examples where corporate involvement in various issues could contribute to environmental problems as a result. Corporations are major entities in the world and thus have an enormous impact (negative and positive) on all our lives. And concerns of overly corporate-led globalization contributing to environmental problems are increasing, as reported and documented by countless environmental and social justice groups around the world.

Environmental Concerns and Corporations

It is not that managers of corporations are necessarily "evil" and want to degrade the environment. One might argue that when they operate in countries or regions that they don't live, they might not care, but the other aspect which may be more fundamental is that it is perhaps a result of the nature of today's businesses and how they feel compelled to operate, compete and stay alive, which might have an enormous impact here. In some respects, many corporations are also victims of the ideologies that are prevalent in current mainstream economics that treat the environment in certain regards. Some corporations might wish to be more environmentally friendly but are unable to do so due to fears that their competitors will get away with it.As the Simultaneous Policy highlights, "Over" competition may be detrimental in this regards too. It is hard for an individual corporation or even group of corporations to effectively break out of this cycle due to fear of competitors being able to take the advantage. Hence this becomes a political as well as economic and environmental issues.

On the political side of things, there have been countless measures pushed and lobbied for that favors corporations directly or indirectly getting out of some of their responsibilities on environmental issues by passing on the costs to others. Various environmental groups constantly campaign on such issues, so this comes as no surprise to state this.

In 1991, then Chief Economist for the World Bank Lawrence Summers, had been a strong backer of the controversial adjustment policies.

Furthermore, corporations are afforded excuses to avoid refitting factories in the first world with their costly environmentally oriented measures and protections, and move elsewhere where regulations have been reduced or removed thanks to economic "agreements"'. As a result, we may see a relatively cleaner environment in the industrialized world, but it is not all explainable by using newer technologies. Due to the centrality of corporations in many issues as important players, they can greatly influence the impact on the environment.

For example, in many cases corporate lobbies have pushed for policies that will benefit them and let them get away with harming the environment. Yet other political processes or even misguided development projects may in some way employ corporations to perform the actual tasks which are damaging to the environment and corporations. This may not be the corporation's fault, per se, however, though in some cases companies do push for such projects, as it is in their interest to gain those lucrative accounts. Many corporate lobbies and think tanks that they fund push for policies which favor such actions in order to make more money. Corporations therefore can also be positive engines for the environment as well.

- That is, if the environment and related factors were central concerns in politics, media, and so forth, then public pressure and other factors would of course require corporations to be more accountable.
- Furthermore corporations typically have a lot of capital, knowledge, and resources to research, pursue, develop, and market environmentally friendly/sustainable products, but only if that is the political driver.
- If the current economic and political systems allow corporations to socialize such costs while they benefit, then there is no real or effective interest in being environmentally friendly as it hurts rather than improves profits and public opinion.

History of Environmentalism

Between 1730 and 1850, the Industrial Revolution sparked an unparalleled wave of mining, forest clearance, and land drainage. It was also a period of the building of great factories. Jobs and economic development ruled. The oceans and rivers seemed unlimited in size and were the sewers of the world.

Reacting to this onslaught, a few scattered individuals began to speak out. But it took 150 years for environmentalism to mature into the public movement we know today. The focus of environmental concerns has changed over the decades, but one debate has barely altered – what is the reason for protecting the planet? For some it's for the benefit of humans, for others it's because nature, like a work of art, has its own value. Still, the movement has become a force to be reckoned with since the days of those pioneers, one and a half centuries ago.

1850-1900 – Environmentalists find their tongue

By 1850, nature writers were evoking the power of the land and talking in terms of a respect for nature. American Henry David Thoreau (1817-1862) published his classic book Walden in 1848. It told of Thoreau's two-year living experiment in woods near Walden Pond, Massachusetts, USA. He spent his time walking, reading and growing food. His intention was to sense then describe the harmony that humans can experience when living with nature.

The idea of a harmonious philosophy was taken up by early conservationists such as naturalist and writer John Muir (1838-1914). This Scottish-born visionary founded the US conservation organization the Sierra Club in 1892. Through the Club, he successfully used his literary gifts to encourage the US government to protect some of the great wildernesses of the country.

Wilderness lovers like Muir and the hikers that enjoyed the land wanted large areas simply left alone. But they met with opposition from the outset. Those with economic interests, like timber companies and politicians, agreed that large areas should be reserved, but only as a future resource of timber, oil, minerals, coal and water. Muir recognized the need to use natural resources and accepted that some forests would have to be sacrificed for their timber. But for him, wildernesses were spiritual places. So loss of wilderness meant a spiritual loss to humanity.

Thus arose a division of beliefs that continues today. One claiming the only considerations are economic, the other arguing that there are other values to consider, such as spiritual value.

Inspired by visionaries like Thoreau and Muir, environmental awareness began to spread through the western world. At about this time, national parks were created in Australia, New Zealand and Canada. And Britain began to establish its first conservation-based organisations, like the RSPB (Royal Society for the Protection of Birds) in 1893 and the National Trust in 1894.

1900-1950s – The growing awareness

In 1914, Martha, the world's only living passenger pigeon, died in Cincinnati Zoo. The species was once the most populous bird on the planet, but it had been hunted to extinction in just 50 years. The plight of this and other decimated species, like the North American buffalo, prompted William Hornaday (1854-1937) to write Our Vanishing Wildlife (1913). Hornaday was one of the first conservationists to draw attention to the plight of endangered wildlife.

Then, in 1949, Aldo Leopold (1887-1948) published A Sand County Almanac – often regarded as the most influential book on conservation ever written. Leopold, a former US Forestry Service official and University of Wisconsin and Iowa State University professor, eloquently and passionately wrote of our duty to protect the balance of nature. He believed humans should extend to nature the same ethical sense of responsibility that we extend to each other. Whether we can or should expand the ethical circle to encompass nature is a subject of continuing debate. (From Prof. Schmidt: We have the Leopold Center for Sustainable Agriculture at Iowa State University where I have been a Prof for the past 36 years and we still push his ideals!

In 1951, somewhat behind the US, Britain designated 10 national parks. Not exactly the wilderness areas that constitute America's parks (in Britain wildernesses had long since disappeared), but the British parks afforded protection from further development.

1960s – The movement is born

Within 100 years a small number of concerned people had done much to raise awareness of environmental destruction. But it wasn't until the 1960s that concern for the environment was galvanized into an organized force. Many would agree that the milestone marking the birth of the environmental movement was Rachel Carson's 1962 book Silent Spring.

Carson, a nature lover and former marine biologist, told of how chemicals like pesticides and insecticides, used on farms, forests and gardens, were contaminating the environment. Wildlife was being poisoned, she said. The insect life was dying (and not just the pest species) which meant no food for the birds. No birds, no bird song = a silent spring. People were in grave danger too. She described in detail how the chemicals, like the insecticide DDT, enter the food chain and accumulate in the fatty tissues of animals, humans included, resulting in higher risks cancer.

Despite media criticism and attempts by the chemical industry to ban the book, many reputable scientists backed her up and her work was validated. President John F Kennedy ordered an investigation into the issues highlighted in the book. Carson was found to be correct – DDT was banned, and the effects of other chemicals were scrutinised.

But the real legacy of Silent Spring was a new public awareness that the environment was being damaged by humans. Previously, degradation of the planet had been the concern of just a few people – those that were bothered by the loss of wilderness. But the news had now spread that our own lives were at risk and the issues could no longer be ignored. The necessity to regulate our behaviour in order to protect the environment became a widely debated notion. Modern environmentalism was born.

1970s – International co-operation

Environmental pressure groups Friends of the Earth and Greenpeace were both established in 1971. They introduced flagship campaigns for threatened species like pandas and tigers and they informed the world of the trade in elephant ivory, rhino horn and seal fur.

The year 1972 saw the first of the 10-yearly Earth Summits. Held in Stockholm, Sweden, it is generally considered to be the primary defining event of international environmentalism. The Earth Summit (officially called the United Nations Conference on the Human Environment) was initiated by the developed world to address the environmental effects of industrialization (113 nations attended). Sweden was concerned about acid rain. Japan was concerned about the industrial poisoning of their seas. Oil tankers spilling their cargoes were a concern worldwide.

The conference produced some successes, including the 26 principles of the Declaration of the United Nations Conference on the Human Environment, an Action Plan for the Human Environment and an Environment Fund. Another significant outcome was the establishment of UNEP (United Nations Environment Programme), designed to promote environmental practices across the globe. UNEP has coordinated the subsequent Earth Summits.

But the summit exposed a rift between the developed (First World) and the developing (Third) world. The issue that caused this was that supposedly the developed world's exploitation of natural resources in a way that not only degraded the environment, but also perpetuated the unequal distribution of wealth. This social (economic) divide remains in place today and has arguably widened.

During the 1970s, philosophers joined the debate and a new branch of ethics was born – environmental philosophy. Up till now, barring the scribblings of a few maverick writers, it was taken as read that we were concerned about caring for the Earth for self-interested purposes. What's bad for the Earth was bad for us too. But now, some philosophers were calling for other values in nature to be recognised. Yes, they said, a healthy planet is good for humans, but wildlife has its own value too – a value that exists independently of its value to humans. This ethical conundrum surfaces with almost every environmental decision we face. Do we protect nature for our sake or for its sake?

1980s – Small steps

The year 1982 was Earth Summit time again. But the Cold War was at its height, the world was distracted, and the meeting, held in Nairobi, Kenya, was considered ineffective.

But the problems didn't stop accumulating. And more voices had joined the clamour. Astronomers complained of light pollution, making it difficult to observe the night sky. Surfers protested against raw sewage being piped into the seas they played in. Marine biologist talked about the noise pollution threat from motor craft to the sonar navigation of whales and dolphins.

Many of these concerns had an effect only on a minority, and hence were easier to ignore. However, when we heard of the hole in the ozone layer, and how we were all going to die from skin cancer we promptly stopped using CFCs in our deodorants and other canister sprays.

In 1983, the UN General Assembly created the UN World Commission on Environment and Development. It appointed Dr. Gro Harlem Brundtland, the first woman prime minister of Norway, as chairperson. Four years later, she published the Brundtland Report, and coined the term 'sustainable development'. The Report combines environmental and economic considerations, and famously defines sustainability as: 'Development that meets the needs of the present without compromising the ability of future generations to meet their own needs. "Sustainability" became the buzzword.

1990s – The warming planet

This decade's Earth Summit occurred in Rio, Brazil, in 1992. It emphasised how the planet's environmental problems are linked to the economy and to social justice issues. The world leaders agreed to combat global warming, protect biodiversity and stop using dangerous poisons.

But Global warming was the major issue at Rio. Carbon dioxide gas, released from burning fossil fuels like petrol (gasoline and diesel), coal, oil and gas, was causing the planet to heat up. The resulting melting ice caps and rising sea levels threatened the whole world. The Kyoto Protocol, introduced at Rio, required signatories to cut carbon dioxide emissions by 5% between 2008 and 2012. Many nations signed up to it, but some developed countries were putting their short-term interests first. Countries with an economy that rests on the oil trade, like the US and Saudi Arabia, were concerned how the agreement would cost them. The US, in particular, refused to commit to anything too binding on the carbon emissions front. Moreover, developing countries like China and India were exempted from most of the Kyoto deadlines and yet they are growing at exceptional rates, using dirty coal and cow dung as fuel, and are now the fastest growing consumers of fossil fuels as prosperity brings automobiles on the scene.

Meanwhile, lack of landfill space in which to bury our rubbish and a need to conserve resources meant that, during the 90s, slowly but surely, recycling bins began to appear in our towns and backyards. Simultaneously, green products grew in number and range on the supermarket shelves. We could feel green as we wash with eco-friendly soaps, write on recycled paper, and eat 'dolphin-friendly' tuna.

Ecotourism was being proposed as a great new way to save the world. The potential being high – in 2006 close to 1 billion people travelled to another country (one tenth of the world's population). But some argued that the damage done by tourism outweigh the benefits. They encourage the development of new resorts in wild places, the over development of fragile beaches in particular (Click on these links for Prof. Schmidt's classes on Coastal Policy, International Integrated Coastal Zone Management and Internship in Coastal Policy) and increase the amount of aviation fuel burned. Yet sometimes both humans and wildlife do get a good deal. Whale-watching, for example, is worth £700 million to the tourist industry, much more lucrative than whale-killing and has thus created a counter weight to whale hunting.

2002 – Johannesburg Earth Summit (Joburg 02)

We go back to Africa for the fourth Earth Summit. In August 2002, 65,000 politicians, numerous NGOs (non-government organizations), and plane loads of media flew in to Johannesburg, South Africa to review the situation. Five areas were identified by the UN for particular attention – water and sanitation, energy, health, agriculture and biodiversity. Previous summits had been dominated by the European Union and the US, but now the developing countries are becoming more vocal demanding their interests be given greater consideration.

There were some achievements. A commitment to halve the number of people in the world who lack basic sanitation by 2015; to halt the loss of fish and forests stocks; and to reduce the agricultural and energy subsidies in the West.

But this Summit has been roundly condemned by environmentalists, claiming the event was hijacked by corporate interests. They say that the US, Japan and the oil companies once again discouraged the promotion of renewable energy sources, like wind and solar power, in order to favour their own economic interests.

Environmental Preservation

ENVIRONMENT - AWARENESS - ENFORCEMENT

The protection and preservation of environment is a pressing issue. Every person, organization and institution has an obligation and duty to protect it. Environmental consciousness deserves to be propagated at all levels. Environmental conservation can be achieved if we all share a single thought, the thought of creating a better world to live in, the thought to give a better deal to everyone, human or otherwise, to the present as well as to the future generation who all have to share the Almighty's great gifts of clean environment and abundant natural resources on this planet earth. Environmental protection encompasses not only pollution but also sustainable development and conservation of natural resources and the eco-system. Environmental degradation can be either localized such as the depletion of a nation's forest resources, or global. such as destruction of the ozone layer. The focus of discussion today revolves around examining the extent to which awareness about the environment has percolated into public consciousness, and making a frank appraisal of enforcement measures adopted so far in protecting the environment. The Government of India as well as our Parliament is increasingly supportive of stringent environmental legislations and Regulations. Various legislations have been enacted by Indian Parliament in last about 30 years to tackle the problem of environmental protection. Various Rules and Regulations have also been framed. Despite these legislations, Rules and Regulations, protection and preservation of environment is still a pressing issue. Today, the necessity of environmental awareness and enforcement is more demanding and urgent than ever before. The first question we have to ask ourselves is why despite provisions in Indian Constitution providing for Environmental Protection and many statutory provisions, the environment degradation continues. The answer to this question is quite simple. The main cause for environment degradation is lack of effective enforcement of various laws. The Supreme Court's orders and directions cover long range of areas whether it be air, water, solid waste or hazardous waste. The field covered is very vast such as –vehicular pollution, pollution by industries, depletion of forests, illegal felling of trees, dumping of hazardous waste, pollution of Rivers, illegal mining. List can be unending.

The Supreme Court has passed orders for closure of polluting industries and environmentally harmful aqua-farms, mandated cleaner fuel for vehicles, stopping illegal mining activity, and protecting forests and architectural treasures like Taj Mahal. Landmark Judgment of 1996 expanding the definition of forest to its ordinary dictionary meaning, ban imposed on all non-forest activities on forest land without prior approval of the Central Government, the directions to constitute Expert Committee in each State to identify forests, directions for movement and disposal of timber, constitution of High Power Committee to deal with forest, the order constituting Central Empowered Committee for monitoring the implementation of orders in forest matters, orders on commercial vandalism indulged by various companies including multinational companies by painting advertisements on rocks around Rohtang Pass and Manali area in Himachal Pradesh, and the constitution of Environmental Protection Control Authority.

The propagation and real and effective implementation of all these can go a long way in motivating people which would help in tackling the problem of environmental degradation. Various High Courts in the country have also passed similar orders. Various government records recognize the problem of environment degradation. Number of Annual Forest Reports issued by the Government of India mention about rapid depletion of forests though the said reports also mention that there has been some check because of the orders of the Supreme Court.

The environmental problems of today whether it is air and water pollution, ozone depletion, land degradation, deforestation, destruction of ecosystem or mismanagement of waste all damage our natural environment and life on earth. None can afford to be complacent considering enormity of the problem and large area to cover. Take for example, threat to forest and wildlife. There is tremendous pressure on forests and unsustainable removals and threat of massive destruction and wild life habitat. Every person and institution has to play the assigned role to the best of one's capability to save India's forest and wild life. What is needed most is commitment and dedication to the cause of protection, preservation and conservation of environment. While many people recognize that environmental pollution is an extremely urgent problem but when placed in the context of seemingly more immediate problems such as poverty crime, corruption and religious and social conflicts, the environment often loses.

The inter-relationship between environmental degradation and many of India's serious problems is often over-looked. It is necessary to stress on the relationship between destruction of environment on one hand and social as well as health problems on the other. It is especially the poor and illiterate who are most exposed to environmental pollution. It is necessary to enlighten them of the link between social and environmental problems. This realization can propel environmentalism to the top of national agenda. Who has suffered the most whether it be Bhopal Gas Tragedy or any other similar disaster? It is the poor and illiterate. It is this class which is exploited most – whether in case of illegal felling of trees or of killing of animals – vested interest mislead them – misguide them. This class has to be educated about the need to protect environment for their self-preservation as well. It can be done by medium of Television, Radio and Print Media. They can increase environmental awareness or even help remedying environmental problems. The communication media can play a positive role in the protection and preservation of environment. They can play an active role in alerting people about environmental damages, corporate failure to meet its legal obligations and truthful analysis of new legislations. The basic responsibilities of the communication media may include: reporting and publishing the truth;

- Conducting thorough probes into issues relating to violations;
- Highlighting the failure of government officials;
- Not succumb to the pressure tactics adopted by governmental officials/anti-social elements; and
- Forcing others to avoid making political mileage from issues relating to the violations.

The emergence of the Internet as a source of information, with its vast reach and accessibility, has been an extremely important development. The only drawback is the difficulty in ascertaining the reliability of source. Also this medium is available to only a limited population in our country. In the light of this, audience in the rural areas. Issues such as forestry, nutrition, women's health, children's rights, overall development, could occupy a top slot on a regular basis. Audio-visual media could relay on various documentaries on the environmental abuses, and facilitate awareness by interviews with environmental activists.

Environmental education became an integral component of the National Policy on Education in 1986. It was declared that there is a need to create consciousness of the environment which must permeate all ages and all sections of the society beginning with the child. Environmental consciousness should inform teaching in schools and colleges and should be integrated in the entire education process. Though environmental education has been integrated into the National Curriculum Frame Work, and as a result of directions issued by the Supreme Court, Environmental Science was made mandatory for undergraduates and Environmental Studies was introduced as a subject for students of Class 1 to 5, but environmental education problems are still far from over. The question still being examined is whether environment should be taught as a separate subject or it should be infused with other subjects. These problems require early solution. A child right from the beginning has to be taught how to act in a more environmental friendly manner for which besides schools ,the village elders and government officials can also play a pivotal role.

The emergence of NGOs represents an organized response by the civil society, especially in those areas in which the State has either failed to reach or done so inadequately. The importance of Public Awareness and NGOs involvement in environmental protection is acknowledged worldwide. It was also highlighted in Rio-Conference in 1992. UNCED supported NGO involvement in an unprecedented manner.

On 29 April 1999, the United Nations Secretary General, Kofi Annan, while addressing the NGOs Forum on Global Issues, specifically recognized the importance and role of NGOs and said that NGOs have a long and proud history of fighting against tyranny and providing humanitarian assistance to the victims of conflict and natural disasters. NGOs armed with e-mail and Internet have been proved more powerful than landmine. The Nobel Committee has recognized their work, awarding its peace prize to NGOs, the Church and academic groups and others. But NGOs have also come in for a less welcome sort of recognition. They have been denied access to meetings and information.

NGOs have been taking a number of steps to promote discussion and debate about environmental issues, outside the broad spheres of popular media and the educational system. Advocacy and awareness is especially crucial in promoting concepts such as sustainable development, natural resource conservation and the restoration of ecosystems. NGOs can sensitize policy makers about the local needs and priorities. They can often intimate the policy makers about the interests of both the poor and the ecosystem as a whole. In providing training facilities, both at community and government levels, NGOs can play a significant role. They can also contribute significantly by undertaking research and publication on environment and development related issues. It is necessary to support and encourage genuine, small, local level NGOs indifferent parts of the country which can provide much needed institutional support specific to the local needs. NGOs can make the following contributions:

- Conducting education and citizen awareness programmes in the field of environment; fact-finding and analysis;
- Filing public interest litigations;
- Innovation and experimenting in areas which are difficult for government agencies to make changes in;
- Providing expertise and policy analysis;
- Providing factual and reliable information with a network of professional expert staff;
- Remaining independent while passing relevant information to the public and governmental bodies;
- Solidarity and support to environmental defenders;
- Working in collaboration with the government for capacity building and promotion of community participation in environmental awareness and protection; and
- Working out at the grass roots level and reaching far-flung areas with or without the government invitation.

International Issues

Environmental problems are often international by nature. Threats to our environment caused by climate change, loss of biological diversity or pollution of the marine environment are examples of problems which can only be solved through cooperation with other countries. The Finnish environmental administration participates in international co-operation to contribute to solving global and regional environmental problems. Some important international issues are listed below:

1. ***Climate change:*** Global warming • Global dimming • Fossil fuels • Sea level rise • Greenhouse gas • Ocean acidification • Shutdown of thermohaline circulation • Environmental impact of the coal industry • Urban Heat Islands.

2. ***Conservation:*** Species extinction • Pollinator decline • Coral bleaching • Holocene extinction • Invasive species • Poaching • Endangered species.

3. ***Energy:*** Energy conservation • Renewable energy • Efficient energy use • Renewable energy commercialization • Environmental impact of the coal industry • Environmental impact of hydraulic fracturing.

4. ***Environmental degradation:*** Eutrophication • Habitat destruction • Invasive species.

5. ***Environmental health:*** Air quality • Asthma • Environmental impact of the coal industry • Electromagnetic fields • Electromagnetic radiation and health • Indoor air quality • Lead poisoning • Sick Building Syndrome • Environmental impact of hydraulic fracturing.

6. ***Genetic engineering:*** Genetic pollution • Genetically modified food controversies.

7. ***Intensive farming:*** Overgrazing • Irrigation • Monoculture • Environmental effects of meat production • Slash and burn • Pesticide drift • Plasticulture.

8. ***Land degradation:*** Land pollution • Desertification.

9. ***Soil:*** Soil conservation • Soil erosion • Soil contamination • Soil salination.

10. ***Land use:*** Urban sprawl • Habitat fragmentation • Habitat destruction.

11. ***Nanotechnology:*** Nano toxicology • Nano pollution.

12. ***Nuclear issues:*** Nuclear fallout • Nuclear meltdown • Nuclear power • Nuclear weapons • Nuclear and radiation accidents • Nuclear safety • High-level radioactive waste management.

13. ***Overpopulation:*** Burial • Water crisis • Overpopulation in companion animals • Tragedy of the commons • Gender Imbalance in Developing Countries • Sub-replacement fertility levels in developed countries.

14. ***Ozone depletion:*** CFC • Biological effects of UV exposure.

15. ***Pollution:*** Environmental impact of the coal industry • Nonpoint source pollution • Point source pollution • Light pollution • Noise pollution • Visual pollution.

16. ***Water pollution:*** Environmental impact of the coal industry • Acid rain • Eutrophication • Marine pollution • Ocean dumping • Oil spills • Thermal pollution • Urban runoff • Water crisis • Marine debris • Microplastics • Ocean acidification • Ship pollution • Wastewater • Fish kill • Algal bloom • Mercury in fish • Environmental impact of hydraulic fracturing.

17. ***Air pollution:*** Environmental impact of the coal industry • Smog • Tropospheric ozone • Indoor air quality • Volatile organic compound • Atmospheric particulate matter • Environmental impact of hydraulic fracturing.

18. ***Reservoirs:*** Environmental impacts of reservoirs.

19. ***Resource depletion:*** Exploitation of natural resources • Overdrafting.

20. ***Consumerism:*** Consumer capitalism • Planned obsolescence • Over-consumption.

21. ***Fishing:*** Blast fishing • Bottom trawling • Cyanide fishing • Ghost nets • Illegal, unreported and unregulated fishing • Overfishing • Shark finning • Whaling.

22. ***Logging:*** Clearcutting • Deforestation • Illegal logging.

23. ***Mining:*** Acid mine drainage • Environmental impact of hydraulic fracturing • Mountaintop removal mining • Slurry impoundments.

24. ***Toxins:*** Chlorofluorocarbons • DDT • Endocrine disruptors • Dioxin • Toxic heavy metals • Environmental impact of the coal industry • Herbicides • Pesticides • Toxic waste • PCB • Bioaccumulation • Biomagnification• Environmental impact of hydraulic fracturing.

25. ***Waste:*** Electronic waste • Litter • Waste disposal incidents • Marine debris • Medical waste • Landfill • Leachate • Environmental impact of the coal industry • Incineration • Great Pacific Garbage Patch • Exporting of hazardous waste• Environmental impact of hydraulic fracturing.

Sustainable Development

Sustainable development has been defined in many ways, but the most frequently quoted definition is from Our Common Future, also known as the Brundtland Report:

Sustainable development is development that meets the needs of the present without compromising the ability of future generations to meet their own needs. It contains within it two key concepts:

- The concept of needs, in particular the essential needs of the world's poor, to which overriding priority should be given; and
- The idea of limitations imposed by the state of technology and social organization on the environment's ability to meet present and future needs.

Sustainable development is defined as balancing the fulfillment of human needs with the protection of the natural environment. A common definition of sustainable development is "development that meets the needs of the present without compromising the ability of future generations to meet their own needs." The field of sustainable development can be conceptually broken into three constituent parts: environmental protection, economic sustainability, and social justice.

The Declaration on the Human Environment was adopted at the United Nations (UN) Conference on Human Environment (Stockholm Conference) that was held between 5-16 June 1972 and brought together countries of different socio-economic structures, convening to evaluate the environment for the first time.

The term "sustainable development" was first used in the Brundtland Report, prepared by the World Commission on Environment and Development in 1987 in which it is defined as "development that meets the needs of the present without compromising the ability of future generations to meet their own needs".

In very broad terms, the Brundtland Report defined the relationship of poverty eradication, equitable distribution of benefits derived from natural resources, population policies and the development of environmentally sound technologies with the principles of sustainable development. In this regard, the Brundtland Report maintained that it was possible to achieve economic growth with an environmentally sound approach and called for the commencement of a new long-term growth era, in which the developing nations had important roles to play and restructuring was made possible, in order to solve the environmental problems of the world and to eliminate poverty.

The UN Conference on Environment and Development (Rio Conference) held in Rio de Janeiro between 3-14 June 1992, constituted a big step towards the adoption of a set of principles to enable a sound management of the environment by governments. During the Conference, Agenda 21, a comprehensive plan of action, as well as Rio Declaration on Environment and Development and Statement on Forest Principles are adopted. In addition, the UN Framework Convention on Climate Change and Convention on Biological Diversity were opened for signature during the Conference. The outcome of the Rio Conference also led to the preparation of the UN Convention to Combat Desertification that was opened for signature in 1994.

The Millennium Development Declaration and the Millennium Development Goals (MDGs) adopted by the governments during UN Millennium Summit in 2000, have become a universal framework for 'development" and are considered as a means for developing countries to work together with developed ones in the pursuit of a shared future. MDGs are eight goals to be achieved by the target year 2015. These include eradication of extreme poverty and hunger, promotion of gender equality, reduction of child mortality as well as ensuring environmental sustainability. The target of "ensuring environmental sustainability" envisages the integration of the principles of sustainable development into country policies and programme and reversing of loss of environmental resources

In order to take a step further the decisions taken in Rio Conference and to render efforts of governments and stakeholders coherent for the achievement of MDGs, the World Summit on Sustainable Development was held in Johannesburg between the dates 26 August - 4 September 2002. Two principal documents were adopted as a result of the Summit: the Johannesburg Implementation Plan and Political Declaration in which the political will of world leaders was expressed.

The Implementation Plan covers a wide range of issues including, inter alia, poverty eradication, changing unsustainable patterns of consumption and production, protecting and managing the natural resource base of economic and social development and health. Some of the targets set out in the Plan are listed below:

Halve by the year 2015, the proportion of the world's people whose income is less than 1 dollar a day and the proportion of people who suffer from hunger and by the same date, to halve the proportion of people without access to safe drinking water,

Promote women's equal access to and full participation in, on the basis of equality with men, decision-making at all levels

Increase investment in cleaner production and eco-efficiency in all countries,

Diversify energy supply by developing advanced, cleaner, more efficient, affordable and cost-effective energy technologies, including fossil fuel technologies and renewable energy technologies, hydro included, and their transfer to developing countries on concessional terms as mutually agreed,

Provide incentives for investment in cleaner production and eco-efficiency in all countries,

Halve by the year 2015 the proportion of world's people without access to safe drinking water and who do not have access to basic sanitation,

Achieve a significant reduction in the current rate of loss of biological diversity.

During the World Summit on Sustainable Development, Turkey presented "National Report on Sustainable Development" prepared with a participatory approach involving the relevant institutions as well as all other stakeholders and a booklet comprised of the best practices of Turkey implemented in the context of sustainable development between 1992-2002.

The Concept of Sustainable Development

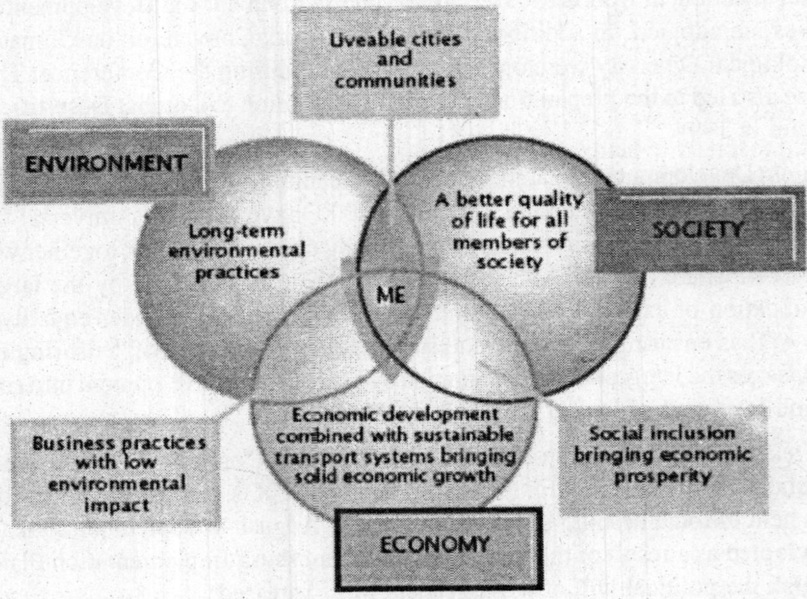

Mobility is our fundamental necessity of 21st century living and brings access to primary services and leisure. But today, current patterns of provision and consumption of mobility are unsustainable and cities all over the world suffer from high levels of traffic related congestion, pollution and the degradation of communities and social dysfunction.

Addressing the issue of climate change is a key topic for all, and for transport in particular. At present CO2 (one of the seven greenhouse gas emissions) from transport are growing despite improvements in technology and fuels mainly due to the sheer increase of the number of trips made.

For the first time in human history more than 50% of the world's population now lives in urban areas (UN-HABITAT 2007). As cities grow their ecological impact increases, and despite the unparalleled flexibility and freedom a car might bring, a city cannot function without public transport. Public transport is vital for future development and the sector is making significant efforts to ensure that it is able to help ensure that citizens today can enjoy a high quality of life in a safe and healthy environment.

Costs and Benefits of Environmental Regulation

Cost-benefit analysis of environmental regulation plays a key role in determining how to achieve our environmental goals without imposing unnecessary costs on the economy. This paper proposes three reforms that address several problems that undermine the role played by cost-benefit analysis in environmental regulation. First, agencies should be required to use a checklist of good empirical practices and should promote decentralized evaluations of data and research. Second, absent compelling systematic evidence to the contrary, agencies should presume that consumers are best able to make their own energy-saving decisions, and should focus on regulations that address the harm that people impose on others. Third, a six-month early regulatory review process should be established for particularly important regulations to allow sufficient time for a thorough cost-benefit analysis and the incorporation of the results into the final regulations.

Industrial Pollution

Industrial pollution is pollution which can be directly linked with industry, in contrast to other pollution sources. This form of pollution is one of the leading causes of pollution worldwide; in the United States, for example, the Environmental Protective Agency estimates that up to 50% of the nation's pollution is caused by industry. Because of its size and scope, industrial pollution is a serious problem for the entire planet, especially in nations which are rapidly industrializing, like China.

This form of pollution dates back to antiquity, but widespread industrial pollution accelerated rapidly in the 1800s, with the start of the Industrial Revolution. The Industrial Revolution mechanized means of production, allowing for a much greater volume of production, and generating a corresponding increase in pollution. The problem was compounded by the use of fuels like coal, which is notoriously unclean, and a poor understanding of the causes and consequences of pollution.

There are a number of forms of industrial pollution. One of the most common is water pollution, caused by dumping of industrial waste into waterways, or improper containment of waste, which causes leakage into groundwater and waterways. Industrial pollution can also impact air quality, and it can enter the soil, causing widespread environmental problems.

Because of the nature of the global environment, industrial pollution is never limited to industrial nations. Samples of ice cores from Antarctica and the Arctic both show high levels of industrial pollutants, illustrating the immense distances which pollutants can travel, and traces of industrial pollutants have been identified in isolated human, animal, and plant populations as well.

Industrial pollution hurts the environment in a range of ways, and it has a negative impact on human lives and health. Pollutants can kill animals and plants, imbalance ecosystems, degrade air quality radically, damage buildings, and generally degrade quality of life. Factory workers in areas with uncontrolled industrial pollution are especially vulnerable.

A growing awareness of factory pollution and its consequences has led to tighter restrictions on pollution all over the world, with nations recognizing that they have an obligation to protect themselves and their neighbors from pollution. However, industrial pollution also highlights a growing issue: the desire of developing nations to achieve first world standards of living and production. Those countries that are already industrialized want to keep their place in the World Economy, and those that aren't want a better position in the world economy e.g. China. As these countries industrialize, they add to the global burden of industrial pollution, triggering serious discussions and arguments about environmental responsibility and a desire to reach a global agreement on pollution issues.

Industrial pollution is unwanted liquid or solid wastes dumped (intentionally or unintentionally) in the environment.

Causes of Industrial Pollution

1. Indiscriminate burning of bushes and discharge of dangerous chemicals in the environment.
2. Industrialization is the main cause of pollution, because more industries increase than there would be more pollution itself.
3. Not maintaining industrial machines which create a lot of friction in machines.
4. Use of low quality coal.

5. By human activities which throw there waste in & around lakes, rivers which are surrounded by industries.

Effects of Industrial Pollution

Global Warming

Global warming is one of the most common and serious consequences of industrial pollution. The emission of various greenhouse gases such as CO2, methane (CH4), among others from various industries, increases the overall temperature of the earth, resulting in global warming. Global warming has various serious hazards, both on the environment as well as on human health. It results in melting of glaciers and snow-capped mountains, causing an increase of the water levels in seas and rivers, thereby increasing the chances of flood. Apart from this, global warming also has numerous health risks on humans, such as increase of diseases such as malaria and dengue, cholera, Lyme disease and plague, among others.

Air Pollution

Industrial pollution, as stated above, is one of the major causes of air pollution. With the increase in the number of industries and factories due to the industrial revolution; air pollution also has increased significantly. The emissions from various industries contain large amounts of gases such as carbon dioxide, sulphur and nitrogen, among others. These gases, when present in elevated levels in the atmosphere, often result in various environmental and health hazards such as acid rain, and various skin disorders in individuals.

Water Pollution

Pollution emitted from the industries is also one of the major factors contributing towards water pollution. Dumping of various industrial waste products into water sources, and improper contamination of industrial wastes, often result in polluting the water. Such water pollution disturbs the balance of the ecosystem inside, resulting in the death of various animal and plant species present in the water.

Soil Pollution

Soil pollution is defined as a phenomenon is which the soil loses its structure and fertility due to various natural and artificial reasons. Dumping of industrial wastes is one of the prime factors contributing towards soil pollution. Industrial wastes contain large amounts of various chemicals which get accumulated on the top layer of the soil, resulting in loss of fertility of the soil. Such loss of fertility ultimately results in changes in the ecological balances of the environment due to reduction in plant growth.

Other Common Effects

Certain other common effects of industrial pollution include damaging buildings and structures, increasing the risk of various occupational hazards such as asbestosis, pneumoconiosis, among others.

1. Air gets polluted so people can't breath easily
2. Water gets polluted by throwing of chemicals in river etc by industries
3. Land also gets polluted because there is too much waste from industries which is not taken care of and causes certain diseases.

Role of Corporate in Environmental Management

Along with the global trend of green business and green living, more and more companies have been attaching great importance to protecting the environment. An effective means to achieve and demonstrate sound environment performance is to adopt an Environmental Management System (EMS) and produce environmental performance reports.

Before the 1980s, environmental regulation in India was almost non-existent. In pursuit of economic development, the Government of India (GoI) kept environmental regulation of multinational corporations to a minimum in order to attract foreign direct investment. Multinational corporations have often been blamed for taking advantage of weak enforcements in India; however, in recent years, many of them have started to self-regulate and often set their environmental standards above the minimum compliances enforced by the GoI.

Benefits of Corporate Environmental Management

The benefits of corporate environmental management are many. In the view of management, it can fulfill supply-chain requirements, ensure continual environmental improvement, help to reduce legislative non-compliance, promote staff environmental awareness and increase financial savings resulting from resource saving and cost reduction. From the public relations perspective, it can improve the company image, and enhance favourable customer relationships.

Environmental Management System

An Environmental Management System (EMS) can help a corporation to improve its environmental performance and thus stay competitive in the environmentally conscious world business market. In general, a corporation will go through 3 steps in setting up its EMS. Conduct an initial environmental audit to evaluate the current environmental performance.Set its own environmental policy as well as objectives and targets.

EMS Certification

The ISO 14000 EMS certification is internationally recognised. To assist the Small and Medium Enterprises (SMEs) to develop their own EMS, the Environmental Protection Department (EPD) has launched support packages on environmental management information and ISO 14001 EMS specifically for SMEs of the construction and electrical/electronic sectors.

A successful EMS also involves periodic audit and review to ensure its effectiveness and achieve continual environmental improvement. EPD also launched a simple guide helping SMEs to conduct environmental audits.

Waste Management

Waste management is not a minor issue for a country but it is a huge accountability on country to reuse and dispose the waste products from different sources properly. It is the conscientiousness of local government authorities to manage non-hazardous residential and institutional waste in metro areas. On other hand the management for non-hazardous commercial and industrial waste is done by the generator. Production of any substance not only new substances there is always waste associated with it. For instance production of clothes, needle, meal, bicycle, car etc waste production is always there.

Not only the techniques but also the location where waste has to be disposed also plays a gigantic role in waste management. If it is disposed in open place there are probability of outbreak of diseases like malaria, dengue, skin allergies, infections and other health risk. If it is disposed in oceans, rivers etc. then there is big jeopardy to aquatic life. The waste generated from nuclear power plants should not be disposed in open place. There are an assortment of methods of waste disposal including integrated waste management, plasma gasification, Landfill, Supercritical water decomposition and Incineration. In other US states, waste management in Phoenix or waste management in Texas a directory of waste management services as well as reviews, maps, websites and information are provided.

The recycling process is widely used for waste management. In this process the products that are in good state are reused or recycled by different techniques resulting less waste production. The traditional method to deal with waste was landfills. In landfills waste was buried into lands but due to limited space and pollution this technique failed.

Pollution Control

The Pollution Control Measures undertaken by the government of India are:

Adoption of cost effective cleaner technologies should be encouraged

- Implementation of waste minimization techniques and adoption of appropriate pollution control measures.
- Discard and discourage technologies which do not conform to the quality of products.
- Spreading awareness messages through programs for the prospective and existing entrepreneurs on usage of cleaner technologies and pollution control.
- Waste minimization for improvement of productivity and creation of Waste minimization circle.
- Assistance for sustainable development to be facilitated by the Government of India through fiscal incentives, technology, training etc.
- An additional system of taxation to be introduced based on concentration of waste.
- Encourage industry to regard 'pollution' as an economic problem.
- To decide the cost of water, power, fuel, etc through market instruments.
- Tax exemption on waste selling, resource recovery and reuse to be introduced.
- Incentives may be introduced on waste selling, resource recovery, reuse, etc.
- Scattered business units to follow stringent pollution control regulations.
- Allowance for capital investment and cleaner technology from foreign and private players.
- Simplification of Environmental clearance procedures for the industries located in industrial estates.
- Encourage Common Effluent Treatment Plant.
- Encourage common captive power plant and steam generation unit.
- During relocation of units detailed action plan to be prepared based on.
- environmental risk assessment.

- Small industries to get assistance from government.
- Further Research and development of cleaner technologies is proposed.

Key Strategies for Pollution Prevention

Pollution prevention describes activities that reduce the amount of pollution generated by a process, whether it is consumer consumption, driving, or industrial production. In contrast to most pollution control strategies, which seek to manage a pollutant after it is formed and reduce its impact upon the environment, the pollution prevention approach seeks to increase the efficiency of a process, thereby reducing the amount of pollution generated at its source. Although there is wide agreement that source reduction is the preferred strategy, some professionals also use the term pollution prevention to include recycling or reuse.

Meaning

Pollution is the contamination of air, soil, or water by the discharge of harmful substances. Pollution prevention is the reduction or elimination of pollution at the source (source reduction) instead of at the end-of-the-pipe or stack. Pollution prevention occurs when raw materials, water, energy and other resources are utilized more efficiently, when less harmful substances are substituted for hazardous ones, and when toxic substances are eliminated from the production process. By reducing the use and production of hazardous substances, and by operating more efficiently we protect human health, strengthen our economic well-being, and preserve the environment.

Source reduction allows for the greatest and quickest improvements in environmental protection by avoiding the generation of waste and harmful emissions. Source reduction makes the regulatory system more efficient by reducing the need for end-of-pipe environmental control by government.

NPPR supports multi-media P2 approaches which work to solve environmental problems holistically and do not only focus on pollution in a single medium (air, land, or water). Well-intentioned rules, regulations and solutions that are not multi-media sometimes exacerbate existing conditions by creating larger problems to other media that are not accounted for by a single media-specific solution. Many times this can result in the transfer of pollution from one medium to another. For example, in some cases, by requiring hazardous air emission controls for industrial facilities, other problems might result, such as pollutants being transferred to underground drinking water through the residual sludge.

What are the Economic Incentives for Pollution Prevention?

Adopting pollution prevention practices and techniques often benefits industry by lowering a company's operational and environmental compliance costs. By preventing the generation of waste, P2 can also reduce or eliminate long-term liabilities and clean-up costs. Furthermore, disposal costs are reduced when the volume of waste is decreased. This can also lead to a reduction in workplace exposures to hazardous materials which can affect workers' health and hence, their productivity. If less waste is produced, there will also be a diminished need for on-site storage space. Furthermore, by preventing pollution there will be a greater likelihood that a company will be in compliance with local, state, and federal compliance statutes. Finally, as community pillars, businesses shoulder an important responsibility for protecting the environment and natural resources for their own good as well as that of society.

Pollution Prevention Methods

Pollution prevention can be accomplished by the following methods:

- ***Design:*** Products, buildings and manufacturing systems can be made resource-efficient throughout their life cycle by incorporating environmental considerations into their design.

  Example: A conference center in eastern Washington was designed, constructed and is operated to reduce its environmental "footprint." Features include a computerized energy management system, efficient lighting and windows, reuse of waste heat for water heating, bathroom flooring made of plant material composites, preservatives-free decking made of recycled plastic bags and wood waste, and native plant landscaping that can get along with reduced irrigation.

- ***Process Changes:*** Rethinking manufacturing processes can turn up ways to reduce production waste, cutting both pollution and costs.

  Example: An Everett, Washington electronic equipment manufacturer found a non-chemical technique to extend by a factor of five the life of a cleaning bath used in circuit board production. As a result, the company has reduced the quantity of chemicals it uses and then discards for the cleaning process. Workers like the change because they don't have to handle as many hazardous chemicals. Additionally, the innovation saved 300 person-hours in maintenance labor costs.

- ***Materials Substitution:*** Alternative materials for cleaning, coating, lubrication and other production processes can provide equivalent results while preventing costly hazardous waste generation, air emissions, and worker health risks.

  Example: A Seattle metal fabricator replaced a high-solvent paint for coating products with a low-solvent paint. While the replacement paint's purchase cost was higher, each gallon coated more product. As a result, the company reduced its painting costs per square foot of coated product. The low-solvent paint emits fewer smog-forming VOCs, enabling the company to avoid the need for a costly air emissions permit.

- ***Materials Reuse:*** One company's wastes may be another company's raw materials. Finding markets for them can reduce solid waste, lessen consumption of virgin resources, increase income for the sellers, and provide an economical resource supply for the buyers.

  Example: An Idaho potato processor markets waste starch to paper producers. Discarded potato peelings are used for cattle feed and pet food production. The peelings also are used to manufacture biodiesel, an alternative vehicle fuel that greatly reduces sulfur, particulate and carbon monoxide emissions.

- ***Resource Efficiency:*** Using energy, water and other production inputs more efficiently helps keep air and water clean, reduces emissions of greenhouse gases, cuts operating costs, and improves productivity.

  Energy Example: A Portland grocery store is saving $65,000 per year in energy costs as a result of upgrading the store's lighting, refrigeration, heating, ventilation and air conditioning systems. Greater energy efficiency reduces the impacts of electricity generation on air, water, fish and wildlife.

  Water Example: An eastern Oregon onion grower experienced a 13 percent increase in yield, 30 percent increase in crop quality, and reduced fertilizer costs as a result of installing a water-efficient drip irrigation system. Reduced water waste lessens consumption pressure on streams, and helps keep them healthy for salmon and other fisheries.

- ***Improved Work Practices:*** Rethinking day-to-day operations and maintenance activities can help managers root out wasteful management practices that drive up costs and cause pollution.

  Example: Two hospitals and a university in a Portland neighborhood worked out an employees trip reduction plan that alleviated congestion, increased transit and car pool ridership, and reduced commute trips by 3.7 million miles. Gasoline consumption was cut by 174,000 gallons per year, and as a result, carbon dioxide emissions were reduced by 3.4 million pounds annually.

  Example: A military facility on Kodiak Island, Alaska stopped changing fleet vehicle oil on a set schedule, and instead changes oil only when an analysis indicates it is necessary. The new practice cut waste oil volume in half and saves the base $11,000 per year.

How to Prevent Water Pollution

- Release of harmful chemical into rivers or seas by the industries and certain house hold activities, needs to be brought to the forefront.
- Never wash off any synthetic products into the water, and dumping garbage into water bodies should not only be reduced, but needs to be stopped completely.
- Ensure proper sewage treatment, and the treated wastes that are generally released from the factories into the rivers and lakes, should be reused by these industries; this will help reduce few cycles.
- Plant water hyacinths in rivers and lakes within your reach, this will help prevent the water from getting polluted by metallic pollutants.
- Recycle inorganic as well as organic wastes, so that they can be transformed and reused as various products.
- Avoid making use of synthetic fertilizers in the farm. These chemicals get washed away with rain water, and pollute nearby water bodies. Make use of natural fertilizers made from recycling wastes.

Preventing Air Pollution

Air pollution is caused due to release of harmful pollutants such as carbon dioxide, carbon monoxide, nitrous oxide, methane, sulfur dioxide and many other gases, which constitute the greenhouse effect. The release of gaseous pollutants in air causes significant imbalance in the ecosystem, and has resulted in a substantial rise in Earth's surface temperature. While minimizing the level of smoke from vehicles and household activities is what the corporations stress upon, governing bodies seem to be waiting for some "right time" to implement preventive measures to control industrial emissions. Following are few steps that you can take in order to help prevent pollution.

- Do not burn your garbage, dispose it in garbage bins, thus ensuring proper treatment.
- Use alternative pollution free sources of fossil fuels. Renewable sources such as solar energy, and the use of windmills for generating energy should be preferred over burning wood, coal, and fossil fuels.
- Plant trees by the sides of the road and encourage your friends and colleagues to join your cause.

Trees help in absorbing carbon dioxide from the atmosphere, and purifies the air surrounding them.

- Proper maintenance of vehicles is very important. Look for advanced smoke controlling devices in the market, and upgrade your vehicles to ensure that they don't emit large amounts of soot.
- Limit the use of electricity, air conditioners, water heaters, and coolers; they emit gases that heat the atmosphere.
- Use a small amount of ethanol in petrol for your vehicles, this reduces the emission of harmful gases in the atmosphere.

Air pollution in the major cause of depletion of protective layer Ozone, which keeps us from potentially harmful ultraviolet radiations.

How to Prevent Sound Pollution:

- Keep the volume of your television and music systems low.
- Horns are provided in your vehicles for emergency purposes, so use them sparingly and only when absolutely necessary. Some people may be under the delusion that honking horns instigates the other person to drive faster, thus paving way for you to reach your destination faster. Continuous honking of horns affects our senses, and eventually cause a dimming effect.
- Loudspeakers need to be handled with care, so that those who are in close proximity will not get affected.
- Check that your vehicles do not emit excessive sound. Upgrade them with sound controlling devices.

How to Prevent Soil Pollution:

- Do not use harmful chemicals for fertilizers, as they enter the food chain, and thus affect the entire ecological system.
- Use of organic manure should be preferred over those that are synthetic.
- Avoid spraying pesticides on the crops, this is one of the major causes of chemical infestation.
- DDT is the most harmful pesticide used in farms. Although the use of DDT has been banned in many countries, there are still some farmers who use it.
- Avoid throwing plastic and non-degradable wastes anywhere but trash bins, so that they undergo recycling. Also, these materials gain access into the soil, and since these wastes don't decompose for years, they eventually cause infertility.

Besides the steps mentioned above, we can take extra efforts in preventing pollution, such as restrict the use of products without which we can survive, such as hair dryers, make up products, jewelry, decorative items etc, and maybe make it a habit to deny marketing brochures that are circulated. Whatever we use results in depletion of resources, and we need to understand that we can indeed use these resources more efficiently. For example, instead of using gold, silver, platinum, titanium, and gemstones for jewelry, the nation can use them for trade, which will in turn reduce the amount of paper required for currency production. Now, since we cannot expect for such a change to happen globally, we need to take measures that will at least limit the amount of such products being manufactured. We need to stop buying such products, which will in turn cause havoc for businesses, and eventually force them to lower their production rate.

Perhaps you are not aware, but enormous amounts of trees are being razed down, so as to facilitate the production of paper. And as we all know, most of the paper in circulation are used for cigarettes, currency, stationary, and marketing. Now, marketing being an extra element of a business, where the only aim is to promote the brand or boost the business, we can certainly raise a voice against the use of paper for marketing or advertising. In the age of digital advancement, we need to use resources optimally, and thus aid our planet's restoration.

Environmental Audit

Environmental auditing originated in the United States in the 1970s. At first reactive in focus, environmental considerations were dealt with by 'end of pipe' solutions. Control measures were heavily influenced by the need to reduce remediation costs and fines which might stem from industrial accidents, and from the need to manage environmental liabilities.

Environmental auditing was introduced to the UK and elsewhere mainly by multi-national companies who began to apply the audit procedures corporately and via subsidiaries (horizontally). It is now being encouraged down the supply chain when large companies demand that their suppliers have green credentials (vertically). Environmental auditing has also become more proactive as organisations have recognised potential market and stakeholder benefits, efficiency gains, financial savings, and the importance of improved public relations.

Historically, environmental auditing has been developed for industrial (chemical and manufacturing) applications. Interest has also occurred in the public sector, resulting from the various Charter initiatives to open up activities to greater public scrutiny. Local authorities now apply auditing in their work. This can be expected to grow more rapidly as a result of new commitments towards sustainable development and the implementation of Local Agenda 21.

Definitions

The term 'environmental auditing' is broad. Many definitions cover auditing in the private and public sector. Private sector environmental auditing has been variously defined as:

A management tool comprising a systematic, documented, periodic and objective evaluation of the performance of the organization, management system and processes designed to protect the environment with the aim of: (1) facilitating management control of practices which may have impact on the environment, and (2) assessing compliance with company policies. (CEC, 1993); and the systematic examination of the interaction between any business operation and its surrounding. This includes all emissions to air, land and water legal constraints; the effects on the neighboring community, landscape and ecology; and the public's perception of the operating company in the local area' (CBI, 1990).

Many types of audit have been carried out by companies (ERM, 1996, Thompson and Therivel, 1991):

- ***Compliance audit:*** The most common type of audit consisting of checks against environmental legislation and company policy;
- ***Issues audit:*** An evaluation of how a company's activities relate to an environmental issue or (e.g.

global pollution, energy use) or an evaluation of a specific issue (e.g. buildings, supplies);

- ***Health and safety audit:*** An assessment of risks and contingency planning (sometimes merged with environmental auditing because of the interconnected impacts of industrial processes and hazards);
- ***Site audit:*** An audit of a particular site to examine actual or potential environmental problems;
- ***Corporate audit:*** An audit of the whole company and its polices, structures, procedures and practices;
- ***Due diligence audit:*** An assessment of potential environmental and financial risks and liabilities carried out before a company merger or site acquisition or divestiture (e.g. contaminated land remediation costs);
- ***Activity or operational audit:*** An assessment of activities that may cross company departments or units (e.g. energy or waste management) and product or life cycle audit - an analysis of environmental impacts of a product throughout all stages of its design, production, use and disposal, including its reuse and recycling (cradle to grave).

Environmental Auditing Practice and Procedures

The more specific type of environmental audit involves the collection, collation, analysis, interpretation, and presentation of information which is used to:

Assess performance against a set of requirements or targets, related to specific issues; Evaluate compliance with environmental legislation and corporate policies; and Measure performance against the requirements of an environmental management system standard.

The systematic, periodic, documented and objective aspects of environmental auditing are fundamental to effectiveness. It is fast developing as an important and powerful tool in the corporate environmental assessment and management toolkit. The requirement periodically to repeat audits ensures that there is an ongoing commitment and a systematic process to improve environmental performance (Grayson, 1992). The scope of repeat audits can also broaden to become more comprehensive as experience and expertise are accrued or as new issues or legislation emerges.

Sometimes the terms assessment, appraisal, monitoring or review have been used interchangeably with audit. Audit implies detailed statistical verification with a periodic cycle between audits. An assessment or review is usually a one-off event which is carried out in less detail and with less direct checking of data.

Environmental Reviews provide a baseline overview of current environmental effects or impacts, relevant environmental legislation and a statement of existing environmental performance. The Reviews provide a basis for establishing a management action plan. They can become part of an environmental management system to help implement the plan. When they are undertaken as the first of a series of periodic environmental audits they have been referred to as a 'Baseline Environmental Audit'.

Environmental audits should be appropriate to the particular circumstances. As environmental auditing draws upon various methodologies, each organization will define its own system depending upon its size, its activities and its corporate culture.

The scope and style of audits vary, but common stages and activities include:

Pre-audit stage

- Full management commitment;
- Setting overall goals, objectives, scope and priorities;
- Selecting a team to ensure objectivity and professional competence;

Audit stage

- On-site audit, well defined and systematic using protocols or checklists;
- Review of documents and records;
- Review of policies;
- Interviews;
- Site inspection;

Post- audit stage

- Evaluation of findings;
- Reporting with recommendations;
- Preparation of an action plan; and
- Follow-up.

Benefits of Auditing

While environmental audits are designed to identify environmental problems, there may be widely differing reasons for undertaking them: compliance with legislation, pressure from suppliers and customers, requirements from insurers or for capital projects, or to demonstrate environmental activities to the public. The benefits of environmental auditing include:

- Ensuring compliance, not only with laws, regulations and standards, but also with company policies and the requirements of an Environmental Management System (EMS) standard;
- Enabling environmental problems and risks to be anticipated and responses planned;
- To demonstrate that an organization is aware of its impact upon the environment through providing feedback;
- Increased awareness amongst stakeholders; and
- More efficient resource use and financial savings.

Laws Governing Environment

Environmental laws

In the Constitution of India it is clearly stated that it is the duty of the state to 'protect and improve the environment and to safeguard the forests and wildlife of the country'. It imposes a duty on every citizen 'to protect and improve the natural environment including forests, lakes, rivers, and wildlife'. Reference to the environment has also been made in the Directive Principles of State Policy as well as the Fundamental Rights. The Department of Environment was established in India in 1980 to ensure a healthy environment for the country. This later became the Ministry of Environment and Forests in 1985.

The constitutional provisions are backed by a number of laws – acts, rules, and notifications. The EPA (Environment Protection Act), 1986 came into force soon after the Bhopal Gas Tragedy and is considered an umbrella legislation as it fills many gaps in the existing laws. Thereafter a large number of laws came into existence as the problems began arising, for example, Handling and Management of Hazardous Waste Rules in 1989.

Following is a list of the environmental legislations that have come into effect:

1. General
2. Forest and wildlife
3. Water
4. Air

1. General

1986 - The Environment (Protection) Act authorizes the central government to protect and improve environmental quality, control and reduce pollution from all sources, and prohibit or restrict the setting and /or operation of any industrial facility on environmental grounds.

- 1986 - The Environment (Protection) Rules lay down procedures for setting standards of emission or discharge of environmental pollutants.
- 1989 - The objective of Hazardous Waste (Management and Handling) Rules is to control the generation, collection, treatment, import storage, and handling of hazardous waste.
- 1989 - The Manufacture, Storage, and Import of Hazardous Rules define the terms used in this context, and sets up an authority to inspect, once a year, the industrial activity connected with hazardous chemicals and isolated storage facilities.
- 1989 - The Manufacture, Use, Import, Export, and Storage of hazardous Micro-organisms/ Genetically Engineered Organisms or Cells Rules were introduced with a view to protect the environment, nature, and health, in connection with the application of gene technology and microorganisms.
- 1991 - The Public Liability Insurance Act and Rules and Amendment, 1992 was drawn up to provide for public liability insurance for the purpose of providing immediate relief to the persons affected by accident while handling any hazardous substance.

1995 - The National Environmental Tribunal Act has been created to award compensation for damages to persons, property, and the environment arising from any activity involving hazardous substances.

- 1997 - The National Environment Appellate Authority Act has been created to hear appeals with respect to restrictions of areas in which classes of industries etc. are carried out or prescribed subject to certain safeguards under the EPA.
- 1998 - The Biomedical waste (Management and Handling) Rules is a legal binding on the health care institutions to streamline the process of proper handling of hospital waste such as segregation, disposal, collection, and treatment.
- 1999 - The Environment (Siting for Industrial Projects) Rules, 1999 lay down detailed provisions relating to areas to be avoided for siting of industries, precautionary measures to be taken for site selecting as also the aspects of environmental protection which should have been incorporated during the implementation of the industrial development projects.
- 2000 - The Municipal Solid Wastes (Management and Handling) Rules, 2000 apply to every municipal authority responsible for the collection, segregation, storage, transportation, processing, and disposal of municipal solid wastes.
- 2000 - The Ozone Depleting Substances (Regulation and Control) Rules have been laid down for the regulation of production and consumption of ozone depleting substances.
- 2001 - The Batteries (Management and Handling) Rules, 2001 rules shall apply to every manufacturer, importer, re-conditioner, assembler, dealer, auctioneer, consumer, and bulk consumer involved in the manufacture, processing, sale, purchase, and use of batteries or components so as to regulate and ensure the environmentally safe disposal of used batteries.
- 2002 - The Noise Pollution (Regulation and Control) (Amendment) Rules lay down such terms and conditions as are necessary to reduce noise pollution, permit use of loud speakers or public address systems during night hours (between 10:00 p.m. to 12:00 midnight) on or during any cultural or religious festive occasion.
- 2002 - The Biological Diversity Act is an act to provide for the conservation of biological diversity, sustainable use of its components, and fair and equitable sharing of the benefits arising out of the use of biological resources and knowledge associated with it

2. Forest and Wildlife

- 1927 - The Indian Forest Act and Amendment, 1984, is one of the many surviving colonial statutes. It was enacted to 'consolidate the law related to forest, the transit of forest produce, and the duty leviable on timber and other forest produce'.
- 1972 - The Wildlife Protection Act, Rules 1973 and Amendment 1991 provides for the protection of birds and animals and for all matters that are connected to it whether it be their habitat or the waterhole or the forests that sustain them.
- 1980 - The Forest (Conservation) Act and Rules, 1981, provides for the protection of and the conservation of the forests.

3. Water

- 1882 - The Easement Act allows private rights to use a resource that is, groundwater, by viewing it as an attachment to the land. It also states that all surface water belongs to the state and is a state property.

- 1897 - The Indian Fisheries Act establishes two sets of penal offences whereby the government can sue any person who uses dynamite or other explosive substance in any way (whether coastal or inland) with intent to catch or destroy any fish or poisonous fish in order to kill.
- 1956 - The River Boards Act enables the states to enroll the central government in setting up an Advisory River Board to resolve issues in inter-state cooperation.
- 1970 - The Merchant Shipping Act aims to deal with waste arising from ships along the coastal areas within a specified radius.
- 1974 - The Water (Prevention and Control of Pollution) Act establishes an institutional structure for preventing and abating water pollution. It establishes standards for water quality and effluent. Polluting industries must seek permission to discharge waste into effluent bodies.

  The CPCB (Central Pollution Control Board) was constituted under this act.
- 1977 - The Water (Prevention and Control of Pollution) Cess Act provides for the levy and collection of cess or fees on water consuming industries and local authorities.
- 1978 - The Water (Prevention and Control of Pollution) Cess Rules contains the standard definitions and indicate the kind of and location of meters that every consumer of water is required to affix.
- 1991 - The Coastal Regulation Zone Notification puts regulations on various activities, including construction, are regulated. It gives some protection to the backwaters and estuaries.

4. Air

- 1948 – The Factories Act and Amendment in 1987 was the first to express concern for the working environment of the workers. The amendment of 1987 has sharpened its environmental focus and expanded its application to hazardous processes.
- 1981 - The Air (Prevention and Control of Pollution) Act provides for the control and abatement of air pollution. It entrusts the power of enforcing this act to the CPCB .
- 1982 - The Air (Prevention and Control of Pollution) Rules defines the procedures of the meetings of the Boards and the powers entrusted to them.
- 1982 - The Atomic Energy Act deals with the radioactive waste.
- 1987 - The Air (Prevention and Control of Pollution) Amendment Act empowers the central and state pollution control boards to meet with grave emergencies of air pollution.
- 1988 - The Motor Vehicles Act states that all hazardous waste is to be properly packaged, labeled, and transported.

The Pepsico Case Study

Company Profile:

Pepsico, Inc. is an American Fortune 500 company headquartered in Purchase, New York. Founded in Chicago in 1965, the company spans 200 countries. It offers over 80 products worldwide, including local variations in the different countries of operation. PepsiCo owns five different food and beverage brands: Frito-Lay, Quaker, Pepsi-Cola, Tropicana and Gatorade. A complete profile of PepsiCo's products is presented. Given the wide range of products under PepsiCo's food and beverage brands, this paper narrows its evaluation to environmental management of PepsiCo's beverage products in India.

Pepsico entered India in 1989 by a joint venture (JV) with the Punjab-government-owned Punjab Agro Industrial Corporation (PAIC) and Voltas India Limited. In 1994, Pepsi ultimately bought out its partners, becoming a fully owned subsidiary and ending the joint venture (Kaye, 2004). The company's beverage portfolio in India consists of carbonated and non-carbonated drinks and packaged mineral water. The iconic beverages such as Pepsi, Mountain Dew, 7 Up, and Mirinda fall under the soft drinks (carbonated) segment. PepsiCo's non-carbonated segment broadly consists of sports drinks (Gatorade), fruit juices (Tropicana), and hydrating beverages such as Aquafina drinking water. The group has built on its expansive beverage business to support the operations at its 43 bottling plants in India (Pepsi Foods, 2010). As seen in figure 3, during 2007-08, the sales from non-alcoholic beverage sector made up 72% of its total sales worldwide.

PepsiCo enjoys a 13% market share of the Indian beverage industry, and over the years its presence has got bigger-especially in the carbonated drinks (soft drinks) sector. In 2003, India was one of the top five markets for growth in the soft drinks sector. PepsiCo has invested more than $1 billion US in its Indian subsidiary (Pepsi Foods, 2010).

Environmental issues at pepsi Co and the Indian Regulatory Environment:

The two most contested environmental issues of PepsiCo India are the quality and quantity of water extracted for its beverages, and the resulting water pollution due to the company's industrial residue. Another challenge faced by the company is the amount of plastic use and waste generated in bottling and packaging of its products.

1. Industrial water use

According to Indra Nooyi, CEO of PepsiCo Inc., soft-drinks and bottle water account for only 0.04% of the total industrial water usage in India (Brady, 2007). However, given the scarcity of drinking water in India, this use still has a large impact on the population that does not have access to clean drinking water. For each liter of soft-drink produced, PepsiCo uses 10 liters of water. In total, the company uses 30 million liters of ground water per year (Shiva, 2004). The company has been alleged to practice "water piracy" for exploitation of ground water resources, resulting in scarcity of drinking water for the residents of the Palakkad district in Kerala, India. A study done by the Kerala groundwater department reported that the factory extracted 366,000 liters more than the permissible limits (Down to Earth, 2007). The company's factory has also been known to cause water pollution by adding toxic sludge containing heavy metals such as lead and cadmium into the nearby streams (Shiva, 2006). Under the Clean Water Act of 1974, the GoI has not set any formal standards for the industrial use of "clean" and "portable" water in their food and beverages, and neither does it have any formal regulation for nonpoint source of industrial pollution (Kaye, 2004). In addition, neither the Prevention of Food Adulteration (PFA) Act of 1954 nor the Fruit Products Order of 1955-the mandatory acts for regulating the quality of beverage contents in India-regulate pesticide content in soft drinks (CSE, 2003).

In 2003, a study led by the Center for Science and the Environment (CSE), an environmental NGO in New Delhi, nationally released reports confirming that soft drinks of Pepsi and Coca-Cola contained pesticides. The samples were found to be 24 times above the general standards finalized (but not notified) by the Bureau of Indian Standards (InfoChange, 2006). Observing an outright disregard of BIS standards, in 2005, the Drinks and Carbonated Beverages Sectional Committee of the BIS introduced higher standards. However, it is alleged that the Union Ministry of Consumer Affairs may have asked the BIS to defer setting standards, since there was no significant improvement in the level of pesticides in the following batches (InfoChange, 2006). Snowballing into a national public health scare, in 2006, seven out of 24 states in India, including government-run schools and colleges, banned both Pepsi as well as Coca Cola (Kaye, 2004).

2. Industrial plastic waste management

PepsiCo India has been criticized both by consumers and environmental NGOs for the environmental waste created by bottling their drinks. In 1994, the beverage giant experienced national antagonism over its alleged contamination of the country's environment through the dumping of plastic waste. Indian environmentalists, along with Greenpeace's Toxic Trade Project, investigated Pepsi Co's involvement in both production and disposal of plastic waste in India. The study found that in 1992, out of the 10,000 metric tons of plastic waste generated as well as imported by Pepsi and other companies, only 60 to 70 percent could be processed. The remaining 3,000 to 4,000 metric tons of plastic garbage was not recyclable . India still lacks a system of closed loop recycling, and therefore the same problems persist today.

At the national policy level, the Ministry of Environment and Forests of India established new Municipal Solid Waste Management Rules in 2000. These rules have failed to manage waste as a cyclic process, instead treating waste as a linear system of collection and disposal and thereby creating health and environmental hazards (Gupta, 2004). The current rules and regulations are inadequate to assess the environmental impact of waste generated at the industrial level. At its headquarters in New York, PepsiCo has been criticized for environmental waste created by bottling a drink (water) that people can get from the tap; especially because only 24.6% of PET (polyethylene terephthalate) plastic bottles used for soda, water, and other products are recycled in the US. As a result, PepsiCo has launched its new Eco-Fina bottle that uses 50% less plastic than its traditional Aquafina bottle. Even Coca-Cola's Dasani brand and Nestle's Poland Springs is known to have been steadily shrinking the weight of their PET plastic bottles (Bauerlein, 2009).

In dealing with the issue of water pollution with toxic waste and pesticides, PepsiCo changed its environmental management based on a host of drivers. The formal institutional drivers are media comment, investor pressure due to fall in sales, and the GoI regulation that established new standards for industrial water use and disposal. The informal drivers attributed to the change are protection of brand image, consumer pressure, and the pressure of domestic NGOs and environmental agencies. For changes made in PepsiCo's packaging, headquarter environmental policies and reports revealed by Greenpeace can be identified as the two main institutional drivers. The informal drivers for this move are: protection of brand image, rise in environmental concerns of its consumers, competition, risk management as a result of its falling shares, and attainment of eco-efficiency.

Review Questions

Conceptual Type

1. Give the meaning of environmentalism.
2. What is environmental preservation?
3. What is environmental degradation?
4. Give the meaning of overpopulation.
5. Give the meaning of ozone depletion.
6. What is sustainable development?
7. What is industrial pollution?
8. What is environmental management system?
9. What are pollutants?
10. Define environmental pollution.
11. Give the meaning of thermal pollution.
12. What is a Green House-effect?
13. What is environmental audit?

Analytical Type

1. Write note on: environmental preservation.
2. Explain the concept of sustainable development.
3. Explain cost and benefits of environmental regulations.
4. State the causes of industrial pollution.
5. What is waste management? What are the causes for waste management?
6. What is waste management? Explain the importance of waste management.
7. Define environmental pollution. What are the types or causes of environmental pollution?
8. Explain the causes and control measures of air pollution.
9. Explain the role of an individual in prevention of pollution.
10. Discuss key strategies for prevention of pollution.
11. Write note on: Laws governing environment.

Descriptive Type

1. Explain the history of environmentalism.
2. Discuss international issues on environmental concern.
3. Explain the effects of industrial pollution.
4. Give the role and benefits of corporate in environmental management.
5. Discuss environmental auditing practices and procedures.

******

Module-6

Business Ethics

Syllabus

Meaning of ethics, business ethics, relation between ethics and business ethics, evolution of business ethics, nature of business ethics, scope, need and purpose, importance, approaches to business ethics, sources of ethical knowledge for business roots of unethical behavior, ethical decision making, some unethical issues, benefits from managing ethics at workplace, ethical organizations.

Introduction

Ethics can be defined as the evaluation of moral values, principles, and standards of human conduct and its application in daily life to determine acceptable human behavior.

Business ethics pertains to the application of ethics to business, and is a matter of concern in the corporate world. Business ethics is almost similar to the generally accepted norms and principles. Behavior that is considered unethical and immoral in society, for example dishonesty, applies to business as well. Discussion on ethics in business is necessary because, business can go unethical, and there are plenty of evidences as in today on unethical corporate practices. Even Adam Smith, in whose name neo-liberallaissez-faire is advocated opined that 'People of the same trade seldom meet together, even for merriment and diversion, but the conversation ends in a conspiracy against the public, or in some contrivance to raise prices'

Business does not operate in vacuum. Firms and corporations operate in the social and natural environment. By virtue of existing in the social and natural environment, business is duty bound to be accountable to the natural and social environment in which it survives.

Irrespective of the demands and pressures upon it, business, by virtue of its existence is bound to be ethical, for at least two reasons: one, because whatever the business does affects its stakeholders and two, because every juncture of action has trajectories of ethical as well as unethical paths wherein the existence of the business isustified by ethical alternatives it responsibly chooses.

One of the conditions that brought business ethics to the forefront is the demise of small scale, high trust and face-to-face enterprises and emergence of huge multinational corporate structures capable of drastically affecting everyday lives of the masses.

Business Ethics

Ethics, the search for 'a good way of being' for a wise course of action, as it could be practiced by business firms is called business ethics.

Ethics in business deals with the ethical path business firm sought to adopt. Afflicting the least suffering to humans and the nature in its entirety, achieving the greatest net benefit to the society and economy enriching the capability of the system in which it is functioning being fair in all its dealings with its proximate and remote stakeholders being prepared to correct its mal-habits and nurturing an enduring virtuous corporate character in totality, can be called business ethics

It is often suggested from extended utilitarian/ consequentialist position that businesses can often attain short-lived gains by acting in an unethical fashion; however, such behaviours tend to undermine the economy over time. For those who uphold the principles of virtue ethics, all that matters is corporations maintaining character of honesty, fairness and humaneness than being ethical for the sake of better consequences. On the other hand experts of deontological ethics and virtue ethics postulate that what matters is the motive to be ethical than the consequential fallout.

Definitions of Business Ethics

According to ***Andrew Crane***, "Business ethics is the study of business situations, activities, and decisions where issues of right and wrong are addressed."

According to ***Raymond C. Baumhart***, "The ethics of business is the ethics of responsibility. The business man must promise that he will not harm knowingly."

Features of Business Ethics

The characteristics or features of business ethics are:

1. Code of Conduct
2. Based on Moral and Social Values
3. Gives Protection to Social Groups
4. Provides Basic Framework
5. Voluntary
6. Requires Education and Guidance
7. Relative Term
8. New concept

- ***Code of conduct:*** Business ethics is a code of conduct. It tells what to do and what not to do for the welfare of the society. All businessmen must follow this code of conduct.
- ***Based on moral and social values:*** Business ethics is based on moral and social values. It contains moral and social principles for doing business. This includes self-control, consumer protection and welfare, service to society, fair treatment to social groups, not to exploit others, etc.
- ***Gives protection to social groups:*** Business ethics give protection to different social groups such as consumers, employees, small businessmen, government, shareholders, creditors, etc.
- ***Provides basic framework:*** Business ethics provide a basic framework for doing business. It gives the social cultural, economic, legal and other limits of business. Business must be conducted within these limits.
- ***Voluntary:*** Business ethics must be voluntary. The businessmen must accept business ethics on their own. Business ethics must be like self-discipline. It must not be enforced by law.
- ***Requires education and guidance:*** Businessmen must be given proper education and guidance before introducing business ethics. The businessmen must be motivated to use business ethics. They must be informed about the advantages of using business ethics. Trade Associations and Chambers of Commerce must also play an active role in this matter.

- ***Relative term:*** Business ethics is a relative term. That is, it changes from one business to another. It also changes from one country to another. What is considered as good in one country may be taboo in another country.
- ***New concept:*** Business ethics is a newer concept. It is strictly followed only in developed countries. It is not followed properly in poor and developing countries.

Business Ethics Factors

During the mid-1960s and 1970s, social awareness movements raised expectations of businesses to use their financial and social influence to address social issues such as poverty, literacy, women rights, public health, and environmental protection. It was argued that these businesses used community resources and profits generated by public participation to address social issues. Hence, there arose a need for managers to take up the responsibility to understand and address social issues guided by high ethical standards.

In this unit, let us learn the different factors that influence the ethics of a business and its managers. Managers are influenced by three factors affecting ethical values. These factors have unique value systems that have varying degrees of control over managers.

- ***Religion:*** Religion is one of the oldest factors affecting ethics. Despite the differences in religious teachings, religions agree on the fundamental principles and ethics. All major religions preach the need for high ethical standards, an orderly social system, and stress on social responsibility as contributing factors to general well-being.
- ***Culture:*** Culture refers to a set of values and standards that defines acceptable behavior passed on to generations. These values and standards are important because the code of conduct of people reflects on the culture they belong to. Civilization is the collective experience that people have passed on through three distinct phases: the hunting and gathering phase, agriculture phase, and the industrial phase. These phases reflect the changing economic and social arrangements in human history.
- ***Law:*** Law refers to the rules of conduct, approved by the legal system of a country or state that guides human behavior. Laws change and evolve with emerging and changing issues. Every organization is expected to abide the law, but in the pursuit of profit, laws are frequently violated. The most common breach of law in business is tax evasion, producing inferior quality goods, and disregard for environmental protection laws.

Importance of Business Ethics

Ethics is significant in all areas of business and plays an important role in ensuring a successful business. The role of business ethics is evident from the conception of an idea to the sale of a product. In an organization, every division such as sales and marketing, customer service, finance, and accounting and taxation has to follow certain ethics.

- ***Public image:*** In order to gain public confidence and respect, organizations must ascertain that they are honest in their transactions. The services or products of a business affect the lives of thousands of people. It is important for the top management to impart high ethical standards to their employees, who develop these services or products.

A company that is ethically and socially responsible has a better public image. People tend to favor the products and services of such organizations. Investors' trust is just as important as public image for any business. A company that practices good ethical creates a positive impression among its stakeholders.

- ***Management's credibility with employees:*** Common goals and values are developed when employees feel that the management is ethical and genuine. Management's credibility with employees and the public are intertwined. Employees feel proud to be a part of an organization that is respected by the public. Generous compensations and effective business strategies do not always guarantee employee loyalty; organization ethics is equally significant. Thus, companies benefit from being ethical because they attract and retain good and loyal employees.
- ***Better decision-making:*** Decisions made by an ethical management are in the best interests of the organization, its employees, and the public. Ethical decisions take into account various social, economic and ethical factors.
- ***Profit maximization:*** Companies that emphasize on ethical conduct are successful in the long run, even though they lose money in the short run. Hence, a business that is inspired by ethics is a profitable business. Costs of audit and investigation are lower in an ethical company.
- ***Protection of society: In*** the absence of proper enforcement, organizations are responsible to practice ethics and ensure mechanisms to prevent unlawful events. Thus, by propagating ethical values, a business organization can save government resources and protect the society from exploitation.

International Business and Ethics

In the previous section, you learned about ethics and its importance in business. Now let us discuss the effects of ethics in international business.

Most countries have similar ethical values, but are practiced differently. This section deals with the way individuals in different countries approach ethical issues, and their ethically acceptable behavior. With the rise in global firms, issues related to ethical values and traditions become more common. These ethical issues create complications to Multi-National Companies (MNCs) while dealing with other countries for business. Hence, many companies have formulated well-designed codes of conduct to help their employees.

Two of the most prominent issues that managers in MNCs operating in foreign countries face are bribery and corruption and worker compensation.

- ***Bribery and corruption:*** Bribery can be defined as the act of offering, accepting, or soliciting something of value for the purpose of influencing the action of officials in the discharge of their duties. Corruption is the abuse of public office for personal gain. The issue arises when there are differences in perception in different countries. For example, in the Middle East, it is perfectly acceptable to offer an official a gift. In Britain it is considered as an attempt to bribe the official, and hence, considered unlawful.
- ***Worker compensation:*** Businesses invest in production facilities abroad because of the availability of low-cost labour, which enables them to offer goods and services at a lower price than their

competitors. The issue arises when workers are exploited and are underpaid compared to the workers in the parent country who are paid more for the same job. The disparity arises due to the differences in the regulatory standards in the two countries.

Managing Ethics

Earlier, we believed that ethics is a prerogative of individuals, but now this perception has immensely changed. Many companies use management techniques to encourage ethical behavior at an organizational level. Various techniques of managing ethics like practicing ethics at the top level management, special training on ethics, forming committees to oversee ethical issues, and defining and implementing code of ethics are:

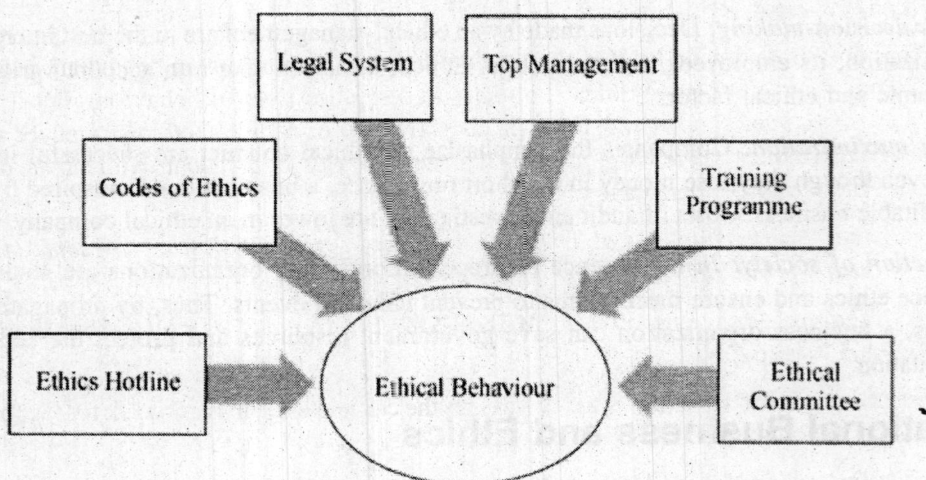

Fig: *Techniques of Managing Ethics*

(i) ***Top management:*** The senior management of a company must be committed to ensure that ethical standards are met. The chief executive of the company must not engage in business practices harmful to employees, or the society. The top management must focus on ethical practices while informing employees of their intention.

(ii) ***Code of ethics:*** One of the best practices for ethics is creating a 'corporate ethical statement' and communicating it within the company. Such practices enhance the company's public image. Almost all Fortune 500 companies have such codes.

(iii) ***Ethics committee:*** There are ethics committees in many firms to help them deal with and advise on work related ethical issues. The Chief Executive Officer can head the committee that includes the Board of Directors. Such a committee answers employee queries, helps the company to establish policies in uncertain areas, advises the Board on ethical issues, and oversees the enforcement of the code of ethics.

(iv) ***Ethics hotline:*** A company's ethical hotline helps its employees report any ethical issues they face at work. The ethics committee then investigates these issues. Such hotline calls are treated confidential, where the caller's identity is protected to encourage employees to report on ethical issues.

(v) The act of reporting illegal, immoral, or illegitimate practices by former or current employees involving its employees is known as Whistle-blowing. Whistle-blowing is favourable to a company because employees can alert the management on possibly deviant behaviour rather than reporting it to the media, which adversely affects the company. A case of whistle-blowing in Xerox corporation (a pioneer in copier machines), led its Chief Financial Officer to be fined $ 5.5 million and banned from practicing accountancy after reports of falsified financial statements emerged.

(vi) ***Ethics training programs:*** Most firms take ethics seriously and provide training for its managers and employees. Such training programs help the employees become familiar with the official policy on ethical issues. These programs demonstrate the use of these ethic policies in everyday decision-making. Ethics training is most effective when conducted by managers and when focused on work environment.

(vii) ***Ethics and law:*** Both law and ethics focus on defining the perfect human behaviour, but they are not the same. Law is the government's attempt to formalise rightful behaviour, but it is rarely possible to enforce written laws. It depends on individual or business ethics to reduce unlawful incidents. Ethical concepts are more complex than written rules since it deals with human dilemmas that go beyond the formal language of law.

Legal rules seek to promote ethical behaviour in companies. The following are some of the Acts which seek to ensure fair business practices in India:

- ***Foreign Exchange Management Act (FEMA) of 1999*** - FEMA regulates the cross border movement of foreign and local currencies.
- ***Companies Act of 1956*** - Companies Act provides the complete legal framework for the formation, running, and winding up of a company.
- ***Consumer Protection Act of 1986 (CPA)*** - CPA provides and regulates the framework for the protection of consumer rights.
- ***Essential Commodities Act of 1955*** - This act defines the goods and services that are essential for the people at all times and provides a legal framework for the uninterrupted supply of the same.

Free Market Ethics

In this section, we will discuss the ethical aspects of competition used to explain free market ethics. Competition is an important element that differentiates free market from command market. Competition is a mechanism for free market production and distribution of goods and services that are in demand. Competition in business is seen as an essential cultural trait of a free market society. Most activities of the free market can be viewed as a competitive contest in which businesses engage to provide products and services for a profit.

In addition to the economic nature of the free market system, there are ethic- related issues as well. The three widely accepted factors of ethics in the free market are market ethics, the Protestant ethics, and the liberty ethics. These three ethics set the stage for the industrial revolution and the accompanying growth in business. During this period, industrial capitalists were allowed to freely operate businesses, build large organizations, exploit workers, and engage in fiercely competitive practices for profit and economic expansion.

- ***Market ethics:*** Market ethics is the basic system of ethics followed by a business in a free market scenario. It covers the entire spectrum of business including sales, pricing, and competitor issues.
- ***The Protestant ethics:*** The Protestant ethics considered ideology as an important factor along with the moral aspects in a capitalist scenario. As an ideology, this ethic served to legitimise the capitalistic system by providing a moral justification for the pursuit of profit and distribution of income.
- ***Liberty ethics:*** Liberty ethics encourages a person to play a participatory role on government, encourages private property, and introduces more freedom and individualism in all spheres of life.

National Differences in Ethics

In the previous section we examined how ethics is significant in international ethics. In this section, let us consider the differences in understanding ethics across countries. The differences in national cultures have an impact on the social and ethical practices of multinational firms. Cultural norms and values that usually influence business practices are attitudes towards women, minorities, bribery, and law. Religion and law are the key social factors that influence the type of ethical issues.

In MNCs, managers play a key role in managing ethics. While working in a foreign country, you cannot expect a manager to have a comprehensive knowledge of that country's culture and social factors that affect business. Therefore, the international manager needs to acquire adequate knowledge of a country's cultural, legal, and social scenarios to ascertain the important ethical issues and to manage these issues. The approaches to understand national differences in ethics are ethical relativism, ethical universalism, and ethical convergence. Let us discuss each of them in detail.

Ethical relativism and Ethical Universalism

Ethical relativism means that each country's outlook on ethics must be considered valid and ethical. This implies that if bribery is not unethical in a foreign country, then it is acceptable for an MNC to encourage bribery even if it is illegal in its home country. Ethical relativism means that when a company deals with a host country for business, the international managers must follow the ethical norms of the host country. Another example is the attitude towards women employees in certain Arab countries. The attitude differs to a large extent compared to western countries. In Saudi Arabia, women employees are segregated from their male counterparts at the work place. All companies, MNCs or local, must comply with these rules.

The principle of ethical universalism states that there are basic moral principles that are valid across all cultural and political boundaries. For example, all countries forbid unethical accounting practices and tax evasion.

Both these principles have drawbacks when in international business. Ethical relativism is a convenient way to indulge in unethical practices with cultural differences as an excuse. The universal approach can be perceived as cultural imperialism, since business managers may regard business practices in some countries as inferior or immoral.

Ethical Convergence

Ethical convergence is defined as the practice of a uniform system of ethical codes in different countries that are culturally and socially different.

There is a growing pressure on international business to follow a uniform set of guidelines in managing ethical behavior and social responsibility across the countries in which they operate. The following are some of the advantages of ethical convergence:

The growth of international trading blocks, such as North American Free Trade Agreement (NAFTA) and the European Union promotes common ethical practices across national cultures and borders to reduce institutional differences. Predictable interaction and behavior among trading partners from different countries makes trade more efficient.

People from different cultural backgrounds increase their interactions and exposure to varying ethical traditions. They adopt, adjust to, and imitate new behavior and attitudes which leads to acceptance of best practices.

International businesses have employees from different cultural backgrounds. The companies rely on their corporate culture to provide consistent norms and values that govern ethical issues to set common standards for employees from different cultural backgrounds.

Negotiating Across Cultures

Negotiations in international businesses face cultural barriers. When people from two different countries try to discuss commercial issues, they have to understand and acknowledge any ethical issues that may come up. These standards of conduct and moral judgement are the basis of an outcome. They can create bring mistrust when the messages and views are misinterpreted. The basic concepts of fairness, dependability, politeness, and punctuality have to be followed at all times. There are two models of negotiating as presented by Solomon and Bertrand. They are the following:

- Linear model.
- Encompassing model.

- ***Linear model:*** Linear model relates to the Chinese culture. Figure 4.2 depicts this model. The first stage is the discussion of the goals and principles. In China, this stage is emphasised so that foreigners understand their commitments. The second stage deals with bargaining positions, which are the offers that are proposed. The third stage clarifies details and the last stage involves implementing the process.

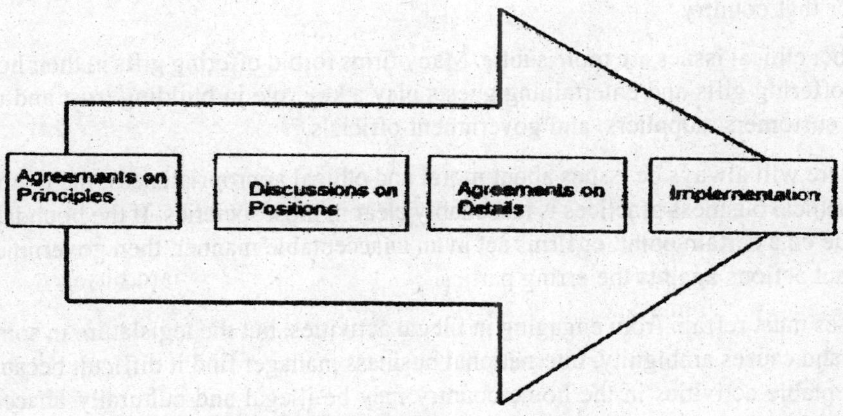

Fig: *Linear Model of Negotiation*

- ***Encompassing model:*** The encompassing model is more descriptive and includes stages that are identical to the linear model, but focuses on the extent to which each stage is presented. Figure 4.3 illustrates this model. The Chinese base their negotiations on improving their national goals which include national development, growth, and improvement of the overall quality of life in China. The western companies that operate in China are expected to sacrifice their goals whenever necessary, so that the Chinese goals are achieved.

  Firms base their negotiations on corporate objectives such as product quality, profit, and maximizing shareholder value. Sacrificing such goals is against corporate responsibility, hence is the main reason for negotiations.

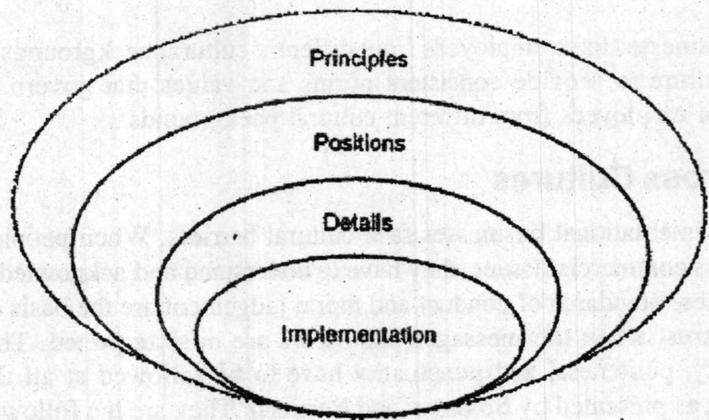

Fig: *Encompassing Model of Negotiation*

Ethical Issues

International business managers face ethical issues that vary based on the market and geographic region. Some of these issues have been widely publicized in the past. Most of these issues are related to the safety and compensation practices of manufacturing plants in emerging countries. Ethical considerations also tend to be connected to political situations. For example, the decision to move a company's headquarters elsewhere to reduce taxes becomes a political issue due to the potential loss of tax revenue for that country.

Some other ethical issues are more subtle Many firms forbid offering gifts in their home countries. But in Japan, offering gifts and entertaining guests play a key role in building trust and understanding with potential customers, suppliers, and government officials.

While there will always be issues about moral and ethical appropriateness, the boundary between ethical and unethical business practices is reasonably clear in most societies. If the boundary is not clear, the law is vague on a certain point, or firms act in an unacceptable manner, then governments may have to taken relevant actions against the erring parties.

Businesses must refrain from engaging in illegal activities, but the legislature in some countries is not very clear and causes ambiguity. International business manager find it difficult because legally and culturally acceptable activities in the home country may be illegal and culturally unacceptable in the foreign country. The international manager has to make prudent decisions at such occasions. MNCs deal with issues related to ethics in foreign country. Some of the issues are the following:

- Conduct business in a country where the government violates human rights.
- Market a product in a country that lacks adequate consumer protection and product liability laws.
- Sell products with harmful side effects, where there is a high level of illiteracy that prevents the customers from following the directions for safe usage of a product.
- Be responsible for the end-user behavior that may not be legal.
- Bribe officials in a country where corruption is widespread.
- Follow local laws in areas such as employee safety and environmental protection that are not as strict as in the home country.
- Change attitude towards female employees in a country where women do not enjoy the same rights as men.
- Use tax avoidance strategies.
- Accomplish business goals with a firm engaged in practices that are illegal in the home country.

Multinational firms should have a moral and ethical responsibility to ensure a safe, fair, environmentally sustainable, and legal work environment in emerging markets irrespective of the local laws. These are the issues that international businesses face when they conduct business in other parts of the world, where the laws are different from their home countries.

Ethical Decision Making

In the previous section you learned about the various ethical issues to be considered in an international scenario, let us discuss the process of ethical decision making.

The competitive nature of business and the emphasis on profit causes managers to violate business ethics. For example, employing workers in a foreign country, where wages are low and working conditions are sub-standard. Ideally, a manager must consider all the choices available to him and make a decision that does not violate the ethics of business.

There are many differences in opinion concerning business ethics. The following are four approaches that help managers make the right decision.

- ***Utilitarian:*** Maximum benefit to the most number of people' is the basis of this approach. For example, in the case of low-wage foreign workers, the cost savings helps the company perform better, but results in layoffs in the home country. If the manager is not willing to employ low-wage workers, the company becomes uncompetitive which in turn results in both foreign and domestic workers being laid off. On the other hand, lower wages tend to bring down the level of wages for everyone, which decreases their purchasing power and affects the sale of the company's goods.
- ***Moral rights:*** Morality is the basis of this approach without considering the consequences. Paying someone extremely low wages is morally wrong. Those who accept this approach believe that a business must not exist if the workers are not paid adequately.
- ***Universalism:*** There are two steps in this approach. First, one needs to decide if the action being considered has to apply to everyone under all situations. Second, the same action must be applied to the manager.

- *Cost-benefit:* The profitability of every action is analyzed. *For example,* the negative publicity of paying extremely low wages weighed against being more competitive.

In conclusion, it is evident that a manager has several approaches to choose from. The manager must take the time to analyze all the possibilities, in order to make the right decision.

Ethics

Ethics is a branch of social science. It deals with moral principles and social values. It helps us to classify, what is good and what is bad? It tells us to do good things and avoid doing bad things.

Ethics separate, good and bad, right and wrong, fair and unfair, moral and immoral and proper and improper human action. In short, ethics means a code of conduct. It is like the 10 commandments of holy Bible. It tells a person how to behave with another person. So, the businessmen must give a regular supply of good quality goods and services at reasonable prices to their consumers. They must avoid indulging in unfair trade practices like adulteration, promoting misleading advertisements, cheating in weights and measures, black marketing, etc. They must give fair wages and provide good working conditions to their workers. They must not exploit the workers. They must encourage competition in the market. They must protect the interest of small businessmen. They must avoid unfair competition. They must avoid monopolies. They must pay all their taxes regularly to the government.

Definition of Ethics

The basic concepts and fundamental principles of right human conduct. It includes study of universal values such as the essential equality of all men and women, human or natural rights, obedience to the law of land, concern for health and safety and, increasingly, also for the natural environment.

Ethics, also known as moral philosophy, is a branch of philosophy that involves systematizing, defending, and recommending concepts of right and wrong conduct. It comes from the Greek word ethos, which means "character". Major areas of study in ethics may be divided into 4 operational areas:

- Meta-ethics, about the theoretical meaning and reference of moral propositions and how their truth values (if any) may be determined;
- Normative ethics, about the practical means of determining a moral course of action;
- Descriptive ethics, also known as comparative ethics, is the study of people's beliefs about morality;
- Applied ethics, about how moral outcomes can be achieved in specific situations

Relationship between Ethics and Business Ethics

The relationship between business and ethics is intrinsically entwined. A successful company is one which can effectively recognize and cultivate the relationship which exists between the two.

Businesses that exhibit and promote strong corporate codes of ethics are more prosperous in the long run ' ecause they show a commitment to an expectation of sound moral behavior. This demonstrates a dedication to society, customers, employees and the business itself. It also enhances a company's reputation if they become commonly known as an ethical company, and this brings more value to the organization.

The highly competitive environment in today's global economy puts pressures on company leaders to remain profitable and to show a good return to stakeholders. Often this pressure can result in unethical decisions being made in order to deliver positive results. When this occurs it usually results in a pattern that gets passed down through the organization.

As leaders show unethical behavior and perhaps even justify it even though they know to be wrong, this eventually becomes a part of organizational culture. People follow by example, and the lack of moral judgment will spread. It's easy to blame "the system", yet many fail to realize the "system" is comprised of decision making individuals. The relationship between business and ethics is inherently linked, but there are some who fail to make this connection. To determine "business is business" is not accurate as responsible (ethical) decision making is an important component of doing good business.

Today's society is an instant gratification one and people expect immediate results. This is perhaps part of the reason why some companies exhibit bad business practices. Not the only reason, but perhaps a common one. Obviously one's individual moral compass impacts choices made in a business, and when the cultural environment nurtures sound moral philosophies and does not tolerate bad business practices, the immoral acts will decline.

Granted the unethical companies may initially make significant gains financially and deliver the profits, but at what cost? When companies make unethical decisions it can result in defective or rushed products, unsubstantiated firing of employees, and false presentations of products to consumers. Is this good for the company? The fact is it's an illusion. Yes, these factors will all cut costs and give the appearance of profit, but it's inevitable that poor choices will negatively impact the business

Evolution of Business Ethics

The study of business ethics evolved through five distinct stages;

(1) Before 1960

(2) The 1960's,

(3) The 1970's

(4) The 1980's, and

(5) The 1990's, and continues to evolve in the twenty-first century.

Before the 1960's, business ethics were discussed primarily through a religious perspective. It was in 1962 that John F. Kennedy established the Consumer's Bill of Rights, in which he outlined four basic consumer rights: the right to safety, the right to be informed, the right to choose and the right to be heard.

In the 1970's, business professors began to write and teach about social responsibility, an organization's obligation to maximize its positive impact on stakeholders and minimize its negative impact. Companies became more concerned with their public image and wanted to address ethical issues more directly.

In the 1980's, centers of business ethics provided publications, courses, conferences, seminars, ethics committees, and social policy committees. The Defense Industry Initiative on Business Ethics and Conduct was developed to guide corporate support for ethical conduct. Its principals had a major impact on corporate ethics. This effort established a method for discussing best practices and working tactics to link organizational practice and policy to successful ethical compliance.

In the 1990's businesses with international operations set up new ethical issues. The Federal Sentencing Guidelines for Organizations was approved by Congress in 1991 to reward organizations for taking actions to prevent misconduct, such as developing effective internal legal and ethical compliance programs.

In 2002, Congress passed the Sarbanes-Oxley Act which made securities fraud a corporate offense and stiffened penalties for corporate fraud. Top executives are now required to sign off on their firms' financial reports, and they risk heavy fines and long prison sentences if they misrepresent their company's financial position. The term ethical culture can be viewed as the character or decision making process that employees use to determine whether their responses to an ethical issue are right or wrong. An ethical culture creates shared values and support for ethical decisions and is driven by top management. Research demonstrates that building an ethical reputation to the public provides benefits that include increased efficiency in business operations, employee commitment, investor trust, customer trust and better financial performance. The reputation of a company has a major effect on its relationships and has the potential to affect its bottom line.

Need or Importance of Business Ethics

These below discuss the need, importance of business ethics:

1. Stop business malpractices
2. Improve consumers confidence
3. Survival of business
4. Protecting consumers rights
5. Protecting employees, shareholders, etc.
6. Develops good relations between business and society
7. Creates good image of business
8. Smooth functioning of business
9. Consumer movement
10. Consumer satisfaction
11. Importance of labour
12. Healthy competition

1. ***Stop business malpractices:*** Some unscrupulous businessmen do business malpractices by indulging in unfair trade practices like black-marketing, artificial high pricing, adulteration, cheating in weights and measures, selling of duplicate and harmful products, hoarding, etc. These business malpractices are harmful to the consumers. Business ethics help to stop these business malpractices.
2. ***Improve customers' confidence:*** Business ethics are needed to improve the customers' confidence about the quality, quantity, price, etc. of the products. The customers have more trust and confidence in the businessmen who follow ethical rules. They feel that such businessmen will not cheat them.
3. ***Survival of business:*** Business ethics are mandatory for the survival of business. The businessmen who do not follow it will have short-term success, but they will fail in the long run. This is because they can cheat a consumer only once. After that, the consumer will not buy goods from that businessman. He will also tell others not to buy from that businessman. So this will defame his image and provoke a negative publicity. This will result in failure of the business. Therefore, if the businessmen do not follow ethical rules, he will fail in the market. So, it is always better to follow appropriate code of conduct to survive in the market.
4. ***Safeguarding consumers' rights:*** The consumer has many rights such as right to health and safety, right to be informed, right to choose, right to be heard, right to redress, etc. But many businessmen do not respect and protect these rights. Business ethics are must to safeguard these rights of the consumers.
5. ***Protecting employees and shareholders:*** Business ethics are required to protect the interest of employees, shareholders, competitors, dealers, suppliers, etc. It protects them from exploitation through unfair trade practices.
6. ***Develops good relations:*** Business ethics are important to develop good and friendly relations between business and society. This will result in a regular supply of good quality goods and services at low prices to the society. It will also result in profits for the businesses thereby resulting in growth of economy.
7. ***Creates good image:*** Business ethics create a good image for the business and businessmen. If the businessmen follow all ethical rules, then they will be fully accepted and not criticized by the society. The society will always support those businessmen who follow this necessary code of conduct.
8. ***Smooth functioning:*** If the business follows all the business ethics, then the employees, shareholders, consumers, dealers and suppliers will all be happy. So they will give full cooperation to the business. This will result in smooth functioning of the business. So, the business will grow, expand and diversify easily and quickly. It will have more sales and more profits.
9. ***Consumer movement:*** Business ethics are gaining importance because of the growth of the consumer movement. Today, the consumers are aware of their rights. Now they are more organized and hence cannot be cheated easily. They take actions against those businessmen who indulge in bad business practices. They boycott poor quality, harmful, high-priced and counterfeit (duplicate) goods. Therefore, the only way to survive in business is to be honest and fair.
10. ***Consumer satisfaction:*** Today, the consumer is the king of the market. Any business simply cannot survive without the consumers. Therefore, the main aim or objective of business is consumer satisfaction. If the consumer is not satisfied, then there will be no sales and thus no profits too.

Consumer will be satisfied only if the business follows all the business ethics, and hence are highly needed.

11. ***Importance of labour:*** Labour, i.e. employees or workers play a very crucial role in the success of a business. Therefore, business must use business ethics while dealing with the employees. The business must give them proper wages and salaries and provide them with better working conditions. There must be good relations between employer and employees. The employees must also be given proper welfare facilities.

12. ***Healthy competition:*** The business must use business ethics while dealing with the competitors. They must have healthy competition with the competitors. They must not do cut-throat competition. Similarly, they must give equal opportunities to small-scale business. They must avoid monopoly. This is because a monopoly is harmful to the consumers

Purpose of Business Ethics

The purpose of business is to generate maximum returns for its owners and shareholders. So therefore should the business pursue all activities that enhance profitability and increase the value of the business for the owners and shareholders.

Business ethics serve a purpose of defining how a business conducts its activities' both internally and externally with an aim of ensuring that all stakeholders receive maximum benefit from the Business. Different businesses develop their ethics to be in line with their nature of business among other considerations.

Business ethics is how a company relates to the public, environmental and employees. You can compare it to morals that people have to follow.

Business ethics are put in place to protect consumers, employees, and to build trust. Business ethics ensure everyone involved, a level of comfort in business dealings, making the entire business more successful, especially internally

By having real policies in place that take care of your employees and the local community it might be argued that long term this will enhance your business brand and over time lead to higher profitability.

By constantly training members of staff and wherever possible promoting from within the organization will lead to employees that feel empowered to work harder and make better decisions. Having regards to the true wellbeing of your employees will lead to a healthier and therefore happier workforce.

By reducing waste and promoting recycling at every opportunity, overheads will be reduced and in the longer term lead to better shareholder value. It is staggering how much resources including energy are wasted by larger companies. Having a regular energy audit and investing long term to reduce demand can only serve to make the business more efficient.

Many businesses try to serve their community by supporting local charities and sponsoring local people to better their lives. There are many ways to do this including education, sports and the environment. In the short term there will be very few perceivable benefits in terms of profitability but these actions will serve to enhance the business brand and increase profitability over the longer term.

Greed is no longer good and focusing purely on profits is unacceptable to your existing and potential customers. By embracing business ethics and social responsibility the business can benefit from increased goodwill.

Approaches to Business Ethics

According to the philosophies, environment means humanity. Today's ethics approaches note depending on keeping human wants under pressure for the benefits of all human beings. By these words environment includes not only men, but also animals, plants i.e., the nature. Ethics occurs by relations of humans with themselves and their physical and social environment. Therefore, the origin of the problems and solution is human. The philosophies note many approaches in these relations. *These approaches can be grouped into three groups:*

- The human-oriented approach
- The living oriented approach
- The environment oriented approach.

Every approach describes one of parts of the whole environmental ethics. But the common point of these approaches is that all human beings and their equal rights take place in the ecosystem. By the each in the concept of deep ecology it is accepted that the diversity of the ecosystem has an internal value and no one has any right to decrease this diversity and difference.

For centuries, people have established a lot of establishments to achieve these goals. Human beings have seen that producing something by cooperation is more productive and effective than doing it alone, so they have established enterprises. They have seen unlimited needs, increasing wants and scarcity of objects and they have also seen establishing enterprises as a way of producing more. But in this century humans saw a lot of impacts from our living. Air, water and soil pollution, the danger of consuming natural resources, acid rain, and gas, dust, and liquids industries caused, soiling of natural foods, industrial pollution, and dangerous wastes, just to mention a few problems we face.

These environmental problems make us reconsider the goals of organizations and their responsibilities to the society and nature. The organizational goals are often not environmentally friendly. In some events the goal of the establishment is opposite to the environment and sometimes organizational activities damage the environment in achieving the goals. In this process, we should emphasize the reasons why they should have responsibility. First, they use environmental resources and resources are limited. Second, they damage the environment by their activities. Third, they use common assets of mankind.

Finally, the enterprises have various forces to influence the environment: Economic force, social and cultural force, technological force, politic force, forces on individuals and physical environment.

In spite of these impacts and forces of establishments, there is no social control system on the activities of enterprises. This point emphasizes business ethics terms as an institutional framework, i.e., social ethics. As an institutional term, social ethics means searching ethical norms to protect the social benefits, and determining the possibilities for achieving a kind society. Then, business ethics means, the norms, duties, responsibilities, courses of actions of enterprises to protect the benefits of whole society.

In a broader view, because of the impacts on the natural and social environment, business ethics concepts determine the responsibilities towards s ecosystem. It is the common denominator of business ethics and environmental ethics is the interrogation of relations and dilemmas between economy and nature, man and society.

According to the common classification of conceptual approaches on business ethics, The approaches three are there. The first approach reconciles ethical values with economic goals. The second approach gives priority to the ethical values. According to Ul rich, a new multidimensional goal system should replace to the profit maximization. And the third approach is pragmatic approach. In this approach, the attitudes model of business managers is the focus of interests.

The last two approaches are very important for us to develop a new concept and term on business ethics. The approach which gives priority to the ethical values is important, because the enterprises are not a purpose, they are only a tool which we use to get benefits. If this tool causes various damages on the ecosystem to get profit, then we should revise our organizational goals, targets and activities. A pragmatic approach is characterized with the importance of individual conscience and discussion of alternative individual courses of actions.

Therefore, these two approaches define the new term business ethics as an institutional concept. This concept includes both organizational responsibility and individual duties as business managers, also covered the ecosystem. We can name this concept as "environment oriented business ethics" or "enterprise ethics" and As determined above, if people are the focus of the problems and solution, educating people becomes our great responsibility. People should be educated as a member of business organizations. This education process should begin in childhood continue during our life.

Ethics is a Normative Science

Ethics is a normative science. It means it lay down the norms or standard of what is good and what is bad. It specifies what we ought to do and what we ought not to do, in a certain situation. Normative ethics is the branch of philosophical ethics that investigates the set of Questions that arise when we think about the question "how should one act, morally speaking?" Normative ethics is the discipline that produces moral norms or rules as it end product. Normative ethics prescribe moral behavior. It is a branch of ethics concerned with classifying actions as right and wrong, attempting to develop a set of rules governing human conduct, or a set of norms for action'. Traditionally, normative ethics (also known as moral theory) was study of what makes actions right and wrong. These theories offered an overarching moral principle to which one could appeal in resolving difficult moral decisions'.

Normative ethical systems can generally be broken down into three categories: deontological, teleological and virtue ethics. The first two are considered deontic or action-based theories of morality because they focus entirely upon the actions which a Person performs. When actions are judged morally right based upon their them consequences we have teleological or consequentiality ethical theory. When actions are judged morally right, based upon how well they conform to some set of duties; we have a deontological ethical theory.

Prescriptive Ethics

Business ethics is a branch of ethics which prescribes standards of how the business is to be carried out. It lays down guidelines for the company's response and accountability to its various stakeholders. It has to maintain a fine balance and take care of the interest of the shareholders on one hand and other like the employees, suppliers, customers and community at large on the other hand. All the stakeholders have different objective of what they expect from the company and at times these objectives may be conflicting in nature.

Applied Ethics

Applied ethics is a branch of ethics that deals with specific, often controversial moral issues such as abortion, female feticide and infanticide, displacement of tribal people due to huge hydro- electric projects, cloning, testing drugs on animals, etc. Business too faces many controversial moral choices such as misleading advertising, insider trading bribery, corruption etc. Ethical theories lay down certain moral standards that provide a reference point for judging the moral value of a decision. When applied to business, these theories should enable the manager to distinguish between right and wrong and to make morally acceptable decision

Sources of Ethical knowledge for Business roots of Unethical Behavior

However there is one very large assumption that is being made in relationship to the capability of the knowledge worker, the service sector worker and those involved in employment in the manufacturing and farming industry.

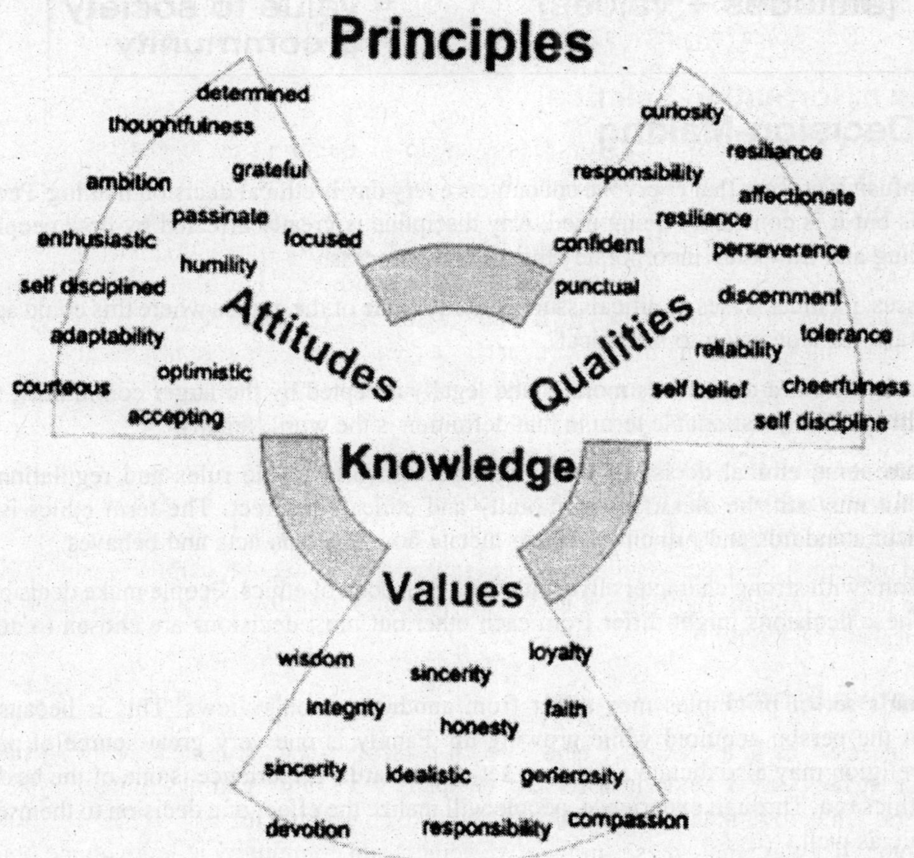

It is all very well to understand, think laterally, generate new ideas, solve complex problems and be good decision makers, accessing, processing and synthesizing large quantities of information in a wide variety of formats, BUT if those same people lack the necessary attitudes, qualities and values which provide that person with the capability to transmit, share, empower and provide leadership and in so doing allow their very clever ideas to blossom, mature and provide processes, systems, products and environments which will benefit their entire community then we are all in trouble.

Knowledge without appropriate attitudes, values and qualities is almost valueless to the society that the person lives in. Without appropriate attitudes, qualities and values the ideas, concepts and the outworking of these will go nowhere.

It is all very well to have a good set of values and attitudes but it is how that person's personality displays the interplay between their values and attitudes to the world via their personal qualities that can make that person invaluable in a wide range of situations, whether it be an emergency and heroic action is required or whether the office needs someone who is light-hearted and fun to be around in order to generate a cordial environment to work or socialise in.

If a person can display their values and attitudes with confidence, tolerance, cheerfulness and a measured sense of self belief then their role in society will become enhanced exponentially. The equation below provides a measure of the importance of someone's personal qualities:

$$[\text{attitudes} + \text{values}]^{\text{qualities}} = \text{value to society } \& \text{ community}$$

Ethical Decision Making

One confusing process that everyone encounters every day is ethical decision making. People may not notice this but it is constantly being used. Any discipline is greatly affected by how people utilize decision making and how they incorporate ethics in that process.

Businesses, medical issues, political issues are only some of the genres where this could apply. But what does it take for a decision to be ethical?

Experts say that if a decision is morally and legally accepted by the larger community, then that decision is ethical. The questionable term in that definition is the word 'legally'.

There are some ethical decisions that might not conform to the rules and regulations of the government but may still be classified as morally and ethically correct. The term ethics is used to describe a set of standards and principles which dictate how a person acts and behaves.

All persons with strong characters live with their own code of ethics. People make decisions every single day. These decisions might differ from each other but most decisions are chosen to do what is right.

A person's set of principles may differ from another person's views. This is because of the influence that the person acquired while growing up. Family is one very great source of principles. Culture and religion may also dictate a person's set of standards. Experience is one of the best ways to learn about ethics too. Through experience, people will realize the effect of a decision to themselves and to other people as well.

Professionally speaking, a formal code of ethics is usually rolled out by companies to assist employees in their decision making dilemmas. These codes are created by the company to make sure that everybody is treated equally and employees respect each other's rights. Since ethical decision making is very helpful in the business level, it is imperative for companies to create an ethics team who will formulate a code of ethics.

There are also ways on how to effectively make an ethical decision. The very first thing to do is to identify if there is an actual problem. This is important so that you will be aware that this problem needs your attention. Then identify if it is an ethical issue or not. Relevant and accurate information must be gathered carefully. Remember, jumping into conclusions because of personal intuition is not what ethical decision making is all about. Evaluate all of the alternatives based on the information that has been gathered.

Different approaches like Rights Based approach, Utilitarian approach, Common Good approach, Virtue approach and Fairness or Justice Approach can be used. After thorough thinking, make the decision. The process of thinking may take some time but making the actual decision should not be delayed. Longer periods of evaluating the problem will just lead to mental exhaustion which will hinder a person from thinking correctly. After the decision has been made, examine the effects of the choice that you have made. Reflect on the lessons that you have learned from the experience and apply it to the next challenges.

Also, think about how your decision would affect the other parties. Before choosing which.decision to make, examine who will benefit and harm from this action. Always make sure that the final decision will end up reducing harm. Check your core values for accuracy. Are you sure that what you thought was right and wrong are correct? Do not be afraid to ask for help from a third party who is not involved in the process. A good test if you were successful in ethical decision making is the Golden Rule. The effect of your decision to others will also affect their decisions on you.

Individuals are often required to make decisions in the business environment every day. Working for a company often requires following an ethical model or framework when making these decisions. Business ethics outlines the acceptable behavior companies expect to see from their employees. Strong decision making and business ethics can also help companies select the best business opportunities.

Facts

Decision making in business ethics usually requires companies to identify specific ethical standards, which often means different things to different people. As organizations continue to grow and expand, new individuals are hired who may not have the same ethical standards as individuals already working in the company. A difference in ethics often changes how individuals approach the decision-making process. Companies often use the organization's mission statement to build a framework for helping individuals make ethical business decisions.

Types

There are five types of ethical standards: utilitarian, rights, fairness or justice, common good, and virtue. Utilitarian ethics is a standard that attempts to do the most good and limit the amount of harm for each individual. A rights approach protects and respects the moral rights of individuals impacted by decisions. The fair or just style seeks to create equality among all individuals while the common good method focuses on bettering society as a whole. The virtue tactic centers on the ideal virtues necessary for promoting individuals for the company.

Functions

Business ethics is a tool companies use to ensure managers, directors, or executive officers act responsibly in various business situations. Ethical decision making attempts to promote the company as a whole, rather than letting one individual profit from business decisions. Individuals who consistently make decisions based on their personal benefit may create legal liabilities for a company that can lead to bankruptcy.

Considerations

Creating an ethical business environment does not happen overnight. Companies may need to spend time and money training and promoting business ethics among managers and employees. Companies may also find implementing an ethical decision-making process may lead to negative feedback from managers or employees. Combating this negative feedback may be a difficult part of implementing business ethics.

Expert Insight

Companies may use professional consultants, seminars, or other training methods to educate employees on decision making in business ethics. These outside sources may also be able to provide companies with an objective review of their current operations and offer advice on how to implement a strong ethical code in their business operations. While these professional resources may be expensive, it often helps companies develop an ethical business environment.

Some Unethical Issuse

1. Wal-Mart

Lack of compassion

Tip of the iceberg can describe the story below. Wal-Mart is company No. 1 in the world. It has the most revenue over any other company ($421 Billion). But its riches equal its controversies. This story is probably the most apt at describing the unethical treatment of its workers, because of the sheer senselessness of it.

In 2000, a collision with a semi-trailer left 52-year-old Deborah Shank with permanent brain damage and in a wheelchair. Her husband and three sons were fortunate for a $700,000 accident settlement from the trucking company. After legal costs and other expenses, the remaining $417,000 was put in a special trust to care for Mrs. Shank. However, six years later the providers of Mrs. Shank's health plan, Wal-Mart, sued the Shanks for the $470,000 it had spent on her medical care.

Wal-Mart was fully entitled to the money; in the fine print of Mrs. Shank's employment contract it said that money won in damages after an accident belonged to Wal-Mart. A federal judge had to rule in favor of Wal-Mart, and the family of Mrs. Shank had to rely on Medicaid and social-security payments for her round-the-clock care. Wal-Mart may be reversing the decision after public outcry.

However this case pinpoints Wal-Mart's often criticized treatment of employees as a commodity and its sometimes inhuman business ethics.

2. Trafigura: Dumping Toxic waste on the Ivory Coast and gagging the media

Earlier in the year, there was media frenzy in the U.K. over celebrities getting court injunctions to silence the press from reporting on their various misdeeds and grubby encounters. This story actually stems from a far more serious beginning, in 2006. Trafigura is a multinational formed in 1993, trading in base metals and energy, including oil. It makes almost 80 billion USD a year. In 2006, it caused a health crisis affecting 108,000 people, after a ship leased by the company was told that, due to toxicity levels higher than expected, the price of transferring the waste on board to the processing plant in the Netherlands had increased twenty-fold. To avoid the charge, Trafigura ordered the ship to dock at other seaports until they could find someone who would dump the waste. At Abidjan, Côte d'Ivoire, one of Africa's largest seaports, the waste was handed over to a newly formed dumping company, Companies Tommy, which illegally dumped the waste, instead of processing it. Many people there became sick due to exposure to the waste, and investigations began to determine whether it was intentionally dumped by Trafigura. Trafigura said in a press statement that their tests showed the waste not to be as toxic as had been claimed. This was proven false by a 2009 UN report posted by Wikileaks.

When newspapers came to publish their own findings, which proved that Trafigura was guilty of releasing toxic waste, they "lawyered up" and started firing legal notices to all news outlets which were saying there was a connection between the dumping and the injuries reported in the Ivory Coast. The Guardian newspaper had conclusive evidence that Trafigura knew of the dumping, and had a report they were ready to publish, however the libel firm hired by Trafigura, Carter Ruck, applied for a super-injunction so that the paper couldn't publish the report until a court decision was made. This caused MP Evan Harris to question the freedom of the press in the country. However, after a twitter campaign that spread the story in a matter of hours, the libel firm responsible backed down and allowed the report to be published.

Carter Ruck are still pursuing a libel case against BBC News night for allegations made on television (later proven true by an independent report).

3. Thomas Edison/Radio Corporation of America: Attempting a monopoly of patents

The ability for inventors and aspiring minds to call an idea their own, and theirs alone, is a very important mark of a fair society. Unfortunately, history is littered by examples of intellectual property being swallowed up by big corporations. In particular, Thomas Edison and the companies he formed with his vast wealth (RCA, General Electric) have always had a habit of trying to abuse the patent system for profit. The reason that Hollywood is the home of the movie industry is that filmmakers in the 1920s were forced to abandon the east-coast because of the high royalties that Edison charged them for use of camera technologies. Edison even had hired goods to harass them for money.

But it was a policy of the RCA (Radio Corporation of America) that caused untold damage for inventors of the 20th century. The official company policy was that "The Radio Corporation doesn't pay royalties" and, allegedly, David Sarnoff, the proud general manager of the company, boasted "we collect them [royalties]". They repeatedly steamrolled inventors and small businesses to acquire their patents without licensing them, forcing the companies to collapse into the RCA's arms because of the mounting legal fees. However, there is one notable exception – the inventor of electronic television, Philo T. Farnsworth, had his patent for electronic television and other components (notably the image dissector) approved in the early 30s, and no matter what the RCA did, they couldn't get round Farnsworth's patents. In 1939, a month after the war had started, the RCA accepted to pay, for the first time in their corporate history, a $1,000,000 patent license for Farnsworth's electronic television. Legend has it there were tears in the eyes of the RCA men as they signed the document.

This whole practice was extremely unethical in terms of the technologies these companies prevented from reaching the market. Farnsworth hoped that "television would bring people together and prevent war", but because of the RCA's actions and endless lawsuits, television never got going until the 50s.

4. Dyncorp:Sex trafficking, reckless chemical usage

The first Private Military Company on the list, and certainly not the last, Dyncorp is a medium sized PMC with revenues of $3 Billion. PMC's are probably the most likely company to become involved in unethical situations. They are being paid by governments to protect areas, and often take the same roles as soldiers. Mixing money with killing is never going to be straightforward; the laws that apply to a PMC soldier are always a gray area, so the law often doesn't catch those that commit a crime.

DynCorp has been employed in "Plan Colombia" (part of the war on drugs) and, in 2001, a group of Ecuadorian farmers filed a class-action lawsuit against DynCorp under the Alien Tort Claims Act, the Torture Victim Protection Act and state law claims in US federal court in the District of Columbia. The plaintiffs claimed that from January to February 2001, DynCorp sprayed herbicide almost daily, in a reckless manner, causing severe health problems (high fever, vomiting, diarrhea, dermatological problems) and the destruction of the food crops and livestock of approximately 10,000 residents of the border region. In addition, the plaintiffs alleged that the toxicity of the fumigant caused the deaths of four infants in this region. Although the usage of herbicides was sanctioned by US congress, Dyncorp never mapped out areas of civilian crops to avoid.

When Dyncorp was employed in Bosnia at the turn of the 21st century, it was revealed, by whistle-blower Ben Johnston that DynCorp employees and supervisors engaged in sex with 12 to 15 year old children, and sold them to each other as slaves. Ben Johnston ended up fired, and later forced into protective custody. According to Johnston, none of the girls were from Bosnia itself, but were kidnapped by DynCorp employees from Russia, Romania and other places. DynCorp has admitted it fired five employees for similar illegal activities, prior to Johnston's charges. In the summer of 2005, the United States Defense department drafted a proposal to prohibit defense contractor involvement in human trafficking for forced prostitution and labor. Several defense contractors, among others, DynCorp, stalled the establishment of a final proposal that would formally prohibit defense contractor involvement in these activities.More allegations of this sort appeared in 2009, involving employees hiring Afghan "dancing boys" for their pleasure.

5. Chevron: Hiring military force for use on native peoples

Ever since attainable petroleum oil was discovered in 1956, in the Niger Delta, Nigeria, companies such as Royal Dutch Shell and Chevron have been making the most of the poor area. In the 70s, the Nigerian government began forcing them to abandon their land to oil companies without consultation, and offering negligible compensation.

The government took control of this land so that it could be distributed to the oil companies. Resistance movements from the native people turned violent in the early 90s, and were threatening to disrupt the operations with mass action. This led to the government declaring that disturbing oil production was an act of treason.Chevron had a military base at their Escravos facility, in the Delta State of Nigeria, which housed over a hundred soldiers. In 1999, when leaders of the Ikiyan people came to negotiate with the soldiers, who were already attacking different villages, they were shot at and up to 62 people were killed by the soldiers, including a seven-year-old girl. The soldiers proceeded to set the villages ablaze, kill livestock and destroy fishing equipment.

Blackwater

The biggest security PMC in the world and, like Dyncorp, is a minefield (sometimes literally) of ethical problems. However, treatment of its workers is what will be shown here. Blackwater's employee contracts routinely include clauses such as:

1) If you defy a direct order, for any reason, you will be abruptly terminated and Blackwater will withhold all back salary and bring legal action against your family.

2) If you die or are injured on a mission due to the negligence of Blackwater, you can't sue them. If you sue them, they will withhold all your back salary and bring legal action against you and your family.

3) It can be terminated for any reason whatsoever, and if you sue them for wrongful dismissal they will withhold all your back salary and bring legal action against you and your family.

Basically, their contracting system holds employees in a state of legal servitude until they quit, and if they have a problem with Blackwater they will be sued by them until they go away. An infamous picture has circulated on the Internet of two Blackwater contractors dead, strung up after they dangerously went through Fallujah in a Jeep. Their superiors at Blackwater ordered them to do the run, even though they objected and the US Army had deemed it "operationally dangerous", and refused to allow soldiers to enter. Blackwater also failed to provide a heavy gunner who was promised to the men to safeguard their trip. As a result, and the fact they couldn't refuse the order without bankrupting themselves and their families, they ended up like that. Blackwater show that they often ignore safety protocol to fulfill a defense contract and get paid. Though Backwater's main source of controversy are the constant allegations of arms smuggling and connections in the government securing them no-bid contracts.

6. Matthias Rath: Alternative treatments for HIV/AIDS

Matthias Rath is a doctor turned vitamin entrepreneur. He runs the Dr. Rath Health Foundation and founded the Dr. Rath Research Institute. He has been called "the most powerful crackpot on the Earth" due to the large amount of funds he has gotten from investors who can see the value of selling "vitamin pills" to cure the most serious of ailments.

In the UK, his adverts claimed that "90 per cent of patients receiving chemotherapy for cancer die within months of starting treatment", and suggested that three million lives could be saved if cancer patients stopped being treated by conventional medicine. The pharmaceutical industry was deliberately letting people die for financial gain, he explained. These advertisements are highly detrimental to cancer sufferers and cancer research groups, it can be easy to look at someone who has lost all their hair to chemotherapy and think that it is a poison, but it is scientifically proven to fight cancer.

Before advertising standards agencies from all over Europe were finally able to stop some of the dishonest adverts (challenging alternative medicine claims are always difficult due to the very nature of the topic), Rath had made his fortune and walked into South Africa with all the acclaim and wealth he needed to place full page advertisements in newspapers saying "The answer to the AIDS epidemic is here". "Anti-retroviral drugs were poisonous, and were a conspiracy to kill patients and make money". Tragically, Matthias Rath had taken these ideas to exactly the right place. Thabo Mbeki, the President of South Africa at the time, was well known as an "AIDS protester", and to international horror, while people died at the rate of one every two minutes in his country, he gave credence and support to the claims of a small band of campaigners who state that AIDS does not exist, that it is not caused by HIV, that anti-retroviral medication does more harm than good, and so on.

So, throughout the turn of the 21st Century, when the AIDS epidemic was at its peak, the South African government was arguing that HIV is not the cause of AIDS, and that anti-retroviral drugs are not useful for patients. They refused to roll out proper treatment programmes, and they refused to accept free donations of drugs. One study estimates that if the South African national government had used anti-retroviral drugs for prevention and treatment at the same rate as the Western Cape province (which defied national policy on the issue), around 171,000 new HIV infections and 343,000 deaths could have been prevented between 1999 and 2007. Rath profited from all this anti-science feeling with his vitamin pills, which sold very well even though they were not supported by any trusted medical research. Matthias is constantly suing medical professionals for slander, when they say that his pills are useless and should not be seen as an alternative to tested medicines.

7. Dow Chemical/Union Carbide: Rejecting liability of Bhopal Disaster

Dow Chemical already had a sinister reputation before they acquired Union Carbide, in 2001. Dow Chemical put a lot of money into its development and manufacturing of napalm for the U.S. military, a chemical which was infamous in the Vietnam War for giving people horrific burns and damaging a generation of unborn babies.

Union Carbide, though, is directly responsible for the deaths of around 8,000 Indian people in December 1984, and the birth defects that followed. The Bhopal disaster occurred when a pesticide factory in Bhopal, India, owned and operated by Union Carbide Corporation, leaked large and deadly amounts of Methyl isocyanate, a highly poisonous gas. So many people were affected because the workers at the plant were so poor that their families set up homes outside the factory gates.

Union Carbide offered $350 million in compensation, the Government of India said that the damages cost $3.3 billion; the Government, in the end, had to settle for $470 million. Throughout the years, UCC have had to fund hospitals and response centers after being nagged by officials, but many still say that what UCC have donated is negligible when compared to the human cost of the disaster. Dow Chemical, who are the wealthier new owners of Union Carbide, have yet to make significant reparations to the people of Bhopal.

8. Siemens: Aiding the Final Solution

During World War Two, Siemens was a major player in the Nazification of Germany, rebuilding the army, creating a giant infrastructure: railways, communications and power generation.

More significantly for this list, they built factories at the camps Auschwitz and Buchenwald. It was typical for a slave worker to build electrical switches for Siemens in the morning, and be snuffed out in a Siemens-made gas chamber in the afternoon. The allies destroyed four fifths of Siemens operated buildings to destroy the brand of the Nazis; Siemens was seen as an icon of Nazi industry.

Siemens is one of the few companies that still exist today, with the same name as when it exploited Jewish labor in the 40s. They are still paying up in lawsuits filed by holocaust survivors. In a move destined for failure, Siemens tried to trademark the name "Zyklon" in 2002, with the intent of marketing a series of products under the name. Including gas ovens.

9. Congo Free State: Genocide

Profiting from genocide and turning a blind eye to it is one thing, but only one organization has committed what can be called genocide for the sake of industry. Founded in 1885, by Leopold II, King of the Belgians, the Congo Free State garnered control over areas now known as the Congo, Rwanda and Burundi through a non-governmental organization, the Association Internationale Africaine. Leopold had acquired the Congo at the Berlin Conference of 1884, which was to regulate the European colonization of Africa.

While under the pretense of conducting humanitarian efforts, e.g. building churches and educating the people, it established an industry of collecting ivory, en masse, using huge amounts of slave labor. Surveyors hired by Leopold found that the greatest riches that the tribe's people could access was ivory. Employing the Force Publique (a combination of a police force, tax collector and gang of enforcers, who had been drafted from able-bodied Congolese men to serve the State), the men would troop along rivers finding villages, separating the men, women and children (rape was exceedingly common) and telling the men that if they did not find a certain amount of ivory they would never see their families again, though a lot of the time the families had already died of disease. Collecting ivory became harder once the elephant population had been decimated, so the FP changed tactics to frightening the villagers away and taking any supplies left behind, then burning everything to the ground.

The other chief export was rubber, Leopold wanted the workers to be proficient and highly motivated so this meant that failing to meet rubber collection quotas was punishable by death. The officers in charge of a particular village would have to bring the hands of those who didn't reach their quotas as proof that the officers hadn't used the bullets to hunt for food. Some soldiers "cheated" by simply cutting of the hand, and leaving them to die, saving ammunition. This even caused small wars between villages; hands had become a valuable item to have, as they can be handed into the officer when they couldn't fill their unrealistic quota.

The entire control of the nation was put under very few people and King Leopold was the definite ler (he ditched the façade of the Association Internationale Africaine soon into his rule). He directly naintained the country more than just about all other dictators before, and since, and it was his policy hat for each bullet fired, a hand must be represented as proof it was used to kill a Congolese worker. This was purely for the sake of cost-cutting. He was running the most cost-efficient company the world had seen. The rubber and ivory industry was grinding to a halt due to the lack of motivation for slaves and the dwindling supply of ivory. Leopold was amassing severe debts, until the rubber boom of he 1890s, which was needed for telegraph wire and car tyres. Rubber overtook ivory as the country's nain export, and profits went through the roof. Estimates of the number of deaths that King Leopold II and the Congo Free State caused range from 10 million to 22 million, both valid claims. It also should be noted that, at the time, Africa's entire population was between 90 and 133 million people.

The Congo Free State ended in 1908, after whispers of the crimes happening in the Congo became houts. The Congo Reform Movement, which included among its members Mark Twain, Joseph Conrad, Booker T. Washington and Bertrand Russell, led a vigorous international movement against the mistreatment of the Congolese population. The European nations had finally decided that Leopold was abusing the Berlin Treaty, and so it was annexed to Belgium, who retained it until 1960. Leopold never intended to keep the nation for a long time, it was his twenty year get-rich-quick scheme, and it worked. Leopold died the wealthiest man in Europe after living the high-life, spending the massive profits on his favorite luxuries: expensive homes, yachts and teenage prostitutes.

Benifits from managing Ethics at Workplace

Ethics, also known as moral philosophy, is a branch of philosophy that involves systematizing, defending, and recommending concepts of right and wrong behavior.

Business Ethics is the concept has come to mean various things to various people, but generally it's coming to know what it right or wrong in the workplace and doing what's right -- this is in regard to effects of products/services and in relationships with stakeholders. Wallace and Pekel explain that attention to business ethics is critical during times of fundamental change -- times much like those faced now by businesses, both nonprofit and for-profit. In times of fundamental change, values that were previously taken for granted are now strongly questioned. Many of these values are no longer followed. Consequently, there is no clear moral compass to guide leaders through complex dilemmas about what is right or wrong. Attention to ethics in the workplace sensitizes leaders and staff to how they should act. Perhaps most important, attention to ethics in the workplaces helps ensure that when leaders and managers are struggling in times of crises and confusion, they retain a strong moral compass. However, attention to business ethics provides numerous other benefits, as well.

Business Ethics and Social Responsibility

Large organizations or publicly held companies often use corporate governance to promote business ethics and social responsibility. This governance creates the framework of policies, procedures, and guidelines for all individuals financial invested in a company.

Sometimes, an industry group can give awards to companies to promote a cause within a field of business. Corporate social responsibility awards can be given by industry leaders to draw attention to or raise standards in a certain area of social responsibility.

Ethics Training

The ethics program is essentially useless unless all staff members are trained about what it is, how it works and their roles in it. The nature of the system may invite suspicion if not handled openly and honestly. In addition, no matter how fair and up-to-date is a set of policies, the legal system will often interpret employee behavior (rather than written policies) as de facto policy. Therefore, all staff must be aware of and act in full accordance with policies and procedures (this is true, whether policies and procedures are for ethics programs or personnel management). This full accordance requires training about policies and procedures.

Business ethics is now a management discipline

Business ethics has come to be considered a management discipline, especially since the birth of the social responsibility movement in the 1960s. In that decade, social awareness movements raised expectations of businesses to use their massive financial and social influence to address social problems such as poverty, crime, environmental protection, equal rights, public health and improving education.

An increasing number of people asserted that because businesses were making a profit from using our country's resources, these businesses owed it to our country to work to improve society. Many researchers, business schools and managers have recognized this broader constituency, and in their planning and operations have replaced the word "stockholder" with "stakeholder," meaning to include employees, customers, suppliers and the wider community.

Benefits of Managing Ethics in the Workplace

- Attention to business ethics has substantially improved society.
- Ethics programs help maintain a moral course in turbulent times
- Ethics programs cultivate strong teamwork
- Ethics programs support employee growth and meaning.
- Ethics programs are an insurance policy-they help ensure that policies are legal.
- Ethics programs help avoid criminal acts "of omission" and can lower fines
- Ethics programs help manage values associated with quality management, strategic planning and diversity management-this benefit needs far more attention.
- Ethics programs promote a strong public image.
- Overall benefits of ethics programs
- Formal attention to ethics in the workplace is the right thing to do.

Ethical Organizations

An organization is formed when individuals from different backgrounds and varied interests come together on a common platform and work towards predefined goals and objectives. Employees are the assets of an organization and it is essential for them to maintain the decorum and ambience of the workplace.

The way an organization should respond to external environment refers to organization ethics. Organization ethics includes various guidelines and principles which decide the way individuals should behave at the workplace.

It also refers to the code of conduct of the individuals working in a particular organization.

Every organization runs to earn profits but how it makes money is more important. No organization should depend on unfair means to earn money. One must understand that money is not the only important thing; pride and honor are more important. An individual's first priority can be to make money but he should not stoop too low just to be able to do that.

Children below fourteen years of age must not be employed to work in any organization. Childhood is the best phase of one's life and no child should be deprived of his childhood.

Employees should not indulge in destruction or manipulation of information to get results. Data tampering is considered strictly unethical and unprofessional in the corporate world. Remember if one is honest, things will always be in his favor.

Employees should not pass on company's information to any of the external parties. Do not share any of your organization's policies and guidelines with others. It is better not to discuss official matters with friends and relatives. Confidential data or information must not be leaked under any circumstances.

There must be absolute fairness in monetary transactions and all kinds of trading. Never ever cheat your clients.

Organizations must not discriminate any employee on the grounds of sex, physical appearance, age or family background. Female employees must be treated with respect. Don't ask your female employees to stay back late at work. It is unethical to discriminate employees just because they do not belong to an affluent background. Employees should be judged by their work and nothing else.

Organization must not exploit any of the employees. The employees must be paid according to their hard work and efforts. If individuals are working late at night, make sure overtimes are paid. The management must ensure employees get their arrears, bonus, incentives and other reimbursements on time. Stealing office property is strictly unethical.

Organization must take care of the safety of the employees. Individuals should not be exposed to hazardous conditions.

Never lie to your customers. It is unprofessional to make false promises to the consumers. The advertisements must give a clear picture of the product. Do not commit anything which your organization can't offer. It is important to be honest with your customers to expect loyalty from them. It is absolutely unethical to fool the customers. The products should not pose a threat to environment and mankind.

Employees on probation period can be terminated anytime but organizations need to give one month notice before firing the permanent ones. In the same way permanent employees need to serve one month notice before resigning from the current services. Employees can't stop coming to office all of a sudden.

Review Questions

Conceptual Type

1. Define ethics and business ethics.
2. Mention any two features of the nature of business ethics.
3. State the various perspectives in business ethics.
4. What are the sources of ethical values?
5. Trace the evolution of business ethics.
6. What is participatory ethics?
7. What is recognitional ethics?
8. What is code of conduct? What is genetic inheritance?
9. What is the difference between values and ethics?
10. What is the role of corporate culture in business ethics?
11. Explain various objectives of ethics.
12. Ethics is a normative science. Discuss.

Analytical Type

1. Write about the history of business ethics
2. Explain need for business ethics? Why ethics is important in business?
3. Give the relation between ethics and business ethics.
4. What is the relationship between ethics and business?
5. Explain needs for business ethics.
6. Explain purpose of business ethics.
7. What is ethical decision making? Explain the framework for ethical decision making process.
8. State some unethical issues for ethics.
9. Write note on: Ethical organization.

Descriptive Type

1. Discuss evaluation of business ethics.
2. Discuss nature and scope of business ethics.
3. Discuss various approaches to business ethics.
4. What are the various sources of ethics? Explain in detail.
5. Explain the factors influencing business ethics.
6. Explain various issues of business ethics.
7. "Is business just another form of war"-discuss.
8. Explain sources of ethical knowledge for business routes of unethical behavior.
9. Discuss benefits from managing ethics in the work place.

*****

Module-7

Corporate Social Responsibility

Syllabus

Types and nature of social responsibilities, CSR principles and strategies, models of CSR, Best practices of CSR, Need of CSR, Arguments for and against CSR, CSR Indian perspective, Indian examples

Introduction

Corporate social responsibility is a form of corporate self-regulation integrated into a business model. CSR policy functions as a built-in, self-regulating mechanism whereby a business monitors and ensures its active compliance with the spirit of the law, ethical standards, and international norms. CSR is a process with the aim to embrace responsibility for the company's actions and encourage a positive impact through its activities on the environment, consumers, employees, communities, stakeholders and all other members of the public sphere who may also be considered as stakeholders.

The term "corporate social responsibility" came into common use in the late 1960s and early 1970s after many multinational corporations formed the term stakeholder, meaning those on whom an organization's activities have an impact. It was used to describe corporate owners beyond shareholders as a result of an influential book by R. Edward Freeman; Strategic management: a stakeholder approach in 1984. Corporate Social Responsibility (CSR) can be understood as a management concept and a process that integrates social and environmental concerns in business operations and a company's interactions with the full range of its stakeholders. The Global Compact asks companies to embrace, support and enact, within their sphere of influence, a set of core values in the areas of human rights, labor standards, the environment and anti-corruption.

The practice of CSR or Corporate Social Responsibility as a paradigm for firms and businesses to follow has evolved from its early days as a slogan that was considered trendy by some firms following it to the present day realities of the 21st century where it is no longer just fashionable but a business requirement to be socially responsible.

This evolution has been necessitated both due to the myriad problems that we as a race face which has changed the environment under which firms operate as well as a realization among business leaders that profits as the sole reason or raison d'être for existence can no longer hold good.

Corporate Social Responsibility is a management concept whereby companies integrate social and environmental concerns in their business operations and interactions with their stakeholders. CSR is generally understood as being the way through which a company achieves a balance of economic, environmental and social imperatives while at the same time addressing the expectations of shareholders and stakeholders. In this sense it is important to draw a distinction between CSR, which can be a strategic business management concept, and charity, sponsorships or philanthropy. Even though the latter can also make a valuable contribution to poverty reduction, will directly enhance the reputation of a company and strengthen its brand, the concept of CSR clearly goes beyond that.

Promoting the uptake of CSR amongst SMEs requires approaches that fit the respective needs and capacities of these businesses, and do not adversely affect their economic viability. UNIDO based its CSR programme on the Triple Bottom Line (TBL) Approach, which has proven to be a successful tool for SMEs in the developing countries to assist them in meeting social and environmental standards without compromising their competitiveness. The TBL approach is used as a framework for measuring and reporting corporate performance against economic, social and environmental performance. It is an attempt to align private enterprises to the goal of sustainable global development by providing them with a more comprehensive set of working objectives than just profit alone. The perspective taken is that for an organization to be sustainable, it must be financially secure, minimize (or ideally eliminate) its negative environmental impacts and act in conformity with societal expectations.

Key CSR issues: environmental management, eco-efficiency, responsible sourcing, stakeholder engagement, labour standards and working conditions, employee and community relations, social equity, gender balance, human rights, good governance, and anti-corruption measures.

A properly implemented CSR concept can bring along a variety of competitive advantages, such as enhanced access to capital and markets, increased sales and profits, operational cost savings, improved productivity and quality, efficient human resource base, improved brand image and reputation, enhanced customer loyalty, better decision making and risk management processes.

Corporate Social Responsibility (CSR)

CSR stands for "corporate social responsibility "In general CSR or business responsibility can be described as an approach by which a company:

- Recognizes that its activities have a wider impact on the society in which it operates; and that developments in society in turn impact on its ability to pursue its business successfully;
- Actively manages the economic, social, environmental and human rights impact of its activities across the world, basing these on principles which reflect international values, reaping benefits both for its own operations and reputation as well as for the communities in which it operates,
- Seeks to achieve these benefits by working closely with other groups and organizations - local communities, civil society, other businesses and home and host governments
- There are four main parts to CSR:

Economic	Responsibility to earn profit for owners
Legal	Responsibility to comply with the law
Ethical	Not acting just for profit, but doing what is right, just and fair
Voluntary and philanthropic	Promoting human welfare and goodwill Being a good corporate citizen contributing to the community and quality of life

While Corporate Social Responsibility (CSR) has no single, commonly accepted definition, it generally refers to a business vision that links respect for ethical values, people, communities and environment.

Leader companies see CSR not just as collection of discrete practices, occasional gestures, or initiatives motivated by marketing, public relations or other business benefits. Rather, they view it as a comprehensive set of policies, practices and programs, integrated throughout business operations and decision-making processes .

Over the past decade, a growing number of companies have recognized the business benefits of CSR policies and practices. Their experiences are bolstered by a growing body of empirical studies that demonstrate CSR is a positive impact on business economic performance, which can be measured in several ways.

Companies have also been encouraged to adopt or expand CSR efforts as a result of pressure from customers, suppliers, employees, communities, investors, social activists and other stakeholders. CSR has been systematically growing in companies of all sizes and across all sectors. Those companies have developed innovative strategies within their programs in areas such as:

- Workplace
- Environment
- Responsible Marketing
- Community Involvement

1. Workplace

Generally speaking, workplace refers to human resources policies that connect directly to the employees: contracts, compensations and benefits, career development, diverse initiatives that promote work-fair environment balance, flexible work schedules, health and wellness programs, job security, family plans and benefits for domestic partners. Beyond specific policies, workplace encompasses corporate culture, values and an organizational design.

Several leading socially responsible companies are crafting innovative workplace policies and practices that closely reflect and respect the needs of all employees in order to meet core business objectives, including attracting and retaining the most talented employees.

The dramatic changes in business that characterize the New Economy are reshaping the workplace. Global competition forces corporations to foster innovative, diverse, and flexible workplaces. In addition , consumers and investors groups are demanding that companies create fair, productive and empowering workplaces. Media coverage of workplace issues has also increased, constantly challenging companies to change.

2. Environment

Over the past years, environmental responsibility has expanded to involve substantially more than compliance with all applicable laws and government regulations. Currently, many leadership companies define environmental responsibility as a process that involve participation and dialog with their community and non-governmental organizations.

Companies must consider the impact that their operations have on the environment, which involves a comprehensive approach towards the company's processes and operations, products and services; waste disposal and emissions; maximizing the efficiency and productivity of all assets and resources; and minimizing practices that might have negative impact for the planet's resources putting in risk the future generations. For example, initiatives such as recycling and energy efficiency regulations have become frequent practices.

Important amount of companies in a wide sectorial range and different geographic regions have found added value and competitive advantage in environmental initiatives. Those initiatives are in several categories; pollution prevention, energy efficiency, design for the environment, supply-chain management, industrial ecology and sustainable development. Leadership companies have integrated environmental responsibility as a core for business value at all levels of their operations and practices.

3. Responsible Marketing

Marketplace issues extend across a wide range of business activities that define a company's relationship with its customers. These activities may be grouped into different categories:

- Product manufacture and integrity
- Labeling and packaging
- Marketing and advertising
- Selling practices
- Prices
- Distribution

In each of these areas, companies, which face increased scrutiny by consumers and non-governmental organizations, are reorganizing their business strategies to address new issues, especially privacy and technology, marketing to children, heightened expectations of product safety and environmental impact.

The scope of marketplace issues has expanded in recent years to include an ever-widening array of topics, including environmental sustainability and a firm's relationship to its competitors. In general, there has been a shift away from "buyer beware" towards an ethos in which companies are expected to accomplish a greater responsibility for the integrity, use and consequences of their products and services.

While businesses must first satisfy customers' key buying criteria-such as price, quality, appearance, taste, availability, safety and convenience-other marketplace factors are taking on growing importance. The globalization of commerce and competition has placed increasing value on companies and brands that are not only trusted by customers; also to which customers feel, a sense of loyalty and commitment.

To achieve this relationship companies had to examine their operations, from customer service, to community relations to cause-related marketing, in view of how they may be directly or indirectly perceived by customers and employees. Overall, this situation has opened broader levels of issues which are driving companies to recognize that their success depends in the relationship with their customers, built as much on their reputation and practices as on the nature of their goods and services.

4. Community Involvement

Community involvement refers to a wide range of actions taken by companies to maximize their beneficial impact on the communities in which they operate. Involvement includes providing money, time, products, services, influence, management knowledge and other resources. When strategically designed and executed, those initiatives not only bring value to recipients, they enhance the reputation of companies and their brands, products and value in local communities where they have significant commercial interests, as well as around the world. For many years, companies have been involved with their local communities, playing significant roles through philanthropy. At present time, companies are engaging in the community in a variety of ways (including donating products or services, creating global employee volunteer projects, lending executives and managers, creating projects to support social issues, etc.), and for a broader variety of reasons. One of the mains reason is that stakeholders are holding companies to a higher standard of citizenship, demanding a positive net impact on society. Added to this, companies' efforts are further motivated by the business benefits of communitarian involvement. This involve increased sales, improved employee morale, an the enhanced ability to compete for valued employees in the local labor arena and being seen as a "good neighbor" within the community. CSR is about how companies manage the business processes to produce an overall positive impact on society.

Definitions of CSR

According to ***Lord Holme and Richard Watts,*** Corporate Social Responsibility is the continuing commitment by business to behave ethically and contribute to economic development while improving the quality of life of the workforce and their families as well as of the local community and society at large

Corporate Social Responsibility is the company's sense of responsibility towards the community and environment (both ecological and social) in which it operates. Companies express this citizenship:

(i) Through their waste and pollution reduction processes

(ii) By contributing educational and social programs, and (3) by earning adequate returns on the employe dresources. See also corporate citizenship.

CSR is an obligation, beyond that required by the law, for a business to pursue long term goals that are good for society.

Types of Social Responsibility

Since all businesses operate in a society they have their responsibility towards various sections of the society. The responsibility may be towards the customers, the society or the community, the Environment and so on. Various types of social responsibilities are mentioned below:

1. Responsibility towards the customers

Customer satisfaction is the most important factor in any business organization. To satisfy the customers, good quality products are to be designed and produced using quality materials, apt technology and well trained, motivated and committed human resources. Toyota's 'customer first policy' has paid it rich dividends and is also being followed by other organizations worldwide. Japanese companies strive towards customer satisfaction. Mantra for the marketing has moved on from 'customer satisfaction' to 'customer delight'. The job of the manager is to identify the actual demand and target customers, ensuring them satisfaction and delight. Workers in the Japanese companies fully cooperate with the management for improving production methods, so that they can satisfy the customers. Japanese products such as high-definition TVs, fuel efficient automobiles, latest consumer electronics and the likes are highly customer oriented things/products. They are being sold at affordable prices to customers. Japanese corporations have become successful in fulfilling and maximizing the customer satisfaction. This has been the result of success of Japanese employees.

2. Social responsibility to prospects

'Prospects' are the possible or probable customers, they may also be called "expected" customers. A good company will always identify its existing customers and make a forecast about the expected customers. At the initial stage i.e. the product planning stage, every company should think of the present market and the expected market. For this the company would take into account the needs, wants, tastes and preferences of the present market and the expected market. This helps the company to offer maximum satisfaction to the customers.

When a company decides to take up a welfare project, the most urgent things must be given priority. Appropriate priorities at the appropriate time help the organization to do well. Especially in social welfare projects it is very important for a company to decide and prioritize things as what comes first, what next, what last and what never at all. Setting up wrong priorities may result into abandoning the important projects.

3. Social responsibility to community

A company is a part of the community. A community is a part of society at large, which provides the immediate social environment to the company. A company has an important role to play in the community; hence it must be committed to the welfare of the environment. The two important social roles of the company are (a) it should play a leading role in the community welfare and (b) it should help society for a pollution free environment. By using friendly technology, conservation of trees and forests, using fuel efficient automobiles and the likes, a company can support society. Many business organizations support the community indirectly by providing employment opportunities by putting up shops, township, transport development, markets and so on.

4. Responsibility towards human resources

The social responsibility of an organization can be first known from its approach to the internal environment. An organization's internal environment mainly consists of its human resources. A company which cares forits internal environment may be able to care for its external environment- society also. A business organization must be willing to maintain the dignity of every employee as a human being, provide enough opportunities to each individual to develop to its maximum potential, satisfy his needs and aspirations. A proper organizational philosophy and human resource policy is needed to fulfill the responsibilities towards the employees. Fair wages, proper organizational climate, good working conditions, career prospects, proper facilities for development and the likes are essential for the growth of the company. All these aspects enhance the sense of belonging and confidence of the workers in the organization. The vision of Mr. Jamshedji Tata was the same in 1907. Some welfare schemes followed by TISCO since its operation in 1911 are as enumerated below:

a) In India an eight hour shift was first introduced by TISCO in 1912.

b) In 1915, free medical aid to employees and their families was started, while the ESI act came into force only in 1948.

c) A welfare department was introduced and welfare activities started in 1917.

d) School for the children of employees was started in 1917, although such a provision is not enforced statutorily even now.

e) For training of employees, a technical training institute was started in 1921.

f) Leave with pay, provident fund and accident compensation was introduced in 1912 much before the Act was passed in 1952.

g) TISCO started the maternity benefit scheme in 1928.

h) Bonus was introduced in 1934, whereas the payment of bonus act was passed in 1965.

i) Retirement gratuity was introduced in 1937, while the payment of gratuity Act was passed in 1972.

j) Ex-gratia payment for road accidents was introduced by the company in 1979.

Housing schemes, transport facility, games and sports facility, worker's education, counseling, career guidance and the likes are the list of items which an organization can include in its employee welfare programmes in addition to the statutory welfare programmes. The most important task of an organization is to recognize the worth and contribution of its employees. Social responsibility of a business organization begins with its own people on the one hand and its customers on the other.

5. Responsibility to society and ecological environment

An organization has responsibility towards its community, society and ecological environment. In this age of globalization, the whole globe can be the society for a business enterprise. A company's society may be the countries or cities wherever it operates, its suppliers, dealers, wholesalers, and retailers. A company has responsibility towards all these sections of society. It can help society to solve its socio-economic problems like poverty, unemployment etc. A company can even adopt villages for concentrated development activities.

6. Responsibility towards government

A business organization has a social responsibility towards the government. It can pay its taxes and duties in time, help the government with social projects and so on. Business enterprises can cooperate with the government's social policies and programmes. They can support the government by following the rules and regulations laid down by the government.

Business organizations can improve their corporate image by paying taxes in time, participating in social welfare projects and policies. Laws such as Industrial law, Labour law and anti-pollution law are some of the laws which have to be abided by business organizations.

7. Social responsibility to Global business environment

Global business environment includes global markets, global operation and technology, global corporate citizenship and global policies and strategies. In today's world, globalization of business is necessary to sustain the market. Global business environment provides healthy competition and a free market operation. Every business enterprise, whether operating globally or indigenously has to follow the conditions of a global environment. It also has social responsibility towards it.

It is the responsibility of a business enterprise to fulfill the needs of worldwide customers. They need a globally approved quality, a globally competitive price and a globally approved technology. Even indigenous companies have to maintain the global quality standards and global social responsibility. Otherwise they may not be able to remain in the global market environment.

Globalization results in the faster and larger growth of industrialization, hence business organizations have greater global social responsibility towards society. Expansion of business through takeovers, acquisitions and merger are common nowadays. Corporate houses make large allocations for social welfare projects in order to gain greater corporate images.

The advent of large business houses and multi-nationals lead to innovative projects for social development. They take measures to tackle pollution and environmental problems in society to improve their social image. Above all, government also introduces rules and regulations for ensuring social responsibility of business. This leads to a greater social awakening in the industrial circles.

The company and its social responsibilities

Corporate social responsibility is a form of corporate self-regulation integrated into a business model. CSR policy functions as a built-in, self-regulating mechanism whereby business monitors and ensures its active compliance with the spirit of the law, ethical standards, and international norms. The goal of CSR is to embrace responsibility for the company's actions and encourage a positive impact through its activities on the environment, consumers, employees, communities, stakeholders and all other members of the public sphere. The term "corporate social responsibility" came into common use in the late 1960s and early 1970s after many multinational corporations formed the term stakeholder, meaning those on whom an organization's activities have an impact.

Corporate Social Responsibility is a concept whereby companies integrate social and environmental concerns into their business operations and in their interaction with their stakeholders (employees, customers, shareholders, investors, local communities, government), on a voluntary basis.

Sustainability

CSR is closely linked with the principles of Sustainability, which argues that enterprises should make decisions based not only on financial factors such as profits or dividends, but also based on the immediate and long-term social and environmental consequences of their activities.

A Global Issue

CSR has become prominent in the language and strategy of business and by the growth of dedicated CSR organizations globally. Governments and international governmental organizations are increasingly encouraging CSR and forming CSR partnerships. CSR is rapidly becoming a major part of all business management courses and a key global issue.

How companies benefit from the CSR concept

No matter the size of an organization or the level of its involvement with CSR, every contribution is important and provides a number of benefits to both the community and business. Contributing to and supporting CSR does not have to be costly or time consuming and more and more businesses active in their local communities are seeing significant benefits from their involvement:

- CSR Benefits
- Reduced costs
- Increased business leads
- Increased reputation
- Improved relationships with stakeholders
- Managing the risks a company faces

- Innovation in processes, products and services
- Social responsibilities for economic growth

In today's world, globalization of business is necessary to sustain the market. Global business environment provides healthy competition and a free market operation. Every business enterprise, whether operating globally or indigenously has to follow the conditions of a global environment. It also has social responsibility towards it. It is the responsibility of a business enterprise to fulfill the needs of worldwide customers. They need a globally approved quality, a globally competitive price and a globally approved technology. Even indigenous companies have to maintain the global quality standards and global social responsibility. Otherwise they may not be able to remain in the global market environment. Globalization results in the faster and larger growth of industrialization, hence business organizations have greater global social responsibility towards society. Expansion of business through takeovers, acquisitions and merger are common nowadays. Corporate houses make large allocations for social welfare projects in order to gain greater corporate images.

Nature of CSR

CSR may include responsibilities in legal sense and in moral or ethical sense. Since the Factory Rule Movement, the specific implementing method of CSR takes mainly multinational enterprises as the implementing principal to place checks on labor standards of a company, the responsibility in moral or ethical sense is more stressed in the society. In fact, the multinational enterprises are passive to a certain extent in implementing the Factory Rules, which takes labor standards as the main content. Their immediate purpose is to maintain their business credit amongst the trade barriers of labor. Specifically, their purpose is to keep their brand name image and avoid negative legal proceedings, avoid consumers' resistance, drop of stock prices, trade sanctions, improve production efficiency, and optimize the management of supply chains.

Obviously, the fact that multinational enterprises implement the Factory Rules is not because they are driven by moral sense of responsibility or pursuit of ethical values. Rather, in more direct sense, it is a business act with business purpose. If as a pure business conduct, the CSR Movement will change its social nature. Therefore, the legal nature of corporate social responsibility must be recognized and stressed. In fact, it is because of the requirement of the legal nature of this movement, transnational enterprises are forced to do so and try all their best to turn the movement commercialized for their own interests.

CSR, especially the factory rules as the basic operation mode of present CSR movement, so far as its nature is concerned, is the legal responsibility of an enterprise or an obligation of an enterprise in the labor relationship. The significance of proposing the obligation of an enterprise in the legal labor relations as its CSR lies in the fact that this legal norm is better combined with social norms to promote the implementation of this legal norm. As a legal norm, the basic requirement to the social responsibility a company takes is to substantiate the obligations undertaken in the legal labor relations. This obligation an employer undertakes is conditioned upon his enjoyment of his rights at the same time. These rights include recruitment right in individual labor relationship, right of labor instruction, right of work dispatch, right of reward and punishment and right of plant closure in the legal collective labor relations. These rights are regarded as the user's rights in contrast to the rights of the laborers. But at the same time, employers must undertake relevant obligations. This means employers must carry out and implement relevant labor standards to enforce the protection on laborers during the laboring process. Specifically, employers' obligation in an individual legal labor relation should be first of all to make payment, which is also the obligation of an employer in the law of property; secondly it is the obligation of labor protection. Secondly, it is the obligation of labor protection. This obligation is one as prescribed in the law of personality, mainly including the moral rights of protecting laborers' life and health during production process and their personal dignity during production management. In collective legal labor relations, the obligation of an employer is mainly not to hinder the workers to exercise their right of unity. During the process that the workers establish their trade unions, hold collective bargaining and take collective actions, employers should not antagonize by means of resorting to improper labor act. Generally speaking, in individual legal labor relations, the obligation of an employer is mainly an obligation of action, i.e. to take appropriate act to ensure the fulfillment of individual workers' right of labor. In the collective legal labor relations, the obligation of an employer is shown to be one of non-action, i.e. the employer should not take actions to hinder or harm the exercise and fulfillment of laborers collective rights and interests.

The obligation of an enterprise in the legal labor relation is mainly realized through legal adjustment of the labor relationship. The conventional legal adjustment of labor relations is done by two ways: one is to have the state to stipulate and implement labor standards; the other one is to have workers to organize trade unions and hold collective negotiations and bargaining. Employment rules or factory rules, in conventional legal adjustment of labor relations serves only as a supplement.

In actual practice, people often ignore the form and nature of CSR as legal adjustment of labor relations. One outstanding issue is that the idea and method of human resources management is entirely used to enforce CSR. Though in reality, the management of human resources and that of labor-management relations is crisscross and inseparable, still, the labor-management relation cannot be dealt with entirely by the method of human resources management. The legal adjustment of human resources management and that of labor relations are two completely different idea and norm systems. The human resource management is a business management method focusing on the interests of an enterprise and aiming at improving the competitiveness of the enterprise. The power principal of management is the enterprise and workers are merely the passive objects of management. On the other hand, the legal adjustment of labor relation is to coordinate and balance the labor relationship in an enterprise with protecting laborers rights and interests as their basic rationale. The principals of the rights and interests are the two parties of workers and management. The basic method of adjustment involves reciprocal handling and voluntary participation by the two parties of workers and management.

CSR Principles and Strategies

The UN Global Compact's ten principles in the areas of human rights, labour, the environment and anti-corruption enjoy universal consensus and are derived from:

i. The Universal Declaration of Human Rights

ii. The International Labour Organization's Declaration on Fundamental Principles and Rights at Work

iii. The Rio Declaration on Environment and Development

iv. The United Nations Convention Against Corruption

- The UN Global Compact asks companies to embrace, support and enact, within their sphere of influence, a set of core values in the areas of human rights, labour standards, the environment and anti-corruption:

A. Human Rights

Principle 1: Businesses should support and respect the protection of internationally proclaimed human rights;

Why Human Rights Are Important for Business

Governments have the primary responsibility for human rights. However, individuals and organizations also have important roles to play in supporting and respecting human rights. The business community has a responsibility to respect human rights, that is, not to infringe human rights. Operating context, company activities and relationships can pose risks that the company might negatively impact human rights, but they also present opportunities to support or promote the enjoyment of human rights while also advancing one's business.

Promoting the rule of law

Societies where human rights are respected are more stable and provide a better environment for business. Businesses whether operating outside their country of origin or at home may have the opportunity to promote and help raise standards in countries where protection of human rights issues is insufficient, especially in ways that are strategically relevant to its core business.

Addressing consumer concerns

Access to global information means that consumers are increasingly aware of where their goods come from and the conditions under which they are made.

Value chain management

Global sourcing and distribution means that companies need to be aware of potential human rights issues both upstream and downstream.

Increasing worker productivity and retention

Workers who are treated with dignity and given fair and just remuneration for their work are more likely to be productive and remain loyal to an employer. New recruits increasingly consider the social, environmental and governance record of companies when making their choice of employer.

Building good community relationships

Companies that operate on a global basis are visible to a large audience world-wide as a result of advances in communications technologies. Addressing human rights issues positively can bring rewards at site level, within local communities, as well as in the broader global commons in which companies operate.

Respecting Human Rights

Respect for human rights is part of Principle 1 of the United Nations Global Compact. In 2008, the UN Human Rights Council adopted the UN Protect, Respect, Remedy Framework, the second pillar of which is that business everywhere has the responsibility to respect human rights. To respect rights essentially means not to infringe on the rights of others-put in other words-to refrain from having a negative impact on the enjoyment of human rights. Business has the potential to impact-positively and negatively-virtually all human rights. Accordingly, business should consider their potential impact on all rights. However, some actual or potential impacts will require special consideration, for example, where the actual or potential impacts are very serious and/or there is a strong connection between the company and the abuse.

For the content of human rights, at a minimum, companies should look to the International Bill of Human Rights and the core International Labour Organization (ILO) Conventions. The publication Human Rights Translated elaborates the main internationally proclaimed human rights from a business perspective and offers practical examples of how companies have infringed on human rights and, as a result, ended up in trouble, as well as examples of how businesses have supported the enjoyment of the rights. Although some rights will be more relevant than others in particular circumstances, situations change, so broader periodic reassessment is necessary.

Business must ensure that its operations are consistent with the legal principles applicable in the country of operation. If national law falls short of international standards, companies should strive to meet international standards and not infringe on human rights. In the rare situation that national law directly conflicts with international standards, companies are not expected to violate national laws. Instead, there may be other ways to support the spirit of international human rights standards.

Importantly, the corporate responsibility to respect exists independently of States' human rights duties. Among other things, this means that businesses have a responsibility to respect human rights whether they are operating in an area of weak governance or in a more stable context. In areas where there is weak governance, the risks of infringing human rights may be greater because of the context. Because the responsibility to respect is a baseline expectation, a company cannot compensate for infringing human rights in one aspect of their business by performing good deeds elsewhere, such as through philanthropic acts, supporting human rights in other areas or by good performance on other issues, such as the environment.

Determining the scope of responsibility

Companies should consider three sets of factors in determining the scope of their responsibility to respect human rights or, in other words, the risk of potential negative impacts on human rights in connection with the conduct of their business.

1. The first is to consider the country and local context in which it is operating for any human rights challenges that context might pose. Information about these is available from NGOs, Government, international trade unions and international organizations.

2. The second set of factors involves considering actual or potential human rights impacts the business' own activities may have within that context-for example, in their capacity as producers, service providers, employers and neighbours. Companies should determine which policies and practices might infringe human rights and adjust those actions to prevent the infringement from occurring. An illustrative list of activities with direct impact might include the production process itself; the products or services the company provides; labour and employment practices; the provision of security for personnel and assets; and the company's lobbying or other political activities.

3. The third set of factors is an analysis of the company's relationships with Government, business partners, suppliers and other non-State actors to consider whether they might pose a risk for the company in terms of implicating it in human rights abuse. Look particularly at the provision or contracting of goods, services and even non-business activities, such as lending equipment or

vehicles. Consider the track records of those entities your company deals with to assess whether the company might contribute to or be associated with abuse caused by those entities.

Due diligence

In order to ensure and demonstrate (i.e. to know and show) that a company is meeting its responsibility to respect human rights it should undertake due diligence. Human rights due diligence is the ongoing process taken to identify, prevent and mitigate negative human rights impacts. By undertaking due diligence, companies not only ensure compliance with national laws but also manage the risk of infringing human rights with a view to identifying, preventing and mitigating it. Tools and guidance materials are very helpful in this process. Comparable processes are typically already embedded in companies to assess and manage financial and related risks. The poster A Human Rights Management Framework-available in all six official UN languages at the UN Global Compact's tools and guidance page-shows the elements of a comprehensive management approach to human rights. Particularly important elements are:

1. ***A statement of policy (integrated or stand alone):*** Companies should adopt a statement of policy as a public commitment to fulfill their responsibility to respect human rights, approved by their board or equivalent. It can be a stand-alone statement or integrated into a broader corporate sustainability policy or code of conduct. Broad inspirational language may be used to describe respect for human rights, but more detailed guidance in specific functional areas is necessary to give those commitments practical meaning. The policy should give meaningful guidance to those within the organization and those significantly linked to the organization. Developing a human rights policy can be an important opportunity for stakeholder engagement on the topic of human rights, which can be almost as important as the policy that results from the process..
2. ***Assessing human rights impacts:*** Many corporate human rights issues arise because companies do not consider the potential implications of their activities and relationships within their operating context. Companies should take proactive steps to understand how existing and proposed activities may affect human rights. The scale of the review will depend on the industry, company size and national and local context and should be commensurate with the level of risk. Based on the information uncovered, companies should refine their plans to address and avoid potential negative human rights impacts on an ongoing basis.
3. ***Integration of human rights policies throughout a company:*** The integration of human rights policies throughout a company may be the biggest challenge in respecting human rights. If awareness of human rights issues and their importance is not fully integrated within the company's management practices, inconsistent or contradictory actions can result. For example, product developers may not consider human rights implications; sales or procurement teams may not know the risks of entering into relationships with certain parties; and company lobbying may contradict commitments to human rights. Leadership from the top is essential to embed respect for human rights throughout a company, as is training to ensure consistency, as well as having the capacity to respond appropriately when unforeseen situations arise.
4. ***Tracking and reporting performance:*** Monitoring and auditing processes permit a company to track ongoing developments. The procedures may vary across sectors and even among company departments, but regular reviews of human rights impact and performance are crucial. Tracking generates information needed to create appropriate incentives and disincentives for employees,

ensure continuous improvement and to make necessary adjustments in priorities and approaches. Confidential means to report non-compliance, such as hotlines, can also provide useful feedback. Reporting is a driver for change, externally as well as internally: It shapes stakeholders' perceptions of a company and helps to build trust; and it is increasingly acknowledged that reporting also acts as a stimulus for internal development with a positive impact on business decisions and outcomes. Global Compact participants are required to communicate their progress (COP) on an annual basis.

Another key element of due diligence is having in place effective company-level grievance mechanisms so that employees, contractors, local communities and others can raise their concerns and have them be considered. This can help companies to identify risks of negative impacts and avoid escalation of disputes.

Supporting Human Rights

In practice, respect and support for human rights are often closely inter linked in terms of the management steps that are taken to enable and ensure respect and support for human rights. For example, corporate policies on human rights often make positive commitments to support human rights, especially rights that may be strategically relevant to their business. Analyses of context, activities and relationships are likely to yield opportunities to promote human rights as well as possible risks of infringing rights. And companies often include in their reports information about the positive contribution they are making to human rights.

Supporting human rights involves making a positive contribution to human rights, to promote or advance human rights. Socially responsible organizations will typically have a broader capability and often desire to support the promotion of human rights within their sphere of influence especially in ways that link strategically to their core business activities. The business case for supporting human rights can be as strong as the business case for respecting human rights. Likewise, stakeholder expectations often extend to the belief that organizations can and should make a positive contribution to the realization of human rights where they are in a position to do so.

There are at least four ways business can support or promote human rights:

- Through their core business activities in support of UN goals and issues
- Strategic social investment and philanthropy
- Advocacy and public policy engagement
- Partnership and collective action.

Some examples of how companies are supporting and respecting human rights through their daily activities:

- **In the workplace:**
- By providing safe and healthy working conditions,
- By guaranteeing freedom of association,
- By ensuring non-discrimination in personnel practices,
- By ensuring that they do not use directly or indirectly forced labour or child labour,

- By providing access to basic health, education and housing for the workers and their families, if these are not provided elsewhere,
- By having an affirmative action programme to hire victims of domestic violence, and
- By making reasonable accommodations for all employees' religious observance and practices.
- **In the community:**
- By preventing the forcible displacement of individuals, groups or communities,
- By working to protect the economic livelihood of local communities,
- By contributing to the public debate. Companies interact with all levels of government in the countries where they operate. They therefore have the right and responsibility to express their views on matters that affect their operations, employees, customers and the communities of which they are a part,
- Through differential pricing or small product packages create new markets that also enable the poor to gain access to goods and services that they otherwise could not afford.
- By fostering opportunities for girls to be educated to empower them and also helps a company to have a broader and more skilled pool of workers in the future, and
- Perhaps most importantly, a successful business which provides decent work, produces quality goods or services that improve lives, especially for the poor or other vulnerable groups, is an important contribution to sustainable development, including human rights.
- If companies use security services to protect their operations, they must ensure that existing international guidelines and standards for the use of force are respected.

Addressing Human Rights

The topic of human rights can sometimes be challenging for a company to talk about with its managers and employees and/or those outside the company. However, promoting understanding about what human rights are, their relevance to business and what, in practical terms, business can do to address human rights issues can help to make action to respect human rights easier.

Some businesses find that looking at opportunities to support human rights as well as the risks of infringing human rights helps to motivate managers and staff to address risks too. Another approach some businesses find helpful is to start by looking at what the business is already doing to respect and support human rights, such as by having good human resources policies and practices, implementing policies on non discrimination and promoting diversity in the workforce, respecting the privacy of customers and workers, undertaking efforts to make essential products more accessible to the poor and implementing effective occupational health and safety policies and practices. This helps to demystify human rights by showing that respecting human rights does not require starting from the very beginning. Nor does it need a whole new management system. Human rights can be integrated into existing business processes and procedures. Some companies find it helpful to look for the right entry point and language to discuss risks and opportunities with managers and staff. Sometimes it might be easier to begin the discussion by talking about familiar concepts like respect, dignity, fairness and equality, and specific scenarios with which managers and employees may be confronted.

Principle 2: make sure that they are not complicit in human rights abuses.

Complicity

Complicity basically means being implicated in human rights abuse that another company, government, individual, group etc is causing.

Respecting human rights includes avoiding complicity, which is another way, beyond their own direct business activities, that businesses risk interfering with the enjoyment of human rights.

The risk of complicity in human rights abuse may be particularly high in areas with weak governance and/or where human rights abuse is widespread. However, the risk of complicity exists in every sector and every country. The risk of an allegation of complicity is reduced if a company becomes aware of, prevents and mitigates risks of complicity through adopting a systematic management approach to human rights, that is, by exercising due diligence. Complicity is generally made up of 2 elements:

1. An act or omission (failure to act) by a company, or individual representing a company, that "helps" (facilitates, legitimizes, assists, encourages, etc.) another, in some way, to carry out a human rights abuse, and
2. The knowledge by the company that its act or omission could provide such help.

The risk of an allegation of complicity is reduced if a company becomes aware of, prevents and addresses risks of complicity through adopting a systematic management approach to human rights issues, including exercising due diligence.

Allegations of complicity are not confined to situations in which a company could be held legally liable for its involvement in the human rights abuse committed by another. The media, civil society organizations, trade unions and others may allege complicity in a far broader range of circumstances. The better view is that the presence of a company in an area and payment of taxes where egregious and systematic human rights abuses are occurring, without more, is not enough to make the organization complicit in those abuses. However, some societal actors take a different view and may lobby business to play an advocacy role in such circumstances.

Accusations of complicity can arise in a number of contexts:

- *Direct complicity:* when a company provides goods or services that it knows will be used to carry out the abuse.
- *Beneficial complicity:* when a company benefits from human rights abuses even if it did not positively assist or cause them.
- *Silent complicity:* when the company is silent or inactive in the face of systematic or continuous human rights abuse.

Contemporary Issues

Human rights issues have become increasingly important as the nature and scope of business has changed. Different actors have different roles to play, and it is important for business to be aware of the contemporary factors that have made human rights an organizational issue.

- *Globalization:* The growth in private investment has witnessed companies expanding operations to countries previously untouched by global markets. In some instances, these countries have poor human rights records and/or the capacity of the state to address these issues is limited. In these cases the role of business in promoting and respecting human rights is particularly important.

- *Growth of civil society:* In some instances the capacity of the state to address human rights issues has diminished. As a result, a steady alienation of people has occurred towards the public institutions that were established to serve them. Non-governmental organizations of all types and sizes have grown to fill the void, progressively influencing both public policy and the market agenda. They include new human rights, labour and corporate accountability organizations.
- *Transparency and accountability:* The need for transparency in business practice has been highlighted both by globalization, the growth of civil society interests and some recent problems in the corporate sector. Advances in information technologies and global communications mean that companies can ill afford to conceal poor or questionable practices.
- *Crime:* Where an international crime is involved, complicity may arise where a company assisted in the perpetration of the crime, the assistance had a substantial effect on the perpetration of the crime and the company knew that its acts would assist the perpetration of the crime even if it did not intend for the crime to be committed.
- *State-owned enterprises:* State-owned enterprises should be aware that because they are part of the state, they may have direct responsibilities under international human rights law.

Possible Actions by Business

An effective human rights policy will help companies avoid being implicated in human rights violations. In order to avoid such situations, companies may wish to consider the following:

- Has the company made a human rights assessment of the situation in countries where it does, or intends to do, business so as to identify the risk of involvement in human rights abuses and the company's potential impact on the situation?
- Does the company have explicit policies that protect the human rights of workers in its direct employment and throughout its supply chain?
- Has the company established a monitoring system to ensure that its human rights policies are being implemented?
- Does the company actively engage in open dialogue with stakeholder groups, including civil society organizations?
- Does the company have an explicit policy to ensure that its security arrangements do not contribute to human rights violations? This applies whether it provides its own security, contracts it to others or in the case where security is supplied by the State.

Actions that may be particularly helpful in avoiding complicity include:

- Respect international guidelines and standards for the use of force (e.g. the UN Basic Principles on the Use of Force and Firearms by Law Enforcement Officials and the UN Code of Conduct for Law Enforcement Officials);
- If financial or material support is provided to security forces, establish clear safeguards to ensure that these are not then used to violate human rights and make clear in any agreements with security forces that the business will not condone any violation of international human rights laws;
- Privately and publicly condemn systematic and continuous human rights abuses;

- Continually consult within and outside the company with relevant stakeholders during both pre-investment and post-investment stages;
- Raise awareness within the company of known human rights issues within the company's sphere of influence;
- Identify those functions within the firm that are most at risk of becoming linked to human rights abuses, possibly even at the pre-investment/project exploration and planning stage, and where there might be opportunities to advance human rights;
- Conduct a human rights impact assessment consisting of an analysis of the functions of a proposed investment and the possible human rights impacts (intended and unintended) they may have on the community or region; and
- Identify internal 'functional risks' in the post-investment situations. This may involve looking at such functions as purchasing, logistics, government relations, human resource management, HSE (health, safety and environment), sales and marketing.

B. Labour

Principle 3: Businesses should uphold the freedom of association and the effective recognition of the right to collective bargaining

Freedom of Association

Freedom of association implies a respect for the right of all employers and all workers to freely and voluntarily establish and join organizations of their own choice. These organizations have the right to carry out their activities in full freedom and without interference, including the promotion and defense of their occupational interests. Employers have the right to freedom of expression provided that its exercise does not infringe a worker's right to make a free decision on whether or not to join a trade union. Employers should not interfere in an employee's decision to associate, or discriminate against the employee or their representative. "Association" includes activities of rule formation, administration and the election of representatives. The freedom to associate involves employers, unions and workers representatives freely discussing issues at work in order to reach agreements that are jointly acceptable. These freedoms also allow for industrial action to be taken by workers (and organizations) in defense of their economic and social interests.

Collective Bargaining

Collective bargaining refers to a voluntary process or activity through which employees and workers discuss and negotiate their relations, in particular terms and conditions of work and the regulation of relations between employers, workers and their organizations. Participants in collective bargaining include employers themselves or their organizations, and trade unions or, in their absence, representatives freely designated by the workers. An important part of the effective recognition of the right to collective bargaining is the "principle of good faith". This is important for the maintenance of the harmonious development of labour relations. This principle implies that the social partners work together and make every effort to reach an agreement through genuine and constructive negotiations, and that both parties avoid unjustified delays in negotiations. The principle of good faith does not imply a pre-defined level of bargaining or require compulsory bargaining on the part of employers or workers and their organizations.

Why are Freedom of Association and Collective Bargaining important?

Businesses face many uncertainties in this rapidly changing global market. Establishing genuine dialogue with freely chosen workers' representatives enables both workers and employers to understand each other's problems better and find ways to resolve them. Freedom of association and the exercise of collective bargaining provide opportunities for constructive rather than confrontational dialogue. This harnesses energy to focus on solutions that result in benefits to the enterprise, its stakeholders, and society at large and is often more flexible and effective than state regulation. It can thus help in anticipating potential problems and advance peaceful mechanisms for dealing with them. A number of studies indicate that the dynamic resulting from freedom of association can set in motion a "decent work" cycle that increases productivity, incomes and profits for all concerned. The guarantee of representation through a "voice at work" facilitates local responses to a globalized economy, and serves as a basis for sustainable growth and secure investment returns. The results help bridge the widening representational gap in global work arrangements, and facilitate the input of those people, regions and economic sectors-especially women and informal sector workers-who otherwise may be excluded from participating in processes that build decent work environments.

Strategies for Business

The Global Compact does not require that employers change their industrial relations frameworks and expresses no view on whether any particular national law meets international standards. However, as organizations such as the International Organization for Employers have indicated, some high performance companies have recognized the value of using dialogue and negotiation to achieve competitive outcomes.

What companies can do:

In the workplace

- Ensure that all workers are able to form and join a trade union of their choice without fear of intimidation or reprisal, in accordance with national law.
- Put in place non-discriminatory policies and procedures with respect to trade union organization, union membership and activity in such areas as applications for employment and decisions on advancement, dismissal or transfer.
- Do not interfere with the activities of worker representatives while they carry out their functions in ways that are not disruptive to regular company operations. Practices such as allowing the collection of union dues on company premises, posting of trade union notices, distribution of union documents, and provision of office space, have proven to help build good relations between management and workers, provided that they are not used as a way for the company to exercise indirect control.
- Provide workers' representatives with appropriate facilities to assist in the development of effective collective agreement.

At the bargaining table

- Recognize representative organizations for the purpose of collective bargaining.
- Use collective bargaining as a constructive forum for addressing working conditions and terms of employment and relations between employers and workers, or their respective organizations.

- Address any problem-solving or other needs of interest to workers and management, including restructuring and training, redundancy procedures, safety and health issues, grievance and dispute settlement procedures, disciplinary rules, and family and community welfare.
- Provide information needed for meaningful bargaining.
- Balance dealings with the most representative trade union to ensure the viability of smaller organizations to continue to represent their members.

In the community of operation

- Preserve the confidentiality of the trade unions and leaders in countries where the government does not permit respect for human rights (including rights at work) or does not provide a proper legal and institutional framework for industrial relations and collective bargaining.
- Support the establishment and functioning of local/national employers' organizations, and trade unions.
- Inform the local community, media and public authorities of your company's endorsement of the UN Global Compact and its intention to respect its provisions, including those on fundamental workers' rights.

Principle 4: the elimination of all forms of forced and compulsory labour;

What does Forced and Compulsory Labour mean?

Forced or compulsory labour is any work or service that is exacted from any person under the menace of any penalty, and for which that person has not offered himself or herself voluntarily. Providing wages or other compensation to a worker does not necessarily indicate that the labour is not forced or compulsory. By right, labour should be freely given and employees should be free to leave in accordance with established rules.

Why should companies be concerned about Forced and Compulsory Labour?

Forced labour does not only constitute a violation of fundamental human rights, but it also deprives societies of the opportunity to develop skills and human resources, and to educate children for the labour markets of tomorrow. So the debilitating consequences of forced labour are not only felt by individuals, in particular children, but also by society and the economy at large. By retarding the proper development of human resources, forced labour lowers the level of productivity and results in less secure investments and slower economic growth. The loss of income due to disruption of regular jobs or income-generating activities reduces the lifetime earnings of potential breadwinners and is thus likely to lead to the loss of food, shelter, and health care of whole families.

While companies operating legally do not normally employ such practices, forced labour can become associated with enterprises through their business links with others, including contractors and suppliers. As a result, all employers should be aware of the forms and causes of forced labour, as well as how it might occur in different industries.

Both the State and private agents have been implicated in the use of forced labour. State-imposed labour includes compulsory participation in public works, and the imposition of forced labour for ideological or political purposes. Forced labour exploitation by private agents can take the forms of slavery, bonded labour or debt-bondage, and other types of coercion. Employers need to be aware that forced labour can take a number of forms. Situations of forced labour are generally characterized by a lack of consent to work (the route into forced labour) and the menace of a penalty (the means of keeping someone in forced labour).

- Slavery (e.g. by birth/ descent into "slave" or bonded status)
- Bonded labour or debt bondage , an ancient practice still used in some countries where both adults and children are obliged to work in slave-like conditions to repay debts of their own or their parents or relatives
- Child labour in particularly abusive conditions where the child has no choice about whether to work
- Physical abduction or kidnapping
- Sale of a person into the ownership of another
- Physical confinement in the work location (in prison or in private detention)
- The work or service of prisoners if they are hired to or placed at the disposal of private individuals, companies or associations involuntarily and without supervision of public authorities
- Labour for development purposes required by the authorities, for instance to assist in construction, agriculture, and other public works
- Work required to punish opinion or expression of views ideologically opposed to the established political, social or economic system
- Exploitative practices such as forced overtime or
- The lodging of deposits (financial or personal documents) for employment
- Physical or psychological (including sexual) violence as a means of keeping someone in forced labour (direct or as a threat against worker, family, or close associates)
- Full or partial restrictions on freedom of movement
- Withholding and non-payment of wages (linked to manipulated debt payments, exploitation, and other forms of extortion)
- Deprivation of food, shelter or other necessities
- Deception or false promises about terms and types of work
- Induced indebtedness (by falsification of accounts, charging inflated prices, reduced value of goods or services produced, excessive interest charges, etc.), and
- Threats to denounce workers in an irregular situation to the authorities

Strategies for Business

Organizations need to determine whether forced labour is a problem within their business sector. It is important to mention that, although high profile cases are typically reported as occurring in developing countries, forced labour is also present in developed countries and should be viewed as a global issue. Understanding the causes of forced labour is the first step towards taking action against forced labour. Where forced labour is identified, the concerned individuals should be removed from work and facilities and services should be provided to enable them to make adequate alternatives. In general, a comprehensive set of interventions, including both workplace and community actions, is needed to help ensure the eradication of forced labour practices.

What companies can do:

In the workplace

- Have a clear policy not to use, be complicit in, or benefit from forced labour.
- Where adherence to forced labour provisions of national laws and regulations is insufficient, take account of international standards.
- Ensure that all company officials have a full understanding of what forced labour is.
- Make available employment contracts to all employees stating the terms and conditions of service, the voluntary nature of employment, the freedom to leave (including the appropriate procedures) and any penalties that may be associated with a departure or cessation of work.
- Write employment contracts in languages easily understood by workers, indicating the scope of and procedures for leaving the job.
- Be aware of countries, regions, industries, sectors, or economic activities where forced labour is more likely to be a practice.
- In planning and conducting business operations, ensure that workers in debt bondage or in other forms of forced labour are not engaged and, where found, provide for the removal of such workers from the workplace with adequate services and provision of viable alternatives.
- Institute policies and procedures to prohibit the requirement that workers lodge financial deposits with the company.
- If hiring prisoners for work in or outside prisons, ensure that their terms and conditions of work are similar to those of a free employment relationship in the sector involved, and that they have given their consent to work for a private employer.
- Ensure that large scale development operations do not rely on forced labour in any phase.
- Carefully monitor supply chains and subcontracting arrangements.

In the community of operation

- Establish or participate in a task force or committee on forced labour in your representative employers' organization at the local, state or national level.
- Work in partnership with other companies, sectoral associations and employers' organizations to develop an industry-wide approach to address the issue, and build bridges with trade unions, law enforcement authorities, labour inspectorates and others.
- Support and help design education, vocational training, and counseling programmes for children removed from situations of forced labour.
- Help develop skills training and income-generating alternatives, including micro-credit financing programmes, for adults removed from situations of forced labour.

- Encourage supplementary health and nutrition programmes for workers removed from dangerous forced labour, and provide medical care to assist those affected by occupational diseases and malnutrition as a result of their involuntary work.
- Where use is made of prison labour, ensure that the terms and conditions of work are beneficial to the prisoners (particularly with regard to occupational health and safety), and that they have given consent to work for a private employer.

Principle 5: The effective abolition of child labour; and

Child Labour

The term "child labour" should not be confused with "youth employment" or " student work." Child labour is a form of exploitation that is a violation of a human right., and it is recognized and defined by international instruments. It is the declared policy of the international community and of almost all governments to abolish child labour.

While the term "child" covers all girls and boys under 18 years of age, not all under-18's must be removed from work: the basic rules under international standards distinguish what constitutes acceptable or unacceptable work for children at different ages and stages of their development. ILO conventions (Minimum Age Convention No. 138 and the Worst Forms of Child Labour Convention No. 182) provide the framework for national law to prescribe a minimum age for admission to employment or work that must not be less than the age for completing compulsory schooling, and in any case not less than 15 years. Lower ages are permitted for transitional periods – in countries where economic and educational facilities are less well-developed the minimum age for regular work generally is 14 years, and 12 years for "light work". The minimum age for hazardous work is higher, at 18 years for all countries.

Minimum Age for Admission to Employment or Work

Developed countries		Developing countries	
Light Work	13 Years	Light Work	12 Years
Regular Work	15 Years	Regular Work	14 Years
Hazardous Work	18 Years	Hazardous Work	18 Years

ILO Convention No. 182 requires governments to give priority to eliminating the worst forms of child labour undertaken by all children under the age of 18 years. They are defined as:

- All forms of slavery-including the trafficking of children, debt bondage, forced and compulsory labour, and the use of children in armed conflict.
- The use, procuring or offering of a child for prostitution, for the production of pornography or for pornographic purposes.
- The use, procuring or offering of a child for illicit activities, in particular the production and trafficking of drugs.
- Work which is likely to harm the health, safety or morals of the child as a consequence of its nature or the circumstances under which it is carried out.

Convention 182 is explicitly complementary to Convention 138 and must not be used to justify other forms of child labour.

Why should companies be concerned about Child Labour?

Child labour is damaging to a child's physical, social, mental, psychological and spiritual development because it is work performed at too early an age. Child labour deprives children of their childhood and their dignity. They are deprived of an education and may be separated from their families. Children who do not complete their primary education are likely to remain illiterate and never acquire the skills needed to get a job and contribute to the development of a modern economy. Consequently, child labour results in under-skilled, unqualified workers and jeopardizes future improvements of skills in the workforce.

Children have the same human rights as adults. But by virtue of their age and the fact that they are still growing and gaining knowledge and experience, they have some distinct rights as children. These rights include protection from economic exploitation and work that may be dangerous to their health, safety or morals and that may hinder their development or impede their access to education. The complexity of the issue of child labour means that companies need to address the issue sensitively, and must not take action which may force working children into more exploitative forms of work. Nevertheless, as Principle 5 states, the goal of all companies should be the abolition of child labour within their sphere of influence.

Association with child labour will likely damage a company's reputation. This is especially true in the case of transnational companies who have extensive supply and service chains, where the economic exploitation of children, even by a business partner, can damage a brand image and have strong repercussions on profit and stock value.

Strategies for Business

Developing an awareness and understanding of the causes and consequences of child labour is the first step that a company can take toward action against child labour. This means identifying the issues and determining whether or not child labour is a problem within the business. Companies sourcing in specific industry sectors with geographically distant supply chains need to be particularly vigilant. However, child labour also exists less visibly in developed, industrialized countries where it occurs, for example, in some immigrant communities.

Discovering if child labour is being used can be difficult, for example in the case where documents or records are absent, and companies may consider using local non-governmental organizations, development organizations or UN agencies to assist in this process.

If an occurrence of child labour is identified, the children need to be removed from the workplace and provided with viable alternatives. These measures often include enrolling the children in schools and offering income-generating alternatives for the parents or above-working age members of the family. Companies need to be aware that, without support, children may be forced into worse circumstances such as prostitution, and that, in some instances where children are the sole providers of income, their immediate removal from work may exacerbate rather than relieve the hardship.

What companies can do:

In the workplace

- Be aware of countries, regions, sectors, economic activities where there is a greater likelihood of child labour and respond accordingly with policies and procedures.
- Adhere to minimum age provisions of national labour laws and regulations and, where national law is insufficient, take account of international standards.
- Use adequate and verifiable mechanisms for age verification in recruitment procedures.
- When children below the legal working age are found in the workplace, take measures to remove them from work.
- Help to seek viable alternatives and access to adequate services for the children and their families.
- Exercise influence on subcontractors, suppliers and other business affiliates to combat child labour.
- Develop and implement mechanisms to detect child labour.
- Where wages are not determined collectively or by minimum wage regulation, take measures to ensure that wages paid to adults take into account the needs of both them and their families.

In the community of operation

- Work in partnership with other companies, sectoral associations and employers' organizations to develop an industry-wide approach to address the issue, and build bridges with trade unions, law enforcement authorities, labour inspectorates and others.
- Establish or participate in a task force or committee on child labour in your representative employers' organization at the local, state or national level.
- Support and help design educational/ vocational training, and counseling programmes for working children, and skills training for parents of working children.
- Encourage and assist in launching supplementary health and nutrition programmes for children removed from dangerous work, and provide medical care to cure children of occupational diseases and malnutrition.

Principle 6: the elimination of discrimination in respect of employment and occupation.

What does Discrimination in Respect of Employment and Occupation mean?

Discrimination in employment and occupation means treating people differently or less favourably because of characteristics that are not related to their merit or the inherent requirements of the job. In national law, these characteristics commonly include: race, colour, sex, religion, political opinion, national extraction, social origin, age, disability, HIV/AIDS status, trade union membership, and sexual orientation.

However, Principle 6 allows companies to consider additional grounds where discrimination in employment and occupation may occur.

Discrimination can arise in a variety of work-related activities. These include access to employment, to particular occupations, promotions and to training and vocational guidance. Moreover, it can occur with respect to the terms and conditions of the employment, such as:

- Recruitment

- Remuneration
- Hours of work and rest/Paid holidays
- Maternity protection
- Security of tenure
- Job assignments
- Performance assessment and advancement
- Training and opportunities
- Job prospects
- Social security
- Occupational safety and health

In some countries, additional issues for discrimination in the workplace, such as age and HIV status, are growing in importance. It is also important to realize that discrimination at work arises in a range of settings, and can be a problem in a rural agricultural business or in a high technology city-based business.

Non-discrimination means simply that employees are selected on the basis of their ability to do the job and that there is no distinction, exclusion or preference made on other grounds. Employees who experience discrimination at work are denied opportunities and have their basic human rights infringed. This affects the individual concerned and negatively influences the greater contribution that they might make to society.

Direct and Indirect Discrimination

Discrimination can take many forms, both in terms of gaining access to employment and in the treatment of employees once they are in work.

It may be direct, such as when laws, rules or practices explicitly cite a reason such as sex or race to deny equal opportunity. Most commonly, however, discrimination is indirect and arises where rules or practices have the appearance of neutrality but in fact lead to exclusions. This indirect discrimination often exists informally in attitudes and practices, which if unchallenged can perpetuate in organizations. Discrimination may also have cultural roots that demand more specific approaches.

Why should companies be concerned about Discrimination?

From a business point of view discrimination does not make sense. It leads to social tensions that are potentially disruptive to the business environment within the company and in society. A company that uses discriminatory practices in employment and occupation denies itself access to talents from a wider pool of workers, and thus skills and competencies. The hurt and resentment generated by discrimination will affect the performance of individuals and teams in the company. Increasingly, Young graduates and new employees also increasingly judge companies on the basis of their social and ethical policies at work. Discriminatory practices result in missed opportunities for development of skills and infrastructure to strengthen competitiveness in the national and global economy. Finally, discrimination isolates an employer from the wider community and can damage a company's reputation, potentially affecting profits and stock value.

Strategies for Business

First and foremost, companies need to respect all relevant local and national laws. Any company introducing measures to promote equality needs to be aware of the diversities of language, culture and family circumstance that may exist in the workforce. Managers and supervisory staff, in particular, should seek to develop an understanding of the different types of discrimination and how it can affect the workforce. For example, women constitute a growing proportion of the world's workforce, but consistently earn less than their male counterparts. Disabled employees may have particular needs that should be met, where reasonable, in order to ensure that they have the same opportunities (e.g. for training and advancement) as their peers.

What companies can do:

Companies can put in place specific activities to address the question of discrimination and eliminate it within the workplace. Some examples are:

In the workplace

- Institute company policies and procedures which make qualifications, skill and experience the basis for the recruitment, placement, training and advancement of staff at all levels.
- Assign responsibility for equal employment issues at a high level, issue clear company-wide policies and procedures to guide equal employment practices, and link advancement to desired performance in this area.
- Work on a case by case basis to evaluate whether a distinction is an inherent requirement of a job, and avoid application of job requirements that would systematically disadvantage certain groups.
- Keep up-to-date records on recruitment, training and promotion that provide a transparent view of opportunities for employees and their progression within the organization.
- Where discrimination is identified, develop grievance procedures to address complaints, handle appeals and provide recourse for employees.
- Be aware of formal structures and informal cultural issues that can prevent employees from raising concerns and grievances.
- Provide staff training on non-discrimination policies and practices, including disability awareness. Reasonably adjust the physical environment to ensure health and safety for employees, customers and other visitors with disabilities.
- Establish programs to promote access to skills development training and to particular occupations.

In the community of operation

- Encourage and support efforts to build a climate of tolerance and equal access to opportunities for occupational development such as adult education programs and health and childcare services.
- In foreign operations, companies may need to accommodate cultural traditions and work with representatives of workers and governmental authorities to ensure equal access to employment by women and minorities.

C. Environment

Principle 7: Businesses should support a precautionary approach to environmental challenges

What is the precautionary approach?

Introducing the precautionary approach, Principle 15 of the 1992 Rio Declaration states that "where there are threats of serious or irreversible damage, lack of full scientific certainty shall not be used as a reason for postponing cost-effective measures to prevent environmental degradation".

Precaution involves the systematic application of risk assessment (hazard identification, hazard characterization, appraisal of exposure and risk characterization), risk management and risk communication. When there is reasonable suspicion of harm and decision-makers need to apply precaution, they have to consider the degree of uncertainty that appears from scientific evaluation. Deciding on the "acceptable" level of risk involves not only scientific-technological evaluation and economic cost-benefit analysis, but also political considerations such as acceptability to the public. From a public policy view, precaution is applied as long as scientific information is incomplete or inconclusive and the associated risk is still considered too high to be imposed on society. The level of risk considered typically relates to standards of environment, health and safety.

Why is the precautionary approach important for business?

The key element of a precautionary approach, from a business perspective, is the idea of prevention rather than cure. In other words, it is more cost-effective to take early action to ensure that irreversible environmental damage does not occur. Companies should consider the following:

- While it is true that preventing environmental damage entails both opportunity-and implementation -costs, remediation environmental harm after it has occurred can cost much more, e.g. for treatment costs, or in terms of company image.
- Investing in production methods that are not sustainable (i.e. that deplete resources and degrade the environment) has a lower, long-term return than investing in sustainable operations. In turn, improving environmental performance means less financial risk, an important consideration for insurers.
- Research and development related to more environmentally friendly products can have significant long-term benefits

What steps could companies take in the application of the precautionary approach?

Issues for the company to deal with under this approach include providing better information to he consumer, communicating potential risk for the consumer, the public or the environment. It also ncludes obtaining prior approval before certain products, deemed to be potentially hazardous, may be laced on the market.

Steps that the company could take in the application of this approach include the following:

Develop a code of conduct or practice for its operations and products that confirms commitment to care for health and the environment.

Develop a company guideline on the consistent application of the approach throughout the company.

- Create a managerial committee or steering group that oversees the company application of precaution, in particular risk management in sensitive issue areas.
- Establish two-way communication with stakeholders, in a pro-active, early stage and transparent manner, to ensure effective communication of information about uncertainties and potential risks and to deal with related enquiries and complaints. Use mechanisms such as multi-stakeholder meetings, workshop discussions, focus groups, public polls combined with use of website and printed media.
- Support scientific research, including independent and public research, on the issue involved, working with national and international institutions concerned.
- Join industry-wide collaborative efforts to share knowledge and deal with issues, in particular production processes and products around which high level of uncertainty, potential harm and sensitivity exist.

Principle 8: undertake initiatives to promote greater environmental responsibility

What is environmental responsibility?

In Chapter 30 of Agenda 21, the 1992 Rio Earth Summit spelled out the role of business and industry in the sustainable development agenda as: "Business and industry should increase self regulation, guided by appropriate codes, charters and initiatives integrated into all elements of business planning and decision-making, and fostering openness and dialogue with employees and the public."

The relevant principle in the Rio Declaration says we have the responsibility to ensure that activities on our own yard should not cause harm to the environment of our neighbours. Society also expects business to be good neighbours. Business gains its legitimacy through meeting the needs of society, and increasingly society is expressing a clear need for more environmentally sustainable practices.

What steps could companies take to promote environmental responsibility?

Steps that the company could take to promote environmental responsibility would be the following:

- Re-define company vision, policies and strategies to include the 'triple bottom line' of sustainable development-economic prosperity, environmental quality and social equity.
- Develop sustainability targets and indicators (economic, environmental, social).
- Establish a sustainable production and consumption programme with clear performance objectives to take the organisation beyond compliance in the long-term.
- Work with suppliers to improve environmental performance, extending responsibility up the product chain and down the supply chain.
- Adopt voluntary charters, codes of conduct or practice internally as well as through sectoral and international initiatives to confirm acceptable behaviour and performance.
- Measure, track and communicate progress in incorporating sustainability principles into business practices, including reporting against global operating standards.
- Ensure transparency and unbiased dialogue with stakeholders.

In doing the above, the existence of appropriate management systems is crucial in helping the company to meet the organizational challenge. Key mechanisms or tools for the company to use would be (a) assessment or audit tools (such as environmental impact assessment, environmental risk assessment, technology assessment, life cycle assessment); (b) management tools (such as environmental management systems and ecodesign) and (c) communication and reporting tools (such as corporate environmental reporting and sustainability reporting).

Principle 9: encourage the development and diffusion of environmentally friendly technologies.

"Businesses should encourage the development and diffusion of environmentally friendly technologies."

What is an environmentally friendly technology?

Environmentally sound technologies, as defined in Agenda 21, should protect the environment, are less polluting, use all resources in a more sustainable manner, recycle more of their wastes and products and handle residual wastes in a more acceptable manner than the technologies for which they were substitutes. They include a variety of cleaner production process and pollution prevention technologies as well as end-of-pipe and monitoring technologies. Moreover, they can be considered total systems including know-how, procedures, goods and services and equipment as well as organizational and managerial procedures. Where production processes that do not use resources efficiently generate residues and discharge wastes, environmentally sound technologies can be applied to reduce day-to-day operating inefficiencies, emissions of environmental contaminants, worker exposure to hazardous materials and risks of technological disasters.

What are the key benefits of developing and diffusing environmentally friendly technologies?

The key benefits of environmentally friendly technologies are the following:

- Implementing environmentally friendly technologies helps a company reduce the use of raw materials leading to increased efficiency.
- Technology innovation creates new business opportunities and helps increase the overall competitiveness of the company.
- Technologies that use materials more efficiently and cleanly can be applied to most companies with long-term economic and environmental benefits.

How can business promote the use and diffusion of environmentally friendly technologies?

- At the basic factory site or unit level, improving technology may be achieved by (i) changing the process or manufacturing technique, (ii) changing input materials, (iii) changes to the product and (iv) reusing materials on site.

Strategic level approaches to improving technology include the following:

- Establishing a corporate or individual company policy on the use of environmentally sound technologies.
- Making information available to stakeholders that illustrates the environmental performance and benefits of using such technologies.

- Refocusing research and development towards 'design for sustainability'.
- Use of life cycle assessment (LCA) in the development of new technologies and products.
- Employing Environmental Technology Assessments (EnTA).
- Examining investment criteria and the sourcing policy for suppliers and contractors to ensure that tenders stipulate minimum environmental criteria.
- Co-operating with industry partners to ensure that 'best available technology' is available to other organizations.

D. Anti-Corruption

Principle 10: Businesses should work against corruption in all its forms, including extortion and bribery.

Origin of the 10th principle

On 24 June 2004, during the UN Global Compact Leaders Summit it was announced that the UN Global Compact henceforth includes a tenth principle against corruption. This was adopted after extensive consultations and all participants yielded overwhelming expressions of support, sending a strong worldwide signal that the private sector shares responsibility for the challenges of eliminating corruption. It also demonstrated a new willingness in the business community to play its part in the fight against corruption.

Underlying legal instrument

With the adoption of the United Nations Convention against Corruption in Merida, Mexico in December 2003, an important global tool to fight corruption was introduced. The Convention is the underlying legal instrument for the 10th principle against corruption and entered into force on 14 December 2005.

Objectives of the 10th principle

The adoption of the tenth principle commits UN Global Compact participants not only to avoid bribery, extortion and other forms of corruption, but also to develop policies and concrete programs to address corruption. Companies are challenged to join governments, UN agencies and civil society to realize a more transparent global economy.

How to define corruption?

Corruption can take many forms that vary in degree from the minor use of influence to institutionalized bribery. Transparency International's definition of corruption is "the abuse of entrusted power for private gain". This can mean not only financial gain but also non-financial advantages.

What is meant by extortion?

The OECD Guidelines for Multinational Enterprises define extortion in the following way: "The solicitation of bribes is the act of asking or enticing another to commit bribery. It becomes extortion when this demand is accompanied by threats that endanger the personal integrity or the life of the private actors involved."

Bribery

Transparency International's Business Principles for Countering Bribery define "bribery" in the following way: "Bribery: An offer or receipt of any gift, loan, fee, reward or other advantage to or from any person as an inducement to do something which is dishonest, illegal or a breach of trust, in the conduct of the enterprise's business."

Practical steps to fight corruption

The UN Global Compact suggests to participants to consider the following three elements when fighting corruption and implementing the 10th principle.

1. Internal: As a first and basic step, introduce anti-corruption policies and programs within their organizations and their business operations;
2. External: Report on the work against corruption in the annual Communication on Progress; and share experiences and best practices through the submission of examples and case stories;
3. Collective: Join forces with industry peers and with other stakeholders

Models of CSR

Corporate social responsibility is the commitment a company has to the community outside of its shareholders and employees. The subject isn't without controversy, with some claiming corporations have no role in social responsibility and others asserting that they can't escape it. Business researcher Elizabeth Redman proposed the three models of corporate social responsibility as a way of understanding this often contentious conversation. In her work on corporate social responsibility, published in the Roosevelt Review, Redman contends that the discussion often involves one of three conceptual models for CSR: a conflict model, an added value model and a multiple goals model.

Traditional Conflict Model

In the traditional conflict model for corporate social responsibility, social values and benefits are seen as in conflict with shareholder profits. Under this model, corporations opting to practice forms of social responsibility are likely to see added costs for doing so. Proponents of this conceptual model generally argue that the nature of business is one of trade-offs between economic and moral values, and corporate managers will inevitably be forced to decide between their social and fiduciary responsibilities or their commitment to shareholder equity value.

Added Value Model

A second model for conceptualizing corporate social responsibility is to see social and environmental commitments as a means to increase profit. While proponents of this model tend to acknowledge that conflicts persist in business decisions, they also believe that CSR investments are also capable of generating new revenues. This model tends to focus on issues like the value of CSR in attracting socially conscious consumers, finding socially conscious employees and managing the risks of negative press.

Multiple Goals Model

Finally, a third model for corporate social responsibility posits a role for social values in corporate decisions that are untethered to economic values. Under this model, corporations have goals beyond shareholder value, including the enhancement of their community without respect to monetary gain.

According to Redman, this model is thought to be relatively radical, though some corporate officers have expressed support for it. Proponents of this model emphasize quality of life as the basis of economic activity.

Best Practices of CSR

Corporate Responsibility (CR) is an issue that, in recent years, has moved further up the agenda in terms of importance for organisations. The increasing public awareness of the need to be 'responsible', the development of the role of Corporate Responsibility Manager, and the expansion of the number of CR reporting indices are demonstrative of this.

It is a concept where an organisation takes responsibility for the impact of its activities in relation to all aspects of its operations. This obligation is seen to extend beyond the current statutory obligation to comply with legislation and sees organisations voluntarily taking further steps to improve performance in relation to key components of CR:

- Corporate governance
- True governance should provide all stakeholders with:
- Clarity, openness and democracy in all the organization's policies, procedures or strategies and
- CR report
- Sustainable communities

CR has become increasingly more than a side issue, owing to recent episodes of business mis-management. With globalisation, the power and impact of trans-national organisations have increased, as have the demands for space and resources, both of which show trends towards becoming more scarce. This has led to the need and desire for greater responsibility and safeguards. Current media focus can be seen to be concentrated upon environmental issues.

In the UK the 2006 Companies Act requires all directors for the first time to have regard for the interests of their staff, their suppliers and customers, the community, and the environment. This legislation also requires that quoted companies produce a business review that includes information about environmental matters, employees and social and community issues.

The Business Case

There is a clear business case for CR. Stakeholders and customers are increasingly concerned about the environmental and social impacts of the products and services they buy. There are numerous recognised benefits from an effective business-led approach to CR:

Reputation Management

In addition to factors such as quality of product and financial performance, CR is a somewhat intangible asset that has the potential to enhance the brand. Reputation for integrity and respect can build customer loyalty based on distinct values differentiating the brand from the competition.

Risk Management

CR provides a means by which companies better understand and manage risk. Establishing a comprehensive CR policy and strategy can offset these risks, spanning legal, financial, environmental, and societal risks.

Recruitment and Retention

Increasingly CR is a key factor in attracting and retaining a talented and diverse workforce. Graduates look for CR records when considering who to work for. CR can also help to improve the perception of an organisation amongst its employees.

Innovation and Learning

Environmental and social constraints restrict how an organisation can make a profit, or bring about continuous improvement. Effective CR can create innovative ways to become profitable, or raise sufficient funds, within those constraints.

Access to Capital

Potential investors in organisations are increasingly using CR performance as an indicator for the quality of management and approach to risk management in a company, when taking decisions on investment of capital into a business.

Licence to Operate

Taking substantive voluntary steps can result in aspects of light-touch regulation being applied where discretion from the regulator is available.

Financial Performance

Effective CR policies should also improve market positioning and profitability. For example many energy saving measures as well as being environmentally friendly also save money.

Reasons against Corporate Responsibility

There are questions over the genuineness of CR to fundamental business strategy. Milton Friedman (1970) argued that 'there is one and only one social responsibility of business: to use its resources and engage in activities designed to increase its profits'.

A company can be accused of 'whitewashing', whereby disinformation is presented by an organisation so as to support a responsible public image, especially if it only communicates CR successes, and not failures, to stakeholders or 'green-washing' where it is trying to present misleading environmental credentials.

The dangers of whitewashing can be evidenced in the example of ENRON. Once a front-runner in terms of CR, the company was held in high regard for its CR reports and environmental and community programmes. However, the scandal of concealment of debts, to give the appearance of profitable company accounts, led to the realisation that good CR records were not relevant if they only existed on a surface level; CR initiatives need to be fully embedded within a company.

If a CR report is to add value to an organisation it should report the weaknesses along with action plans on how to address them. There is also a charge that CR programmes might be focused to draw away the majority attention from the ethical considerations at the core of the operation.

Good Practice Principles for Corporate Responsibility Reporting

There is a growing public demand for information about the impacts a company has on the society in which it operates. Thus, reporting on responsible business performance to stakeholders (whether a legislative requirement or not) creates a shared understanding of responsible business and helps to integrate such practices into the 'fabric' of an organisation.

By sharing relevant information about the risks and opportunities it faces, as well as its social, environmental and economic performance, a company can enhance its reputation and build confidence among investors, analysts, employees and customers. CR reports can be published in print or online, with summary or overview documents for certain stakeholder audiences, such as employees.

Alternatively, an organisation might have a CR section on its corporate website, or include responsible business in its annual report and accounts.

Whatever format is used, a CR report should be a consolidated view of management and performance on responsible business issues. It should also define the reporting period, contain policy statements, objectives and targets, and review performance to enable a year-on-year comparison.

Need of CSR

Corporate Social responsibility in a business organization is very important and need in the following ways:

a) Societal approach is very important to business organizations, which demand that they should be responsive to the social problems of society.

b) To establish a good corporate image, business organizations include social responsibility as a corporate objective.

c) Social welfare terms are included in the collaborative agreements, which require the company to take up the social responsibility of business.

d) Legal provisions like pollution and environmental laws also direct a company to take up social problems.

e) Donations to approved NGOs are also exempted from the income tax.

f) Commitment to social responsibility by an organization also enhances its image, resulting in better business environment.

g) Companies undertaking social responsibility can position their products better and increase their market share.

h) In case a situation demands, due to natural calamities or accidents, a company has to compensate the victims or provide medical treatment to the affected people.

i) For extraneous consideration also, some time, some organizations are forced to take up social responsibility.

j) In some organizations the culture is so strong that they take up social responsibility as their moral responsibility.

Arguments for and against CSR

The major arguments for the assumption of social responsibilities by business are:

1) ***Public expectations:*** Social expectations of business have increased dramatically since the 1960s. Public opinion in support of business pursuing social as well as economic goals is now well solidified.

2) ***Long run profits:*** Socially responsible businesses tend to have more and secure long run profits. This is the normal result of the better community relations and improved business image that responsible.

3) ***Ethical obligation:*** A business firm can and should have a conscience. Business should be socially responsible because responsible actions are right for their own sake.

4) ***Public image:*** Firms seek to enhance their public image to gain more customers, better employees, access to money markets, and other benefits. Since the public considers social goals to be important, business can create a favorable public image by pursuing social goals.

5) ***Better environment:*** Involvement by business can solve difficult social problems, thus creating a better quality of life and a more desirable community in which to attract and hold skilled employees.

6) ***Discouragement of further government regulation:*** Government regulation adds economic costs and restricts management's decision flexibility by becoming socially responsible, business can expect less government regulation.

7) ***Balance of responsibility and power:*** Business has a large amount of power in society. An equally large amount of responsibility is required to balance it. When power is significantly greater than responsibility, the imbalance encourages irresponsible behavior that works against the public good.

8) ***Stockholder interests:*** Social responsibility will improve the price of a business's stock in the long run. The stock market will view the socially responsible company as less risky and open to public attack. Therefore, it will award its stock a higher price earning ratio.

9) ***Possession of resources:*** Business has the financial resources, technical experts, and managerial talent to provide support to public and charitable projects that need assistance.

10) ***Superiority of prevention over cures:*** Social problems must be dealt with at sometime. Business should act on them before they become serious and costly to correct and take management's energy away from accomplishing its goal of production goods and services.

The major arguments against the assumption of social responsibilities by business are:

1) ***Violation of profit maximization:*** This is the essence of the classical viewpoint. Business is most socially responsible when it attends strictly to its economic interests and leaves other activities to other institutions.

2) ***Dilution of purpose:*** The pursuit of social goals dilutes business's primary purpose: economic productivity. Society may suffer as both economic and social goals are poorly accomplished.

3) ***Costs:*** Many socially responsible activities do not pay their own way. Someone has to pay these costs. Business must absorb these costs or pass them on to consumers in higher prices.

4) ***Too much power:*** Business is already one of the most powerful institutions in our society. If it pursued social goals, it would have even more power. Society has given business enough power.

5) ***Lack of skills:*** The outlook and abilities of business leaders are oriented primarily toward economies. Business people are poorly qualified to cope with social issues.

6) ***Lack of accountability:*** Political representatives pursue social goals and are held accountable for their actions. Such is not the case with business leaders. There are no direct lines of social accountability from the business sector to the public.

7) *Lack of broad public support:* There is no broad mandate from society for business to become involved in social issues. The public is divided on the issue. In fact, it is a topic that usually generates a heated debate. Actions taken under such divided support are likely to fail.

CSR Indian Perspective

The European Union defines Corporate Social Responsibility (CSR) as "a concept that an enterprise is accountable for its impact on all relevant stakeholders. It is the continuing commitment by business to behave fairly and responsibly and contribute to economic development while improving the quality of life of the workforce and their families as well as the local community and the society at large." In broader terms, CSR means a collection of policies, programs and practices adopted,

An Indian perspective of corporate social responsibility followed and recognized by a company that is based on certain values, including respect for people, communities (in which the company operates) and the environment.

Corporate plays a vital role in shaping the quality of life of the society as a whole in today's globalized economy. According to Nobel Laureate Amartya Sen, "Market forces alone are not sufficient for equitable distribution, and some sort of intervention is required, be it political or from business houses, towards society."

CSR covers various issues, like human rights, working conditions, equality and diversity, consumer protection, environment and health impacts, economic development, ethical business practices and lobbying and political influence.

Today, companies are increasingly adopting socially responsible practices because of their long-term benefits. Some of the benefits are:

- Creating and maintaining a high reputation;
- Securing strong relationship with stakeholders;
- Creating a better, safer and more stimulating work culture;
- Improving business management efficiency;
- Protecting from boycott actions; Making access to funding easier;
- Benefiting from fiscal advantages and administrative facilitation;
- Reducing enterprise risk. Indian Context: The Evolution and Growing Interest

Companies funded education and other social welfare activities even during the pre-independence era in India.

CSR Indian Examples

Corporate Social Responsibility: Initiatives and Examples

Today, businesses are expected to extend their attention beyond stockholders, customers and employees to include other stakeholders such as the community and environment. The concept of corporate social responsibility (CSR) emerged expectations and consists of transparent organizational management; careful consideration of the global environment, human rights, employment and in particular, compliance with ordinances, regulations, and laws. CSR can lead to more sustainable corporations by encouraging good relationships with society. it is not easy for all to achieve the required level of CSR. Establishing CSR is not a simple task, nor is it free from risks and problems. CSR requires support not only from shareholders and investors but also from customers, employees, and communities. Salman Khurshid, Minister of state for corporate Affairs, Government of India, made his standpoint on CSR very clear. Mr.Khurshid said that CSR should be quantifiable like carbon credits as corporate cannot behave irresponsibly in social responsibility and should act in, "enlightened self interest". The ministry review of CSR projects to ensure that the funds are used in the genuine progress of society. CSR projects include encouragement of literacy and higher education ,grant of scholarship and aid to deserving young pupils of less privileged sections of society ,facilities for constructing schools, renovation of school buildings and other infrastructure .Besides ,the company also pays out for healthcare and family welfare development .The emphasis is also on development of infrastructure facilities –improvement of roads ,bridges ,street lighting ,draining system and progress of agriculture and cottage industries.

Meaning of CSR

Corporate social responsibility (CSR) is also known as corporate responsibility, corporate citizenship, responsible business, sustainable responsible business (SRB), or corporate social performance. It is a form of corporateself-regulation integrated into a business model. Ideally, CSR policy would function as a built-in, self-regulating mechanism whereby business would monitor and ensure its adherence to law, ethical standards, and international norms. Consequently, business would embrace responsibility for the impact of its activities on the environment, consumers, employees, communities, stakeholders and all other members of the public sphere. CSR-focused businesses would proactively promote the public interest by encouraging community growth and development, and voluntarily eliminating practices that harm the public sphere, regardless of legality.

General Issues in CSR: There are three groups of issues: legal compliance, ethical practices, and social contributions.

1. ***Legal Compliance:*** The compliance section is mainly concerned with establishing the legal way to avoid the application of laws. The objective is to find the loophole that makes it possible to avoid the reach of the law. If international agreements are ratified and codified into domestic laws, companies at this level will try to comply with international agreements; but other than that, companies will not comply with such agreements willingly.
2. ***Ethical Practices:*** Companies try to avoid any action resulting in a negative impact on others and any action that might cause harm or damage to others. Companies comply with not only the letter but also the spirit of the law. Even if international agreements are not ratified or codified into domestic laws, companies at this level will try to understand and put those spirits into practice.
3. ***Social Contributions:*** Companies exert positive influences and impacts to help others or, for example, develop environmentally friendly technologies.

Important Driver of CSR: The first relates to globalization. Business corporations are trying to develop CSR policies to establish internal systems that make it possible to reduce negative impacts and increase the positive influences over external stakeholders. Globalization is the creation of a new business era when a business corporation can enjoy an enormous amount of freedom. There is no single government or single law enforcement body to apply the same laws and regulations to all players. International agreements exist but can easily be ignored in a number of countries. The second driver of CSR varies from country to country and region to region. Each society has different issues to be solved with the help of a business corporation.

Role of Public Sector Unit: The corporate sector will slowly become more involved in social development and with its huge financial, technical and human resources will be able to bring in far – reaching social changes. Public sector oil companies spend a minimum of 2 percent of their net profits of the previous year on CSR activities. Oil & Natural Gas Corp(ONGC)and Indian Oil Corporation(IOC)has been spending 0.75-1 percent of their net profit of CSR activities .In 2007-08, Rs. 246.70 crore was spent by oil PSU on CSR activities including Rs 124.01 crore by ONGC and Rs. 64.27 crore by IOC .Oil India Ltd. spent Rs 28.93 crore on CSR activities in 2007-08 ,Hindustan Petroleum Rs. 6.67 crore, Bharat Petroleum Rs 7.38 crore and GAIL Rs. 15.44 crore .In first nine months of 2008-09, ONGC spent Rs 59.96 crore and IOC Rs 25.71 crore on CSR activities .OIL spent Rs 12.73 crore ,HPCL Rs. 6.48 crore ,BPCL Rs.12.93 crore and GAIL Rs. 7.09 crore on CSR activities in April -December 2008-09. And then in May last year ONGC increased its allocation for CSR activities to Rs 300 crore ,which is 2% of its net profit in the previous fiscal ,from Rs 145 crore. GAIL India, which is involved in gas transportation, had also allocated Rs. 25 crore, 2% of its profits in 2008-09. The petroleum ministry has indicated that oil PSUs are expected to spend Rs 700 crore in 2009-10 on CSR.

Some Important examples of CSR activities

Anand Corporate Services Limited

Anand has a long standing commitment to addressing the needs of the society, in view of its belief that for any economic development to be meaningful, the benefits from the business must trickle down to the society at large. Anand is of the firm view that the corporate goals must be aligned with the larger societal goals. 25 years ago, the SNS Foundation, an expression of Anand's corporate social responsibility, was born. The objective of SNS foundation was comprehensive community development. The Foundation has created programs in the fields of health, education, natural resource management and life skills training, only to make sure that fellow humans could breathe easy.

The long term goal of Anand CSR is to implement concepts like 'Zero Tolerance Zone for Child Labour', 'Zero Waste Zone' using strategies like Reduce, Recycle and Reuse not only at Anand/SNSF locations but extend to Anand residential areas.

Aptech Limited

Aptech Limited, a leading education player with a global presence, has played an extensive and sustained role in encouraging and fostering education throughout the country since inception. As a global player with complete solutions-providing capability, Aptech has a long history of participating in community activities. It has, in association with leading NGOs, provided computers at schools, education to the underprivileged and conducted training and awareness-camps.

Aptech students donated part of the proceeds from the sale of their art work to NGOs. To propagate education among all sections of the society throughout the country, especially the underprivileged, Aptech fosters tie-ups with leading NGOs throughout the country, including the Barrackpur-based NGO, Udayan, a residential school for children of leprosy patients in Barrackpur, established in 1970. The company strongly believes that education is an integral part of the country's social fabric and works towards supporting basic education and basic computer literacy amongst the underprivileged children in India.

Avon Cycle Limited

The poor and ignorant of India's rural population turn to nearest towns and cities for healthcare. They face in difference and exploitation. Hope gives way to despair. This gave inspiration to AVON for locating MATAKAUSHALYADEVI, PAHWA CHARITABLE HOSPITAL. Mr. Sohan Lal Pahwa, AVON's Chairman and Principal Trustee of the hospital, spent a good part of his working life devoted to philanthropy. The hospital, in its 5th year of inception, has risen to serve a model healthcare facility boasting of some bold experiments in its very early years of existence. It's support since inception has been of the order of Rs. 3 crore to date and it continues uninterrupted. Reaching out to the needy farther afield, the hospital holds regular camps in surrounding villages to propagate scientific approach to healthcare. Recently the hospital took the social responsibility concept a step further and formulated a scheme titled 'Celebrated Female Child' to enable and inspire positive and enduring environment for society's all–consuming passion for 'sons only' to end

CISCO System Inc.

Philanthropy at Cisco is about building strong and productive global communities - communities in which every individual has the means to live, the opportunity to learn, and the chance to give back. The company pursues a strong "triple bottom line" which is described as profits, people and presence. The company promotes a culture of charitable giving and connects employees to nonprofit organizations serving the communities where they live. Cisco invests its best-in-class networking equipment to those nonprofit organizations that best put it to work for their communities, eventuating in positive global impact. It takes its responsibility seriously as a global citizen. Education is a top corporate priority for Cisco, as it is the key to prosperity and opportunity.

ICICI Bank Ltd

The Social Initiatives Group (SIG) of ICICI Bank Ltd works with a mission to build the capacities of the poorest of the poor to participate in the larger economy. The group identifies and supports initiatives designed to break the intergenerational cycle of poor health and nutrition, ensure essential early childhood education and schooling as well as access to basic financial services. Thus, by promoting early child health, catalyzing universal elementary education and maximizing access to micro financial services, ICICI Bank believes that it can build the capacities of India's poor to participate in larger socio-economic processes and thereby spur the overall development of the country. The SIG works by understanding the status of existing systems of service delivery and identifying critical knowledge and practice gaps in their functioning. It locates cost effective and scalable initiatives and approaches that have the potential to address these gaps and supports research to understand their impact. This is undertaken in collaboration with research agencies, nongovernmental organisations (NGOs), companies, government departments, local stakeholders and international organisations.

Infosys Technologies Limited

Infosys is actively involved in various community development programs. Infosys promoted, in 1996, the Infosys Foundation as a not-for-profit trust to which it contributes up to 1%PAT every year. Additionally, the Education and Research Department (E&R) at Infosys also works with employee volunteers on community development projects. Infosys leadership has set examples in the area of corporate citizenship and has involved itself actively in key national bodies. They have taken initiatives to work in the areas of Research and Education, Community Service, Rural Reach Programme, Employment, Welfare activities undertaken by the Infosys Foundation, Healthcare for the poor, Education and Arts & Culture.

ITC Limited

ITC partnered the Indian farmer for close to a century. ITC is now engaged in elevating this partnership to a new paradigm by leveraging information technology through its trailblazing 'e-Choupal' initiative. ITC is significantly widening its farmer partnerships to embrace a host of value-adding activities: creating livelihoods

by helping poor tribals make their wastelands productive; investing in rainwater harvesting to bring much-needed irrigation to parched drylands; empowering rural women by helping them evolve into entrepreneurs; and providing infrastructural support to make schools exciting for village children. Through these rural partnerships, ITC touches the lives of nearly 3 million villagers across India.

Mahindra & Mahindra

The K. C. Mahindra Education Trust was established in 1953 by late Mr. K. C. Mahindra with an objective to promote education. Its vision is to transform the lives of people in India through education, financial assistance and recognition to them, across age groups and across income strata. The K. C. Mahindra Education Trust undertaken number of education initiatives, which make a difference to the lives of deserving students. The Trust has provided more than Rs. 7.5 Crore in the form of grants, scholarships and loans. It promotes education mainly by the way of scholarships. The Nanhi Kali project has over 3,300 children under it. We aim to increase the number of Nanhi Kalis (children) to 10,000 in the next 2 years, by reaching out to the underprivileged children especially in rural areas.

Tata Consultancy Services

The Adult Literacy Program (ALP) was conceived and set up by Dr. F C Kohli along with Prof. P N Murthy and Prof. Kesav Nori of Tata Consultancy Services in May 2000 to address the problem of illiteracy. ALP believes illiteracy is a major social concern affecting a third of the Indian population comprising old and young adults. To accelerate the rate of learning, it uses a TCS-designed Computer–Based Functional Literacy Method (CBFL), an innovative teaching strategy that uses multimedia software to teach adults to read within about 40 learning hours.

Dalmia Cement (Bharat) Limited

The water source for the villages in and around the Dalmia Cement factory is dependent on rains. During summer months, the villagers, particularly women folk, travel long distances to fetch water for drinking and other purposes. Considering the difficulties and hardship faced by the people, the company, after discussing with the village elders and concerned Government authorities, took the initiative of making water available by:

Providing deep bore wells. So far, 45 bore wells have been provided in various villages, namely Kallakudi, Palanganathan, Malvoi, Elakkurichi, Muthuvathur, Pullabmadi, Edayathankudi etc. Approximately, 300 to 400 people get adequate drinking water from each bore well.

Water tanks to store the water.

Rain and seepage water is harvested in the quarries of the company is pumped into a tank and supplied to inhabitants. 44,000 trees were planted and nurtured over a period

of eight years. The presence of large trees and vast greenery has considerably improved the ecology in the area.

DCM Shriram Consolidated Limited

Shriram Fertilisers and Chemicals, is a unit of DSCL, located at Kota, 475 kms. Over the last 3 decades, various initiatives have been undertaken by the unit, in the Hadoti region (Kota, Bundi, Jhalawar districts) in ICU, ambulances, family planning, medical assistance; schools, scholarships, emphasis on girl child education; water to people and infrastructure.

Goodearth Education Foundation (GEF)

Work of GEF was initiated in 1996 with a project in the Rai Bareilly district in Uttar Pradesh. The four-year project covered 63 government schools and benefited 15,000 children. GEF is currently implementing projects in Thane district, Maharashtra (in 56 schools & balwadis), Alwar District, Rajasthan (this Project is being implemented in partnership with the NGO Bodh Shiksha Samiti, covering 71 schools & balwadis) and Solan district, Himachal Pradesh (10 Balwadis). GEF Objectives include providing equal opportunities in pre-primary& primary education to all children, and quality of education by ensuring that it is relevant, effective and activity based.

Hindustan Construction Company (HCC)

HCC plays an active role in CSR initiatives in the fields of Health, Education, Disaster Management, and Environment. Disaster Resource Network DRN is a worldwide initiative, promoted by the World Economic Forum (WEF). Trained volunteers and equipment resources from Engineering Construction & Logistics companies will complement the existing efforts of Government, NGO's and International Organizations in disaster management. It was during the WEF annual meet that the massive earthquake struck Gujarat in January 2001. The need for a trained and effective participation from industry was first felt there. The members of Engineering and Logistics segment of WEF came together to establish this network. The idea was further strengthened during the 9/11 incident where again the industry participated in the relief operations. DRN Worldwide was formally launched in New York in January 2002. And shortly thereafter, DRN - India Initiative was launched.

India Aluminium Company Limited

The Women's Empowerment project was initiated by Indal-Muri in Jharkhand where the Company operates an alumina refining plant. It was implemented in collaboration with an NGO, CARE-Jharkhand. The central problem this project has attempted to address is the very low socio-economic condition of the rural and tribal population of Silli block caused by low agricultural productivity,lack of or low cash income, unresponsive health/ Integrated Child Development Services (ICDS)schemes. Project has helped set up around 100 Self Help Groups so far, which are running successfully with members trained in various vocational income–generating skills, agricultural methods for better yields and health care initiatives. About 2000 women have been brought into the fold of this activity helping to improve not justtheir own lives but the quality of life of their children and families as well.

JCB India Ltd.

JCB India adopted a Government school, in the vicinity of the company premises as its social responsibility. They strongly believe that children are the foundation of our nation and they could be helped, we could build a better community and society tomorrow. The reason for adopting this particular school was the poor management of the school in terms of infrastructure, resources and quality of education. The company's commitment to the school goes much beyond just providing monetary support towards infrastructure and maintenance of school building.

Review Questions

Conceptual Type

1. What is Corporate Social Responsibility?
2. What is sustainability?
3. Give the meaning of complicity.
4. Give the meaning of contemporary issues.

Analytical Type

1. Explain nature of Corporate Social Responsibility.
2. What are the principles of Corporate Social Responsibility?
3. Write note on: Best practice of Corporate Social Responsibility.
4. Explain needs for Corporate Social Responsibility.
5. State the general issues of CSR

Descriptive Type

1. Discuss various types of Corporate Social Responsibility.
2. Give the strategies for Corporate Social Responsibility.
3. Discuss various models of Corporate Social Responsibility.
4. Give the major argument against CSR.
5. Discuss Indian perspectives of CSR with example.

*****

Module-8

Business Law

Syllabus

Law of contract, meaning of contract, agreement, essential elements of a valid contract, classification of contracts, proposal and acceptance, free consent, void agreements.

Negotiable instruments act 1881: Nature and Characteristics of Negotiable instruments, Kinds of Negotiable Instruments – Promissory Notes, Bills of Exchange and Cheques. Parties to Negotiable Instruments, Negotiation, Presentment, Discharge and Dishonor of Negotiable Instrument, Law of agency, Bailment & Pledge: 36

Sale of goods act 1930: Definition of Sale, Sale v/s Agreement to Sell, Goods, price and Time, Condition and Warranties, Express and Implied Condition, "Doctrine of Caveat Emptor", Performance of Contract of sale, Right of Unpaid Seller.

Intellectual property law, law relating to patents, law relating to copyrights, law relating to trade mark.

Law of Contract

Introduction

Law is a main contributory factor for man's welfare and wellbeing. The study of law is of enormous practical value and vital and ever-present force in modern life. Every individual and even more a business man needs even more through knowledge of the law than the person not so engaged. As he carried his business, he is confronted with problems arising out of contract, sale of goods, bailment, agency, negotiable instruments, cyber-crimes environmental issues, international dealing and so on. At present situation business are facing a lot of formidable problems as every activity of the business is vigilantly watched by the public and law. In economics is started developing in the positive direction and exposed to global competition and followed the path of economic liberalization to the greater extent. This made compulsory to study 'Business Law' or to the knowledge of various legal aspects as a part of commerce, management and business study curriculum with different titles.

With the growth of people's social and economic behavior has assumed a multi-dimensional character. Most civilized societies, therefore, provide and enforce different set of rules, regulations and principles for different kind of social behavior. In this connection there are different branches of law both for social, individual and business such as constitutional law, civil procedure codes, criminal procedure codes, International law, Mercantile law/Business law and so on. The mercantile law is referred to the branch of law which comprises laws concerning trade, industry, business or commerce with the increasing complexities of modern business world, the scope of mercantile law has enormously widened. Since the business is related to society, any activity related society and main's welfare are directly related, hence it is now termed as business law or legal aspects of business or business regulations.

Prior to the enactment of the various acts like the contract acts, sales of goods acts, companies act, the negotiable instrument act, Insurance act, etc., business transactions were regulated by the personal laws of the parties to the suit. The rights of Hindus and Muslims were governed by their respective laws and usages. Where both parties were Hindus, they were regulated by the Hindu Law and where both parties were Muslims, the Mohammedan Law was applied. In cases where one party was a Hindu and the other was of Muslims, the personal law of the defendant was applied. In case of persons other than Hindus and Muslims, and also where laws and usages of Hindus and Muslims were silent on any point, the courts generally applied their principles of English law.

In the present era the General law applicable to all sort of persons in the society irrespective of any religious differences. The applications are based on nature and type of situation faced every man in the society. Hence the study on different activity and the practices of an individual man is essential.

Man is a rational and social being who comes into contact with various types and varieties of people with different capabilities and dimensions.

Meaning of Law

Law is a rule of action evolved to regulate social life and to avoid conflict of interests. Law is enacted or customary in a community and recognised as commanding or avoiding certain action.

Law is:

- Commanding or influencing of certain actions;
- Collectively as a social system or subject of study;
- Binding force on individuals or society;
- Rule of action and procedure;
- Regularity in natural occurrences;
- Judicial remedy.

The above different meaning of law reflection on man and has different connotations for different people as;

• A citizen	A set of rules which he must obey.
• A lawyer	Profession/vocation.
• A legislator	Something created by him.
• A judge	Guiding principles applicable for decisions
• A social scientist	Social control.

Thus the meaning of law differs from person to person according to the individual's perception. It is, therefore very difficult to give one confirmed and accurate definition of Law. It is often preceded by an adjective to give it a more precise meaning, example: Civil Law, Criminal Law, Commercial Law, Labour Law, Industrial Law, Social Law, International Law and so on. However, in the legal sense, the word "Law" includes all the rules and principles which regulate our relations with other individuals, with the society and with the state.

It is the duty of the state to regulate the conduct of people by a set of rules. Intern the people of the state to follow these rules directly or indirectly and implicitly or explicitly. Such rules of conduct after its recognition by the state and enforced by it on people, are termed as 'Law'. This is to confirm, the reference can be taken from the Salmond, an eminent jury as "Law is the body of principles recognised and applied by the state in the administration of justice".

The meaning of law can be justified with some of the following definitions:

- ***Woodrow Wilson,*** " Law is that portion of the established habit and thought of mankind which has gained distinct and formal recognition in the shape of uniform rules backed by the authority and power of the government".
- ***Austin,*** " A law is a rule of conduct imposed and enforced by the sovereign".
- ***Scotland,*** " Law as rules of external human action enforced by the sovereign political authority i.e., the state".
- ***Oxford Dictionary,*** " Law is rule made by authority for the proper regulation of a community or society or for correct conduct of life".

From the above discussions and definitions, it is clear that the law can be applicable as the following:

(i) Body of rules which includes Statute Law like;

(a) The Indian contract Act 1872,

(b) The Indian partnership Act 1932

(c) The Companies Act 1956

(d) Case Laws

(e) Customs and Usages.

(ii) Guide to human conduct.

(iii) Imposed by some authority in whom special power is vested, like;

(a) Municipal bodies.

(b) State legislative assemblies.

(c) Parliament

(d) All statute law laid down by the state.

(e) Case law laid down by the superior courts.

(f) Customs and usages practiced by the people over period of time.

(iv) Enforcement, which is main characteristic of law, carried by the state. The law which is not enforced ceases to be law.

Object of Law

(1) To incorporate uniformity and social security among all category of people of the society.

(2) To establish socio-economic justice and remove the existing imbalances in the socio-economic structure.

(3) To impose social justice on the basis of social change by considering all round welfare and improvement of the community, through welfare and well-being of the citizens individually and collectively from material, moral and spiritual stand points.

(4) To create awareness of law among the citizen, its contents, purpose, requirements, regulations and manner involves which its serves them. It is able to make them follow the law and respect it.

(5) To make a strong government or state to implement the law positively for the benefit of human-being and for the welfare and well being of the society.

Need for Law

As law is a body of rules passed, and it is guidance which is imposed to certain level to the general public, it is obvious that the law must be known and practiced by each and every person in the society.

"Ignorantia juris non-excusat" is a familiar and well accepted maxim and the meaning of the same is ignorance of law is no excuse. Though it is not possible for any common man to learn every branch of law, yet it is to the advantage of each member of the community to know something of rules and regulations by which he is governed and as such he must acquaint himself with the general principles of the law of the country.

It is understood that, some knowledge of law is necessary for every member of the society in general and particular with the business class. As such no sound businessman would attempt to solve important legal problems affecting his business interest without expert legal advice. A general knowledge of some of the more important legal principles and how they apply to certain problems will definitely help a business man in avoiding conflict with the persons with whom he comes into business contacts. Mercantile Law, Commercial Law or Business Law are in particular importance to business people or general public to certain extent engaged in economic and social activities.

Commercial Law or Business Law

The term commercial law is used to denote that branch of law which is concerned with the matters of commercial or business nature. Many a time it deals with contractual situations, rights and obligations arising out of commercial or business transactions.

The term commercial is used to denote the aggregate body of those legal rules which are contracted with trade, industry and commerce.

It is also defined as, " that branch of law which comprises laws concerning trade industry and commerce".

Mercantile Law or Business Law is also known as a body of legal rules which relates to the conduct of business.

According to ***Slaters, " The phrase***

Mercantile Law or Commercial Law, is generally used to denote those portions of the law which deal with the rights and obligations arising out of transactions between mercantile persons". It also comprises a vast number of transactions pertaining to business transactions, and these laws govern the relation of business to society. There is no separate statute entitled 'Mercantile law' or 'Commercial law' or 'Business law' but for the shake of convenience some of the acts related to men and society and men in business are grouped together and called Mercantile Law or Business Law.

These laws are part of civil law which is connected to society directly. Some of them are like, Law of Contracts, Sales of Goods Act, Consumer Protection Act, Environmental Protection Act, Intellectual Property Act and so on.

Scope of Commercial or Business Law

Most civilized societies provide and enforce different sets of rules and guiding principles for different kinds or social behaviour. Hence there are several branches of law such as Constitutional Law, Criminal Law, Civil Law, Industrial Law, Labour Law, Commercial Law or Business Law and so on.

The scope of commercial or business law is fairly large. It includes the law relating to contracts, sale of goods, partnership, negotiable instruments, insurance, insolvency, carriage of goods, company's activities and so on. In respect of Business Law in particular which is also dealing with the activities pertaining with the any class of people who are directly or indirectly connected with the business activities. Hence the scope of business law can be broadly classified as:

(i) **Law of contract** Deals with any agreement which may be in particular or general with the individuals belonging to the society and also of various commercial activities.

(ii) **Law of sale of goods** Deals with the agreement between one trader to another trader with only commercial transactions.

(iii) **Economic and other Legislation** Are termed as 'General Law', deals with both the business and society which sets the rules towards rights, duties and obligations for any category of people in the society. Some of the law of this nature which are termed as 'Act' are:

(a) The Monopolies and Restrictive Trade Practices Act 1969.

(b) The Environment (Protection) Act 1986.

(c) The Patents Act 1970.

(d) The Sick Industrial Companies (Special Provision) Act 1985.

(e) The Consumer Protection Act of 1986.

(f) The Securities Contracts (Regulation) Act 1956.

(g) The Foreign Exchange Management Act and so on.

Law of Contract

Business and society go hand in hand, and at the same time Law and society are very closely related. It is often found that law changes with a change in the society. Society lays down rules of conduct for common good, sometimes at the expense of the individuals. Every individual should be a man and he is a social being. Every social being should surrender a part of his freedom to the society especially towards law that in turn ensures him safety, security and peace. So Law aims in bringing and maintaining peace and order in the society. One such law is the Indian Contract Act. The law of contracts forms the oldest branch of the law relating to business and general transactions, as it affects every person in one way or the other, as all of us enter into some kind of agreement or contract everyday. Law of contract is very essential to all merchants, when they are involved with huge money and dealings. At the same time it is also for the general public like a person buys a movable property, hires some goods or services, booking for a marriage hall, putting up of a show and so on. Such contracts create legal relations giving rise to certain rights and obligations.

According to ***Asen***; "The law of contract is intented to ensure that what a man has been led to expect shall come to pass, that what has been promised shall be performed."

Nature of Law of Contract

The law of contract is that branch of law which determines the circumstances in which a promise or an **agreement shall be legally binding on the person making it**. The law relating to contracts in India is confined to the Indian Contact Act, 1872. The Act came into force on the first day of September 1872. Originally this Act was included with general principles of law of contract, contracts relating to sale of goods, special kinds of contracts like indemnity, guarantee and so on. Later the Indian Contract

Act has been divided into two, Part I as general principles of Law of Contract and Sale of goods Act, where as in Part II it is Partnership Act and so an.

Unlike other branches of law, law of contract does not apply, but it determines the circumstance in which a Promise has been made. The parties to an agreement may lay down their own terms and conditions. The Indian Contract Act does not declare to be a complete and exhaustive code, it deals with the general principles of the law of contract and with special contracts only.

The law of contract differs from other branches of law. The Act does not lay down a number of rights and duties which the law will enforce. In this Act the party themselves creates rights and duties which will be supported with a limited principles.

Definition of Contract

Sir John Salmond defines a contract as, "An agreement creating and defining obligations between two parties."

According to ***Sir William Anson***, "A contract **as a legally binding agreement** made between two or more persons, by which rights are acquired **by one or more to acts or forbearance on the part of the other or others.**"

In simple words, a contract is an agreement between two or more parties which is intended to have legal consequences.

According to Halsburey, "A contract is an agreement between two or more persons which is intended to be enforceable at law and is **constituted by the acceptance by one party** of an offer made to him by the other party to do or abstain from doing some act."

Sir Fredirck Pollock defines, "Every agreement and promise enforceable at law is a Contract."

According to the ***Indian Contact Act***, Section 2 (h) "An agreement enforceable by law is a Contract."

According to above definitions, it is clear that a contract should consist of two elements;

(i) Agreement

(ii) Legal obligation or agreement must be enforceable by law.

(i) Agreement

Agreement is an acceptance to a offer. Agreement is considered to be prime element to form any contact. According to the Act, the word 'agreement' is defined under Section 2(e) as, "Every promise or every set of promise, forming the consideration for each other is an agreement." According to this act for agreement there should be a promise then,

What is a promise?

A **Promise** is defined under Section 2 (b) as, "when the person to whom the proposal is made signifies his assent there to, the proposal is said to be accepted. A proposal when accepted, becomes a promise."

Then, how does the word Proposal is defined under the Act? According to the Act again the proposal is also defined under Section 2 (a) as, "When one person signifies to another his willingness to do or to abstain from doing anything, with a view to obtain the **assent of that other to such act** or abstinence, he is said to make a proposal."

So, An **agreement** should have a **Promise** and Promise should have **Proposal.**

From the above it is clear that, an agreement involves **proposal** or **offer** by one party and the acceptance of the same by the other party. It should be understood that the word proposal is an English term, whereas offer is another term for the proposal used in Indian contract. Hence proposal and offer are similar terms.

An agreement requires existence of two or more persons i.e. plurality of persons as a person cannot enter into an agreement with himself.

From the above it can be concluded that an agreement consist of an 'offer' or 'proposal' from one party and its acceptance by the other. It also implies that the parties have a common interest and intention about the subject-matter of their agreement. Thus, Agreement is created through offer and acceptance.

So, Agreement = offer + Acceptance.

(ii) Legal obligation: An agreement to become a contract must give rise to legal obligation. A legal obligation is a duty enforceable by law. That is the common acceptance formed and communicated between two parties, must create legal obligation. It binds the parties to a contract and imposes the necessity of doing or to abstain from doing a definite act. If an agreement does not create a duty enforceable by law, then it is not a contract. Thus, an agreement is a wider term than a contract. But **agreement creating social, religion or moral obligations cannot be taken for a contract.**

For example, A invite B for a dinner and the invitation is accepted by B, the obligation of A is to prepare the dinner and the obligation of B is to attend dinner. These obligations are purely social obligations and they do not create a legally enforceable agreement. If any one of them does not perform his part of the social obligation, the other cannot take any action against the former.

One more example of social contract is a contract or agreement between husband and wife which are purely domestic and not intended to create legal obligations.

In connection with the above circumstance the leading case explain this sort of situations clearly like,

Balfour V/s Balfour (1919)

Mr. Balfour was employed in Ceylon. Mrs. Balfour owing to ill health, had to stay in England and could not accompany him to Ceylon. Mr. Balfour promised to send her £ 30 per month, while he was abroad. But Mr. Balfour failed to pay the agreed amount. Mrs. Balfour filed a suit against her husband for recovering the said amount. The court held that it was a mere domestic agreement and that the promise made by the husband in this case was not intended to create obligation and it was clear from the conduct of the parties.

Thus, from the above, one can decide as, "All contracts are agreements, but all agreements are not contracts. Only these agreements are contracts which give rise to legal obligation.

Therefore; Agreements are wider, which may be constituted both for social and business transactions. Whereas the contract is restricted to create legal obligations. So all contracts should have agreement, where as all agreement need not be termed as contract.

Thus it is said, "All contracts are agreements but all agreements are not contracts."

So, **Contract = Agreement + Legal obligation**

Or

Contract = Agreement + Enforceability at law

Therefore Salmond rightly says, "The Law of contracts is not a whole law of agreements or is it whole law of obligations, it is the law of those agreements which create obligations, and of those obligations which have their source in agreements".

Thus "the law of contract is not the whole law of obligations" The law of contacts is the law of those legal obligations which have their source in agreements. The law of contracts is not concerned with those obligations which do not arise out of agreement.

Example: Obligation arising from judgement of Courts, obligations arising from tort or civil wrong and obligation to maintain wife and children do not arise out of agreement and hence they do not constitute contracts.

Essentials of Valid Contract or Essential Elements of a Valid Contract

All agreements are contracts where as all contracts are not agreement. Hence the word agreement is wider than the contract. To make the agreement to be contract there need to is a the legal obligations. This is clearly given under Sec 10, Chapter II of the Contract Act as, "All agreements are contracts if they are made by the free consent of parties, competent to contract, for a lawful consideration and with a lawful object, and are not hereby expressly declared to be void." "From this it is obvious to make a contract void or valid, there need to be certain conditions to be followed. These conditions are termed as elements which are essential for an agreement into contract.

1. Plurality of Parties.
2. Offer and Acceptance.
3. Legal obligation
4. Lawful consideration
5. Capacity of parties
6. Free consent.
7. Lawful object.
8. Certainty of meaning.
9. Possibility of performance
10. Agreement not declared void or illegal
11. Legal formalities

1. **Plurality of Parties:** An agreement is constituted by means of an offer by one party and an acceptance to that offer by the other party, which is known as plurality of parties for a valid contract. Here, one party may be an offeror and the other party may be the acceptor.

2. **Offer and Acceptance:** An agreement is the result of an offer and its acceptance. In order to create a valid contract both 'lawful offer' and 'Lawful acceptance' are essential. Thus, in agreement there should be two parties i.e. offeror, one who is making the offer and another person acceptor who is accepting or giving his assent for the offer. There are certain rules laid down by the Contract Act to make both offer and acceptance to be valid.

3. **Legal obligation:** An agreement to become a contract must given rise to a legal **obligation.** Section. 10 of the Act, which lays down the essentials of a valid contract does not specify 'intention to create legal relations,' as one of the ingredients. This is also considered as one of the necessary contractual ingredient in English Law. Under Indian Contract Act, an obligation is the legal duty to do or abstain from doing a definite act or acts.

   If the parties do not intend to create legal obligations, there is no contract between them, whereas an agreement for social obligations cannot be a contract.

   As previously referred to Balfour Vs Balfour (1919) In this case, there is an agreement between husband and wife and agreement without the intention of creating legal obligations (refer page 17) same is hold good for the agreement to have lunch at a friend's house.

   In case of commercial transactions, an intention to create legal obligation is presumed. If the parties expressly declare and resolved that their agreement is not intended to create legal relationships, then even a business transaction will not amount to contract.

4. **Lawful consideration:** The legal meaning of consideration is **'quid-pro-quo'** or something in return. Consideration is one of the essential elements of contract. Contradiction is defined as, "Consideration is the price for which the promise of another is brought." (Black stone). Promises made without consideration is not enforceable contract. According to Sec 25 of the Act, that an agreement without consideration is void. An agreement which is not supported by consideration is considered as **'nudum pactum'** (a nude or bare agreement). So it should be supported by the parties. Each party to the agreement must give or promise something and receive something or a promise in return.

   Example: If A offers to sell his vehicle for Rs. 1,00,000, and B accepts the offer, then for A-Rs 1,00,000 is the consideration and for B-vehicle is the consideration. Consideration may take in the form of money, goods or services. Consideration may also be past, present and future, whereas it must be real and unlawful.

5. **Capacity of parties:** When an agreement is formed to make it to be a valid contract, there arises, question of contractual capacity of parties who make the agreement. The parties to an agreement must be competent to a contract, otherwise it cannot be enforced by Court of Law. If either of the parties does not have the capacity to contract, the contract is not valid. Section 11 of the Contract Act also says that, "every person is competent to contract, who is in the age group of majority, according to the law to which he is subject, and who is sound mind, and not disqualified from contracting by any law to which he is subject." (For more detail refers the topic 'capacity of parties)'.

6. **Free consent:** The word consent means the parties must have agreed upon the same thing in the same sense. So, the consent should come from both the parties, that is the offeror and the accepter. The consent must be free and genuine. When the agreement is made between the parties, both the parties should agree upon same-thing with the same sense. This is known as **"Consensus-ad-idem"** in English Law. The consent of the parties should not be obtained by mis-representation, fraud, undue-influence, coercion or mistake, otherwise such of the agreement is invalid under law. Hence an agreement must be made with free consent.

7. **Lawful object:** Object is nothing to do with consideration but it should be lawful. The object for which the agreement has been entered must not be illegal or immoral or opposed to public policy. The purpose or design of the contract is lawful, but, when a party hires a house and use it as a gambling house, then the object of the contract is to run a gambling house, then it is unlawful and it not accepted under law. Hence the object which is not agreeable under law or for defeat of any law, intention of creating fraud, any injury to person and property, any act against the public policy are not lawful objects.

8. **Certainty of meaning:** Agreements to form valid contracts must be certain. As per section 29 of the Act, "Agreements, the meaning of which is not certain, or capable of being made certain, are void. The terms of the contract must be precise and certain. It cannot be left vague. A contract may be void on the ground of uncertainty.

   Example: If A agrees to sell to B, a white horse for rupees five thousand or rupees ten thousand, there is nothing to show which of the two prices was to be given. This sort of agreement will become invalid.

9. **Possibility of performance:** If the act is impossible to act by itself, both physically or legally, it cannot be enforced at law.

   Example: If A agrees with B to discover treasure by magic, such agreement is unenforceable.

10. **Agreement not declared void or illegal:** The agreements must have been expressly declared to be void by any law in force in country, when such agreements if entered into, shall not be enforceable by courts of Law. According to the Law, agreement in restraint of marriage, trade, legal proceedings, uncertainty of meaning and wagering agreement are void, unlawful or illegal.

11. **Legal formalities:** There is no specification for the agreement or contract which should be made in oral or written. An oral contract is a perfectly valid contract, except in those cases where writing, registration etc., are required for some statutes. In India agreement in writing is required in cases of sale, mortgage, lease or gift of immoveable property and so on. If the legal formalities are not followed then there cannot be a valid agreement to form a contract.

Hence from the above essential, it is clear that all the agreement of offer and acceptance alone will not form the contract. To form a valid contract the above mentioned eleven elements, are essentially to be present. Hence it is said that, **"All contracts are agreement but all agreements are not contract."**

Types of Contract

The types of contract can be grouped on the basis of the classification. This can be classified differently connected to Indian Contract Act and English Law.

Classification Under English Law

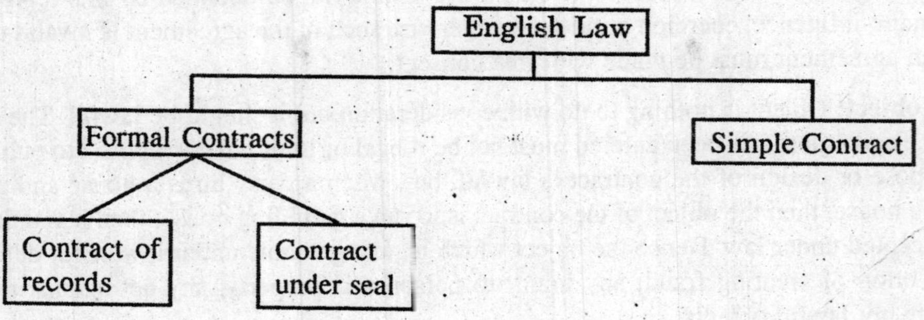

According to the Indian Contract Act contracts may be classified on the basis of their **Validity, formation or performance.** The classification of the same is given below.

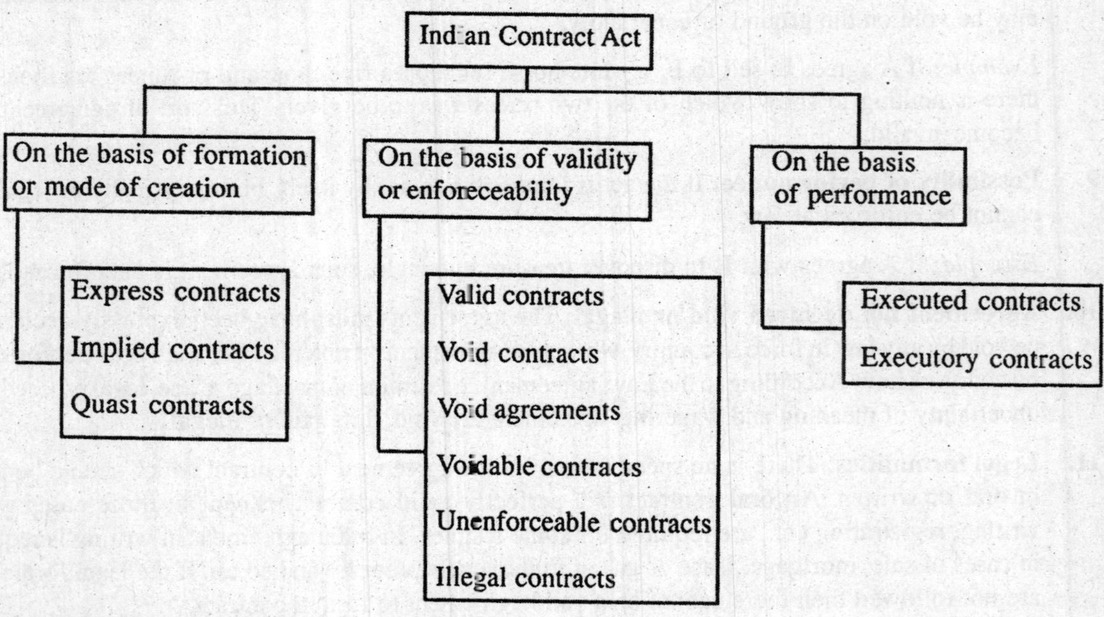

A brief explanation of the above classification is as follows:

1. On the basis of Formation or Mode of Creation

(i) Express Contract:

An express contract is entered into by words which may be either spoken or written, where the proposal and acceptance is made in words, then it is an express contract.

(ii) Implied contract:

When both offer an acceptance is constituted', a contract is made, other than the **words,** the contract is said to be implied contract. Many a times the implied contracts are understood out of the surrounding circumstances and the conduct of the parties who made them; and is fallowed with various legal obligations. So, where a person employs another person to do some work, the law implies that the former agrees to pay for the work.

Example : Mr. A, a coolie in uniform takes up the luggage and carried it out of the railway station without being asked by Mr. B, and B allows him to do so, then the law implies that Mr. B agrees to pay for the services of Mr. A.

(iii) Quasi Contract:

It is also known as constructive contract. Quasi contract is a contract in which there is no intention on either side to make a contract, but the law imposes a contract. In other words quasi contract or constructive contract is not a contract at all. It is created by law and not intentionally entered into by the parties, i.e. 'Quasi-contractual obligations' are imposed by law without offer and acceptance. To be clear in understanding of Quasi contract, under certain circumstances, a person may receive a benefit to which the law regards another person as better entitled, or for which the law considers he should pay to the other person, even though there is no contract between the parties. In this case the parties are put in the same position as if these were formed a contract between them.

Example : A, a merchant, leaves goods at B' house by mistake, B treats the goods as his own. Here B is bound to pay A for the goods used.

The Quasi contract or constructive contract is used in English Law whereas under Indian Contract Act, from section 68 to 72, is explained this sort of situations and ground, in the name of "of certain Relations Resembling those created by contract." In other sense it aims at **"nemo debt locuplatari ex-Liena justua"** that means "a person shall not be allowed to rich himself unjustly at the expenses of another".

Quasi-contracts under Indian Contract Act: The Indian Contract Act refers the Quasi-contract under the heading. *Certain relations resembling those created by contract,* (Section 68 to 72).

1. Claim for necessaries supplied to a person incapable of contracting on his account (Sec. 68).
2. Reimbursement of a person paying money due by another in payment of which he is interested (Sec. 69).
3. Obligation of person enjoying benefit of a non-gratuitous act (Sec. 70).
4. Rights and liabilities of the finder of lost goods (Sec. 71).
5. Liability of persons to whom money is paid or things delivered, by mistake or under coercion (Sec. 72).

2. On the basis of Validity or Enforceability

(i) Valid Contract:

An agreement becomes enforceable by law when all the essential elements of a valid contract are present. In other words an agreement enforceable at law is a valid contract. According to the Contract

Act, under Sec. 10, "all agreement are contracts if they are made by the free consent, competent parties, lawful consideration and lawful object. Such of the contract should not declared to be void."

(ii) Void Contracts:

Void contracts are contracts which not enforceable by law. According to Sec 2(j) of the Contract Act, "Void contract is a contract which cease to be enforceable by law becomes void, when it ceases to be enforceable." According to this section it is clear that, a void contract is a contract which was valid originally, i.e.. at the time of formation but the same becomes void subsequently. The following are the different situation or circumstances to make a contract a void:

(a) **Supervening impossibility [Sec. 56]**

Example: A enters into a contract to import goods from a foreign country. It becomes void subsequently when a war breaks out between the country of import and export.

(b) **Subsequent illegality:** A contract also becomes void by subsequent illegality, for *Example:* A agrees to sell B 1000 bags of wheat at Rs 800 per bag. Before delivery, the Government bans private trading of paddy. In this case the contract become void.

(iii) Void Agreements:

Void agreement is agreements which does not create any legal rights and obligations According to Sec 2(g), "void agreement is an agreement not enforceable by law." Hence the void agreement confers no rights on any person and, creates no obligations. Such an agreement without any legal effect is **void-abinitio** i.e. void at the very beginning

Example : An agreement with a minor and an agreement without considerations, an agreement in restraint of marriage, trade, legal proceedings and so on are void agreements.

(iv) Voidable Contracts:

It is a contract which can be enforced or avoided at the option of the aggrieved party. According to Sec 2 (i), "An agreement which is enforceable by law at the option of one or more of the parties there to, but not at the option of the others is a voidable contract." From this section it is clear that the word used here is **'contract'** and not just **'agreement'**. That is so because the rights and duties are created and contract is valid unit the option to avoid and it is exercised by the person whose consent to the agreement was not free but was obtained by coercion, undue influence, fraud and mis-representation. That is why it is expected to enter into a contract by a person who comes into Equity (i.e. before law) must come with clean hands."

Thus a voidable contract is valid and enforceable until it is repudiated or avoided by the party entitled to avoid it.

A voidable contract continues to be valid till it is avoided or repudiated by the aggrieved party. According to Sec 64, when the aggrieved party avoids the contract, the other party need not to perform any promise, and party avoiding the contract should restore any benefit he has received, under the contract to the other party.

Example: A by misrepresentation forces B to sell 100 bags of rice at Rs 100 per bag, and pays Rs. 4000 in part payment of the price. B, being the aggrieved party, can rescind or cancel the contract. However, he has to pay back Rs. 4000 to B and B need not pay the balance. So here the option is left to B to make it a valid or cancel the contract.

(v) Unenforceable Contracts:

An unenforceable contract is a contract which is valid in itself, but cannot be enforced in the court of Law due to some technical defects, like absence of written form or absence of a proper stamp. Such contracts must be sued upon by one or both of the parties. According to Sir William Anson, "An unenforceable contract is one which is good in substance, though by reason of some technical defect, one or both the parties cannot be sued on it. Many a times the court of law cannot enforce it for the reason for the expiry of date, registration and attestation along with the other reasons given above. If the technical defect could be cured, the contract becomes enforceable, if it cannot be cured, the contract remains unenforceable.

Example: A borrows Rs. 20,000 from B and makes a promissory note and a one rupee stamp is pasted on the pro-note. The agreement though complete is unenforceable because of the technical defect. i.e., Promissory note not being stamped properly and it is undervalued.

(vi) Illegal Contracts:

Illegal contracts are also termed as unlawful contracts. Illegal contract is a contract which is either prohibited by law or otherwise against the policy of law. According to Sec.23, "the consideration or object of an agreement is unlawful if it is forbidden by law, or is of such a nature that if permitted, it would defeat the provisions of law, or is fraudulent or involves or implies injury to the person or property of another, or the court regards it as immoral or opposed to public policy."

Example: A borrows Rs 1,00,000 from B for the purpose of smuggling goods. B knows the purpose of loan by A, the agreement between A and B is collateral to the main agreement which is illegal.

An illegal agreement is void-ab-into. All illegal agreements are void but all void agreements are not illegal. The money paid or Property transferred under an illegal agreement cannot be recovered. No action can be taken for breach of an illegal agreement. With the example given above that the illegal agreement in this collateral transaction, is also void.

3. On the basis of Performance

1. Executed Contract:

An executed contract is one when both the parties have performed their obligations or carried out the terms of the contract. It is referred as a complete contract. In other sense when offeror and acceptor have completely performed their respective obligations under the contract, then such contract is said to be executed contract. That is, it is a contract where under the terms of the contract nothing remains to be done by both the party. For instance, in case of cash sales, the contract is executed at once.

Example: A agrees to sell certain goods to B at a certain price. A delivers the goods and B pays the price. Thus both the parties have performed their respective obligations. Then this contract becomes an executed contract.

2. Executory Contract:

In this type of contract the obligations of the parties are to be performed at a later time, or where the contract is yet to be performed either wholly or partially when one or both parties have their obligation, then such contracts are called as executory contract.

Example: A agrees to make a painting for B for Rs. 10,000. Mr. A has yet to make a painting and Mr. B has not made any payment. So, both the parties are yet to perform their obligations. Suppose if A has made the painting, but B yet to make payment in such cases, it is executed on A' s part and executory on B's part.

Thus, executory contract may be: (a) Unilateral (b) Bilateral.

(a) **Unilateral Contract:** Unilateral contract is one sided contract. In this type, one party would have discharged the obligations. In certain contracts one party has to fullfil his obligations, where as the other party has already performed his obligations. Such contract may also be termed as 'contract with executed consideration' along with 'unilateral' and 'one sided' contracts. Thus, in case of unilateral contract the obligation is outstanding only against one of the parties at the time of formation of contract.

Example: Mr. A has lost his documents which are very valuable. He offers by advertisement a reward of Rs 1,00,000 to any person, who will find and bring the documents very safely and hand over to him. Mr. B who comes across the advertisement, searches and finds the documents and hand it over to Mr. A. As soon as B does this act, the contract comes into existence. Now only, A has to perform his obligation by paying Rs.1,00,000 to B, as B had already performed his part of obligation by finding the documents.

(b) **Bilateral Contract:** Bilateral contracts are the contracts in which the obligation on the part of both the parties to the contract are outstanding at the time of formation of the contract. In such contracts, promise on one side is exchanged for a promise on the other. Thus bilateral contracts, under executory contracts are also known as contracts with executory consideration.

Example: A manufacturer agrees to supply certain goods at a certain price to a retailer after certain time. The payment is to be made at the time of delivery of goods. This is a bilateral contract as the obligations of both the parties are outstanding at the time of formation of the contract.

Classification of Contracts in English Law

As main source of contract Act is from English Law, if is meaningful to study the classification under English Law.

(1) **Formal Contract:** Formal contracts and its validity depends upon their form and they are valid even without consideration. They are two types;

(i) **Contract under seal.** This type of contract are in writing and signed by the parties. The following contracts should be under seal, otherwise they are not valid:

(a) Contracts without consideration.

(b) Lease of land for period of more than three years.

(c) Contracts by corporations and

(d) Contracts with British shipping.

(ii) **Contracts of Records.** This is included in the court judgements and recognisances. Obligations in which cases arise out of court judgements and not under contracts.

(2) **Simple Contract:** All contracts other than the formal ones are called simple contracts or parol contracts. They may be created orally, in writing and which may be implied by conduct.

Offer [Proposal]

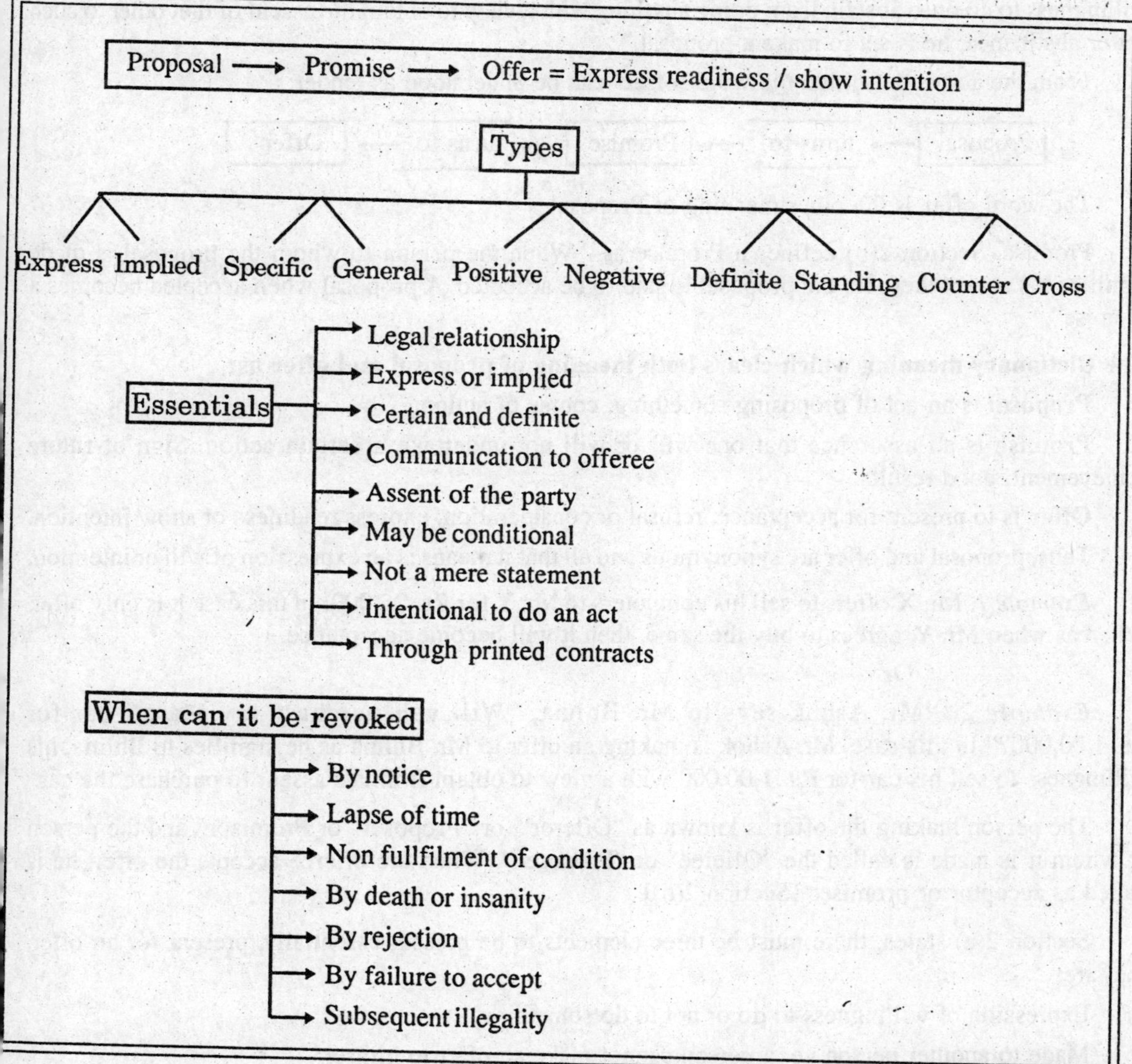

Introduction

Any activity or understanding of two persons begins with some proposal from one person to another. This proposal in turn will be understood as 'Offer'. At the inception of every agreement, there must be a definite offer by one person to another and acceptance of the same person to whom the offer is made.

The term proposal and offer are considered synonymous and are used interchangeably. The word 'Proposal' is used under Indian Law, whereas the same is used as 'Offer' under English Law.

Meaning and Definition of Offer: Offer is basis and one of the major element of essentials of valid contract.

According to the Indian Contract Act, Section 2(a) "When one person signifies to another his willingness to do or to abstain from doing anything with a view to obtain the assent of that other to such act or abstinence, he is set to make a proposal."

From the above definition the word **'offer'** can be understood as lender:

The word offer is the other meaning of Proposal

Promise, Section 2(b) defines a Promise as, "When the person to whom the proposal is made signifies his assent there to, the proposal is said to be accepted. A proposal when accepted becomes a promise".

The Dictionary meaning which clears both meaning of proposal and offer as:

Proposal is an act of proposing something, course of action.

Promise is an assurance that one will or will not undertake a certain action. Sign of future achievement, good results.

Offer is to present for acceptance, refusal or consideration, express readiness or show intention.

Thus, proposal and offer are synonymous and all that it means is an expression of will or intention.

Example 1. Mr. X offers to sell his computers to Mr. Y for Rs. 25,000. In this case it is only offer. Whereas when Mr. Y, agrees to buy the same, then it will become acceptance.

Or

Example 2. "Mr. Ashok says to Mr. Bhima, "Will you purchase my Maruti car for Rs. 1,00,000?" In this case, Mr. Ashok is making an offer to Mr. Bhima as he signifies to Bhima, his willingness to sell his car for Rs. 1,00,000 with a view to obtain Bhima's assent to purchase the car.

The person making the offer is known as "Offeror", or "Proposer" or Promisor" and the person to whom it is made is called the "Offeree" or "Proposee". When the offeree accepts the offer, he is called as acceptor or promisee [Section 2(d)].

Section 2(a) states, there must be three elements to be present essentially, present for an offer, they are:

(a) Expression of willingness to do or not to do something.

(b) Made to another person i.e. a person cannot make an offer to himself.

(c) With the object of giving the consent to the other person to such act or abstinence.

From the above three elements it can be clear that a casual enquiry, information, a statement of fact or statement of mere intention are not offers.

How an offer is made?

An offer can be made by expression of words, spoken or written which is called as "Express offer" "Will you buy my business at Mumbai for 5 crores?" or when A advertises in a newspaper, offering Rs. 5,000 to anyone who returns his lost documents, these are express offer.

An offer may also be implied from the conduct of the parties or the circumstances of the case. This is referred as "implied offer". Thus, when a company runs a cab on a particular route, there is an implied offer by the company to carry passengers for a certain fare. The acceptance of the offer completes as soon as passenger boards the cab.

An offer may be made to a specific person or general public:

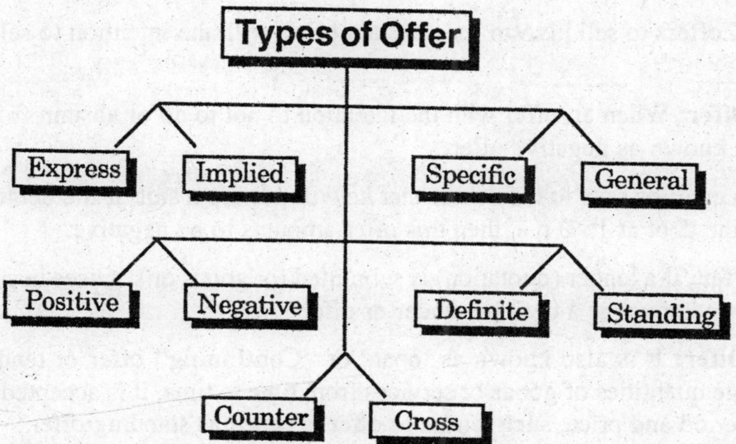

Express Offer: When an offer is communicated by words, spoken or written, then it is termed as an express offer. It can also be communicated through advertisement telephone, messenger or telegram.

Implied Offer: An offer communicated by conduct or act is an implied offer. When a person goes to a consultant for an advice his conduct implies an offer to pay the usual fee to the consultant.

Specific Offer: An offer made to a specific or definite person or class of persons is known as specific offer. Specific offers are also referred to **"Offer to individuals"**, (Case Boulton Vs Jones).

General Offer: An offer made to the world or "Public at large" is known as general offer. It can be accepted by any member of the public. According to Salmond, it is to be referred as **"offer at large"**. An offer of reward for some information, made to the public at large through a public advertisement is an example of general offer.

In respect this a popular case is,

Carlill Vs Carbolic Smoke Ball Co; – (1983)

The company advertised in several news papers that a reward of £ 100 world be given to any person who contact influenza. After using the smoke balls which is medicine in the form of capsules, which is the company's product, according to the printed direction. One, Mrs. Carlill used the smoke balls according to the directions of the company, but contracted influenza; then, Mrs. Carlill demanded the reward, but the company refused to pay the reward. (compensation) She then filed a suit in the court of law. Then the court held that **she could recover reward** offered on the ground that the company's offer through public advertisement amounted to a general offer, and a general offer may be **accepted by any member of the public**. In return the company filed the petition, pleading that Mrs. Carlill had not communicated her intention to accept, then the judge refusing the petition, pointed that in cases like this, communication is not necessary, since, her **doing the required act amounted to an acceptance** of the offer.

This case is referred to both general offer and Implied offer

Positive Offer: When an offer is to dc something focused, then the offer is said to be positive. i.e. an offer is to act or intention to do some act certainly.

Example: X offers to sell his van for a certain price, with the intention to sell the van, is positive offer.

Negative Offer: When an offer with the intention to not to do or abstain from doing something, this offer is known as negative offer.

Example: A creditor says to his debtor that he will not file a suit, if the debtor is prepared to pay interest on the debt at 15% p.a, then this offer amounts to be negative.

Definite Offer: If a tender (quotation) is submitted for goods or services in specified quantity, the tender offer is known as a definite tender or offer.

Standing Offer: It is also known as 'open' or **"Continuing"** offer or tender. When a concern requires large quantities of goods or services from time to time, it is accepted by the supplier over a definite period and price, such tender or offer is called as standing offer.

Cross Offer: When two parties make identical offers to each other, in ignorance of each other's offer, such offers are known as cross offers. They shall not constitute acceptance of one's offer by the other.

Example: A wrote to B on 28th Dec 2005, offering to sell 1,000 tons of irons at Rs. 7,000 per ton. On the same day B wrote to A offering to buy 1,000 tonnes of iron Rs. 7,000 per ton. The two letters crossed in post and neither of them knew anything about the offer to the other. B contended that there was a good contract. It was held that B was not bound as a result of the simultaneous offers, each being made in ignorance of the other.

Counter Offer: A counter offer is a rejection of original offer, it is a new offer which needs acceptance by the original promisor before a contract is made. In case of **Hyde Vs Wrench**; An offer to sell a form for £1,000 was rejected by the plaintiff, who offered £ 950 for it. This was turned down by the offeror and then the plaintiff agreed to pay £ 1,000. It was held that the defendant was not bound by any such acceptance as the original offer was conditionally accepted.

From the above, different types/kinds of offer or proposal may be classified on the basis of Method and Man i.e., (i) How an offer is made? (ii) To whom an offer is made?

What are not offers?

Not all offers are valid offers as they differ from:-

(a) A mere statement of intention. *Example:* An announcement of a forth coming auction sale.

(b) An invitation to offer. *Example:* An advertisement in newspapers, to display of goods for window shopping and so on.

(c) A mere communication of information. *Example:* Book-seller's catalogue.

(d) A casual enquiry.

(e) A prospectus, inviting the public to subscribe to the shares or debenture of a company.

(f) An advertisement for the tenders. *Example:* In; "Harris Vs Nickerson", Nickerson, an **auctioner**, advertised in a newspaper that a sale of office furniture would be held in a specified day. Harris, with an intention of buying some furniture came from a distant place to attend auction but due to some reasons all the furniture was withdrawn from the sale. **Harris thereupon sued Nickerson** for his loss of time and expenses. It was held, that a declaration of intention to do a thing did not create a binding contract with those who acted upon it, so that Harris could not recover any compensation.

Essentials of a valid offer or Rules regarding valid offer

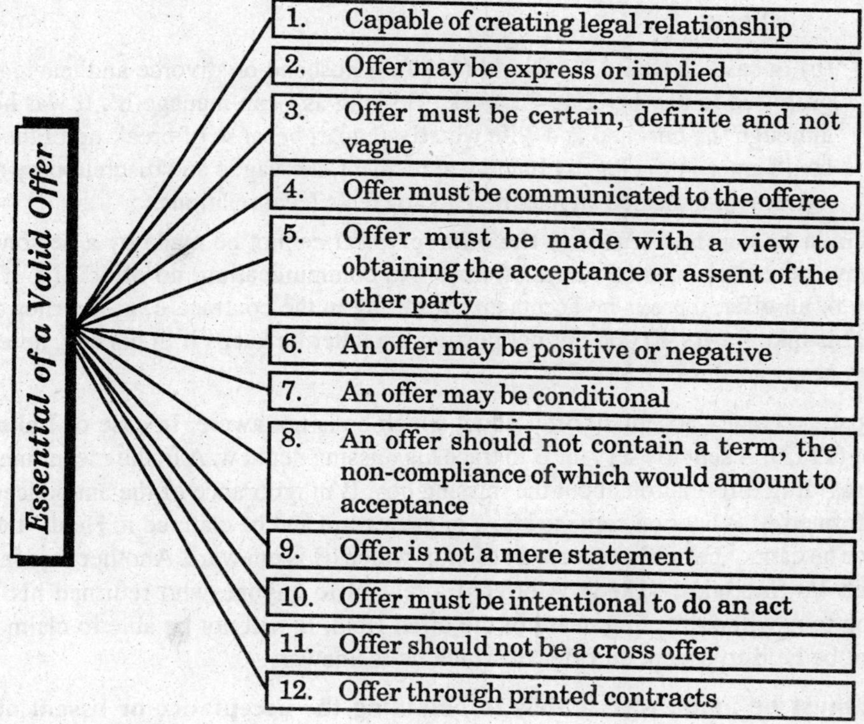

1. Capable of creating legal relationship: Offer must be such that it should create legal elationship. An offeror must intend to create legal bindings and legal relationships. Not all offers will reate legal binding like a social invitation, even if it is accepted, and does not create legal relationship, as is not intended.

xample: A accepts an invitation to dine at B's place on a certain date, but fails to turn up on the ppointed date. Here A cannot be sued for a breach of contract because in contracts regulating social vitation or domestic arrangements cannot create legal binding or legal relationships and it do not tend legal consequences to follow from the breach of a contract. The essential elements is that, an fer therefore must be such as would result in a valid contract when it is accepted.

2. Offer may be express or implied: There is no legal rule that how it must be made. It can be press, which means mere by a word of mouth or implied through understanding. The Contract Act not giving any specification regarding the mode of making contract. Hence it may be express or nplied.

3. Offer must be certain, definite and not vague: Terms of offer must be definite, certain, unambiguous and clear or not loose and vague. Both offeror and offeree should be clear about the legal consequences arising out of contract. Any vague offers does not convey or communicate what it exactly means. According to the famous case, **Taylor Vs Portington (1855)**; A offered to take a house on lease for three years at £ 284 per annum if the house was put into through repair and drawing rooms handsomely decorated according to the present style. It was held that, the offer was too vague to result in a contractual relationship because the term 'Present style' may mean one thing to A and another to B. Hence here the agreement is void.

Example: (a) A says B, "I will sell a house" whereas A owns 5 houses. The offer is not definite.

(b) In case of **Gould Vs Gould (1970)**, A husband on divorce and leaving his wife promised to pay her £ 15- a week, 'So long as I can manage it'. It was held that although the husband and wife who lived apart because of break-up of their marriage, could enter into a legally binding agreement, the vague and discretionary terms of the agreement indicated an intention not to create legal relations.

4. Offer must be communicated to the offeree: Offer cannot be made by a person to himself. It must be always be communicated to the offeree. "No communication, no offer", i.e. if there is no communication of an offer, there is no acceptance resulting in the contract. e. g: A writes a letter to B offering to sell his bike for Rs 40,000 but not posting the letter he keeps it in his bag, here it is not an offer and B can never accept it.

Again a person cannot accept an offer about which he is not aware. In case of **Lalman Shukla Vs Gauri Dutt (1913)**; A sent his servant B to trace his missing nephew. A in the meantime announced a reward for providing information about the missing boy. B in ignorance of the announcement traced the boy and informed A. B later on came to know of the reward and he claimed it. Held – the claim was dismissed, since he cannot be held to accept an offer of which he is unaware. Another case in connection with this **'Fitch Vs Snedakar (1868),** A offered a reward to anyone who returned his lost dog. B brought the dog to A without having heard of the offer. Held, B will not be able to claim the reward, since he cannot be held to accept an offer of which he is unaware.

5. Offer must be made with a view to obtaining the acceptance or assent of the other party. The offer to do or not to do something should have the focus of getting assent from the other party and it is not an offer when it is made merely with a view to disclosing the intention of making an offer.

Announcement of notice of auction sale of certain articles at a certain place on a certain date is merely an invitation of offer and not an actual offer.

The case related to this is, **Harris Vs Nickerson 1873**, according to this, A advertised in the newspaper to effect sale of his goods on a particular day at a particular place. Mr. B, travelled a long distance to bid for the things. On arrival, he found that the sale was cancelled. He sued Mr. A for the breach of contract. It was held that advertisement was merely expression of an intention and not an offer and B could not recover his expenditure.

6. An offer may be positive or negative: A positive offer is an offer to do something. A negative offer is, on the other hand, is an offer not to do something or abstain from doing something and both are accepted.

7. An offer may be conditional: An valid offer can also be conditional. Such offers are offer that can be accepted only subject to that conditions. A conditional offer lapses when the condition is not accepted. In this, a conditional offer by the management of a company to the trade union to pay a certain amount lapses when condition is not accepted. In connection to his there is a case, **Thomson Vs LMS Railway Company (1930)**, according to this case, Mr. A a traveler takes a ticket for a railway journey. On the front of the ticket, it was printed as "for conditions see back". One of the conditions was that the Railway Company would not be liable for the personal injuries to the passengers. A the traveler was injured by a railway accident and sued for the injury. It was held that the travelers were bound by the conditions and could not recover any damages. In this case, the LMS Railway Company is not bound to pay any of the compensation due to the accidents.

Again, one of the recent case in India connected to this is, **Lily white Vs Munuswami (AIR 1966)**, A delivered one new saree to a laundry for washing, on the back of the printed receipt it was stated that the customer would be entitled to recover only 15% of the market price of the article in case of loss. The saree was lost owing to the negligence of the laundry. In a suit by A, it was held that the laundry showed its negligence and is against the public interest. It was held the laundry is to pay full value of the saree.

8. An offer should not contain a term, the non-compliance of which would amount to acceptance: While making the offer should not presumed to be accepted, one cannot say while making the offer that if the offer is not accepted before a certain date, it will be presumed to have been accepted. Thus, an offeror cannot say that if acceptance is not communicated upto a certain date, the offer would be presumed to have been accepted. If the offeree does not reply, there is no contract, as no obligation to reply can be imposed on to him on the ground of justice.

9. Offer is not a mere statement: A mere statement without any intention is not an offer. An invitation or an answer to a question and a statement of price list does not constitute a valid offer. i.e. a price lists, window displays, tenders, invitation by a company to public to subscribe to its shares, railway displays, sign boards, hoarding and so an are not an offer.

10. Offer must be intentional to do an act: An offer without intention of the offeror to commit something is not an offer. That is offeror may not be serious in his expression and the offer is made just like that, but it does not constitute a valid offer.

11. Offer should not be a cross offer: Cross offer does not constitute a valid offer as here two persons make identical offer. The court does not approve one person is offer an offer and another persons offer is not an offer.

12. Offer through printed contracts: An offer through printed matters for the special purpose formulate a valid offer/contract

Example: Life Insurance Corporation of India, Indian Railways, Nationalised banks, Credit Co-operative societies and so on. These are some of the examples of organisation where in thousands of people enter into agreement for their own benefits. It is difficult to make organisations to stand with the different types of offer to different people. This type of offer or contracts are also known as Standard Forms of Contracts.

Revocation of Offer

Revocation means 'cancellation'. Revocation of offer here is withdrawal of offer by the offeror. It can be revoked or cancelled anytime before it is accepted by the offeree. Before acceptance it is not communicated to the concern person, then it can be cancelled.

According to Section 5 of the Indian Contract Act, "A Proposal may be revoked at any time before the communication of its acceptance as against the proposer".

Section 6 of the Act gives the following conditions for the revocation of offer;

1. **Revocation by communications of notice:** An offer may be revoked by the offeror by giving notice of the revocation to the other party before it is accepted. Notice of revocation will take effect only when it comes to the knowledge of the offeree.
2. **Revocation by lapse of times:** An offer can be cancelled when the time given is crossed. i.e, if the time is prescribed by the offeror for the acceptance, of the offeree, if offeree fails to given his consent within that time limit then automatically the offer gets cancelled.
3. **Revocation by non fulfillment of conditions:** An offer lapses or gets cancelled when an acceptor fails to fulfill a condition precedent to the acceptance of the offer. **Example:-** A offers to sell a motor van to B on a condition that B pays a certain amount before a certain date. If B fails to pay the required amount with in given time, then the stands cancelled.
4. **Revocation by the death or insanity of the offeror or offeree:** When either of the party i.e. offeror or offeree dies or become insane before it is accepted, then the offer gets cancelled.
5. **Revocation by rejection:** When the offeree dis-agrees or rejects the offer made by the offeror the offer is cancelled or revoked. Rejection of an offer is effective only when it comes to the knowledge of the offeror.

   Rejection takes place:

   (a) When the offeree communicates his rejection of the offer to the offeror.

   (b) When the offeree makes a counter offer.
6. **Revocation by failure to accept in the mode prescribed:** An offer must be accepted according to the mode prescribed. In absence of the mode prescribed, then it should be on a reasonable or usual mode.
7. **Revocation by subsequent illegality:** An offer lapses, if it becomes illegal after it is made and before it is accepted. Thus, where an offer is made to sell 100 bags of rice for Rs. 25,000 and before it is accepted, a law prohibiting the sale of rice by the private individuals is enacted Here the offer comes to an end.

Acceptance

Overview

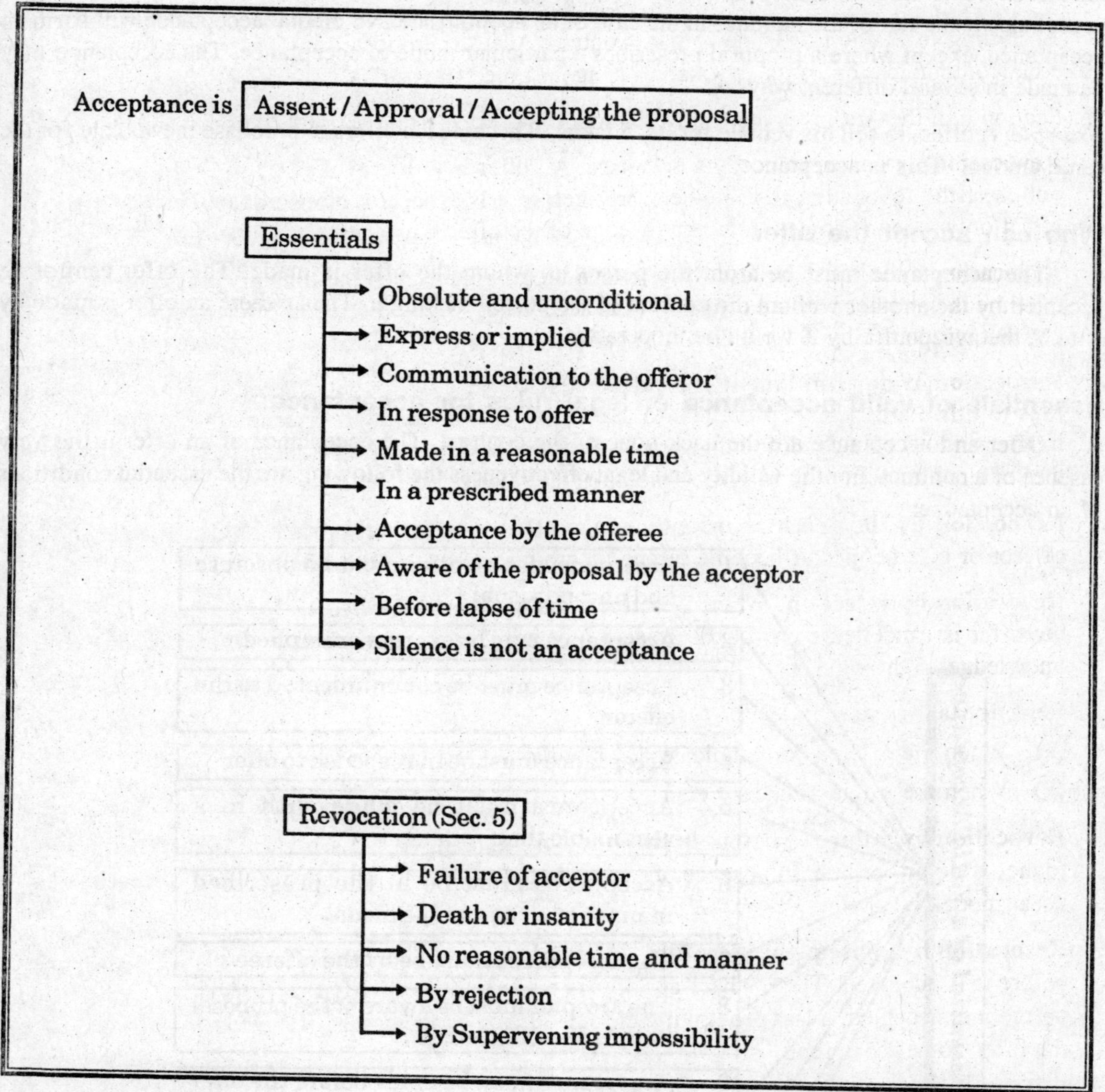

Offer and acceptance go hand in hand, as a contract is formed when an offer is accepted. Acceptance signifies the willingness of the receiving party to whom the offer has been made. The dictionary meaning of acceptance refers to the willingness to accept or affirmative answer to an invitation or approval. When a person to whom the proposal is made signifies his assent, it is an acceptance of the proposal. An accepted proposal is called a promise or an agreement. According to the Section 2(b) of the Indian Contract Act, acceptance is defined as, "when the person to whom the proposal is made signifies his assent thereto, the proposal is to be accepted. A proposal when accepted becomes a promise", Thus, acceptance is the assent or consent given to proposal. The offeree will become acceptor or promisee when he accepts the offer.

Thus, acceptance is the manifestation by the offeree of his assent to the term. The acceptor should do something to signify his intention to accept. A common example of an act amounting to acceptance is the fall of the hammer in the case of an auction sale. No mental acceptance will form an acceptance, except where a proposal prescribes a particular mode of acceptance. The acceptance may be made in several different ways.

Example: A offers to sell his vehicle for Rs. 5 lakhs, B accepts the offers to purchase the vehicle for the same amount. This is acceptance.

Who can accept the offer

The acceptance must be from the person to whom the offer is made. The offer cannot be accepted by the another without the consent of the person making it. Thus, where an offer is made by X to Y, the acceptance by Z would be inoperative.

Essentials of valid acceptance or legal rules for acceptance:

Offer and acceptance are the back-bone of the contract. The acceptance of an offer is the very essence of a contract. For the validity and legal effectiveness the following are the essential conditions of an acceptance:

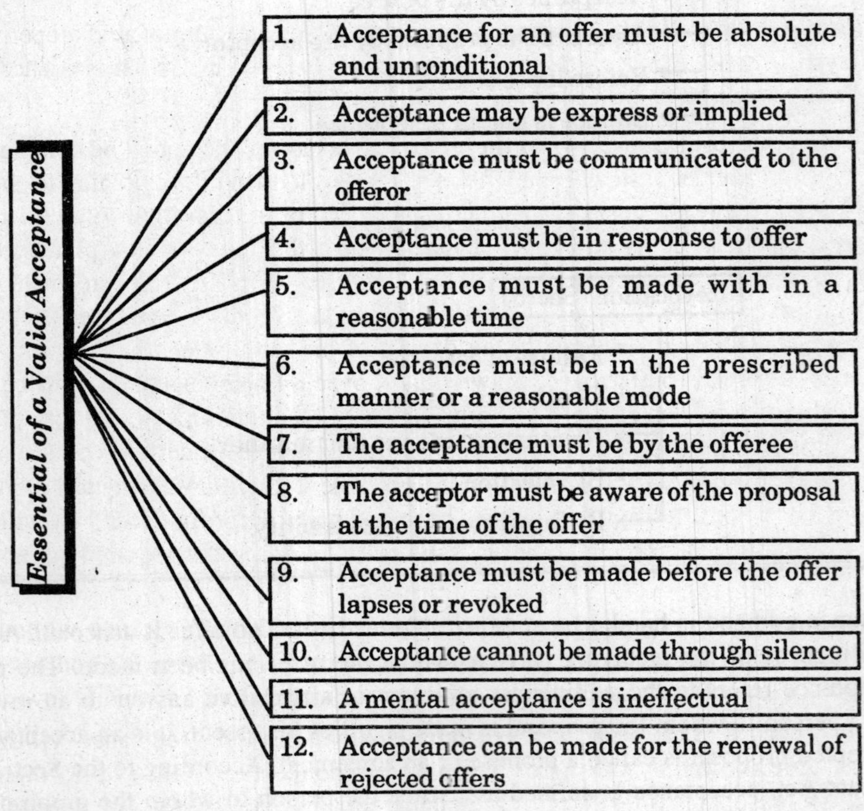

1. Acceptance for an offer must be absolute and unconditional: Section 7(1) of the Act says, "The acceptance must be absolute and unqualified" that is absolute or in full and unqualified or unconditional. A qualified and conditional acceptance amounts to a counter offer and rejection of the original offer. Any alteration or variation, however, small of the offer will make the acceptance invalid. In the case of;

Jordan Vs Norton (1838)

A wrote to B offering to buy his horse if he warranted her sound and quiet in harness by which the horse is fastened and also controlled. B wrote back to A that he accepted the offer and warranted her sound and quiet in double harness. It was held that A was not bound by his offer as B's reply was, in effect, a counter offer and not an unqualified acceptance of A's offer.

Another case, **Neale Vs Merret (1930)** M offered to sell a piece of land to N at £ 280. N accepted and enclosed £ 80 with a promise to pay the balance by monthly installments of £ 50 each. It was held, there is no contract between M and N, **as the acceptance was not unqualified**.

2. Acceptance may be express or implied: When an acceptance is express in words, spoken or written i.e. by word of mouth, by post, by telephone, telegram or through messenger or through any means, it is express acceptance.

When the acceptance is given by conduct, it is implied acceptance. When an acceptance is to be inferred from the circumstances of the case or from the conduct of the parties it is referred to implied acceptance.

In case of **V. Rao Vs A. Rao (1916)**, A widow promised to settle some immovable property to her niece if the niece stayed with her in her residence. Thus, niece stayed with her in her residence till her death. It was held that the niece was entitled to the property.

3. Acceptance must be communicated to the offeror: The acceptance must be communicated to the offeror through some means. Instead if the offeree remains silent and does nothing to show that he has accepted the offer, then no contract is formed. The acceptor should signify his intention to accept. Thus where a person accepts an offer but fails to post the letter of acceptance, it is no acceptances. In case of Brogden Vs Metropolitan Railway Company (1877) A draft agreement relating to the supply of coal was sent to the manager of a Railway Company for his acceptance. The manager wrote the word 'approved' and put the draft in the drawer of his table intending to send it to the Company's solicitor for a formal contract to be drawn up. By oversight the document remained in the drawer. It was held there is no contract. The offeror need not to communicate his acceptance in respect of implied offer and acceptance. It happens when performance of certain conditions takes place, or some required act is done. For this situation the example is **Carlill Vs Carbolic smoke ball Co. (1893)**. In this case, Carlill used smoke balls of the company according to its directions and contracted influenza, it is amounted to acceptance of the offer by doing the required act and could claim the reward.

4. Acceptance must be in response to offer: There can be no acceptance without offer. Acceptance cannot be made before the offer. For example, no allotment of shares in a company can be made unless the allotee has applied for them before hand. As such, acceptance should follow the offer.

5. Acceptance must be made with in a reasonable time: A valid acceptance will be made within the reasonable time allowed by the offeror. When there is no mention of time by the offeror then it can be made within a reasonable time. What is reasonable time is a question of fact depending on a particular circumstance. Acceptance may be made at any time till the offer is alive otherwise such of the acceptance are invalid.

6. Acceptance must be in the prescribed manner or a reasonable mode: Where the offeror precribes mode of acceptance then the acceptor should adopt the same mode. Section 7(2) states that if the acceptance is not made in the manner prescribed, the proposer may within a reasonable time after the acceptance is communicated to him, insist that the acceptance must be made in a manner prescribed. Otherwise the acceptance can be made through other reasonable manner in which it is communicated to the offeror.

In case of, **Surendra Nath Vs Kedarnath AIR(1936)** An offer was made in the following terms, "I intend to sell my house for Rs. 1,00,000, if you are willing to have it, write to 'A' at his address". Instead of writing to A, the purchaser sent an agent to A and agreed to purchase. It was held that the seller was bound by the acceptance and there was no violation of Section 7, when the purchaser, instead of writing to the particular person, met him personally to communicate his acceptance.

7. The acceptance must be by the offeree: An offer can be accepted only by the person or persons to whom it is made. A valid contract arises only if its acceptance is communicated by a person who has the authority to accept. If it is communicated by the unauthorised person, it is not valid acceptance.

In case of **Powel Vs Lee (1908)**, A applied for the post of a Head master in a school. He was selected by the appointing authorities. But the decision of his appointment was not communicated to him. One of the members of the appointing committee informed him of his appointment. But the member was not authorised to communicate the decision and he is communicated the decision in his individual capacity. Subsequently, the appointing authority cancelled his selection. A brought a legal action for the breach of contract. His action was rejected by the court and it was observed that, "There must be notice of acceptance from the contracting party. Information from an unauthorised person is as insufficient and it is considered as over hearing from behind the door".

8. The acceptor must be aware of the proposal at the time of the offer:

(a) Acceptance is made when the offer is created. When an acceptor is not aware of existence of the offer and conveys his acceptance, then there is no valid contract. There must be knowledge of the offer before anyone could consent to it. An act done out of ignorance of the offer for a reward cannot be called an acceptance. Another examples is, case, **"Lalman Shukla Vs Gauri Datt". (1913)**

(b) A sold his business to his manager B without disclosing the fact to his customers. C a customer, who had running an account with A, sent an order for the supply of goods to A by name. B received the order and executed the same. C refused to pay the price. It was held that there was no contract between B and C because C never made any offer to B and as such C was not liable to pay the price to B. The same kind of example is also taken from the case **Boulton Vs Jones (1857)**.

9. Acceptance must be made before the offer lapses or revoked: Acceptance must be given when the offer is in force. Due to the reasons offer may be lapsed or revoked, but the acceptance is to be before the lapse or revoke of an offer.

10. Acceptance cannot be made through silence: Silence is not a mode of acceptance. No contract is formed if the offeree remains silent and does nothing to show that he has accepted the offer.

Silence is not always accepted. Generally speaking, the person to whom the offer is made need not to reply. But his silence cannot be regarded as an acceptance of the proposal. For *Example:* If A expresses to B that if "I don't hear from you by next Monday, I shall presume that you have bought the goods". Here, there is no contract and silence is not acceptance.

11. A mental acceptance is ineffectual: No acceptance can be made by mind without expression or implied. Such of the acceptance is not valid or not effected.

12. Acceptance can be made for the renewal of rejected offers: The acceptor can give his acceptance for the rejected offer, if the same is reviewed.

Revocation of Acceptance

According to Sec. 5 of the Act, acceptance may be revoked at any time before the communication of the acceptance is complete as against the acceptor, but not afterwards. Revocation of acceptance amounts of withdrawal of the acceptance to a proposal by the offeree himself.

Example: A propose, by a letter sent by post, to sell his house to B. B accepts the proposal by a letter sent by post. B may revoke his acceptance any time before the letter communicating it, reaches A, but not afterwards. The following are the additional circumstances for the rejection:

1. The acceptance can be revoked by the failure of the acceptor to fulfill a condition precedent.
2. By death or insanity of the proposer.
3. When it is not in a reasonable time and manner.
4. The acceptance can be revoked by the rejection of the offer.
5. It can be made by supervening impossibility.

Negotiable Instrument Act 1881

The Negotiable Instruments Act was passed in the year 1881. The instrument is mainly an instrument of credit readily convertible into money and easily passable from one hand to another hand. Local usage prevails unless excluded-The Act does not affect any local usage relating to any instrument in an oriental language. However, the local usage can be excluded by any words in the body of the instrument, which indicate an intention that the legal relations of the parties will be governed by provisions of Negotiable Instruments Act and not by local usage.

A negotiable instrument is a document guaranteeing the payment of a specific amount of money, either on demand, or at a set time. According to the Section 13 of the Negotiable Instruments Act, 1881 in India, a negotiable instrument means a promissory note, bill of exchange or cheque payable either to order or to bearer. So, there are just three types of negotiable instruments such as promissory note, bill of exchange and cheque. Cheque also includes Demand Draft.

An instrument can be negotiated any number of times. As per Section 118(e), endorsements appearing on the negotiable instrument are presumed to have been made in the order in which they appear on the instrument, unless contrary is proved. There is no mandatory provision to put date while signing, though advisable to do so. Section 118(d) provides that there is presumption that the instrument was negotiated before its maturity, unless contrary is proved. As per section 60, Bill can be negotiated even after date of maturity by persons other than maker, drawee or acceptor after maturity. However, person getting such instrument is not 'holder in due course' and does not enjoy protections available to 'holder in due course'.

Meaning

'Negotiable' means transferable whereas 'instrument' means a document, therefore negotiable instruments means a transferable document. A negotiable instrument is one which entitles the holder to the receipt of money. It gives him the right to transfer the same by mere delivery or endorsement thereon. The negotiability of the instrument continues till its maturity. A negotiable instrument may be made payable to two or more payees jointly, or it may be made payable in the alternative to one or two, or one or some of several payees.

Definitions

"Negotiable Instrument is a transferable, signed document that promises to pay the bearer a sum of money at a future date or on demand".

The Negotiable Instruments Act 1881, does not define a negotiable instrument but merely states, "a negotiable instrument means a promissory note, bill of exchange or cheque payable either to order or bearer" (Section 13). This section does not prohibit any other instrument that satisfies the essential features of portability".

"A n gotiable instrument is one which is, by a legally recognized custom of trade or by law, transferable by delivery in such circumstances that (a) the holder of it for the time being may sue on it in his own name and (b) the property in it passes, free from equities, to a bona-fide transferee for value, notwithstanding any defect in the title of the transferor."

"A Negotiable instrument means a promissory note, bills of exchange or cheque payable either to order or to bearer". 'Negotiable' means transferable whereas 'instrument' means a document, therefore negotiable instruments means a transferable document. A negotiable instrument is one which entitles the holder to the receipt of money. It gives him the right to transfer the same by mere delivery or endorsement thereon. The negotiability of the instrument continues till its maturity. A negotiable instrument may be made payable to two or more payees jointly, or it may be made payable in the alternative to one or two, or one or some of several payees.

Features of Negotiable Instruments

The features of Negotiable Instruments are as follows :

1. A Negotiable Instrument must be in writing
2. It must be stamped as per Indian Stamp Act.
3. It must contain an order to pay. Words like 'please pay Rs 5,00,000/- on demand and oblige' are not used.
4. The order must be unconditional.
5. The order must be to pay money and money alone.
6. The sum payable mentioned must be certain or capable of being made certain.

Characteristics of a Negotiable Instrument

A negotiable instrument has the following characteristics:

1. ***Property:*** The possessor of the instrument is the holder and owner thereof. A negotiable instrument does not merely give possession of the instrument, but right to property. Who sever gets possession of the instrument becomes its owner and is entitled to the sum mentioned therein as the holder. It passes by mere delivery where instrument is payable to 'bearer.'

2. ***Defects in Title:*** The holder in good faith and for value called the 'holder in due course' gets the instrument free from all defects of any previous holder.

3. ***Remedy:*** The holder can sue upon the negotiable instrument in his own name. All prior parties are liable to him. A holder in due course can recover the full amount of the instrument.

4. ***Right:*** The holder in due course is not affected by certain defenses which might be available against previous holder, for example, fraud to which he is not a party.

5. ***Payable to Order:*** All three negotiable instruments are payable to order which is expressed to a particular person. An instrument which does not restrict its transferability expressly is negotiable whether the word 'order' is mentioned or not. The word 'order' or 'bearer' is no longer necessary to render an instrument negotiable.

   It must be noted that all the three negotiable instrument is endorsed and is expressed to be payable to the order of a specified person, it is nevertheless payable to him or his order.

6. ***Payable to Bearer:*** The negotiable instrument is expressed to be payable or on which the only or last endorsement is an endorsement in blank. It specifies that the person in possession of the bill is a bearer of the instrument which is so expressed payable to bearer.

7. ***Payment:*** A negotiable instrument may be made payable to two or more payees, or it may be payable in alternative to one or two payees.
8. ***Consideration:*** Consideration in the case of a negotiable instrument is presumed.
9. ***Presumptions:*** Certain presumptions apply to all negotiable instruments.

Presumptions as to Negotiable Instrument

For deciding cases in respect of rights of parties on the basis of a bill of exchange, the Court is entitled to make certain presumptions. These are briefly stated as follow :

1. ***Consideration:*** That every negotiable instrument is made or drawn for a consideration. Thus, this need not necessarily be mentioned.
2. ***Date:*** That the negotiable instrument was drawn on the date shown on the face of it.
3. ***Acceptance before maturity:*** That the bill of exchange was accepted before its maturity, i.e., before it became overdue.
4. ***Transfer before maturity:*** That the negotiable instrument was transferred before its maturity.
5. ***Order of Endorsements:*** That the Endorsements appearing upon a negotiable instrument were made in the order in which they appear.
6. ***Stamping of the instrument:*** That an instrument which has been lost was properly stamped.
7. ***Holder is Holder in due course:*** That the holder of a negotiable instrument is the 'holder in due course', except where the instrument has been obtained from its lawful owner or its lawful custodian by means of offence or fraud.
8. ***Proof of dishonour:*** If a suit is filed upon an instrument which has been dishonoured, the Court shall, on proof of the protest, presume the fact of dishonour unless it is disproved.

Payee in a Negotiable Instrument

All three kinds of negotiable instruments mentioned under Section 13 of the Act could be made payable in any of the following ways:

(i) Payable to bearer

The expression "bearer instrument" signifies an instrument, be it promissory note, bill of exchange or a cheque, which is expressed to be so payable or on which the last endorsement is in blank. This character of the instrument can be altered subsequently e.g. an endorsee can convert an 'Endorsement in blank' into an 'Endorsement in full'. In such a case, the holder of the instrument would not be able to negotiate the instrument by mere delivery. He will be required to endorse the instrument before delivering it.

(ii) Payable to order

An instrument is payable to order when it is payable to:

(i) The order of a specified person, or

(ii) A specified person or his order, or

(iii) A specified person without the addition of the words "or his order" and does not contain words prohibiting transfer or indicating an intention that it should not be transferable.

Types of Negotiable Instruments

A negotiable instrument can be of the following types:

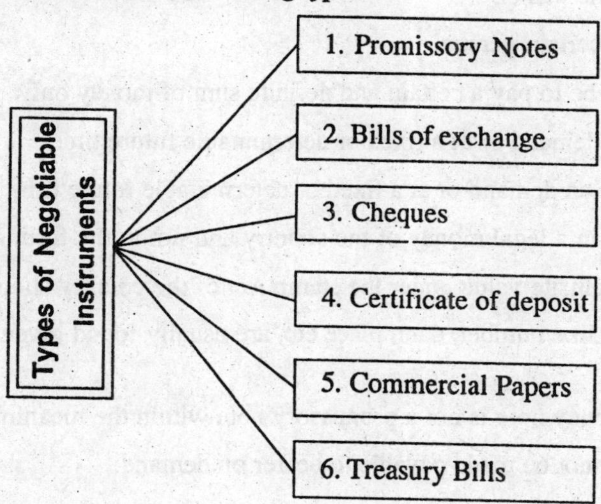

1. Promissory Notes

A "promissory note" is an instrument in writing containing an unconditional under-taking, signed by the maker, to pay a certain sum of money only to, or to the order of, a certain person, or to the bearer of the instrument.

Features of a Promissory Note

(i) A promissory note must be in writing, duly signed by its maker and properly stamped as per Indian Stamp Act.

(ii) It must contain an undertaking or promise to pay. Mere acknowledgement of indebtedness is not enough.

(iii) The promise to pay must not be conditional.

(iv) It must contain a promise to pay money only.

(v) The parties to a promissory note, i.e. the maker and the payee must be certain.

(vi) A promissory note may be payable on demand or after a certain date.

(vii) The sum payable mentioned must be certain or capable of being made certain. It means that the sum payable may be in figures or may be such that it can be calculated.

Essentials of a Promissory Note

1. The promissory note must be in writing.
2. The promissory note must contain an undertaking to pay.
3. The promise to pay must be unconditional one.
4. It must be signed by the maker.
5. The maker must be a certain person.
6. The undertaking must be to pay a certain and definite sum of money only.
7. It must be payable on demand or at a fixed or determinable future time.
8. It should only payable on demand or at a fixed or determinable future time.
9. The payment must be in a legal money of the country and not in the form of food, grain.
10. Revenue stamps or requisite value under the stamp Act of the country should be affixed.
11. Other matters of form like number, date, place etc, are usually found given in notes, but they are not essentials in law.
12. A bank note or a currency note is not a promissory note within the meaning of this section.
13. A promissory note cannot be made payable to bearer on demand.

2. Bills of Exchange

As per statutory definition, "Bill of exchange" is an instrument in writing containing an unconditional order, signed by the maker, directing a certain person to pay a certain sum of money only to, or to the order of, a certain person or to the bearer of the instrument. A cheque is a special type of Bill of Exchange. It is drawn on banker and is required to be made payable on demand.

A Bill of Exchange has been defined under Section 5 of the NI Act as "an instrument in writing containing an unconditional order, signed by the maker, directing a certain person to pay a certain sum of money only to, or to the order of certain persons or to the bearer of the instrument."

Parties to a Bill of Exchange

1. ***The Drawer:*** Is the party that issues a Bill of Exchange in an international trade transaction; usually the seller.
2. ***The Drawee:*** Is the recipient of the Bill of Exchange for payment or acceptance in an international trade transaction; usually the buyer.
3. ***The Payee:*** Is the party to whom the Bill is payable; usually the seller or their bankers.

Characteristics of a Bill of Exchange

(i) ***It must be in writing:*** The Bill of Exchange must be in writing.

(ii) ***Order to pay:*** There must be an order to pay. It is of the essence of the bill that its drawer orders the drawee to pay money to the payee. The term 'order' does not mean command. Any request or

direction or other words, which show an intention of the drawer to cause a payment being made by the drawee is sufficient. Politeness may be admissible but excessive politeness may prompt one to disregard it as an order.

(iii) ***Unconditional order:*** This order must be unconditional, as the bill is payable at all events. It is absolutely necessary for the drawer's order to the drawee to be unconditional. The order must not make the payment of the bill dependent on a contingent event. A conditional Bill of Exchange is invalid.

(iv) ***Signature of the drawer:*** The drawee must sign the instrument. The instrument without the proper signature will be inchoate (unclear or unformed or undeveloped) and hence ineffective. It is permissible to add the signature at any time after the issue of the bill.

(v) ***Drawee:*** A bill, in order to be perfect, must indicate a drawee who should be called upon to accept or pay it.

(vi) ***Parties:*** The drawer, the drawee (acceptor) and the payee- the parties to a bill are to be specified in the instrument with reasonable certainty.

(vii) ***Certainty of amount:*** The sum must be certain.

(viii) ***Payment in kind is not valid:*** The medium of payment must be money and money only. The distinctive order to pay anything in kind will vitiate the bill.

(ix) ***Stamping:*** A Bill of Exchange, to be valid, must be duly stamped as per the Indian Stamp Act.

(x) ***Cannot be made payable to bearer on demand:*** A Bill of Exchange as originally drawn cannot be made payable to the bearer on demand.

Advantages of Bills of Exchange

- Bill of exchange fixes the date of payment. The creditor knows when to expect his money and the debtor also knows when he will be required to make payment.
- A bill of exchange is a negotiable instrument and can be used in settlement of debts.
- it is a written and signed acknowledgement of debt and affords conclusive proof of indebtedness.
- A debtor is free from worries and enjoys full period of credit, as he can never be called upon to pay the amount of the bill before the due to date.
- A creditor can convert the bill into cash by getting it discounted with the bank.

3. Cheques

A Cheque is an instrument in writing, containing an unconditional order, drawn on a specified banker, signed by the drawer, directing the banker, to pay, on demand, a certain sum of money only, to a certain person or to his order or to the bearer of the instrument.

A cheque is a document or instrument that orders a payment of money from a bank account. The person writing the cheque, the *drawer*, usually has a current account, or checking account, or chequing account where their money was previously deposited. The drawer writes the various details including the money amount, date, and a payee on the cheque, and signs it, ordering their bank, known as the *drawee*, to pay that person or company the amount of money stated.

4. Certificate of Deposit

Certificate of deposit is a negotiable financial instrument issued by a bank documenting a deposit; with principal and interest repayable to the bearer at a specified future date.

Importance of Certificate of Deposits

1) These are freely transferable by endorsement and delivery
2) Issued at discount to face value
3) These are document of title to time deposits.
4) Repayable on a fixed date without grace
5) The most convenient instruments to depositors as they enable short term surpluses to earn higher returns
6) CDs offer maximum liquidity as they are transferable by endorsement and delivery. The holder can resell his certificate to another person or party.
7) From the view of issuing bank, it is a means to raise resources in times of need and improve their lending capacity. The CDs are fixed term deposits which cannot be withdrawn until the redemption date.
8) It is an ideal instrument for banks with short term surplus funds to invest at attractive rates.

5. Commercial Paper

A Commercial Paper is an unsecured promissory note issued with a fixed maturity, short-term debt instrument issued by a corporation approved by RBI, typically for the financing of accounts receivable, inventories and meeting short-term liabilities. Maturities on commercial paper rarely range any longer than 270 days. The debt is usually issued at a discount, reflecting prevailing market interest rates. Commercial paper is not usually backed by any form of collateral, so only firms with high-quality debt ratings will easily find buyers without having to offer a substantial discount (higher cost) for the debt issue.

Features of Commercial Papers

1) Commercial Paper is a short term money market instrument comprising usance promissory note with a fixed maturity.
2) It is a certificate evidencing an unsecured corporate debt of short term maturity.
3) Commercial paper is issued at a discount to face value basis bit it can also be issued in interest bearing form.
4) The issuer promises to pay the buyer some fixed amount on some future period but pledges no assets, only his liquidity and established earning power, to guarantee that promise.
5) Commercial paper can be issued directly by a company to investors or through banks/merchant bankers.

6. Treasury Bills

A treasury bill is a kind of finance bill or promissory note issued by the government of the country to raise short term funds. According to one categorisation, Treasury bills are ad hoc, tap, and action bills. India has experimented with 91-day Treasury bills, 182-day Treasury bills, 364-day Treasury bills, and two types of 14-day Treasury bills. The treasury bills are purchases by foreign banks in India scheduled banks, National Co-operative Development organisations, financial institutions, joint stock companies, DFHI and others.

Characteristics of Treasury Bills

The important features of Treasury bills are:

1. High liquidity
2. Absence of risk of default
3. Ready availability on tap
4. Assured yield
5. Low transactions cost
6. Eligibility for inclusion in statutory liquidity ratio (SLR) and
7. Negligible capital depreciation.

Difference between Promissory Note and Bill of Exchange

Promissory Note	Bill of Exchange
i) It contains a promise to pay.	i) It contains an order to pay.
ii) The liability of the maker of a note is primary and absolute.	ii) The liability of the drawer of a bill is secondary and conditional.
iii) It is presented for payment without any previous acceptance by the maker.	iii) If a bill is payable some time after sight, it is required to be accepted either by the drawee himself.
iv) The maker of a promissory note stands in immediate relationship with the payee and is primarily liable to the payee or the holder.	iv) The maker or drawer of an accepted bill stands in immediate relationship with the acceptor and the payee.
v) It cannot be made payable to the maker himself. The maker and the payee cannot be the same person.	v) The drawer and payee or the drawee and the payee may be the same person.

Cheque

History of Cheque

The cheque had its origins in the ancient banking system, in which bankers would issue orders at the request of their customers, to pay money to identified payees. Such an order was referred to as a bill of exchange. The use of bills of exchange facilitated trade by eliminating the need for merchants to carry large quantities of currency (e.g. gold) to purchase goods and services. A draft is a bill of exchange which is not payable on demand of the payee. The ancient Romans are believed to have used an early form of cheque known as pra-scriptiones in the first century BC. During the 3rd century AD, banks in Persia and other territories in the Persian Sassanid Empire issued letters of credit known as bakks.

Muslim traders are known to have used the cheque system since the time of Harun al-Rashid (9th century) of the Abbasid Caliphate. In the 9th century, a Muslim businessman could cash an early form of the cheque in China drawn on sources in Baghdad, a tradition that was significantly strengthened in the 13th and 14th centuries, during the Mongol Empire. Indeed, fragments found in the Cairo Geniza indicate that in the 12th century cheques remarkably similar to our own were in use, only smaller to save costs on the paper. They contain a sum to be paid and then the order "May so and so pay the bearer such and such an amount". The date and name of the issuer are also apparent. Between 1118 and 1307, it is believed the Knights Templar introduced a cheque system for pilgrims travelling to the Holy Land or across Europe. The pilgrims would deposit funds at one chapter house, then withdraw it from another chapter at their destination by showing a draft of their claim. These drafts would be written in a very complicated code only the Templers could decipher.

Meaning of Cheque

A Cheque is an instrument in writing, containing an unconditional order, drawn on a specified banker, signed by the drawer, directing the banker, to pay, on demand, a certain sum of money only, to a certain person or to his order or to the bearer of the instrument.

Parties to a Cheque

There are three parties involved in every cheque or payment order:

(i) ***Drawer:*** The person who gives the order (writes out the cheque)

(ii) ***Drawee:*** The financial institution upon whom the cheque is drawn

(iii) ***Payee:*** The person or organisation named to receive payment.

Characteristics of Cheque

The characteristics of cheque can be summarised as under:

1. A cheque is an unconditional order on a specified banker where the drawer has his account.
2. A cheque can be drawn for a certain sum of money.

3. Cheque is payable by the banker only on demand.
4. A cheque does not require acceptance by the banker as in the case of bill of exchange.
5. A cheque may be drawn up in three forms i.e.:

   (i) Bearer cheque is one which is either expressed to be so payable or on which the last or only endorsement is an endorsement in blank);

   (ii) Order cheque is one which is expressed to be so payable or which is expressed to be payable to a particular person without containing any prohibitory words against its transfer or indicating an intention that it shall not be transferable (Section 18); and

   (iii) Crossed cheque is a cheque which can be collected only through a banker.
6. The cheque is a revocable mandate and the authority can be revoked by countermanding payment.
7. The cheque is determined by notice of death or insolvency of the drawer.
8. All cheques are bills of exchange but all bills of exchange are not cheques.

Types of Cheques

1) ***Open cheque:*** An open cheque is a cheque which is payable at the counter of the drawee bank on presentation of the cheque.

2) ***Bearer cheque:*** A bearer cheque is the one which is issued without the name of the payee and the same can be encashed by any one. Bearer cheque is made payable to the bearer i.e. it is payable to the person who presents it to the bank for encashment.

3) ***Order cheque:*** A cheque which is paid to a named person with the words 'or order' after the payee's name, showing that he or she can endorse it and pass it to someone else if desired.

4) ***Crossed cheque:*** A crossed cheque is a cheque which is payable only through a collecting banker and not directly at the counter of the bank. Crossing ensures security to the holder of the cheque as only the collecting banker credits the proceeds to the account of the payee of the cheque.

Differences between Cheque and Bill of Exchange

Cheque	Bill of Exchange
1. Cheque can be drawn only on a banker.	1. The drawee may be any person.
2. A cheque is payable on demand.	2. A bill may be drawn payable on demand or on expiry of certain period after date or sight.
3. Cheque is payable on demand and no grace period is allowed.	3. While calculating maturity three day's grace is allowed.
4. Notice of dishonour is not necessary.	4. A notice of dishonour is required.
5. A cheque can be drawn to bearer and made payable on demand.	5. A bill cannot be made bearer if it is payable on demand. A bill drawn 'payable to bearer on demand' is void.
6. A cheque is not required to be presented for acceptance.	6. Bills sometimes, require presentment for acceptance.
7. No stamp duty is payable on cheques.	7. Affixation of proper stamps is necessary in case of Bills of Exchange.
8. A cheque may be crossed.	8. A bill of exchange cannot be crossed.
9. There is no system for noting and protesting in case of dishonour.	9. In case of dishonour of a bill proper noting and protesting is necessary.
10. The drawer does not get discharged from his liability because of delay in presenting the cheque to the bank for payment.	10. The drawer of the bill stands discharged from his liability if it is not duly presented for payment.

Liability of the Parties

1. ***Drawer:*** Undertakes that on due presentment, the cheque will be paid.
2. ***Endorser:*** Similar liabilities to the drawer unless the words sans recurs or 'without recourse' are added after the endorser's signature. A person who signs a cheque other than as payer or endorser can still be liable if it can be shown that at the time of signing that was their intention.
3. ***Other people who have possession of the cheque at some time:***

   (i) ***Holder:***

   — Payee or endorser of a cheque who is in possession of it.

   — Bearer of a bearer cheque.

   (ii) ***Holder for value:*** The person to whom the cheque has been negotiated after actual consideration has been introduced into the chain.

Essentials of Valid Cheque

The essential elements of a cheque are as under:

1) ***It must have all essential of a bill of exchange:*** The first requirement of a valid cheque is that it must have all the essential elements of a bill exchange. The reason for the same is that the cheque is primarily a bill of exchange drawn upon a banker.

2) ***It must be drawn on a specified banker:*** The second requirement of a valid cheque is that it must be drawn on a specified banker. A cheque drawn on any person other than a banker is not valid.

3) ***It must be payable on demand:*** The last requirement of a valid cheque is that it must be payable on demand. As a matter of fact, a cheque is always payable on demand.

Crossing of Cheques

A cheque may be a open cheque or a crossed cheque. An open cheque is one that can be paid by the paying banker across the counter while crossed cheque cannot be paid across the counter. Crossing of cheques is a universally adopted practice. Crossing on a cheque is a direction to the paying banker that the payment shall not be made across the counter. The payment on a crossed cheque can be collected only through a banker.

Cheques are usually crossed as a measure of safety. Crossing is made by drawing two parallel traverse lines across the face of the cheque with or without the addition of certain words. The usage of crossing distinguishes cheques from other bills of exchange.

In this regard Section 123 of the Negotiable Instruments Act states:

"Where a cheque bears across its face an addition of the words 'and company' or any abbreviation thereof, between two transverse lines, or of two parallel tranverse lines simply, either with or without the words 'not negotiable' that addition shall be deemed a crossing, and the cheque shall be deemed to be crossed generally".

***Who may cross the cheque*:** Crossing of a cheque is an instance of an alteration which is authorized by the Act. Thus, the following parties may cross a cheque:

1. ***Drawer:*** The drawer of the cheque may cross the cheque generally or specially.

2. ***Holder:*** Where the drawer does not cross the cheque, the holder may cross it generally or specially. Even if the cheque is already crossed the holder may add the words 'not negotiable'.

3. ***Banker:*** Where a cheque crossed specially the collecting banker may again cross it specially to another banker as its agent for collection. This is the only case where the Act allows a second special crossing by a banker and for the purpose of collection

Types of Crossing of Cheque

Crossing can be classified into two categories: (i) General (ii) Special.

(i) General Crossing

Section 123 of the Act refers to general crossing. "Where a cheque bears across its face two traverse lines with or without the words "and Co." or any abbreviation thereof or the words 'not negotiable, the cheque is said to have been crossed generally.

"Where a cheque is crossed generally, the banker on whom it is drawn shall not pay it otherwise than to the banker" (Section 126). The payee may get the cheque collected through a bank of his choice.

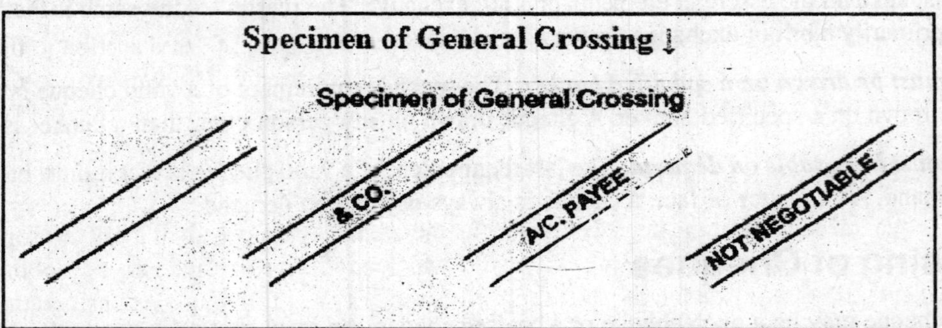

(ii) ***Special Crossing:*** Special crossing implies the specifications of the name of the banker on the face of the cheque. The object of special crossing is to direct the drawee banker to pay the cheque only if it is presented through the particular bank mentioned.

In the case of special crossing the addition of two parallel transverse lines is not essential though generally the name of the bank to which the cheque is crossed specially is written between the two parallel transverse line (Section 124).

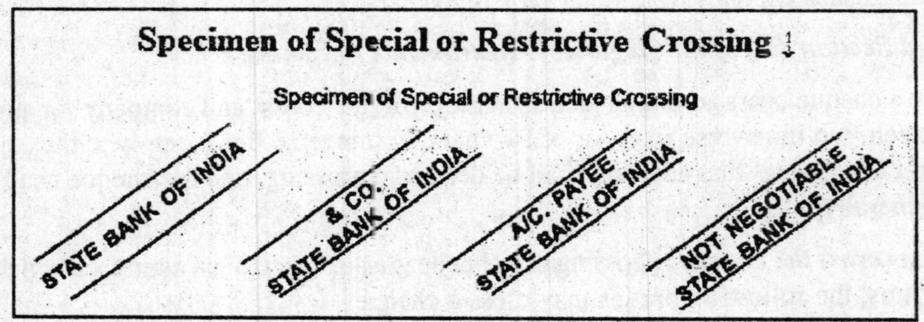

Section 126 of the Act provides that:

"Where a cheque is crossed specially, the banker on whom it is drawn shall not pay it otherwise than to the banker to whom it is crossed, or his agent for collection".

Section 127 of the Act provides that:

"Where a cheque is crossed specially to more than one banker, except when crossed to an agent for the purpose of collection, the banker on whom it is drawn shall refuse payment thereof".

Special crossing may take any of the following shapes:

(i) "Account Payee" crossing or restrictive crossing

(ii) This type of crossing acts as a warning to the collecting bankers that the proceeds are to be credited into the account of the payee.

(iii) These words are a mere direction to the receiving or collecting banker. These do not affect the paying banker who is under no duty to ascertain that the cheque in fact has been collected for the account of the person named as the payee.

(iv) It has been held that crossing cheque with the words "Account Payee" and mentioning a bank is not a restrictive endorsement so as to invalidate further negotiation of the cheque by the endorsee.

(v) It has been decided by the courts that an "account payee" crossing is a direction to the collecting banker as to how the proceeds are to be applied after receipt. The banker can disregard the direction only at his own risk and responsibility.

Cheque marked "Not Negotiable"

The general rule about the negotiability is that the holder in due course of a bill or promissory note or cheque takes the instrument free from any defect which might be existing in the title of the transferor. If the holder takes the instrument in good faith, before maturity and for valuable consideration, his claim is not defeated or affected by the defective title of the transferor. In case of any dispute, it is the transferor with the defective title who is liable. Addition of the words "not negotiable" to the crossing of a cheque, makes the position different.

Section 130 of the Negotiable Instruments Act provides that:

"A person taking a cheque crossed generally or specially bearing in either case the words 'not negotiable' shall not have or shall not be able to give a better title to the cheque than the title of person from whom he took had".

The effect of such a crossing is that the title of the transferee would be vitiated by the defect in the title of the transferor. The transferee of such a crossed cheque cannot get a better title than the transferor himself. The transferee cannot claim the right of a holder in due course by proving that he purchased the instrument in good faith for value.

Banker's liability on payment of crossed cheque in due course

In respect of a crossed cheque it is presumed that the banker, on whom it is drawn, has made payment to the true owner of the cheque, though in fact, the amount of the cheque may not reach the true owner. In other words, the banker making payment in due course is protected, whether the money is or is not, in fact, received by the true owner of the cheque (Section 128). Bankers liability on wrong payment of a crossed cheque section 126 of the Act states that:

(a) In the case of generally crossed cheque the banker shall not pay it otherwise than to a banker, and

(b) In the case of a specially crossed cheque it shall not be paid by the banker otherwise than to the banker to whom it is crossed or to his agent for collection.

Where the drawee banker pays a crossed cheque otherwise than in accordance with the provisions of Section 126 it shall be liable to the true owner of the cheque for any loss he may have sustained (section 129).

Protection of Banker in respect of uncrossed Cheques

Section 85(2) reads: When a banker makes payment on an uncrossed cheque in due course he is authorized to debit the account of his customer with the amount so paid irrespective of the genuineness of the Endorsement thereon.

For example, a cheque is drawn payable to N or order and it is stolen. Thereafter, the thief or someone else forges N's endorsement and presents the cheque to the bank for encashment. On paying the cheque, the banker would be able to debit the drawer's account with the amount of the cheque. The original character of the cheque issued as bearer, is not altered by subsequent endorsements, so far as the paying bank is concerned, provided that the payment is made in due course. Hence the proposition that "once a bearer instrument always a bearer instrument".

Protection in respect of crossed cheques

When a banker pays a cheque drawn by his customer in accordance with section 126 of the Act he can debit the drawer's account with the amount paid, even though the amount of the cheque does not reach the true owner.

Prerequisites for claiming protection

The protection in both the cases referred above can be availed of only if the payment has been made in due course i.e.,

(a) According to the apparent tenor of the instrument,

(b) In good faith and without negligence.

(c) To any person in possession thereof,

(d) In circumstances that do not incite any suspicion that he is not entitled to receive payment of the cheque.

Liability of Drawee of Cheque

Section 31 of the Act states that; the drawee bank is under a duty to pay the cheque, provided he has in his hands sufficient funds of the drawer and the funds are properly applicable to such payment. If the banker refuses payment without sufficient cause being shown, he must compensate the drawer, not the holder, for any loss caused by such improper refusal (Section 31).

The banker must pay the cheque only when he is duly required to do so e.g. if there is an agreement between the drawer and the banker that the former shall not draw more than one cheque every week, the banker is not bound to pay the second cheque.

The amount of compensation that the drawee would have to pay to the drawer is to be measured by the loss or damage say loss of credit, suffered by the drawer. The principle is : "The lesser the value of the cheque dishonoured, the greater the damage to the credit of the drawer".

When banker shall refuse the payment: A banker will be justified or bound to dishonour a cheque in the following cases, viz;

(i) The cheque is undated.

(ii) The cheque is stale i.e. it has not been presented within the validity period of the cheque.

(iii) The instrument is inchoate or not free from reasonable doubt.

(iv) The cheque is post-dated and presented for payment before its ostensible date.

(v) The customer's funds in the banker's hands are not 'properly applicable' to the payment of cheque drawn by the former.

(vi) The customer has credit with one branch of a bank and he draws a cheque upon another branch of the same bank in which either he has account or his account is overdrawn.

(vii) A garnishee or other legal order from the Court attaching or otherwise dealing with the money in the hand of the banker, is served on the banker.

(viii) Authority of the banker to honour a cheque of his customer is determined by the notice of the drawer's death, lunacy and insolvency. However, any payment made prior to the receipt of the notice of death is valid.

(ix) Notice in respect of closure of the account is served by either party on the other.

(x) The cheque contains material alterations, irregular signature of irregular endorsement.

(xi) The customer has countermanded payment.

(xii) Any ambiguity in the material part of the cheque including the defects resulting from the crossing of the cheque.

(xiii) Any difference between the amount of cheque in words and in figures.

(xiv) Any irregular endorsements.

(xv) The cheque is mutilated.

(xvi) Signature of the drawer has been forged.

Dishonour of Cheques

Section 92 of the Act reads as under:

"A promissory note, bill of exchange or cheque is said to be dishonoured by non-payment when the maker of the note, acceptor of the bill or drawee of the cheque makes default in payment upon being duly required to pay the same".

If on presentation the banker does not pay then dishonour takes place and the holder acquired at once the right of recourse against the drawer and the other parties on the cheque. The important point to be noted in connection with the dishonour of a cheque is that its negotiability is lost.

Circumstances for dishonour of cheques and consequences of wrongful dishonour

Following are the circumstances under which a cheque can be dishonoured by a paying banker:

a) When the Banker receives a notice of the drawer's death, insolvency, insanity etc.

b) If a cheque has become stale or bears an impossible or incomplete date

c) When the drawer's signature on the cheque differs from his specimen signatures.

d) If the drawer's funds are subject to Banker's right to set-off.

e) When the Banker receives a prohibitive order from any government organisation.

f) When a garnishee order is attached to the customer's account.

g) When the cheque is a conditional one.

h) If the cheque is not clear or bears any material alteration.

The banker has an obligation to honour customer's cheque as and when they are presented as long as sufficient funds are available at credit in customer's account. Sec 31 of the Negotiable Instruments Act 1881, states that " the drawee of a cheque having sufficient funds of the drawer in his hands, properly applicable to the payment of such cheque, must pay the cheque when duly required to do so , in default of such payment, must compensate the drawer for any loss or damage caused by such a default".

(i) The damages that the banker has to pay will be more in case of wrongful dishonour of cheques of the trader-customer. New Central Hall vs United Commercial Bank Ltd.

(ii) "Smaller the cheque , greater the damage". The customer suffers more when the amount of the cheque dishonoured is small.

(iii) The customer can claim substantial general damages without having any monetary loss.

(iv) In case of trustee account, normally substantial general damages will be awarded for wrongful dishonour.

(v) In case of non trader customer, the damage will be nominal.

(vi) Special damages are also awarded for the financial loss incurred by the customer as a consequence of wrongful dishonour, provided the loss must be proved by the customer.

Types of Dishonour

Dishonour of cheque can be divided into two categories i.e.:

(a) ***Rightful Dishonour:*** Dishonour of cheque by the drawee banker for any of the reasons specified above or for any other rightful reason. In this case there is no remedy available against the banker but the holder in due course has remedy both civil and criminal against the drawer.

(b) ***Wrongful Dishonour:*** Dishonour of cheque by the banker due to negligence or carelessness by its employees. The drawer may bring an action against the bank for losses suffered by him. The payee has no action against the banker in this case.

Dishonour of Cheque is an Offence

Section 138 of the Negotiable Instruments Act states that the return of a cheque by a banker because the money standing to the credit of the accountholder is insufficient to honour the cheque or that it exceeds the amount arranged to be paid from the account by an agreement made with the bank, is a criminal offence. The drawer shall be deemed to have committed an offence and such offence will be punishable with imprisonment for a term up to two years imprisonment or with a fine twice the amount of the cheque or both.

Provisions of section 138 of the Act are applicable only if:

(a) The cheque in question has been issued in discharge of a liability only. Unless contrary is proved, as per the provisions of section 139, a cheque is presumed to have been received by the holder in discharge of a debt or liability. A cheque given as gift will not fall in this category.

(b) The cheque is presented to the bank for payment within six months or its specific validity period, whichever is earlier.

(c) The payee or holder in due course has given notice demanding payment within thirty days of the receiving information of dishonour which should be for a reason other than insufficiency of funds.

(d) The drawer does not make payment within 15 days of the receipt of the notice. The complaint can be made only by the payee/holder in due course, within one month.

Offences by companies: If the person committing an offence under section 138 is a company, every person who was in charge of the affairs of the company and was responsible for the business of the company at the time offence was committed shall be deemed to be guilty of the offence and shall be liable to be proceeded against and punished accordingly. (Section 139) However, a person shall not be punishable under section 139 if it is proved that the offence has been committed without his knowledge or consent and that he had taken all due care to prevent commission of the offence.

Action to be taken: If a cheque is dishonoured for lack of funds, the drawer can be punished with imprisonment up to one year and/ or within a fine up to double the amount of the cheque if:

(i) The cheque has been presented to the bank within a year from the date on which it was drawn or within its validity.

(ii) The payee or holder makes a demand for payment by giving notice in writing to the drawer within thirty days of the receipt of the information.

(iii) The drawer of the cheque fails to make payment within fifteen days of receipt of the notice.

Material Alteration of Cheque

A cheque may be altered by the drawer or by a third party after it is drawn. For example, the date of cheque may be altered or the amount payable may be altered. Alteration may be made genuinely or fraudulently. Alterations may be material or immaterial.

Material Alteration

An alteration is regarded as material when it alters materially or substantially the operation of the instrument and liabilities of the parties thereto. It is defined as "an alteration which alters the business effects of the instrument if used for any business purpose". So any change in an instrument which causes to speak a different language in legal effect from that which it originally spoke, or which changes the legal identity or the relation of the parties to it, is a material alteration.

The following are some of the examples of material alteration:

(a) Alteration of the date of the instrument.

(b) Alteration of the sum payable.

(c) Alteration of the place of the payment.

(d) Alteration of the name of the payee.

(e) Alteration of the crossing marks.

(f) Alteration in the rate of interest.

Under the Negotiable Instruments Act, 1881, the following do not amount to material alterations:

(a) Filling blanks of the instrument.

(b) Conversion of blank endorsement into an endorsement in full.

(c) Making acceptance conditional.

(d) Altering a general crossing into a special crossing.

(e) Crossing of an uncrossed cheque.

(f) Alteration made with the consent of the parties.

Bill Presentment

Presentment for acceptance refers to presenting of a bill of exchange to the drawee named in the bill of exchange for his acceptance and agreement to pay the bill, usually at some time in the future. It is an act which amounts to a notification of the holding of a bill of exchange with a request to accept, accompanied by the bill.

Presentment for Acceptance

Presentment for acceptance must be made:

1. Where the bill is payable after sight, cr any other case where presentment for acceptance is necessary in order to fix the maturity of the instrument; or,

2. Where the bill expressly stipulates that it shall be presented for acceptance; or,

3. Where the bill is drawn payable elsewhere than at the residence or place of business of the drawee.

(a) In no other case is presentment for acceptance necessary in order to render any party to the bill liable:

(i) When failure to present releases drawer and indorser, Except as herein otherwise provided, the holder of a bill which is required by the next preceding section to be presented for acceptance must either present it for acceptance or negotiate it within a reasonable time. If he fails to do so, the drawer and all indorsers are discharged.

(ii) Presentment; how made, Presentment for acceptance must be made by or on behalf of the holder at a reasonable hour, on a business day and before the bill is overdue, to the drawee or some person authorized to accept or refuse acceptance on his behalf; and

(iii) Where a bill is addressed to two or more drawees who are not partners, presentment must be made to them all unless one has authority to accept or refuse acceptance for all, in which case presentment may be made to him only;

(b) Where the drawee is dead, presentment may be made to his personal representative;

(c) Where the drawee has been adjudged a bankrupt or an insolvent or has made an assignment for the benefit of creditors, presentment may be made to him or to his trustee or assignee.

(iv) On what days presentment may be made, A bill may be presented for acceptance on any day on which negotiable instruments may be presented for payment under the provisions of Sections seventy-two and eighty-five of this Act. When Saturday is not otherwise a holiday, presentment for acceptance may be made before twelve o'clock noon on that day.

(v) Presentment where time is insufficient, where the holder of a bill drawn payable elsewhere than at the place of business or the residence of the drawee has no time, with the exercise of reasonable diligence, to present the bill for acceptance before presenting it for payment on the day that it falls due, the delay caused by presenting the bill for acceptance before presenting it for payment is excused and does not discharge the drawers and endorsers.

(vi) Where presentment is excused, presentment for acceptance is excused and a bill may be treated as dishonored by non-acceptance in either of the following cases:

(a) Where the drawee is dead, or has absconded, or is a fictitious person or a person not having capacity to contract by bill.

(b) Where, after the exercise of reasonable diligence, presentment can not be made.

(c) Where, although presentment has been irregular, acceptance has been refused on some other ground.

(vii) When dishonored by non acceptance, A bill is dishonored by non-acceptance:

(a) When it is duly presented for acceptance and such an acceptance as is prescribed by this Act is refused or can not be obtained; or

(b) When presentment for acceptance is excused and the bill is not accepted.

(viii) Duty of holder where bill not accepted, Where a bill is duly presented for acceptance and is not accepted within the prescribed time, the person presenting it must treat the bill as dishonored by non acceptance or he loses the right of recourse against the drawer and endorsers.

(ix) Rights of holder where bill not accepted, When a bill is dishonored by non acceptance, an immediate right of recourse against the drawer and endorsers accrues to the holder and no presentment for payment is necessary.

Rules as to Presentment for a Payment

1. Subject to the provisions of this Act, a bill must be duly presented for payment. If it is not so presented, the drawer and endorsers shall be discharged.

2. A bill is duly presented for payment if it is presented in accordance with the following rules:

   (a) Where the bill is not payable on demand, presentment must be made on the day it falls due.

   (b) Where the bill is payable on demand, then, subject to the provisions of this Act presentment must be made within a reasonable time after its issue in order to render the drawer liable, and within a reasonable time after its endorsement in order to render the endorser liable. In determining what is a reasonable time regard shall be had to the nature of the bill, the usage of trade with regard to similar bills, and the facts of the particular case.

   (c) Presentment must be made by the holder, or by some person authorised to receive payment on his behalf, at a reasonable hour on a business day, at the proper place as hereinafter defined, either to the person designated by the bill as payer, or to some person authorised to pay or refuse payment on his behalf, if by the exercise of reasonable diligence such person can there be found.

   (d) A bill is presented at the proper place:

      (i) Where a place of payment is specified in the bill, and the bill is there presented:

      (ii) Where no place of payment is specified, but the address of the drawee or acceptor is given in the bill, and the bill is there presented:

      (iii) Where no place of payment is specified and no address given, and the bill is presented at the drawee's or acceptor's place of business, if known, and if not, at his ordinary residence, if known:

      (iv) In any other case, if presented to the drawee or acceptor at his last known place of business or residence, or wherever he can be found.

   (e) Where a bill is presented at the proper place, and after the exercise of reasonable diligence no person authorised to pay or refuse payment can be found there, no further presentment to the drawee or acceptor is required.

   (f) Where a bill is drawn upon or accepted by 2 or more persons who are not partners, and no place of payment is specified presentment must be made to them all.

   (g) Where the drawee or acceptor of the bill is dead, and no place of payment is specified presentment must be made to the executor or administrator of the deceased, if any, and if by the exercise of reasonable diligence he can be found.

   (h) Where authorised by agreement or usage, presentment through the post office is sufficient.

When Presenment for Acceptance is Necessary

(1) Where a bill is payable after sight, presentment for acceptance is necessary in order to fix the maturity of the instrument.

(2) Where a bill expressly stipulates that it shall be presented for acceptance, or where a bill is drawn

payable elsewhere than at the residence or place of business of the drawee, it must be presented for acceptance before it can be presented for payment.

(3) In no other case is presentment for acceptance necessary in order to render liable any party to the bill.

(4) Where the holder of a bill drawn payable elsewhere than at the place of business or residence of the drawee has not time, with the exercise of reasonable diligence, to present the bill for acceptance before presenting it for payment on the day that it falls due, the delay caused by presenting the bill for acceptance before presenting it for payment is excused, and does not discharge the drawer and indorsers.

Discharge of Instrument

An instrument is said to be discharged when;

(a) All the rights under it are extinguished.

(b) It ceases to be negotiable

(c) Even a holder in due course does not acquire any right under it.

In short, an instrument is discharged only when the party primarily and ultimately liable on the instrument is freed from liability.

Discharge of a party to an instrument does not discharge the instrument itself. Consequently, the holder in due course may proceed against the other parties liable for payment of the instrument.

Different modes of discharge from liability

Parties to negotiable instruments are discharged from liability when the right of action on the instrument is extinguished. The right of action on a negotiable instrument is extinguished by the following methods;

(a) By payments in due course:

The parties primarily liable to make payment on an instrument are discharged from liability to all parties if the instrument is payable to bearer or endorsed in blank, and such maker, acceptor or endorser makes payment in due course of the amount due thereon i.e when the payments have been made to the holder of the instrument at or after maturity in good faith and without notice of any defect in the title to the instrument.

(b) By cancellation of acceptor's/endor's name:

The maker, acceptor and endorser respectively of a negotiable instrument are discharged form liability to a holder who cancels the acceptor's or endorser's name with the intent to discharge the acceptor/endorser and to all parties claiming under such holder i.e. if the holder of a bill cancels the signature of acceptor with and intention to discharge him, both maker and the acceptor of such negotiable instrument are discharge from the liability to the holder and to all parties claiming under such a holder section 82. How ever, it is to be noted that any cancellation under/by a mistake or without the authority of the holder is inoperative.

(c) By release:

The holder of an instrument may release any of the parties to the instrument by any method other than cancellation of names e.g a separate agreement of waiver or release. The release may be express or implied of section 82. The party so released and all subsequent parties who have a right against the party so released will also stand released and discharged from the liability.

(d) By allowing more than 48 hours to the drawee's for acceptance:

If the holder of a bill of exchange allows the drawee's more than forty eight hours, exclusive of public holidays to decide whether he will accept the bill, all prior parties not consenting to such an allowance of more than 48 hours are discharge from liability to such holder, this is because the holder must treat the instrument as dishonoured if the drawee's fails to signify his acceptance within forty eight hours, and then the holder must five notice to the drawer and to all prior parties, and must not allow time unless they give their consent that more time should be allowed section 83.

(e) Dissenting parties discharged by qualified or a limited acceptance:

The holder of a bill is entitled to unqualified acceptance, if he elects to take a qualified acceptance; he does so at his own peril and discharge all parties prior to himself unless he obtains their consent to such an acceptance. All previous parties are discharged in the following cases;

(1) When acceptance is qualified.

(2) When acceptance is for a part of the sum

(3) When acceptance substitute a different place or time of payment.

(4) When acceptance is not signed by the drawee's not being partners.

But, if the prior parties subsequently approve of such acceptance by the holder, they will not be discharged.

(f) By payment, alteration not being apparent:

If a person makers payment on an altered note, bill or cheque, and the alteration is such that it is not apparent the payment is deemed to have been made in due course and the person (banker or other person) who is liable to pay the amount is protected section 89.

Where the cheque is an electronic image of a truncated cheque, any difference in apparent tenor of such electronic image and the truncated cheque shall be a material alteration and it shall be the duty of the bank or the clearing house, as the case may be, to ensure the exactness of the apparent tenor of electronic image of the truncated cheque while truncating and transmitting the image.

Any bank or a clearing house which receives a transmitted electronic image of a truncated cheque, shall verify from the party who transmitted the image. To it, that the image so transmitted to it and received by it, is exactly the same.

(g) By negotiation back:

If a bill of exchange which has been negotiated is at or after maturity, held by the acceptor in his own right all right to action thereon are extinguished section 90.

(h) By delay in presenting the cheque within a reasonable time:

If a cheque is not presented for payment within a reasonable time after its issue the drawer is not liable for the delay, in Ramesh vs. M Rahul reasonable time was held to be six months. If there was a raid and the cheque was seized then the action of not presenting the cheque was found excusable. However, if the drawer suffers some loss to the failure of the bank, the drawer is discharged as against the holder to the extent of losses suffered by him.

For example, if vivan draws 10 cheques of Rs.250 each, each but when the cheque a ought to be presented, has only Rs. 2000 at the bank and subsequently the bank fails before the cheques a represented ,civil will be released from liability to the extent of Rs. 2500 at the bank, he will be discharged in full.

(i) By operation of law:

A negotiable instrument is also discharged by operation of law under any of the following circumstances;

(a) By lapse of time i.e. when the claim under the instrument becomes barred by the limitation act on the expiry on the period prescribed for the recovery of the amount due on the instrument; or

(b) By merger i.e. when the debt under the instrument is merged in the judgment debt obtained against the acceptor make, or endorser,

(c) Under the law of insolvency i.e. when the acceptor, maker or endorser who becomes insolvent, is discharged by an order of the court made in the insolvency proceedings.

(j) By payment by the drawee's of a cheque payable to order of to bearer:

Payment in due course discharges the bank from liability even if the payment is made to a wrong person, a cheque is said to have been paid in due course when it has been paid in good faith after taking proper care to ascertain the genuineness of the endorsements. But if the drawer's signature is forged, the banker can, under no circumstances, claim discharge on payment.

The bank is discharged by payment in due course to the bearer notwithstanding any endorsement thereon, whether in full or in part and whether or not such endorsement purports to restrict or exclude further negotiation. The endorsee under an endorsement in full cannot recover the amount from the banker who has paid it to the bearer section 85.

(k) By material alteration of the instrument without assent of all parties liable:

Material alteration is that charge in the negotiable instrument which affects the validity of the instrument or right of the parties thereto. Validity of the instrument is affected only when the alteration is material. Any material alteration of a negotiable instrument renders the same void as against any one who is party thereto at the time of making such alteration. Following have been held to be material alteration;

1. Alterations of the date of the instrument.
2. Alterations of the sum playable.
3. Alteration of the time of payment.
4. Alteration in the rate of interest.
5. Alteration in the rate of interest.
6. Alteration by addition of new party.
7. Alteration by adding the place of payment.

Law of Agency

Agent

An "agent" is a person employed to do any act for another or to represent another in dealings with third persons. The person for whom such act is done, or who is so represented, is called the "principal". The function of agent is to bring his principle in contact with third person.

Rules of Agency

(i) Subject to certain acts personal in nature like marriage, whatever a person can do , he can do so through an agent.

(ii) He who acts through an agent , does it himself subject to certain conditions.

Who may Employ Agent

Any person who is of the age of majority according to the law to which he is subject, and who is of sound mind, may employ an agent.

Who may be an Agent

As between the principal and third persons any person may become an agent, but no person who is not of the age of majority and of sound mind can become an agent, so as to be responsible to his principal according to the provisions in that behalf herein contained.

Consideration not Necessary

No consideration is necessary to create an agency.

Creation of Agency

1. By express agreement

The usual form of a contract of agency is a power of attorney on a stamped paper.

2. By implied agreement

Such agency arises when the principal through his conduct leads the third party to believe that certain person is his agent. It includes:

(i) Agency by estoppel

(ii) Agency by holding out

(iii) Agency by necessity

3. By ratification

When a person acts on behalf of another without his consent , and the other person accepts his acts, the acts are said to be ratified. This places the parties in the same position in which they would have been if acts were done with prior authority.

EFFECT OF RATIFICATION

Where acts are done by one person on behalf of another, but without his knowledge or authority, he may elect to ratify or to disown such acts. If he ratifies them, the same effects will follow as if they had been performed by his authority.

RATIFICATION MAY BE EXPRESSED OR IMPLIED

Ratification may be expressed or may be implied in the conduct of the person on whose behalf the acts are done.

KNOWLEDGE REQUISITE FOR VALID RATIFICATION

No valid ratification can be made by a person whose knowledge of the facts of the case is materially defective.

EFFECT OF RATIFYING UNAUTHORIZED ACT FORMING PART OF A TRANSACTION

A person ratifying any unauthorized act done on his behalf ratifies the whole of the transaction of which such act formed a part.

RATIFICATION OF UNAUTHORIZED ACT CANNOT INJURE THIRD PERSON

An act done by one person on behalf of another, without such other person's authority, which, if done with authority, would have the effect of subjecting a third person to damages, or of terminating any right or interest of a third person, cannot, by ratification, be made to have such effect.

4. By operation of law

Sometimes agency arises due to operation of law. Promoters of a company and partners of a firm are agents due to such implication.

AGENT'S AUTHORITY MAY BE EXPRESS OR IMPLIED

The authority of an agent may be express or implied.

DEFINITIONS OF EXPRESS AND IMPLIED AUTHORITY

An authority is said to be express when it is given by words, spoken or written. An authority is said to be implied when it is to be inferred from the circumstances of the case; and things spoken or written, or the ordinary course of dealing, may be accounted circumstances of the case.

EXTENT OF AGENT'S AUTHORITY

An agent having an authority to do an act has authority to do every lawful thing which is necessary in order to do such act.

An agent having an-authority to carry on a business has authority to do every lawful thing necessary for the purpose, or usually done in the course, of conducting such business.

AGENT'S AUTHORITY IN AN EMERGENCY

An agent has authority, in an emergency, to do all such acts for the purpose of protecting his principal from loss as would be done by a person of ordinary prudence, in his own case, under similar circumstances.

SUB-AGENTS WHEN AGENT CANNOT DELEGATE

An agent cannot lawfully employ another to perform acts which he has expressly or impliedly undertaken to perform personally, unless by the ordinary custom of trade a sub-agent may, or from the nature of the agency, a sub-agent must, be employed.

"SUB-AGENT"

A "Sub-agent" is a person employed by, and acting under the control of, the original agent in the business of the agency.

REPRESENTATION OF PRINCIPAL BY SUB-AGENT PROPERLY APPOINTED

Where a sub-agent is properly appointed, the principal is, so far as regards third persons, represented by the sub-agent, and is bound by and responsible for his acts as if he were an agent originally appointed by the principal.

Agent's responsibility for sub-agents: The agent is responsible to the principal for the acts of the sub-agent.

Sub-agent's responsibility: The sub-agent is responsible for his acts to the agent, but not to the principal, except in case of fraud or wilful wrong.

AGENT'S RESPONSIBILITY FOR SUB-AGENT APPOINTED WITHOUT AUTHORITY

Where an agent, without having authority to do so, has appointed a person to act as a sub-agent, the agent stands towards such person in the relation of a principal to an agent, and is responsible for his acts both to the principal and to third persons; the principal is not represented by or responsible for the acts of the person so employed, nor is that person responsible to the principal.

RELATION BETWEEN PRINCIPAL AND PERSON DULY APPOINTED BY AGENT TO ACT IN BUSINESS OF AGENCY

Where an agent, holding an express or implied authority to name another person to act for the principal in the business of the agency, has named another person accordingly, such person is not a sub-agent, but an agent of the principal for such part of the business of the agency as is entrusted to him.

AGENT'S DUTY IN NAMING SUCH PERSON

In selecting such agent for his principal, an agent is bound to exercise the same amount of discretion as a man of ordinary prudence would exercise in his own case; and, if he does this, he is not responsible to the principal for the acts or negligence of the agent so selected.

Termination of Agency

An agency is terminated by the principal revoking his authority; or by the agent renouncing the business of the agency; or by the business of the agency being completed; or by either the principal or agent dying or becoming of unsound mind; or by the principal being adjudicated an insolvent under the provisions of any Act for the time being in force for the relief of insolvent debtors.

1. BY ACT OF PARTIES

(i) Agreement between principal and agent.

(ii) Revocation by the principal : The principal may revoke the authority of the agent any time before the authority has been exercised. When agency is continuous one, notice of termination to agent as well as third parties is essential.

COMPENSATION FOR REVOCATION BY PRINCIPAL, OR RENUNCIATION BY AGENT

Where there is an express or implied contract that the agency should be continued for any period of time, the principal must make compensation to the agent, or the agent to the principal, as the case may be, for any previous revocation or renunciation of the agency without sufficient cause.

NOTICE OF REVOCATION OR RENUNCIATION

Reasonable notice must be given of such revocation or renunciation; otherwise the damage thereby resulting to the principal or the agent, as the case may be, must be made good to the one by the other.

REVOCATION AND RENUNCIATION MAY BE EXPRESSED OR IMPLIED

Revocation and renunciation may be expressed or may be implied in the conduct of the principal or agent Respectively

Duties of Agent

1. To carry out work as per direction of Principal

An agent is bound to conduct the business of his principal according to the directions given by the principal, or, in the absence of any such directions, according to the custom which prevails in doing business of the same kind at the place where the agent conducts such business. When the agent acts otherwise, if any loss be sustained, he must make it good to his principal, and, if any profit accrues, he must account for it.

2. To carry out with care, skill and diligence

An agent is bound to conduct the business of the agency with as much skill as is generally possessed by persons engaged in similar business, unless the principal has notice of his want of skill. The agent is always bound to act with reasonable diligence, and to use such skill as he possesses; and to make compensation to his principal in respect of the direct consequences of his own neglect, want of skill or misconduct, but not in respect of loss or damage which are indirectly or remotely caused by such neglect, want of skill or misconduct.

3. An agent is bound to render proper accounts to his principal on demand

4. It is the duty of an agent, in cases of difficulty, to use all reasonable diligence in communicating with his principal, and in seeking to obtain his instructions.

5. Not to deal in his own account

If an agent deals on his own account in the business of the agency, without first obtaining the consent of his principal and acquainting him with all material circumstances which have come to his own knowledge on the subject, the principal may repudiate the transaction, if the case shows either that any material fact has been dishonestly concealed from him by the agent, or that the dealings of the agent have been disadvantageous to him.

PRINCIPAL'S RIGHT TO BENEFIT GAINED BY AGENT DEALING ON HIS OWN ACCOUNT IN BUSINESS OF AGENCY

If an agent, without the knowledge of his principal, deals in the business of the agency on his own account instead of on account of his principal, the principal is entitled to claim from the agent any benefit which may have resulted to him from the transaction.

AGENT'S RIGHT OF RETAINER OUT OF SUMS RECEIVED ON PRINCIPAL'S ACCOUNT

An agent may retain, out of any sums received on account of the principal in the business of the agency, all moneys due to himself in respect of advances made or expenses properly incurred by him in conducting such business, and also such remuneration as may be payable to him for acting as agent.

6. Agent's duty to pay sums received for principal

Subject to such deductions, the agent is bound to pay to his principal all sums received on his account.

7. To protect and preserve the interest of principal in case of his death or insanity.
8. An agent should not use information obtained in course of agency against the principal.
9. He must not set an adverse title to the goods.
10. He should not put himself in a position where his duties and interest will conflict.
11. He must not delegate his authority subject to certain exceptions.

Rights of Agent

1. AGENT'S LIEN ON PRINCIPAL'S PROPERTY

In the absence of any contract to the contrary, an agent is entitled to retain goods, papers, and other property, whether movable or immovable, of the principal received by him, until the amount due to himself for commission, disbursements and services in respect of the same has been paid or accounted for to him.

2. Right to receive remuneration as per agreement, or if there is no agreement, reasonable remuneration.

WHEN AGENT'S REMUNERATION BECOMES DUE

In the absence of any special contract, payment for the performance of any act is not due to the agent until the completion of such act; but an agent may detain moneys received by him on account of goods sold, although the whole of the goods consigned to him for sale may not have been sold, or although the sale may not be actually complete.

AGENT NOT ENTITLED TO REMUNERATION FOR BUSINESS MISCONDUCTED

An agent who is guilty of misconduct in the business of the agency is not entitled to any remuneration in respect of that part of the business which he has misconducted.

3. The agent has right to be indemnified against all lawful acts done by him in exercise of authority conferred upon him.

4. The agent has right to be compensated for all injuries sustained by him because of negligence or lack of skill on part of principal.

5. The agent has 'right of stoppage in transit' under following circumstances:

(i) If he has bought goods on behalf of principal incurring personal liability. This right is similar to that of an unpaid seller.

(ii) If he is personally liable to principal for price of goods sold, he has this right against buyer incase the buyer becomes insolvent. This right is also similar to that of an unpaid seller.

PRINCIPAL'S DUTY TO AGENT

(1) AGENT TO BE INDEMNIFIED AGAINST CONSEQUENCES OF LAWFUL ACTS

The employer of an agent is bound to indemnify him against the consequences of all lawful acts done by such agent in exercise of the authority conferred upon him.

(2) AGENT TO BE INDEMNIFIED AGAINST CONSEQUENCES OF ACTS DONE IN GOOD FAITH

Where one person employs another to do an act, and the agent does the act in good faith, the employer is liable to indemnify the agent against the consequences of that act, though it causes an injury to the rights of third persons.

.NON-LIABILITY OF EMPLOYER OF AGENT TO DO A CRIMINAL ACT

Where one person employs another to do an act which is criminal, the employer is not liable to the agent, either upon an express or an implied promise, to indemnify him against the consequences of that act.

EFFECT OF AGENCY ON CONTRACT WITH THIRD PERSONS ENFORCEMENT AND CONSEQUENCES OF AGENT'S CONTRACTS

Contracts entered into through an agent, and obligations arising from acts done by an agent, may be enforced in the same manner, and will have the same legal consequences, as if the contracts had been entered into and the acts done by the principal in person.

(3) COMPENSATION TO AGENT FOR INJURY CAUSED BY PRINCIPAL'S NEGLECT

The principal must make compensation to his agent in respect of injury caused to such agent by the principal's neglect or want of skill.

PRINCIPAL HOW FOR BOUND, WHEN AGENT EXCEEDS AUTHORITY

When an agent does more than he is authorised to do, and when the part of what he does, which is within his authority, can be separated from the part which is beyond his authority, so much only of what he does as is within his authority is binding as between him and his principal.

PRINCIPAL NOT BOUND WHEN EXCESS OF AGENT'S AUTHORITY IS NOT SEPARABLE

Where an agent does more than he is authorised to do, and what he does beyond the scope of his authority cannot be separated from what is within it, the principal is not bound to recognise the transaction.

CONSEQUENCES OF NOTICE GIVEN TO AGENT

Any notice given to or information obtained by the agent, provided it be given or obtained in the course of the business transacted by him for the principal, shall, as between the principal and third parties, have the same legal consequence as if it had been given to or obtained by the principal.

AGENT CANNOT PERSONALLY ENFORCE, NOR BE BOUND BY, CONTRACTS ON BEHALF OF PRINCIPAL

In the absence of any contract to that effect, an agent cannot personally enforce contracts entered into by him on behalf of his principal, nor is he personally bound by them.

Presumption of contract to the contrary—Such a contract shall be presumed to exist in the following cases :

(1) Where the contract is made by an agent for the sale or purchase of goods for a merchant resident abroad;

(2) Where the agent does not disclose the name of his principal; and

(3) Where the principal, though disclosed, cannot be sued.

RIGHTS OF PARTIES TO A CONTRACT MADE BY AGENT NOT DISCLOSED

If an agent makes a contract with a person who neither knows, nor has reason to suspect, that he is an agent, his principal may require the performance of the contract; but the other contracting party has, as against the principal, the same right as he would have had as against the agent if the agent had been the principal.

If the principal discloses himself before the contract is completed, the other contracting party may refuse to fulfil the contract, if he can show that, if he had known who was the principal in the contract, or if he had known that the agent was not a principal, he would not have entered into the contract.

PERFORMANCE OF CONTRACT WITH AGENT SUPPOSED TO BE PRINCIPAL

Where one man makes a contract with another, neither knowing nor having reasonable ground to suspect that the other is an agent, the principal, if he requires the performance of the contract, can only obtain such performance subject to the rights and obligations subsisting between the agent and the other party to the contract.

RIGHT OF PERSON DEALING WITH AGENT PERSONALLY LIABLE

In cases where the agent is personally liable, a person dealing with him may hold either him or his principal, or both of them, liable.

CONSEQUENCE OF INDUCING AGENT OR PRINCIPAL TO ACT ON BELIEF THAT PRINCIPAL OR AGENT WILL BE HELD EXCLUSIVELY LIABLE

When a person who has made a contract with an agent induces the agent to act upon the belief that the principal only will be held liable, or induces the principal to act upon the belief that the agent only will be held liable, he cannot afterwards hold liable the agent or principal respectively.

LIABILITY OF PRETENDED AGENT

A person untruly representing himself to be the authorised agent of another, and thereby inducing a third person to deal with him as such agent, is liable, if his alleged employer does not ratify his acts, to make compensation to the other in respect of any loss or damage which he has incurred by so dealing.

PERSON FALSELY CONTRACTING AS AGENT NOT ENTITLED TO PERFORMANCE

A person with whom a contract has been entered into in the character of agent, is not entitled to require the performance of it if he was in reality acting, not as agent, but on his own account.

LIABILITY OF PRINCIPAL INDUCING BELIEF THAT AGENT'S UNAUTHORIZED ACTS WERE AUTHORIZED

When an agent has, without authority, done acts or incurred obligations to third persons on behalf of his principal, the principal is bound by such acts or obligations, if he has by his words or conduct induced such third persons to believe that such acts and obligations were within the scope of the agent's authority.

EFFECT, ON AGREEMENT, OF MISREPRESENTATION OR FRAUD BY AGENT

Misrepresentations made, or frauds committed, by agents acting in the course of their business for their principals, have the same effect on agreements made by such agents as if such misrepresentations or frauds had been made, or committed, by the principals; but misrepresentations made, or frauds committed, by agents, in matters which do not fall within their authority, do not affect their principals.

Irrevocable Agency

An agency is irrevocable in the following circumstances:

(i) Where agency is coupled with interest for the agent over and above his remuneration.

(ii) Where the agent has incurred personal liability.

(iii) Where the agent has already exercised a part of his authority, so far as acts already done.

Bailment and Pleage

"Bailment","Bailor"and"Bailee"

A "bailment" is the delivery of goods by one person to another for some purpose, upon a contract that they shall, when the purpose is accomplished, be returned or otherwise disposed of according to the directions of the person delivering them. The person delivering the goods is called the "bailor". The person to whom they are delivered is called the "bailee".

Explanation: If a person already in possession of the goods of another contract to hold them as a bailee, he thereby becomes the bailee, and the owner becomes the bailor, of such goods, although they may not have been delivered by way of bailment.

From the definition it is clear that 'bailment' is concerned only with goods.

DELIVERY TO BAILEE HOW MADE

The delivery to the bailee may be made by doing anything which has the effect of putting the goods in the possession of the intended bailee or of any person authorized to hold them on his behalf.

Consideration for Bailment

The detriment suffered by the bailor, in parting with the possession of the goods, is sufficient consideration to support the contract of bailment.

BAILOR'S DUTY TO DISCLOSE FAULTS IN GOODS BAILED

The bailor is bound to disclose to the bailee faults in the goods bailed, of which the bailor is aware, and which materially interfere with the use of them, or expose the bailee to extraordinary risks; and if he does not make such disclosure, he is responsible for damage arising to the bailee directly from such faults.

If the goods are bailed for hire, the bailor is responsible for such damage, whether he was or was not aware of the existence of such faults in the goods bailed.

CARE TO BE TAKEN BY BAILEE

In all cases of bailment the bailee is bound to take as much care of the goods bailed to him as a man of ordinary prudence would, under similar circumstances, take of his own goods of the same bulk, quality and value as the goods bailed.

BAILEE WHEN NOT LIABLE FOR LOSS, ETC., OF THING BAILED

The bailee, in the absence of any special contract, is not responsible for the loss, destruction or deterioration of the thing bailed, if he has taken the amount of care of it described in section 151.

TERMINATION OF BAILMENT BY BAILEE'S ACT INCONSISTENT WITH CONDITIONS

A contract of bailment is voidable at the option of the bailor, if the bailee does any act with regard to the goods bailed, inconsistent with the conditions of the bailment.

LIABILITY OF BAILEE MAKING UNAUTHORISED USE OF GOODS BAILED

If the bailee makes any use of the goods bailed, which is not according to the conditions of the bailment, he is liable to make compensation to the bailor for any damage arising to the goods from or during such use of them.

Pledge

A pledge is a contract whereby a good is deposited with the lender as security for repayment of the loan. The delivery of goods may be made by transferring the goods from the owners godown to a banker s godown or the keys of the owners godown be handed over to the lender. The delivery of documents of title relating to goods also creates a valid pledge. The person delivering the goods as security is called the pledge. The person to whom the goods is delivered is known as pledgee'. The essential features of pledge thus are:

(a) There must be bailment of goods (delivery of goods).

(b) The delivery or goods (bailment) must be by way of security.

(c) The security must be for payment of debt.

Rights and Duties of a Banker as a Pledgee

Rights of a banker

The banker has the following rights as a pledgee:

(a) **Right to retain goods:** The pledgee has the right to retain the goods pledged not only for the payment of debt but- also for the interest and other expenses incurred by him.

(b) **Right to recover extra ordinary expenses:** If the banker (pledgee) has incurred extra ordinary expenses on the loan advanced, he has the right to recover the same from the pledger.

(c) **Default in payment;** If the pledger makes default in making payment, the pledgee can dispose of the pledged goods after giving proper notice to the pledger.

(d) **Right of full value of goods:** The pledgee has the right of full value of pledged goods till such time; the entire debt is not discharged.

Duties of a banker as Pledge

(a) A pledgee is required to take reasonable care of goods pledged with him.

(b) The pledgee or anyone else is not authorized to make use of goods pledged with him.

(c) The pledgee is required to return the goods pledged after the full payment of debt

Duties of a Pledge

1. The pledgee is required to take as much care of the goods pledged to him as a person of ordinary prudence would, under similar circumstances, take of his own goods, of a similar nature.
2. The pledgee must not put the goods to an unauthorised use.
3. The pledgee is bound to return the goods on payment of the debt.

4. Any accruals to the goods pledged belong to the pledgor and should be delivered accordingly. Thus, for example, if the security consists of equity shares and the company issues bonus shares to the equity shareholders, the bonus shares are the property of the pledgor and not the pledge

Advantages of Pledge

To a creditor, pledge is perhaps the most satisfactory mode of creating a charge on securities. It offers the following advantages:

1. The goods are in the possession of the creditor and, therefore, in case the borrower makes a default in payment, they can be dispcsed of after a reasonable notice;
2. Stocks cannot be manipulated as they are under the lender's possession and control;
3. In the case of insolvency of the borrower, creditor can sell the goods and prove for the balance of the debt, if any;
4. There is hardly any possibility of the same goods being charged with some other party if actual possession of the goods is taken by the creditor.

Basic law of Pledge

As a pledge is a specie of bailment, all requirements of bailments are applicable to pledges too:

- Delivery of goods by the pawnor to pawnee
- Delivery must be such as to put the goods effectively in the control of the pawnee, and outside the control of the pawnor
- Agreement that the goods will be returned to pawnor when purpose satisfied
- Goods must be movable property, ascertainable
- Since a pledge is a mere bailment and not a hire, hence, pawnee does not get any right of using the goods

Sales of Goods Act, 1930

In trade and commerce, sales and purchase of goods are very common transactions. These transactions may appear to be very simple but the possibilities of complications is always there. Therefore knowledge of basic principles of sale and purchase is very much essential for all the concerned parties as well as for the entire community.

The Sale of Goods Act contains the basic principles as well as the legal framework of transactions of sale and purchase.

Earlier the Sale of Goods Act was a part of the Indian Contract Act. A separate Act was framed in the year 1930.

Basic Concepts

(1) 'Buyer" means a person, who buys or agrees to buy goods,

(2) "Delivery" means voluntary transfer of possession from one person to another.

(3) "Sale" means transfer of property in goods for a price.

(4) "Hire – Purchase Agreement" means the seller delivers the possession of the goods to the other person and he charges rent for the goods. After receiving the price of the goods, the ownership of the goods is passed on to the purchaser

(5) "Barter exchange" means exchange of goods for goods.

(6) "Bailment" means only the possession is transferred from the bailor to the bailee. Such transactions may be for the purpose of keeping the goods in the safe custody or may be for furnishing security.

Definition of Sale

Section 4 defines 'sale' as , A contract of sale of goods is a contract whereby the seller transfers or agrees to transfer the property in goods to the buyer for a price.

1) A contract of sale is made by an offer to buy or sell goods for a price and the acceptance of such offer.

   The contract may provide for the immediate delivery of the goods or immediate payment of the price or both, or for the delivery or payment by installments, or that the delivery or payment or both shall be postponed.

2) Subject to the provisions of any law for the time being in force, a contract of sale may be made in writing or by word of mouth, or partly in writing and partly by word of mouth or may be implied from the conduct of the parties.

Essential of a Contract of Sale

1) There must be at least two parties as a person cannot sale goods to himself. However there may be a contract of sale between one part-owner and another.

2) There must be a transfer or agreement to transfer the ownership of goods from one person to another. Mere transfer of possession is not sale.

(3) The subject matter of sale must be 'goods' and movable. The transfer of immovable property is not governed by Sale of Goods Act, 1930.

(4) The consideration for sale is called price which should be stated in terms of 'money'. Exchange of 'goods' for 'goods' is barter and not sale. However price may be paid partly in terms of money and partly in kind.

(5) All essential elements of a valid contract must be present in a contract of sale.

(6) A contract of sale may be absolute or conditional.

Difference between Sale and Agreement to sale

Sale	Agreement to sale
1. Sale is an executed contract. Property in the goods passes from seller to buyer.	1. It is an executory contract. Transfer of property in goods is to take place at a future date subject to fulfillment of certain conditions.
2. If goods are destroyed, the loss will be borne by the buyer even though they may be in possession of the seller.	2. The loss will be borne by the seller even though the goods may be in possession of the buyer.
3. A sale gives right to the buyer to enjoy the goods against the whole world including the seller.	3. The buyer only can sue the seller for damages.
4. In case of sale, the buyer can be sued for price of goods.	4. The buyer can be used only for damages.
5. If buyer becomes insolvent before payment is made, the seller has to deliver the goods to the official receiver unless he has lien on them.	5. Seller may refuse to deliver the goods to the official receiver.
6. If the seller becomes insolvent after payment of price, the buyer can claim the goods from the official receiver.	6. The buyer cannot claim the goods. He can only claim ratable dividend for the amount paid by him.
7. The seller cannot resale the goods. In this case, if the subsequent buyer takes in good faith and for consideration, he gets a good title.	7. The original buyer may only sue the seller for damages.

Classification of Goods

The goods which form the subject of a contract of sale may be either existing goods, owned or possessed by the seller, or future goods Sec 6(1) or contingent goods [Sec 6(2)].

1. Existing goods are owned by the seller at the time of sale. They are of the following types:

   (i) Specific goods –These are identified and agreed upon at the time of sale.

   (ii) Ascertained goods- These become ascertained after the contract is made.

   (iii) Generic goods-These are not ascertained at the time of contract and is defined only by description.

2. Future goods are not owned by the seller at the time of contract but manufactured or acquired by him subsequent to formation of contract. Where by a contract of sale the seller purports to effect a present sale of future goods , the contract operates as an agreement to sale.

3. Contingent goods: These are goods the acquisition of which by seller depends upon a contingency which may or may not happen.

Effect of Destruction of Goods [Sec 7]

Goods perishing before making of contract (Sec 7) – Where there is a contract for the sale of specific goods, the contract is void if the goods without the knowledge of the seller have, at the time when the contract was made, perished or become so damaged as no longer to answer to their description in the contract.

Goods perishing before sale but after agreement to sell (Sec 8) – Where there is an agreement to sell specific goods, and subsequently the goods without any fault on the part of the seller or buyer perish or become so damaged as no longer to answer to their description in the agreement before the risk passes to the buyer, the agreement is thereby avoided.

Sec (7 & 8) are applicable only in case of specific goods and not uncertained/generic goods.

Price

(Secs. 9 & 10) In a contract of sale 'price' to the consideration for sale of goods and is expressed in terms of money. It forms essential part of contract.

Ascertainment of Price

(1) The price in a contract of sale may be fixed by the contract or may be left to be fixed in manner thereby agreed or may be determined by the course of dealing between the parties.

(2) Where the price is not determined in accordance with the foregoing provisions, the buyer shall pay the seller a reasonable price. What is a reasonable price is a question of fact dependent on the circumstances of each particular case.

Document of title of goods

It symbolizes the goods and confers a right to the owner to take possession of the same or further transfer the right to some other person. A delivery order , railway receipt, bill of lading are some of the examples of document of title to goods.

Agreement to sell at valuation

(1) Where there is an agreement to sell goods on the terms that the price is to be fixed by the valuation of a third party and such third party cannot or does not make such valuation, the agreement is

thereby avoided: Provided that, if the goods or any part thereof have been delivered to, and appropriated by, the buyer, he shall pay a reasonable price therefor.

(2) Where such third party is prevented from making the valuation by the fault of the seller or buyer, the party not in fault may maintain a suit for damages against the party in fault.

Stipulations as to time (Sec 11)

Unless a different intention appears from the terms of the contract, stipulations as to time of payment are not deemed to be of the essence of a contract of sale. Whether any other stipulation as to time is of the essence of the contract or not depends on the terms of the contract.

Condition and Warranty

Definitions

(1) A stipulation in a contract of sale with reference to goods which are the subject thereof may be a condition or a warranty.

(2) As per Sec 12(2) of the sale of Goods Act, a condition is a stipulation essential to the main purpose of the contract, the breach of which gives rise to right to treat the contract as repudiated.

(3) As per Sec 12(3) of the sale of Goods Act, a warranty is a stipulation collateral to the main purpose of the contract, the breach of which gives rise to a claim for damages but not to a right to reject the goods and treat the contract as repudiated.

(4) Whether a stipulation in a contract of sale is condition or a warranty depends in each case on the construction of the contract, a stipulation may be a condition though called warranty in a contract. [Sec 12(4)]

When condition to be treated as warranty

(1) Where a contract of sale is subject to any condition to the fulfilled by the seller, the buyer may way give the condition or elect to treat the breach of the condition as a breach of warranty and not as a ground for relating the contract as repudiated.

(2) Where a contract of sale is not severable and the buyer has accepted the goods or part thereof, the breach of any condition to be fulfilled by the seller can only be treated as a breach of warranty and not as a ground for rejecting the goods and treating the contract as repudiated, unless there is a term of the contract, express or implied, to that effect.

(3) Nothing in this section shall affect the case of any condition or warraty fulfill ment of which is excused by law by reason of impossibility of otherwise.

Conditions and Warranties may be either expressed or implied

When terms of contract expressly provide for them, they are known as express conditions or warranties.

Implied conditions and warranties are incorporated in every contract of sale unless the circumstances show a different intention.

Implied conditions are of the following types :

(i) Condition as to title [Sec 14(a)]

In a contract of sale, unless the circumstances of the contract are such as to show a different intention, there is:

(a) An implied condition on the part of the seller that, in the case of a sale, he has a right to sell the goods and that, in the case of an agreement to sell, he will have a right to sell the goods at the time when the property is to pass.

(b) An implied warranty that the buyer shall have and enjoy quiet possession of the goods.

(c) An implied warranty that the goods shall be free from any charge orencumbrance in favour of any third party not declared or known to the buyer before or at the time when the contract is made.

(ii) Sale by description (Sec 15)

Where there is a contract for the sale of goods by description, there is an implied condition that the goods shall correspond with the description, and, if the sale is by sample as well as by description, it is not sufficient that the bulk of the goods corresponds with the sample if the goods do not also correspond with the description.

(iii) Condition as to quality or fitness (Sec 16)

As per Sec 16 of the Sale of Goods Act Subject to the provisions of this Act and of any other law for the time being in force, there is no implied warranty or condition as to the quality or fitness for any particular purpose of goods supplied under a contract of sale, excepts as follows:-

(1) Where the buyer, expressly or by implication, makes known to the seller the particular purpose for which the goods are required, so as to show that the buyer relies on the seller's skill or judgement, and the goods are of a description which it is in the course of the seller's business to supply (whether he is the manufacturer or producer or not), there is an implied condition that the goods shall be reasonably fit for such purpose:

Provided that, in the case of a contract for the sale of a specified article under its patent or other trade name, there is no implied conditions to its fitness for any particular purpose.

(2) Where goods are bought by description from a seller who deals in goods of that description (whether he is the manufacturer or producer or not), there is an implied condition that the goods shall be of merchantable quality. Provided that, if the buyer has examined the goods, there shall be no implied conditions as regards defects which such examination ought to have revealed.

(3) An implied warranty or condition as to quality or fitness for a particular purpose may be annexed by the usage of trade.

(4) An express warranty or conditions does not negative a warranty or condition implied by this Act unless inconsistent therewith.

(iv) Sale by sample (Sec 17)

(1) A contract of sale is a contract for sale by sample where there is a term in the contract, express or implied, to that effect.

(2) In the case of a contract for sale by sample there is an implied condition:

(a) That the bulk shall correspond with the sample in quality.

(b) That they shall have a reasonable opportunity of comparing the bulk with the sample.

(c) That the goods shall be free from any defect, rendering them un-merchantable, which would not be apparent on reasonable examination of the goods.

Implied warranties are of following types:

(a) Warranty of quiet possession [Sec.14(b)]

If the buyer in any way is disturbed from enjoying the quiet possession of goods purchased because of seller's defective title, the buyer can claim damages from seller.

(b) Warranty of freedom from encumbrances[Sec.14(c)]

The buyer is also entitled to additional warranty that the goods are free from any charge or right of any third party, not declared or known to the buyer.

Goods must be ascertained

Where there is a contract for the sale of unascertained goods, no property in the goods is transferred to the buyer unless and until the goods are sanctioned.

Doctrine of Caveat Emptor-Caveat Emptor means 'let buyer be aware'. It is a fundamental principle of law of sale of goods and implies that the seller is under no obligation to point out the defects in his own goods. The doctrine is however subject to following exceptions:

(i) In case of implied conditions and warranties.

(ii) When the buyer makes it known to seller the purpose and depends on his expertise.

(iii) When the seller commits fraud.

(iv) When there is a usage of trade.

Passing of the Property from the Seller to the Buyer

A Sale is defined as transfer of ownership of the goods from the seller to the buyer for a price .Therefore what is important in a transaction of sale is the transfer of the ownership. It is essential to determine the exact point of time at which the ownership of the goods is transferred in favour of the buyer. Sections 18 to 25 of the Sale of Goods Act, determine when the property passes from the seller to the buyer.

(i) Goods must be ascertained

Where there is a contract for sale of unascertained goods, the property in the goods does not pass to the buyer till the goods are ascertained.

(ii) Intention of the parties for such transfer

(1) Where there is a contract for the sale of specific or ascertained goods the property in them is transferred to the buyer at such time as the parties to the contract intend it to be transferred.

(2) For the purpose of ascertaining the intention of the parties regard shall be had to the terms of the contract, the conduct of the parties and the circumstances of the case.

Specific goods

(i) Specific goods in a deliverable state

Where there is an unconditional contract for the sale of specific goods in a deliverable state, the property in the goods passes to the buyer when the contract is made, and it is immaterial whether the time of payment of the price or the time of delivery of the goods, or both, is postponed.

(ii) Specific goods to be put into a deliverable state

Where there is a contract for the sale of specific goods and the seller is bound to do something to the goods for the purpose of putting them into a deliverable state, the property does not pass until such thing is done and the buyer has notice thereof.

(iii) Specific goods in a deliverable state

When the seller has to do anything thereto in order to ascertain price Where there is a contract for the sale of specific goods in a deliverable state, but the seller is bound to weigh, measure, test or do some other act or thing with reference to the goods for the purpose of ascertaining the price, the property does not pass until such act or thing is done and the buyer has notice thereof.

Unascertained goods

(1) Where there is a contract for the sale of unascertained or future goods by de scription and goods of that description and in a deliverable state are uncondition ally appropriated to the contract, either by the seller with the assent of the buyer or by the buyer with the assent of the seller, the property in the goods thereupon passes to the buyer. Such assent may be expressed or implied, and may be given either before or after the appropriation is made.

(2) Delivery to carrier-Where, in pursuance of the contract, the seller delivers the goods.

Goods on approval or 'on sale or return'

When goods are delivered to the buyer on approval or on sale or return or other similar terms, the property therein passes to the buyer:

(a) When he signifies his approval or acceptance to the seller to does not other actadopting the transaction.

(b) If he does not signify his approval or acceptance to the seller but retains the gods without giving notice of rejection, then, if a time has been fixed for the return of the goods, on the expiration of such time, and, if not time has been fixed, on the expiration of a reasonable time.

Reservation of right of disposal

(1) Where there is a contract for the sale of specific goods or where goods are subsequently appropriated to the contract, the seller may, by the terms of the contract or appropriation, reserve the right of disposal of the goods until certain conditions are fulfilled. In such case, notwithstanding the delivery of the goods to a buyer, or to a carrier or other bailee for the purpose of transmission to the buyer,

the property in the goods does not pass to the buyer until the conditions imposed by the seller are fulfilled.

(2) Where goods are shipped or delivered to a railway administration for carriage by railway and by the bill of landing or railway receipt, as the case may be, the goods are deliverable to the order of the seller or his agent, the seller is prima facie deemed to reserve the right of disposal.

(3) Where the seller of goods draws on the buyer for the price and transmits to the buyer the bill of exchange together with the bill of lading or, as the may be, the railway receipt, to secure acceptance to payment of the bill of exchange, the buyer is bound to return the bill of lading or the railway receipt if he does not honour the bill of exchange, and, if he wrongfully retains the bill of lading or the railway receipt, the property in the goods does not pass to him.

Explanation: In this section, the expression "railway" and "railway administration" shall have the meanings respectively assigned to them under the Indian Railways Act, 1890.

Risk prima facie passes with property

Unless otherwise agreed, the goods remain at the seller's risk until the property therein is transferred to the buyer, but when the property therein is transferred to the buyer, the goods are at the buyer's risk whether delivery has been made or not.

Sale by person not the owner

Where goods are sold by a person who is not the owner thereof and who does not sell them under the authority or with the consent of the owner, the buyer acquires no better title to the goods than the seller had, unless the owner of the goods is by conduct precluded from denying the seller's authority to sell.

However, this is subject to certain exceptions as follows:

(i) Sale by mercantile agent:

Where a mercantile agent is, with the consent of the owner, in possession of the goods or of a document of title to the goods, any sale made by him, when acting in the ordinary course of business of a mercantile agent, shall be as valid as if he were expressly authroised by the owner of the goods to make the same, provided that the buyer act is good faith and has not at the time of the contract of sale notice that the seller has not authority to sell.

(ii) Sale by one of joint owners:

If one of several joint owners of goods has the sole possession of them by permission of the co-owners, the property in the goods is transferred to any person who buys them of such joint owner in good faith and has not at the time of the contract of sale notice that the seller has not authority to sell.

(iii) Sale by person in possession under voidable contract:

When the seller of goods has obtained possession thereof under a contract voidable under Section 19 or Section 19A of the Indian Contract Act, 1872, but the contract has not rescinded at the time of the sale, the buyer acquires a good title to the goods, provided he buys them in good faith and without notice of the seller's defect of title.

(iv) Seller or buyer in possession after sale:

(a) Where a person, having sold goods, continues or is in possession of the goods or of the documents of title to the goods, the delivery or transfer by that person or by a mercantile agent acting for him of the gods or documents of title under any sale, pledge of other disposition thereof to any person receiving the same in good faith and without notice of the previous sale shall have the same effect as if the person making the delivery to transfer were expressly authorised by the owner of the gods to make the same.

(b) Where a person, having bought or agreed to buy goods, obtains with the con sent of the seller, possession of the goods or the documents of title to the goods, the delivery or transfer by that person or by a mercantile agent acting for him, of the goods or documents of tile under any sale, pledge or other disposition thereof to any person receiving the same in good faith and without notice of any lien or other right of the original seller in respect of the gods shall have effect as if such lien or right did not exist.

(v) Sale by estoppel:

Where the owner by his conduct or omission, leads the buyer to believe that the seller has authority to sell, he is estopped from denying the fact afterwards. The buyer thus gets a better title than the seller.

For example A tells B in presence of C that A is agent of C. C maintains silence instead of denying it. Later if A sells C's goods to B , C cannot dispute B's title to the goods.

(vi) Sale by an unpaid seller after exercising his right of lien or stoppage in transit.

(vii) Exceptions in other Acts:

(a) Sale by Official Receiver or Liquidator.

(b) Sale by a pawnee or pledgee in certain cases.

(c) Sale by finder of lost goods in certain cases.

Performance of the Contract of Sale

Performance of a Contract of sale means as regards the Seller, delivery of goods to the buyer. From buyer's side the performance means the acceptance of the delivery of goods and payment for them as per the terms and conditions of sale.

Payment and delivery

Unless otherwise agreed, delivery of the goods and payment of the price are concurrent conditions, that is to say, the seller shall be ready and willing to give possession of the goods to the buyer in exchange for the price, and the buyer shall be ready and willing to pay the price in exchange for possession of the goods.

Delivery

As per the Sale of Goods Act, Delivery is defined as the voluntary transfer of possession from one person to another. Delivery of goods sold may be made by doing anything which the parties agree shall be treated as delivery or which has the effect of putting the goods in the possession of the buyer or of any person authorised to hold them on his behalf.

Rules as to delivery

(1) Delivery of goods and payment of price are concurrent conditions unless otherwise agreed upon.

(2) Effect of part delivery

A delivery of part of goods, in progress of the delivery of the whole has the same effect, for the purpose of passing the property in such goods, as a delivery of the whole, but a delivery of part of the goods, with an intention of severing it from the whole, does not operate as a delivery of the remainder.

(3) Buyer to apply for delivery

Apart from any express contract, the seller of goods in not bound to deliver them until the buyer applies for delivery.

(4) Place of delivery

Whether it is for the buyer to take possession of the goods or for the seller to send them to the buyer is a question depending in each case on the contract, express or implied, between the parties. Apart from any such contract, goods sold are to be delivered at the place at which they are the time of the sale, and goods agreed to be sold are to be delivered at the place at which they are at the time of the agreement to sell, if not then in existence, at the place at which they are manufactured or produced.

(5) Time of delivery

Where under the contract of sale the seller is bound to send the goods to the buyer, but no time for sending them is fixed, the seller is bound to send them within a reasonable time.

Demand or tender of delivery may be treated as ineffectual unless made at a reasonable hour. What is a reasonable hour is a question of fact.

(6) Goods in possession of a third person

Where the goods at the time of sale are in the possession of a third person, there is no delivery by seller to buyer unless and until such third person acknowledges to the buyer that he holds the goods on his behalf.

(7) Cost of delivery

Unless otherwise agreed, the expense of and incidental to putting the goods into a deliverable state shall be borne by the seller.

(8) Mode of delivery

Delivery of goods may be actual, symbolic or constructive.

(9) Delivery of wrong quality

(1) Where the seller delivers to the buyer a quantity of good less than he contracted to sell, the buyer may reject them, but if the buyer accepts the goods so deliv ered he shall pay for them at the contract rate.

(2) Where the seller delivers to the buyer a quantity of goods larger than he contracted to sell the buyer may accept the goods included in the contact and reject the rest, or he may reject the whole. If the buyer accepts the whole of the goods so delivered, he shall pay for them at the contract rate.

(3) Where the seller delivers to the buyer the gods he contract to sell mixed with goods of a different description not included in the contract, the buyer may accept the goods which are in accordance with the contract and reject the rest, or may reject the whole.

(4) The provisions of this section are subject to any usage of trade, special agreement or course of dealing between the parties.

(10) Installment delivery

(1) Unless otherwise agreed, the buyer of goods is not bound to accept delivery thereof by installments.

(2) Where there is a contract for the sale of goods to be delivered by stated installments which are to be separately paid for, and the seller makes no delivery or defective delivery in respect of one or more installments, or the buyer neglects or refuses to take delivery of or pay for one or more installments, it is a question in each case depending on the terms of the contract and the circumstances of the case, whether the breach of contract is a repudiation of the whole contract, or whether it is a sever able breach giving rise to a claim for compensation, but not a right to treat the whole contract as repudiated.

(11) Delivery to carrier or wharfinger

(1) Where, in pursuance of a contract of sale, the seller is authorised or required to send the goods to he buyer, delivery of the goods to a carrier, whether named by the buyer or not, for the purpose of transmission to the buyer, or delivery of the goods to a wharfinger for safe custody, is prima facie deemed to be a delivery of the goods to the buyer.

(2) Unless otherwise authorised by the buyer, the seller shall makes such contract with the carrier or wharfinger on behalf of the buyer as may be reasonable having regard to the nature of the goods and the other circumstances of the case. If the seller omits so to do, and the goods are lost or damaged in course of transit or whilst in the custody of the wharfinger, the buyer made decline to treat the delivery to the carrier or wharfinger as a delivery to himself, or may hold the seller responsible in damages.

(3) Unless otherwise agreed, where goods are sent by the seller to the buyer by a route in-volving sea transit, in circumstances in which it is usual to insure, the seller shall give such notice to the buyer as may enable him to insure them during their sea transit and if the seller fails so to do, the goods shall be deemed to be at his risk during such sea transit.

(12) Risk where goods are delivered at distant place

Where the seller of goods agrees to deliver them at his own risk at place other than that where they are when sold, the buyer shall, nevertheless, unless otherwise agreed, take any risk of deterioration in the goods necessarily incident to the course of transit.

(13) Buyer's right of examination the goods

(1) Where goods are delivered to the buyer which he has not previously examined, he is not deemed to have accepted them unless and until he has a reasonable opportunity of examining them for the purpose of ascertaining whether they are in conformity with the contract.

(2) Unless otherwise agreed, when the seller tenders delivery of goods to the buyer, he is bound, on request, on request, to afford the buyer a reasonable opportunity of examining the goods for the purpose of ascertaining whether they are in conformity with the contract.

(14) Buyer not bound to return rejected goods

Unless otherwise agreed, where goods are delivered to the buyer and he refuses to accept them, having the right so to do, he is not bound to return them to the seller, but it is sufficient it he intimates to the seller that he refuses to accept them.

(15) Liability of buyer for neglecting or refusing delivery of goods

When the seller is ready and willing to deliver the goods and requests the buyer to take delivery, and the buyer does not within a reasonable time after such request take delivery of the goods, he is liable to the seller for any loss occasioned by his neglect or refusal to take delivery and also for a reasonable charge for the care and custody of the goods.

Nothing in this section shall affect the rights of the seller where the neglect or refusal of the buyer to take delivery amounts to a repudiation of the contract :

Delivery are of following types:

Actual- In this case goods are handed over by the seller to the buyer or his authorized agent.

Symbolic- When goods are bulky and actual delivery is not possible, the delivery may be symbolic ,e.g. handing over the keys of the godown.

Constructive - This happens in the ways mentioned below:

(i) When seller holding the possession of goods, agrees to hold them on behalf of the buyer.

(ii) When buyer holding the possession of goods, with seller's consent, holds them as owner.

(iii) When a third person holding the possession of goods on behalf of seller, acknowledges to hold them on behalf buyer.

Rights of an Unpaid Seller

In a transaction of sale it is not possible to avoid credit sales. In credit sales there is a risk of a debtor not paying the price of the goods even after the credit period is over. The seller of the goods therefore must possess some rights which he can use to secure payment of the price. If the recovery of the price is not possible due to the reason of bankruptcy of the buyer, he must have some other remedies. The Sale of Goods Act has made elaborate provisions regarding the rights of an unpaid seller.

Unpaid Seller

(1) The seller of goods is an "unpaid seller":

(a) When the whole of the price has not been paid or tendered.

(b) When a bill of exchange or other negotiable instrument has been received as conditional payment and the conditions on which it was received has not been fulfilled by reason of the dishonour of the instrument or otherwise.

(2) The term "seller" includes any person who is in the position of a seller, as, for instance, an agent of the seller to whom the bill of lading has been endorsed, or a consignor or agent who has himself paid, or is directly responsible for, the price.

Intellectual Property Law

Man is a wonderful being with great imagination, marvelous creation and highly skillful. In some of the situations man is beyond the nature. With the emerging and fast growing business and market environments, computers and information technology, man's contributions and creations are wonderful. These creations are to be protected. In order to protect inventions and creations a separate legislation has been enacted, which is known as Intellectual Property Legislation – Patents Act 1970.

Intellectual Property Legislation – Patents Act 1970

Intellectual Property means "a property created by human brain or human intellect." The subject matter of intellectual property (I.P) is very wide which includes literary and other works like inventions, designs, trade marks, computer programs etc. Earlier I.P were collectively known as "Industrial property".

Scope of Intellectual Property Rights

The convention establishing World Intellectual Property Organization (WIPO) has given a wider definition of IPRs. According to this definition the IPRs shall include the rights relating to:

(i) Literary, artistic and scientific work;

(ii) Performances of performing artists, phonograms and broadcasts;

(iii) Inventions in all fields of human endeavour;

(iv) Scientific discoveries;

(v) Industrial designs;

(vi) Trade marks, service marks and commercial names and designations;

(vii) Protection against unfair competition and; all other rights resulting from intellectual activity in the industrial, scientific, literacy or artistic fields.

Kinds of Intellectual Property

Industrial Property and Intellectual Property

(1) Patents, designs and trademarks are considered as "Industrial Property"

(2) Copyright and Confidential information are considered as "Intellectual Property"

According to World Intellectual Property Organisation (WIPO) intellectual property includes rights relating to:

(1) Industrial designs

(2) Literary, artistic and Scientific works

(3) Protection against unfair competition

(4) Scientific discoveries

(5) Performances of artists and programmes etc.

The concept of 'intellectual property' started gaining its importance since 1992 when the new industrial policies were reformed which gave scope for liberalization and globalisation of trade.

GATT, WTO and TRIPS " GATT " (General Agreement on Trade and Tariff) was established in 1947, with a 22 member state. Since 1947-1993,8 rounds of discussion took place between the member states to formulate rules and regulations relating to international trade. The object of GATT was to reduce the interference of the governments throughout the globe and to develop trade and commerce, especially to develop underdeveloped countries and to protect their rights to do their business without any condition by the developed nations.

For the first time "Intellectual Property" rights were included in the Uruguay Round in 1986.

The last and eight URUGUAY Round held in 1993. During this round the most conflicted "DUNKEL DRAFT" was born.

Sir Arthur Dunkel was the Director General of GATT, who retired on 20-6-1993. The Uruguay Rounds, which was ended on 15-12-93 incorporated the Dunkel Draft. Where three countries signed, including India. P.V Narasimha Rao's government, signed Dunkel Draft along with other countries for which the opposition parties and other persons opposed it. This round was recognized as the biggest negotiation mandate on trade ever agreed. Later GATT was changed into WTO (World Trade Organisations) in 1995. WTO was established in Geneva on a permanent basis.

In connection with intellectual property, the specialized council for Trade Related Aspects of Intellectual Property Rights (TRIPS) came into existence on a permanent basis. w.e.f. form 1.1.95 "TRIP AGREEMENT' has become very popular in relation to the Intellectual property rights throughout the world.

The council of TRIP is an independent body within the WTO. The council implements and monitors the progress of the TRIP's agreement by co-operating with WTO, World Intellectual property organization (WIPO), UNESCO, as well as other International organizations.

The TRIP contains all necessary legal provisions relationed to copy rights, trade marks, Industrial designs, patents, protection of un-disclosed information etc.

The Patent Act, 1970

Meaning of Patent: A patent generally speaking, is a grant from government, which confers on the grantee, for a limited period of time, the exclusive privilege of making, selling and using the invention for which a patent has been granted and also of authorizing others to do so.

Thus "Creative work" based on individual initiative is granted the 'Status of Property' which can be hired, licensed, purchased or sold. Thus, Patent Acts encourages inventions and reduces the risk of pirating or copying.

History of Patent Law

Regarding the original development of all intellectual property rights including patent, England has been considered as an important place in the world history. It has set the base for patent rights internationally. Patents played an important role in the development of Industries in the western countries.

In India, the British Rulers enacted the Patents and Designs Act, 1911 after several amendments since 1856, the first Patent Act in India was passed which gave exclusive rights to the patentees for a period of 14 years. There was no further development of Patent Laws in India as we were under the clutches of British Rule. Then, after independence, the parliament appointed two expert committees headed by Justice Bakshi Teak Chand in 1950 and Justice Raja Gopal Iyangar in 1959. These committees found that the foreign companies misused the Patent Laws of India. This led to a debate in Parliament and finally the bill was passed on 19th Sept 1970 and was notified as the Patent Act 1970. Thereafter the Patent and Design Act 1911 was split into two. Namely

(1) The Design Act 1911 and (2) The Patent Act, 1970

The Patent Act, 1970 has incorporated several new provisions preventing the misuse of patents, which was further amended in 1999 and in 2002.

India is a member State of World Intellectual Property Organisation (WIPO) an International Organisation, responsible for the promotion, protection of Intellectual property throughout the world.

Objective of the Patent Act

The object of Patent Act is to encourage new technology, scientific inventions and research;

Industrial progress;

Grant of right to own,

Use or sell the method or the product patented for a limited period of time.

Definitions: See 2 (1) of the Act defines the various terms used in the Act.

1. "Appellate Board" means the Appellate Board referred to in section 116. [Section 2(1) (a)]
2. "Assignee" includes an assignee of the assignee and the legal representative of a deceased assignee and references to the assignee of any person include references to the assignee of the legal representative or assignee of that person. [Section 2(1) (ab)]
3. "Capable of Industrial application" in relation to an invention, means that the invention is capable of being made or used in an industry. [Section 2(1) (ac)]
4. "Controller" means the Controller General of Patents, Designs and Trade Marks referred to in section 73. [Section 2(1) (b)]
5. "Convention Application" means an application for a patent made by virtue of section 135. [Section 2(1) (c)]
6. "Convention Country" means a country or a country which is member of a group of countries or a union of counties or an Inter-Government organization notified as such under sub-section (1) if section 133. [Section 2(1) (d)]
7. "Exclusive license" means a licence from a patentee which confers on the licensee, or on the license and persons authorized by him, to the exclusion of all other persons (including the patentee), any right in respect of the patented invention, and exclusive license shall be construed accordingly. [Section 2(1) (f)]
8. "Food" means any article of nourishment and includes any substance intended for the use of babies, invalids or convalescents as an article of food or drink. [Section 2(1) (g)]

9. "Government undertaking" means any industrial undertaking carried on-

   (i) By a department of the Government, or

   (ii) By a corporation established by a Central, Provincial or State Act, which is owned or controlled by the Government, or

   (iii) By a Government company as defined in section 617 of the Companies Act, 1956 and includes the Council of Scientific and Industrial Research and any other institution which is financed wholly or for the major part by the said Council. [Section 2(1) (h)]

10. "Medicine or Drug" includes-

    (i) all medicines for internal or external use of human beings or animals;

    (ii) all substances intended to be used for or in the diagnosis, treatment mitigation or prevention of diseases in human beings or animals;

    (iii) all substances intended to be used for or in the maintenance of public health, or the prevention or control of any epidemic disease among human beings or animals;

    (iv) insecticides, germicides, fungicides, weedicides and all other substances intended to be used for the protection or preservation of plants;

    (v) all chemical substances which are ordinarily used as intermediates in the preparation or manufacture of any of the medicines or substances above referred to. [Section 2(1) (l)]

11. "Patents" means a patent granted under this Act and includes for the purposes of specified sections and chapters of this Act, a patent granted and the Indian Patents and Designs Act 1911. [Section 2(1) (m)]

    Generally speaking 'Patent' is a grant from the government, conferring on the granter, for a limited period of time, the exclusive privilege of making, selling and using the invention for which a patent has been granted and also of authorizing others to do so.

    Thus, 'creative work' based on private initiative is granted the status of 'property' which can be sold, hired, licensed or purchased. Thus, patent protection encourages invention by reducing the risk of pirating or copying.

12. "Patent Agent" means a person for the time being registered under this Act as a patent agent. [Section 2(1) (n)]

13. "Patented Article" and "Patented Process" means respectively an article or process in respect of which a patent is in force. [Section 2(1) (o)]

14. "Patentee" means the person for the time being entered on the register as the grantee or proprietor of the patent. [Section 2(1) (p)]

15. "Patent of addition" means a patent granted in accordance with section 54 [section 2(1) (q)]

16. "Person interested" includes a person engaged in, or in promoting, research in the same field as that to which the invention relates. [Section 2(1) (t)]

17. "True and First Inventor" does not include either the first importer of an invention into India, or a person to whom an invention is first communicated from outside India. [Section 2(1) (y)]

18. "Invention" means a new product or process involving an inventive step and capable of industrial application. [Section (1) (j)]

Meaning of Inventions

Patent is granted to inventions. The invention should satisfy the following three tests to get patent.

1. Test of Novelty – The subject matter should be new.
2. Test of Utility – It should be useful.
3. Test of Durability – The subject matter should be capable of being marketed for communication purpose.

What are not inventions: As per section 3 (as amended in 2002), the following are not inventions within the meaning of this Act-

(a) an invention which is frivolous or which claims anything obviously contrary to well established natural laws;

(b) an invention the primary or intended use or commercial exploitation of which could be contrary to public order or morality or which causes serious prejudice to human, animal or plant life or health or to the environment;

(c) the mere discovery of a scientific principle or the formulation of an abstract; theory or discovery of any living thing or non-living substance occurring in nature;

(d) the mere discovery of any new property or new use for a known substance or of the mere use of known process, machine or apparatus unless such known process results in a new product or employs at least one new reactant;

(e) a substance obtained by a mere admixture resulting only in the aggregation of the properties of the components thereof or a process for producing such substance.

(f) the mere arrangement or re-arrangement or duplication of known devices each functioning independently on one another in a known way;

(g) a method of agriculture or horticulture;

(h) any process for the medicinal, surgical, curative, prophylactic diagnostic, therapeutic or other treatment of human beings or any process for a similar treatment of animals to render them free of disease or to increase their economic value or that of their products.

i) plants and animals in whole or any part thereof other than micro-organisms but including seeds, varieties and species and essentially biological processes for production or propagation of plants and animals;

j) a mathematical or business method or a computer program per se or algorithms;

k) a literary, dramatic, musical or artistic work or any other aesthetic creation whatsoever including cinematographic works and television production;

l) a mere scheme or rule or method of performing mental act or method of playing game;

m) a presentation of information;

(n) topography of integrated circuits;

(o) an invention which, in effect, is traditional knowledge or which is an aggregation or duplication of known properties of traditionally known component or components.

Kinds of Patents

Three kinds of patents are granted under different provisions of the Act. These are:

1. **Ordinary Patent:** Is a "Patent" normally obtained by filing application under Sec. 6(1) of the Patent Act 1970.
2. **Patent of Addition:** It is a patent for improvement in or modification of an invention for which a patent application has already been made or it has been granted

   Sec. 54 to 56 of this Act containing provisions regarding application, sealing of patent, renewal fees, terms of patent and validity period of patent of addition.

   A patent of addition remains in force only as long as the patent for the original invention remains in force.
3. **A patent granted in respect of a convention:** Application filed u/s 135 of the Act under reciprocity arrangements the convention application has to be made within one year from the date of the first application made in a convention country in respect of that invention.

Administration of Patent System in India

Under the Patents Act – 1970 – The Head Office is located at Calcutta and has branches at Delhi, Mumbai, and Chennai having jurisdiction over the North, West and South Zones respectively.

Jurisdiction for filing a patent application is decided depending upon where the applicant for patent resides or his place of business or domicile.

Who is a Patentee?

A patentee is a person who enjoys the right of "Patent".

When a person invents and applies for patent and fulfills all the conditions, he gets a patent from the government. According to Sec. 48 of Patent Act 1970, a patentee or his licensee enjoys the following rights.

A patentee shall have exclusive right by himself, his agent or licensee to-

(a) make, use, exercise, sell or distribute the patented article or substance and

(b) use or exercise the patented method or processes in India.

Exclusive Marketing Rights

Under WTO agreement India had to provide "Product Patent" to MNCs for inventions relating to pharmaceutical and agro-chemical products from 1-1-95 and the grant of such patents provided exclusive Marketing Rights for 5 years after attaining marketing approval or grant of patent which ever is earlier.

This applies to inventions for which patent applications are filed on or after 1-1-95 in India or abroad. Thus, "Product Patent" and Exclusive marketing Rights are not available for products developed and patented abroad before 1-1-95.

In order to meet these obligations under Article 70(8) and (a) of TRIP agreement of WTO, the Patent Amendment Act, 1999 in a new chapter IV A on exclusive Marketing Right and the provisions are contained in Sec. 24A to 24E. w.e.f. 1-1-95.

1. Applications for grant of Exclusive Rights (Sec. 24A)
2. Grant of Exclusive Rights (Sec. 24B)
3. Compulsory Licenses (Sec. 24C)
4. Special Provision under public Invent (24D)
5. Suits relating to infringements (24E)
6. Central Govt. and its officers not to be liable (24F)

Procedure for grant of patent

Following are the steps for grant of a patent under this Act:

(1) Filing an application for a patent.

(2) Examination of application.

(3) Acceptance of the application and advertisement of such acceptance in the official gazettee.

(4) Over coming opposition, if any to the grant of patent and

(5) Grant and sealing of patents

Filing an application for a patent

Any person interested in obtaining a patent has to make an application.

(1) An application for a patent for an invention may be made,

(a) by any person who claims to be the true and first inventor of the invention.

(b) by any person being the assignee of the person claiming to be the true and first inventor in respect of the right to make such an application.

(c) by the legal representatives of the deceased person who immediately before his death was entitled to make such an application.

(2) An application under Sub Sec. (1) may be made by any of the person referred to there in either alone or jointly with any other person (Sec. 6)

(a) Applicant need not be citizen of India, it can be made by any person claming to be the true of first inventor of the invention.

(b) A joint stock company or a partnership firm or a corporation can apply for a patent only as an assignee of the inventor. This so because, such bodies cannot invent anything and cannot, therefore, be called "inventors".

(c) Government Servants are at liberty to apply for grant of patent directly to patent office subject to any special conditions of service applicable to employees of any particular department.

(d) Defence Employees are not eligible to apply for patents except in the manners laid down in special regulations applicable to them.

(e) Railway and Research Establishment employees are not eligible to apply for patents or permit other person to apply for patent except with the permission of the govt. and in accordance with the regulations.

(3) U/S 54(1) an application for a patent of addition may be made only by the applicant for the original patent to which it is an addition, if the application for the original patent is pending or by the registered Proprietor of such original patent, if it has been granted.

(4) A convention application may be made by any person who has made an application for a patent in respect of that invention in a convention country or by his assignee or his legal representative.

Application For Patents (Sec. 7)

(1) Every application for a patent shall be for one invention only and shall be made in the prescribed form and filed in the patent office.

(1A) Every international application under the Patent Co- operation Treaty for a patent, as may be filed designating India shall be deemed to be an application under this Act, if a corresponding application has also been filed before the Controller in India.

(2) Where the applications are made by virtue of an assignment there shall be furnished with the application, or within such period as may be prescribed after the filing of the application, proof of the right to make the application.

(3) It shall state that the applicant is in possession of the invention and shall name the owner claiming to be the true and first inventor, and where the person so claiming is not the applicant or one of the applicants, the application shall contain a declaration that the applicant believes the person so named to be the true and first inventor.

(4) Every such application (not being a convention application) shall be accompanied by a provisional or a complete specification.

Term of Patent and Renewal Fees (Section 53 as amended in 2002)

(1) Subject to the provisions of this Act, the term of every patent granted, after the commencement of the Patents (Amendment) Act, 2002, and the term of every patent which has not expired and has not ceased to have effect, on the date of such commencement, under this Act, shall be twenty years from the date of filing of the applicant for the patent.

This is a major change in term of patents. Prior to this amendment, the position was, subject to the provision of this Act, the term of every patent shall-

(a) in relation an invention claiming the method or process of manufacture of a substance, were the substance is intended for use, or is capable of being used, as food or as a medicine or drug, be five years from the date of sealing of the patent, or seven years from the date of the patent whichever period is shorter; and (b)in respect of any invention be 14 years from the date of patent.

(2) A patent shall cease to have effect if renewal fee is not paid within the prescribed period extended period under this section.

(3) The period shall be extended to such period, not being more than six months longer than the prescribed period, as may be specified in a request made to the Controller if the request is made and the renewal fee and the prescribed additional fee paid before the expiration of the period so specified.

(4) Not with standing anything contained in any other law for the time being in force, on cessation of the patent right due to non-payment of renewal fee or on expiry of the term of patent, the subject matter covered by the said patent shall not be entitled to any protection.

Loss or destruction of patents (Section 154) If a patent is lost or destroyed or its non-production is accounted for to the satisfaction of the Controller, the Controller may at any time, on application made in the prescribed manner and on payment of the prescribed fee, cause a duplicate thereof to be sealed and delivered to the applicant.

Rights of Patentees (Section 48) Subject to the other provisions contained in this Act and the conditions specified in section 47, a patent granted under this Act shall confer upon the patentee-

(a) where the subject matter of the patent is a product, the exclusive right to prevent third parties, who do not have his consent, from the act of making, using, offering for sale, selling or importing for those purpose that product in India;

(b)where the subject matter of the patent is a process, the exclusive right to prevent third parties, who do not have his consent, from the act of using that process, and from the act of using, offering for sale, selling or importing for those purposes the product obtained directly by that process in India:

Provided that the product obtained is not a product in respect of which no patent shall be granted under this Act.

Surrender of patents (Section 63)

(1) A patentee may, at any time by giving notice in the prescribed manner to the Controller, offer to surrender this patent.

(2) Where such an offers is made, the Controller shall advertise the offer in the prescribed manner and also notify every person other than the patentee whose name appears in the register as having an interest in the patent.

(3) Any person interested may, give notice to the Controllers of opposition to the surrender.

(4) If the Controller is satisfied after hearing the patentee and any opponent, that the patent may properly be surrendered, he may accept the offer and by order, revoke the patent.

Revocation of Patents (Section 64-66)

A patent confers exclusive rights to the first and true inventor. There is elaborate procedure for grant of patent under this Act and Patent Office will take all possible precautions before granting a 'patent'. Under the provisions of this Act it is open to any person to challenge the validity of patent. If the grounds challenging the grant of patent are valid or the Government in public interest deems it fit, the exclusive rights granted to inventor shall be withdrawn. Any such withdrawal of rights granted to patentee is termed revocation of patent.

Section 64 provides for revocation of patents as follows:

Subject to the provisions contained in this Act, a patent, whether granted before or after the commencement of this Act, may, on the petition of any person interested or of the Central Government or on a counter-claim in a suit for infringements of the patent, be revoked by the High Court on any of the following grounds;

(a) The invention, was claimed in a valid claim of earlier priority date contained in the complete specification of another patent granted in India.

(b) [omitted];

(c) Patent was obtained wrongfully in contravention of the rights of the petitioner or any person under or through whom he claims;

(d) That claim is not an invention within the meaning of this Act;

(e) [omitted];

(f) [e.f omitted];

(g) Invention is not useful;

(h) The complete specification does not sufficiently and fairly describe the invention and the method by which it is to be performed;

(i) That the scope of any claim of the complete specification is not sufficiently and clearly defined;

(j) That the patent was obtained on a false suggestion or representation;

(k) That the subject of any claim is not patentable under this act.

(l) The invention was secretly used in India, otherwise than as mentioned in subsection (3) before the priority date of the claim;

(m) Applicant for the patent has failed to disclose to the Controller the information required by section 8 or has furnished information which in any material particular was false to his knowledge;

(n) Applicant contravened any direction for secrecy passed under section 35 or made or caused to be made an application for the grant of a patent outside India in contravention of section 39.

(o) Leave to amend the completed specification under section 57 or section 58 was obtained by fraud.

(p) That the complete specification does not disclose or wrongly mention the source or geographical origin of biological material used for the invention.

(q) That the invention so far as claimed in any claim of the complete specification was anticipated having regard to the knowledge, oral or otherwise, available within any local or indigenous community in India or elsewhere.

Without prejudice to the provisions contained in sub-section (1) a patent may be revoked by the High Court on the petition of the Central Government, if the High court is satisfied that the patentee has without reasonable cause dialed to comply with the request of the Central Government within the meaning of section 99 upon reasonable terms.

Revocation of patent in public interest. Where the Central Government is of opinion that a patent or the mode in which it is exercised is mischievous to the State or generally prejudicial to the public, it may, after giving the patentee an opportunity to be heard, make a declaration to that effect in the Official Gazette and thereupon the patent shall be deemed to be revoked.

Register of patents (Sections 67-72)

Sealing of Patent is done at patent office at Calcutta. The Controller shall enter in Register of Patent relevant details in respect of patents such as:

(i) Names, addresses and nationality of the patentees,

(ii) Title of the invention,

(iii) Date of the patent, the date of sealing etc.

(iv) Renewal fees and date of renewal

(v) Change of in patentee's address, if any

According to Section 67.

1) There shall be kept at the patent office a register of patents, wherein shall be entered-

(a) The names and addresses of grantees of patents;

(b) Notification of assignments and of transmissions of patents, of licenses under patents, and of amendments, extension, and revocations of patents; and

(c) Particulars of such other matters affecting the validity or proprietorship of patents as may be prescribed.

2) No notice of any trust, whether express, implied or constructive, shall be entered in the register, and the controller shall not be affected by any such notice.

3) The register shall be kept under the control and management of the Controller.

4) Notwithstanding anything contained in sub-section (1), it shall be lawful for the controller to keep the register of patents or any part thereof in computer floppies, diskettes or any other electronic form subject to such safeguards as may be prescribed.

5) In the event the register is kept wholly or partly in computer floppies, diskettes or any other electronic form-

(a) References in this Act to an entry particulars in the register shall be deemed to include reference to a record of particulars kept in computer floppies, diskettes or any other electronic form and comprising the register or part of the register and references to the rectification of the register are to be read as including references to the rectification of the record of particulars kept in computer floppies, diskettes or any other electronic form and comprising the register or part of the register.

A patent is not valid unless it is in writing and registered with the controller within 6 months. ithout registration, there will not be accepted by the court or controller as evidence.

Copyright

U/S 14 "copyright" means the exclusive right subject to the provisions of this Act, to do or authorise the doing of any of the following acts in respect of a work or any substantial part thereof, namely in the case of a computer programme:

1. To reproduce the work in any material form including the storing of it in any medium by electronic means,
2. To issue copies of the work to the public not being copies already in circulation,
3. To perform the work in public, or communicate it to the public,
4. To make any cinematograph film or sound recording in respect of the work,
5. To make any translation of the work
6. To make any adaptation of the work
7. To do, in relation to a translation or an adaptation of the work, any of the acts specified in relation to the work in sub clauses (i) to (vi)

viii to sell or give on hire, or offer for sale or hire, any copy of the computer programme, regardless of whether such copy has been sold or given on hire on earlier occasions

U/S2(ffc) "computer programme" means set of instructions expressed in words, codes, schemes or in any other form, including a machine readable medium, capable of causing a computer to perform a particular task or achieve a particular results.

What is Copyright?

Copyright is a bundle of rights given by the law to creators of literary, dramatic, musical and artistic works and producers of cinematograph films and sound recordings.

Owner of the Copyright

- An individual author who writes a programme is the owner of copyright. A programme developed by several individuals, in which the contribution of one author is not distinct from the contribution of the others, all the individuals are joint authors and own the copyright jointly.
- **Under the Act "author means"**

In relation to any literary, dramatic, musical or artistic work which is computer-generated, the person who causes the work to be created.

- **Contract of service**

In case of programme made under a contract of service as an employee then the employer will be the first owner of the copyright unless there is any agreement to the contrary.

- **Contract for service**

Programmes written by people who have been appointed as independent contractor on contract for service will have the first right as owners unless such copyright is expressly assigned to the party taking their services.

How to protect your Copyright

Copyright subsists in all original published or unpublished compute programmes,

The copyright in computer programmes made within the lifetime of the author until sixty years from the year in which the author dies.

It is not compulsory to register the copyright in India but it can be a good idea to register. But one needs to take proper professional advise before registering.

Registration with the registrar of Copyright is helpful in an infringement suit.

Copyright Notice

As per the Berne Convention(to which India is a signatory) for protection of literary and artistic works,use of copyright notice is optional. It is a good idea to incorporate a copyright notice.

A Copyright notice consists of the following:

1. The symbol © (letter "c" in a circle) or the word "Copyright",
2. The copyright owners name, and
3. The year of first publication.

The copyright notice should be placed on computer programme copies in such a way as to give reasonable notice of the owner of the copyright.

How to register a programme with the Registrar of Copyright

Copyright Office regards computer programmes as literary works for which one has to file the following duly completed along with requisite fees:

1. Form IV-Application for Registration of Copyrights,
2. Statement of Particulars,
3. Statement of Further Particulars ,
4. Three complete copies of the works (one has to be very cautious here to submit appropriate works after taking professional help as giving away whole of the source code can be harmful as after registration your application is open to public for inspection.)

Assignment of the Copyright

U/S 18 The owner of the copyright in an existing work or prospective owner of the copyright in a future in a future work may assign to any person the copyright, either wholly or partially in the following manner:-

1. For the entire world or for a specific country or territory; or
2. For the full term of copyright or part thereof; or
3. Relating to all the rights comprising the copyright or only a part of such rights.

U/S 19. Mode of assignment:

(1) No assignment of the copyright in any work shall be valid unless it is in writing signed by the assignor or his duly authorised agent.

(2) The assignment of copyright in work shall identify such work, and shall specify the rights assigned and the duration and territorial extent of such assignment.

(3) The assignment of copyright in any work shall also specify the amount of royalty payable, if any,

(4) Where the assignee does not exercise the rights assigned to him under any of the other sub sections of this section within a period of one year from the date of assignment, the assignment in respect of such rights shall be deemed to have lapsed after the expiry of the said period unless otherwise specified in the assignment.

(5) If the period of assignment is not stated, it shall be deemed to be five years from the date of assignment.

(6) If the territorial extent of assignment of the rights is not specified, it shall be presumed to extend within India.

Infringement of Copyright

Copyright in work is considered to be infringed:

A. When any person without a license granted by the owner of the Copyright or the Registrar of copyrights or in contravention of the conditions of a license so granted or of any conditions imposed by a competent authority under copyright act-

1. Does anything, the exclusive right to do which is by copyright act conferred upon the owner of copyright, or

2. Permits for profit any place to be used for the communication of the work to public where such communication constitutes an infringement of the copyright in the work.

B. When any person:

1. Makes for sales or hire, or sells or lets for hire, or by way of trade displays or offers for sales or hire, or

2. Distributes either for the purpose of trade or to such an extent as to affect prejudicially the owner of the copyright, or

3. By way of trade exhibits in public, any infringing copies of the work.

4. Imports into India any infringing copies of the work for the private and domestic use of the importer.

Remedies for copyright infringement

Courts are empowered to grant the following relief:

1. Temporary and permanent injunctions
2. Impounding and destruction of all infringing copies, including masters
3. Imprisonment of the accused or imposition of fine or both.
4. Actual monetary damages plus the infringer s profits

U/S 64 of the Copyright Act, any police officer, not below the rank of a sub.- inspector, may if he is satisfied that an offence in respect of copyright in any work has been, is being, or is likely to be committed, seize without warrant, all copies of the work, and all plates used for the purpose of making infringing copies of the work, wherever found and produce them before a Magistrate as soon as practicable.

U/S 66 of the Copyright Act, The Court trying any offence, may, whether the alleged offender is convicted or not, order that all copies of the work in the possession of the alleged offender, which appear to be infringing copies be delivered up to the owner of copyright.

Trade Mark

A trade mark, is an identification mark which may be a word, a device, a label, a name brand, heading or numeral etc. or a combination thereof used to enable the purchaser to distinguish one trader's goods from similar goods of other traders .A trade mark connects particular goods in the minds of people to particular manufacturer.

Computer and computer related products as also Software products can also have trademark that will distinguish the products from the other manufacturers and can be identified by the consumer to be coming from particular manufacturer. e.g. Dell, IBM. Microsoft are all trademarks of their respective manufacturers. In fact these trademarks are very popular and are registered trademarks. Use of these trademarks by others in respect of similar goods may amount to infringement and against which action can be taken.

Selection of a Trade Mark for your products

A trademark may be a word, letter a device or numeral label or any combination thereof.

It shall be distinctive.

If it is a word it should be easy to speak, spell and remember.

The ideal word for a trademark is an invented or coined word.

It should be short.

How to Protect Your Trade Mark

Care should be taken to keep the distinctiveness of the trademark intact by using it in correct ways in written materials, in promotions etc.

It should be used exactly the way it was designed.

"The Trade and Merchandise Marks Act, 1958" is the legislation which deals with trademark law in India. Under this Act registration of trademark is permitted under specified classes of goods. Computer, software products are registered under class 9 (nine) in India.

Once the trademark is registered it helps in action against infringement.

In case of unregistered marks and marks which are not registrable, the only form of protection is the common law remedy of passing off.

The basic difference between the protections available for registered trademarks (infringement action) and unregistered trademarks (action for passing is that the former is a statutory remedy and the latter is a common law remedy. In order to establish infringement with regard to a registered trademark, it is necessary only to establish that the infringing mark is identical or deceptively similar to the registered mark and no further proof is required. In the case of a passing off action, proving that the marks are identical or deceptively similar alone is not sufficient. The use of the mark should be likely to deceive or cause confusion. Further, in a passing off action it is necessary to prove that the use of the trademark by the defendant is likely to cause injury or damage to the plaintiff's goodwill, whereas in an infringement suit, the use of the mark by the defendant need not cause any injury to the plaintiff.

The types of trademarks that can be registered

1. Trademark protection is available for words, names, symbols, or devices that are capable of distinguishing the owner's goods from the goods of others.
2. A trademark that merely describes a class of goods rather than distinguishing the trademark owner's goods from goods provided by others cannot be registered.
3. Trademarks are not registered if:
    - The use of the mark is likely to deceive or cause confusion;
    - The use of the mark is contrary to any law or is disentitled to protection in any court of law;
    - The mark contains scandalous or obscene matter;
    - The mark contains any matter that is likely to hurt the religious sentiments of any section of the citizens of India;
    - The mark is identical or deceptively similar to a trademark already registered in respect of the same goods or goods of the same description;
    - The use of the mark is prohibited under The Emblems and Names (Prevention of Improper Use) Act, 1950.

Procedure for registration of trade marks

- Any person/entity who claims to be the proprietor of a trademark can apply for registration. Before applying for registration, the applicant may apply for a report from the Registrar of Trademarks, as to whether the mark or one similar to it has already been registered or applied for. The applicant can also conduct private searches using the records maintained in the Registry.
- Thereafter, the application for registration should be filed in Form TM-1, under the Trade and Merchandise Marks Rules, 1959.
- After the application is received, the Registrar of Trademarks will examine the same and communicate any objections to the applicant. The objections normally are with regard to distinctiveness and similarity with already registered trademarks. The applicant can put forward his case in writing or at a hearing. If the submissions of the applicant are accepted, the application will be advertised in the Trademarks Journal.
- In case any objections are received, the Registrar will conduct a hearing and give a decision regarding the same.

- If no objections are received, the Registrar will enter the mark in the Register of Trademarks and issue a certificate of registration to the applicant. The certificate of registration is valid from the date of application for registration.

Advantages of registration of the trade mark

The exclusive right to use the trade mark in relation to the goods for which it

is registered and the right to take legal action against others who may infringe the registered trade mark or one resembling it in relation to similar goods.

Renewal of registration

The registration of a trademark is for a period of seven years from the date of the application. Registration of the mark can be renewed for successive period of seven years.

Assignment of trademark

A trademark is recognised as a form of property. It is therefore assignable and transferable as in the case of other forms of property. Assignment of trademark can be made by making a request on form TM-23/24 along with the deed of assignment etc to the trademark registry.

An unregistered trademark can be assigned without the goodwill of the business under the following circumstances:

(i) At the same of assignment it is used in the same business as a registered trademark;

(ii) That both the registered and unregistered trademarks are assigned at the time and to the same person; and

(iii) That the goods in respect of which the assignment is effected are the same for both the marks.

Infringement of a trademark

A registered trademark is infringed if a person uses the same/deceptively similar mark in the course of trade, in respect to the same goods. The test for deceptive similarity is whether the defendant's use of a mark is likely to cause confusion, i.e., whether an appreciable number of reasonably prudent consumers are likely to be confused or deceived as to the source, affiliation or sponsorship of the parties and their goods and services.

Reliefs that the court may grant in an infringement suit are:

- Injunction, restraining the further use of the trademark;
- Damages or an account of profits; and
- An order for delivery of the infringing labels and marks for destruction.

Service marks

Service marks are marks used by people rendering various kinds of services, for e.g.: travel agents, finance companies, consultants etc. At present there is no provision for the registration of service marks in India, and they can only be protected by an action for passing off.

The Trade Marks Bill, 1999

It is passed by both Houses of parliament and has also received the Presidential assent is still to be notified. So far it is not in effect.

Some of the important provisions under the new Act are:

- "Trade mark" shall now include services as well. All 42 international classifications of goods will be applicable in India. Thus service providers will be able to register their service marks.
- The period of registration has been enhanced from 7 years to 10 years.
- "Well known trade mark" can be protected.
- The new Act will empower courts to pass ex-parte injunction orders or other interlocutory orders for (a) discovery of documents, (b) preserving the infringing goods, documents or other evidence, and (c) restraining the offender from disposing off or dealing with his assets in a manner which may adversely affect the plaintiff's ability to recover damages, costs or other pecuniary remedies.
- Trademark violation is now a cognizable and non-bailable offence
- Minimum penalties of a six-month imprisonment term and Rs. 50,000/- have now been prescribed for trademark violations. The maximum penalties have been increased from two years imprisonment to three years and a fine of Rs. 2 million.

Review Questions

Conceptual Type

1. Define the term contract.
2. Define Agreement. What is an offer?
3. Define Promise. Define Proposal.
4. Define consideration.
5. What is unlawful consideration?
6. What are the essential requirement of a contract?
7. What are executed and executory contract?
8. What do you mean by (i) Unenforceable contract? (ii) Implied contract? (iii) contingent contract?
9. What are unilateral contracts? Give example.
10. What do mean by 'bilateral contracts?
11. Define term acceptance. State the any three essentials of valid acceptance.
12. What is Free consent? Define undue influence.

13. Define negotiable instrument. Give an example.
14. What is promissory note?
15. What is a bill of exchange?
16. What do you mean by crossing of cheques? Mention the types of crossing?
17. What is Mutilated cheque?
18. Define sub agent. Who is called substitute agent?
19. Define bailment.
20. Define pledge.
21. Define contract of sale.
22. Define Agreement to sell.
23. Who is called an unpaid seller?
24. Give the meaning of Intellectual Property.
25. Give the meaning of trade mark.

Analytical Type

1. Define agreement. What are the kinds of agreement?
2. Define proposal or offer? What are the essentials of a valid offer?
3. Define acceptance? What are the essentials of a valid acceptance?
4. Who can enter into a contract? Who cannot?
5. Explain the presumptions as to negotiable instrument.
6. What are the essential conditions of promissory note.
7. How are cheques classified.
8. State the circumstances under which a cheque can be dishonoured by a paying banker.
9. Write a note presentation for negotiation.
10. State the methods for discharge of the negotiable instrument.
11. Explain the instant under which an agent is personally liable.
12. What are the essential elements of bailment.
13. Explain the essential elements of pledge. Distinguish between bailment and pledge.
14. What are the rights and duties of pledgee and duties of pledger.
15. What do you mean by contract of sale? Discuss the essential features of contract of sale.
16. What do you mean by Intellectual Property Rights?
17. Mention the inventions that are not patentable.

18. What is a patent? State the steps of obtaining patent.
19. What are advantages of obtaining patent? Explain different kind of patent.
20. State the provisions relating to patent agents.

Descriptive Type

1. Discuss fully the essential elements of a valid contract.
2. Bring out the various classes of contract.
3. Explain briefly the rules regarding minor's agreement.
4. Who are the parties to competent the contract? Discuss who are incapable of contracting.
5. State the various ways in which a contract may be discharged.
6. State the exception of the rule. "An agreement in restraint of trade is void".
7. Define the term negotiable instrument. What are the different types of negotiable instruments. Explain their characteristics.
8. Write a note on Statutory protection given by negotiable instrument act to the collecting banker.
9. What is bill of exchange? How does it differ from promissory note?
10. State and explain the different kinds of agents.
11. Define agent. How is an agency created?
12. Explain the duties and rights of agents towards his principal.
13. What are the rights and duties of the principal towards his agent.
14. What are the rights and duties of bailor and bailee?
15. Explain briefly the rights of unpaid seller against the goods and against the buyer personally.
16. Explain briefly the exceptions to the rule "Nemo dat qui non habet" or "Sale by non-owner".
17. Explain the detail the rules related to the delivery of goods for the performance of contract of sale.
18. What is meant by opposition for grant of patent? What are the rules/ procedure in this regard?
19. What inventions are not Patentable?
20. Explain law related to copyright and trademark.

*****

Case Studies

Case Study 1

Every time the bird Phoenix rose from its ashes, it signified its immortal character. Like wise Tata Steel has always defined the odds, be it the steel downturn of the 90s or Russi Modi, who left the company during turbulent years. But the new decades brings threat from global steel manufacturers like Mittal Steel and Posco in front of whom Tata Steel seems lesser than even half a match. Would Tata Steel be able to fight their might? In reality will Tata Steel even survive?

Tata Steel did not follow old paternalism and refrained from antique management practices. The almost challenges were to hold people together and to streamline business processes. It was named the Best Steel Company by World Steel Dynamics in 2006 for the third time. It has an unquestionable credit to itself that it is amongst the lowest cost producers of steel in the world.

Mittal Steel, which rules the global steel industry has already announced plans to set up a 12 million tonne steel plant in Jharkhand. Total steel production of Tata is only 8% of Mittal Steel. Moreover Posco the world's fifth largest steel company is set to pump in $12 billion into its steel plant in Orissa.

It is not only the competition that is haunting Tata Steel, but also the threat posed by global steel industry. The global steel industry has a production, consumption mismatch resulting in overcapacity, which along with other factors like raw materials shortage would aggravate injuries to global steel sector. Another problem is the dominance of China's Steel industry with Chinese Government as majority stake holder with a steel production of 39.1 metric million tones p.a. where India lags far behind.

Tata Steel is planning to be a major player in 2015 through acquisitions. It is also currently introducing brands and brand positioning.

Questions:

1. Perform SWOT analysis for Tata Steel.
2. Is branding the right strategy for Tata Steel now? Substantiate your answer.
3. What are the strategies the company should follow now to achieve its plant for 2015?

Case Study 2

India's problem is not lack of resources, it is the inability and / or unwillingness to mobilize resources into the public sector. The Indian economy is confronting a fiscal crisis. The reasons for this are the steady decline over the years in the share of direct taxes in spite of the fact that both incomes and savings of the top 10 percent of the households in the country have been steadily increasing. The government does not appear committed to placing greater reliance on direct taxes to mobilize resources. It is unwilling to tax the rich and therefore has no option except to fall back on indirect taxes and rely more than ever on borrowing from those who expect interest and tax concessions from temporarily parting with their resources to enable the government to continue its "development programmes".

Grave inter - sectorial imbalances also exist in India's tax structure because agricultural incomes are tax free. The Raj committee had recommended the introduction of agricultural tax to remove this inequality, but the state governments did noting to implement the recommendation. The long term fiscal policy also did noting to eliminate this inter - sectorial imbalances.

Public sector enterprises failed to generate the untemplated reinvertible surplus and the small surplus that became available from these enterprises was not attributable to improved efficiency. The fiscal deficit thus reflects the total resource gap, which equals the excess of total government expenditure over the government revenue and grants. The fiscal deficit thus, fully indicates the indebtedness of the government.

Questions:

1. What is fiscal policy? And what are its components?
2. Distinguish between direct and indirect taxes.
3. Explain briefly the reasons for fiscal deficit.
4. Suggest remedies for the new fiscal policy to combat fiscal crisis.

Case Study 3

Virgin mobile USA has reason to believe some people will cut back on food before they give up their cell phones. In talking with thousands of their customers who are part of a special online panel, virgin mobile found that 68% of their customers say they are keeping their cell phones, but are cutting back in other ways, for example, 88% are dining out less frequently and 79% are deferring big ticket purchases.

The information from the panel warranted a press release. Press is a high priority for building awareness about the company and its prepaid value; customers who join the panel are asked if they are willing to talk to the media. When the Chicago Tribune expressed interest in the story, virgin mobile directed the newspaper to (suzame) Suzanne peace to talk about her experience as a customer. She used to spend $ 109 per month on her cell phone with sprint. She switched to no - contact with virgin mobile USA to pay by the minute and has never looked back.

Questions:

1. What is the impact of global recession on telecommunication industry?
2. Will virgin mobile able to survive in the present crisis?
3. Give some remedies to tackle the global recession.
4. How do you deal with the unemployment problem during the recession?

Case Study 4

Read the following case and answer the questions given at the end.

You are a director of a Multi National Company based in India, with Headquarters in Swedan. You are told to develop.

a) A code of ethics and conduct for your Co. (with regard to the Indian operations)

b) Develop a training programme for the same for employees.

c) Develop a system for monitoring ethical decision making in the company.

Case Study 5

Exports of a country are in great demand because level of income of people in the importing country is fairly high, such goods will be in a position to command higher price and income level of people in the country exporting those goods will rise. This will mean higher wages in export industries. The rising income of people in export industries will also mean increasing demand for other domestic goods whose prices will also go up therefore, level of income of people producing those goods would also rise.

On the other hand, if in a country, demand for imported goods from the other country is relatively small or elastic people in the importing country will be getting imported goods at relatively lower price. Income of the people producing such goods will be lower. This will also mean lower demand for other domestically produced goods while they will be paying high prices for imported goods.

Questions:

1. "The level of income of people in a country" has great influence on sharing gains from international trade. Justify with reasons.
2. "The demand for such goods is inelastic in the importing country" Do you agree? If yes, give reasons.
3. Determine the relationship between size of a country and gains from international trade.

Case Study 6

"What Ethics Means to Coke" ?

Coca-Cola India has commissioned rainwater harvesting project in three phases within the premises of its bottling plant at Atmakuru village near Vijayweada. The plant can now harvest 100 per cent of rainfall on nearly six acres of constructed area. The plant maintains an additional 34-acre green belt within its premises. The company had earlier donated computers, furniture and books to the village library, besides providing scientific equipment, books and school bags for students in five schools in the neighboring villages.

According to Sanjiv Gupta, CEO and president of Coca-Cola India. "We believe in conducting our business in a manner that benefits the local communities. It is indeed a matter of pride and honor for all of us to receive the support from the villages here".

In 1998, Coca - Cola set up a bottling plant in Perumatti in the southern state of Kerala. Since it opened, local villagers have complained about the fall in the amount of water available to them and have blamed the fall in supplies on Coca - Coca who, they claim, uses up to a million liters per day at the plant. Further, following the cleaning of the bottles, a waste sludge is produced that Coca - Cola has been disposing of on the land of local farmers claiming it was a useful fertilizer. BBC Radio 4 programme reported the details of the contaminants in the sludge Coca - Cola sells as fertilizer, gives away, or sometimes dumps in dry riverbeds are revealed for the first time. Following the programme samples of the sludge were analysed by scientists at Exeter University in the south west of England and found to contain toxic chemicals including lead and cadmium - both of which can be harmful to human and further suggested that there was little or not benefit of the sludge as a fertiliser. Later tests by the local state laboratories find that the levels of toxic chemicals are within safety levels but that it should not be used as a fertilizer.

In a separate development, sales of Coca - Cola have been hit by suggestions that its drinks produced in India contained higher levels of pesticide residues that was healthy A large number of bodies have joined in the campaign for the local community demanding the plant be closed down and that tests are carried on Coca - Cola to assess its safety. A lawsuit to this effect was thrown out which prompted Coca - Cola to issue an angry comment claiming that the reports were scurrilous, unnecessarily scared large numbers of Coca - Cola's customers and put thousands of jobs in its plants throughout India at risk.

Sunil Gupta, Vice - President of Coca - Cola India, says the company has been the target of a handful of extremist protesters and it is lack of rainfall that has caused local water supplies to be exhausted. The company claims to use a maximum of 6,00,000 liters a day. Coca - Cola even sends round tenders of water to the region to help the local community. Mr. Gupta also says Coca - Cola undertook an environmental impact assessment before building the plant. He stood by the claim that the sludge waste from the plant was fertiliser and said the company complied with all local environmental laws and stood for the welfare of the community.

The Charity Action Aid says the crisis facing the once prosperous farming area is an example of the worst kind of inward investment by multinational companies in developing countries. In a report to the World Trade Organization's meeting in Cancun, Mexico the charity says this kind of abuse must be controlled. The report says Perumatti was a thriving agricultural community until Coca - Cola set up the bottling plant in 1998. Conconut groves and vegetable crops have had to be abandoned because of the lack of water. Action Aid says thousands of people worked on the land but now just 141 are employed at the plant with a further 250 as casual laborers.

The team of experts of the Central Water Resources Development and Management Kozhikode, appointed by the High Court of Kerala, has recommended in its final report that the Coca - Cola Beverages Ltd. can safety by permitted to draw 5 - lakhs liters of ground water a day for industrial use, under normal rain conditions. The local economy that the village council which had granted the company a license to operate is now demanding the plant's closure.

Questions:

1. In this case, what is more important - the very product or the location of the plant?
2. What concepts of business ethics are relevant in this case?
3. What are your suggestions for resolving the issue?

Case Study 7

Read the following case and answer questions given at the end. It carries thirteen marks. It is compulsory.

It was a sports stadium. Eight children were standing on the track to participate in the running event.

*Ready!*Steady!*Bang!!!

With the sound of toy pistol, all eight girls started running.

Hardly have they covered ten to fifteen steps, one of the smaller girls slipped and fell down. Due to bruises and pain, she started crying.

When other seven girls heard this sound, they stopped running, stood for a while and turned back, they all ran back to the place where the girl fell down. One among them bent, picked and kissed the girl gently and required Now pain must have reduced.

All seven girls lifted the fallen girl, pacified her, two of them held the girl firmly and they all seven joined hands together and walked together and reached the winning post.

Officials were shocked. Clapping of thousands of spectators filled the stadium. Many eyes were filled with tears and perhaps it had reached the God even!

Yes. This happened in Hyderabad (India) recently!

The sport was conducted by National Institute of Mental Health.

All these special girls had come to participate in this event and they are spoastic children.

Yes, they were mentally retarded! Challenged.

Questions:

1. What did they teach this world?
2. Can you apply this incident to a modern business which is characterized by cut throat competition!
3. In the course of sympathizing with a colleague, whether other members of the team lost the game of play and win? Can you afford this kind of attitude in business?
4. Can you rewrite the above case in a way that suits modern business organization?

Case Study 8

Read the following and analyse the ethical issues involved in each of them.

i) Some business people and other experts argue that bribery helps cut through mounds of red tape. Do you agree? By calling for reforms in nations that condone bribery are international agencies promoting a certain set of values and morals? Are they practising cultural imperialism?

ii) When international firms enter the Indian market, they soon learn about the various ways in which a rigid caste system can affect business activities. Should these companies adjust to local management styles and HR practices? Or should they import their own styles and practices because they are so called "more developed" and equitable?

iii) Companies often relocate factories from industrialised nations with high labour cost to such low wage countries as China, India, Mexico and the nations of Central America. Is there any reasonable response to charges that in so doing, they frequently exploit child labour, force women to work 75 hour week and destroy family units?

Case Study 9

Analyse and comment on the following situations:

a) IT specialists play an increasing role in the lives of individuals and the operations of organisations. The information systems they develop and maintain effect our physical and financial well being tremendously. Are IT specialists professionals? If they are, why don't they comply with a mandatory code of ethics as other professionals (such as physicians and lawyers) do?

b) Professional Management today is at intellectual cross roads. Most of its knowledge base is rooted in "business management". This is primarily because its central concern is with bottomline. In its deep commitment to these ideals, it has largely neglected other concerns.

Case Study 10

Assume that a democratically elected government, after a favourable vote in an election, launches a programme to clear 1,50,000 acres of tropical rain forests in order to promote economic development. To carry out the will of the people, the government issues a request for proposals to international engineering firms for a contract to help clear the acreage. A number of international firms have indicated that they will bid on the project. Your company wants a report from you on the proposal. Prepare a detailed report arguing for and against bidding on the project.

Case Study 11

1. ABC Co. sells to Life Co. 500 bags of sugar each containing 100 kgs. It is agreed that Life Co. shall get two months credit and the price per bag of sugar at Rs. 1,500. Life Co. allows the sugar to remain in ABC Co.'s warehouse. In the meantime, because of huge unaccumulated losses, Life Co. becomes insolvent before the expiry of two months. Official Receiver demands the delivery of the sugar from the ABC Co. without offering to pay. What are the rights of ABC Co.?

2. 'A' offered to sell his house to 'B' for Rs.1,00,000. 'B" accepted the offer by post. On the next day 'B' sent a telegram revoking the acceptance which reached 'A' before the letter. Is the revocation of acceptance valid? Would it make any difference if both the letter of acceptance and the telegram of revocation of acceptance reach 'B' at the same time?

3. 'A' drew cheques in favour of 'B'. A' clerk forged B's endorsement and negotiated the cheques to 'C' who took them in good faith and for value. 'C' received payment of the cheques. 'A' claims to recover the amount from 'C'. Will he succeed?

Case Study 12

Raja stores is a reputed retail store in Punjab. Mr. Laxmi Narayan, the proprietor has seen it grow from strength to strength over the last 20 years. The store prides for quality products and enjoys a good image in the market. In recent times, many departmental stores have come up in the adjoining areas and slowly the competition is hotting up. Mr. Laxmi Narayan's major concern is about losing patronage to the bigger stores as they are offering lower prices. He knows he could not compete on prices though he prides himself on excellent customer service and quality product.

Advice Mr. Laxmi Narayan regarding the new threat posed by competition and ways to beat it.

Case Study 13

Basmati is an aromatic rice grown in Northern India and Pakistan. In September, 1997, Rice Tea., a small food technology company based in texas, United states, was granted a patent by the U.S. patent office to call on aromatic rice variety developed in USA as Basmati. India challenged the case, arguing that basmati is a unique rice grown in Northern India, and not a name Rice Tea. could claim. In fact only inventions can be patented. Consequently, the U.S. patent office accepted India's basic position, and Rice Tech had to drop 15 out of 20 claims that it had made. Of the remaining claims, Rice Tea, managed to evolve three new varieties of rice for which it got a patent from United States Patent and Trademarks Office (USPTO), as India had not objected to these. The ruling has not handed over Rice Tea., the basmati brand. Rather, it provides it provides it a patent for superior three strains of basmati developed by cross-breeding a Pakistani Basmati with a semi-dwarf American variety.

According to the WTO agreement, geographical indications like basmati can be legally protected and their misuse can be thus prevented. The unfortunate thing is that the Government of India has not taken timely steps for protecting our geographical indications and bio-diversity.

Questions:

1. Can any of the following, viz., turmeric, neem and the name basmati be patented? Substantiate your answer.
2. Evaluate the legal implications of the role player by the Government of India (GOI) in preventing the misuse of the name Basmati.

Case Study 14

a. There is a contract for the sale of 25 quintals of ghee within a specified period by A to B . A delivers 20 quintals but does not deliver the residue. A claims the price of the ghee supplied, but refuses to supply the residue unless paid for the quantity supplied. Decide the case.

b. At an auction sale ,A makes the highest bid for a flower vase. Purporting to accept the bid, the auctioneer strikes the vase and breaks it. Who is to bear the loss?

Case Study 15

Black & Co. is a limited company which is 10 years old. The said company is doing a flourishing business in the leather goods and footwear products. The company has employed about 1500 workmen in various capacities.

The company directors in their Board meeting wanted to diversify the business into textile. The board passed the resolution to start the textile business as a subsidiary.

The company's Memorandum of Association, in one of the clauses, is very clear that the company shall only deal with leather products and footwear.

Now the very act of the company is ultra virus the Memorandum of Association. Please explain. Advise the company to overcome this problem.

Case Study 16

a) X, an auctioneer, advertises through newspaper that the sale of office furniture will be held at Bangalore, Y, a broker from Chennai, reaches Bangalore on the stipulated time and date. X, the auctioneer, withdraw all the furniture from the auction sale. Y sues X for the loss of time and expense. Will he succeed?

b) X contracts with Y to buy 50 copies of Business Law authored by A. Y supplies 25 copies of the book written by A, 5 copies written by B and 10 copies written by C. Advise X.

*****